D1083565

The Heart of the Story
Eudora Welty's Short Fiction

The Heart of the Story

Eudora Welty's Short Fiction

PETER SCHMIDT

University Press of Mississippi

Jackson & London

Excerpts from the working papers of *The Golden Apples*, "The Winds" typescript, and "Circe" in *The Bride of the Innisfallen and Other Stories* have been published with the permission of the Harry Ransom Humanities Reserch Center, The University of Texas at Austin.

Some of the material that appears in Chapters 1, 3, and 4 was first published as "Sibyls in Eudora Welty's Stories" in *The Eye of the Storyteller*, edited by Dawn Trouard (Kent, Ohio: The Kent State University Press, 1989). Reprinted with permission of The Kent State University Press.

Excerpts from "Clytie" and "Powerhouse" in *A Curtain of Green and Other Stories*, copyright 1941 and renewed 1969 by Eudora Welty. Reprinted by permission of Harcourt Brace Jovanovich, Inc.

Excerpts from "June Recital" and "The Wanderers" in *The Golden Apples*, copyright 1947 and renewed 1975 by Eudora Welty. Reprinted by permission of Harcourt Brace Jovanovich, Inc.

Excerpts from "The Burning" in *The Bride of the Innisfallen and Other Stories*, copyright 1951 and renewed 1979 by Eudora Welty. Reprinted by permission of Harcourt Brace Jovanovich, Inc.

The paper in this book meets the guidelines for permanence and durability of the Committee on Production Guidelines for Book Longevity of the Council on Library Resources.

Library of Congress Cataloging-in-Publication Data

Schmidt, Peter, 1951–
    The heart of the story : Eudora Welty's short fiction / Peter
Schmidt.
        p.   cm.
    Includes bibliographical references and index.
    ISBN 0-87805-500-2 (cloth). — ISBN 0-87805-501-0 (pbk.)
        1. Welty, Eudora, 1909–   —Criticism and interpretation.
    2. Short story.   I. Title.
    PS3545.E6Z86   1991
    813'.52—dc20   90-21708
                                                    CIP

British Library Cataloging-in-Publication data available

to
Lisa
and
in memory of my mother
and
all the other Mrs. Morrisons

Contents

A Note on the Text

I cite page numbers from *The Collected Stories of Eudora Welty* (New York: Harcourt Brace Jovanovich, 1980) parenthetically, in the body of the text, giving page numbers only. When I cite other relevant Welty texts, such as *One Writer's Beginnings, The Eye of the Story,* or *Conversations with Eudora Welty,* the context will always make it clear that the page numbers given in parenthesis in the text do not refer to *The Collected Stories;* if not, I name the other text in parentheses. As many other texts as possible are cited parenthetically in the text as well. The Works Cited listing at the end of the book contains the relevant bibliographic information for both primary and secondary sources cited in the text and notes.

Manuscripts are cited in the notes using the enumeration system published in Suzanne Marrs's *The Welty Collection: A Guide to the Eudora Welty Manuscripts and Documents at the Mississippi Department of Archives and History* (Jackson: University Press of Mississippi, 1989), citing Marrs's numbers and the collection in which the manuscript is kept, plus the page(s) in that volume in which the manuscript is described (for example: I.A4 Jackson, Marrs 31–32). Marrs's book also covers significant Welty collections outside of those stored at the Mississippi Department of Archives and History in Jackson.

A Note on the Text

Acknowledgments

I would like to say thank-you to friends and colleagues who have been particularly helpful orienting me when I was lost in this book: Rachel Blau DuPlessis, Lawrence Buell, Dawn Trouard, Albert Devlin, Ruth Vande Kieft, Michael Kreyling, Harriet Pollack, Carol Singley, Laurie Langbauer, Phil Weinstein, Chuck James, Kathryn Morgan, T. Kaori Kitao, Wai-chee Dimock, Richard Spear, Peggy Whitman Prenshaw, Louise Westling, Seetha Srinivasan, and Hunter Cole. Some of these people may be surprised to see themselves on this list, but they shouldn't be surprised at what a thoughtful comment or question can do. Readers who enjoy reading between the lines of a book's footnotes (as I do) will notice others who repeatedly sustained me as well. They are not responsible for the creature that emerged from these Morgan's Woods, of course.

I would also like to acknowledge my students at Swarthmore College, particularly for their insights on "Petrified Man" and "The Wide Net" and for their frustration with some of the premises of the myth-symbol school of Welty criticism, which prodded me towards several of the points in the first three chapters of the book. A research grant from Swarthmore enabled me to travel to Mississippi and Texas to look at Welty's manuscripts at a crucial stage in the book's composition; since most of this book was written in the summers and on half-salary during an unpaid leave, such support proved especially helpful. Suzanne Marrs's guide to the Welty collection in Jackson (and Noel Polk's supplement in Marrs on Welty manuscripts elsewhere) made my sleuthing much more efficient than it usually is, as did the knowledgeable staffs of the Mississippi Department of Archives and History in

Jackson and the Harry Ransom Research Library at the University of Texas; I encountered so little frustration in finding what I was looking for, in fact, that I began to wonder whether I was really working. *Writing,* of course, was different.

The book's dedication (*dedicare:* to give out tidings) involves feelings that are beyond words.

Preface

In *One Writer's Beginnings* (1984), Eudora Welty described the early growth of one of her most important volumes of stories, *The Golden Apples* (1949). After writing several separate stories, she suddenly realized that they were all linked: "some of the characters in one story were, and had been all the time, the same characters who had appeared already in another story." Conceived independently, the stories and characters that were to make up *The Golden Apples* gained new clarity and complexity when Welty first imagined them sharing the same world, the imaginary town of Morgana, Mississippi. Revision became, literally, re-seeing identities, not merely re-naming actors; Welty experienced a new understanding of the motives of her characters and of how their lives evolved once she imaged them having interlocking histories and a shared, small-town locale. As she came to see, her characters were all related "by the strongest ties—identities, kinships, relationships, or affinities already known or remembered or fore shadowed. From story to story, connections between the characters' lives, through their motives or actions, sometimes their dreams, already existed: there to be found" (*One Writer's Beginnings* 98–99). It was as if connections among Welty's stories lay waiting to be discovered in the midst of writing them—waiting for the moment of revelation when she could suddenly dare to see her separate stories as part of a story cycle, a larger whole.

The Collected Stories of Eudora Welty (1980) for the first time gathered together her three magisterial volumes of stories from the 1940s—*A Curtain of Green and Other Stories* (1941), *The Wide Net and Other Stories* (1943), and *The Golden Apples* (1949)—along with her 1955 collection, *The Bride of the Innisfallen and Other Stories*, and two stories published in the 1960s, "Where Is the Voice Coming From?" (1963) and "The Demonstrators" (1966). The book includes forty-one stories in all. For a reader reading the stories in order, the *Collected Stories* may be as revelatory as Eudora Welty's experience with the tales that became *The Golden Apples*. As powerful as her stories are individually, they are even more impressive when considered together. Welty's words describing her writer's experience challenge her *readers* as well: "In writing, as in life, the connections of all sorts of relationships and kinds lie in wait of discovery, and give out their signals to the Geiger counter of the charged imagination, once it is drawn into the right field" (99).

Approaching the *Collected Stories* with such a charged imagination does not imply that the stories in that volume will form "one" story or that Welty's vast panorama of characters is reducible to a handful of personality types. Indeed, reading Welty's stories as a group leaves one in awe of a mind that could imagine and give life to voices as diverse as those of Stella-Rondo and Virgie Rainey, Powerhouse and Circe. It also does not assume that the *Collected Stories* represent the final accounting of all Welty's stories: all of her readers look forward to discovering the stories she still may have in store for us (Prenshaw, *Conversations* 198, 210). Considering the published stories collectively allows us to discover hidden connections, affinities, rememberings, and foreshadowings among the tales that cannot be seen as well when the stories are read separately or seen merely as "background" for her novels. It is in order to trace some of those patterns in Welty's stories that I have written this book.

Without slighting Eudora Welty's considerable talent for writing novels, many readers (including myself) feel that the heart of her achievement as an artist lies in her stories. As Welty herself has said, "I think I'm a short story writer naturally. . . . I never intended to write a novel. Every single one of my novels came about accidentally" (Prenshaw, *Conversations* 272). Like the stories of Porter or Hemingway or Faulkner—or, for that matter, James, Twain, Chekhov, and Hawthorne—Welty's tales are indispensable for an understanding of the larger corpus to which they belong. Scholarship on the stories was already a healthy enterprise in the 1970s, but it gained new strength and new directions with the publication of *The Collected Stories* and

One Writer's Beginnings in the 1980s. We have only just begun to discover the "affinities" that Welty's stories share with each other, with the canon of American writers, and with women's writing in general.

This book builds upon previous Welty criticism but questions some of the formalist and archetypal or myth-critical assumptions that have generally guided it. I am hardly alone in this enterprise, of course. Some of the colleagues I know who are raising similar questions and making similar moves are acknowledged in the notes, and I am sure there are many more doing feminist and new historicist writing right now who will be published soon. At a time when the methodologies of formalist and archetypal criticism, whatever their virtues, seem increasingly limited and limiting, Eudora Welty's stories are able to teach us new ways of reading and different ways of defining an artist's historical context and social engagement. Ironically, the writer who in the 1940s through the 1960s was often accused of having too great a concern for formal patterning and too little a concern for social and political issues[1] now in the 1990s seems to have a radically innovative conception of both artistry and ideology. Welty's stories impress because of their volatile, decentering energy, not merely for the (unmistakable) perfections of their surface, and her critiques of social stereotyping—particularly as it involves the shaping of women's identities—have never appeared more timely or more daring.

Over the course of writing this book, in fact, I have come to believe that the stories that Eudora Welty published in the 1940s (*A Curtain of Green* through *The Golden Apples* and "Circe") represent, along with work by Richard Wright and Ann Petry, the most important fiction to appear in the United States in that decade. I base this judgment not only on the intensity and variety with which Welty developed her art of short-story writing in the decade but also on the fact that her stories are immensely empowering for women writing today—for *all* writers working today, really—and because her stories profoundly help us reinterpret earlier writing by American women and the "canon" of American literature itself.

The four chapters of this book include readings of many of Welty's stories. Her first volume, *A Curtain of Green,* is given a full chapter and then some, not only because it has so many stories (seventeen in all), but also because these first stories explore aesthetic and social issues that would be relevant for all her work. Several stories from *A Curtain of Green*—particularly "Flowers for Marjorie," "Petrified Man," and "Why I Live at the P.O."—are discussed in later chapters rather than the first one because this allows for greater continuity and contrast in my argument. My analysis of Welty's early stories focuses on issues of imprisonment and release, especially as they are raised by the fates of Welty's female characters, many of whom, like Lily Daw, Old Addie, Clytie, and Mrs. Larkin in the volume's title story, are thought by the townspeople to be madwomen. These characters and others engage in furious activity within enclosed spaces symbolized not only by physical walls but by gender divisions—in Mrs. Larkin's case, the town's expectations for how she will conduct herself as a widow. Several issues in particular are provocative here: the sexual politics of the family, the ironic links between "proper" behavior for women and madness, the rage many of the stories' younger heroines feel toward older female authority figures, and the ways in which the narrative voice in several of the stories—most notably "Clytie"— seems in the end to punish the heroine for her rebelliousness. Hovering behind all the topics listed above is an even more intriguing one, the extent to which Welty's early stories exploring the different fates available to eccentric or "mad" women were an attempt to confront her own anxieties about how to validate her imaginative activity as a writer. She has not particularly stressed such a topic in her critical prose or her interviews, admittedly, but the stories tell a different story: they return to this issue almost compulsively. Much has been written recently in feminist criticism concerning how to interpret motifs of the madwoman in women's writing, but few of these insights have yet been applied to Welty's early stories, which seem tailor-made to test such generalizations. Chapter One closes with readings of three stories in *A Curtain of Green* that suggest possible alternative fates other than stigmatization for independent-minded characters, via two female characters who appear to be weak but are not (Ruby Fisher and Phoenix Jackson) and one male character (Powerhouse) who is compared to a powerful female figure, a sibyl, during crucial moments in the story.

The linked but contrasting themes of imprisonment and release in Chapter One become the basis for a look at Welty's later tragic and comic stories in the next chapters. Chapter Two focuses on Welty's later tragic stories and considers whether "tragedy" may have a slightly different plot for women than for men and, if so, why. It considers the recurrent motif in Welty's stories of male tragic characters doing violence to women, contrasted with women tragic characters doing violence to themselves: Ran MacLain and Miss Eckhart from *The Golden Apples* are the two most extended portraits that fit this pattern. Both feminist literary criticism and so-called "new historicist" criticism (much of it written by feminist critics, of course) has much to teach us about how firmly Welty grounds these dramas within a richly detailed social and historical context. Studies by psychologists such as Freud, Karen Horney, and Nancy Chodorow are invaluable as well. By the same token, however, Welty's stories have much to teach contemporary criticism and recent psychoanalytical writing, since her work anticipates by several decades many of the current debates about the social construction of gender, genre, difference, and ideology.

Chapter Three asks whether Welty's sense of comedy is as inflected with a sense of gender difference as her tragic stories are, especially in regard to the changing ways her stories satirize stereotypical behavior by men and women. The chapter begins by pairing a well-known comedy, "Why I Live at the P.O.," with "*Women!!* Make Turban in Own Home!" a barely-known piece of comic journalism written during the same year (1941), in order to define two contrasting modes of comedy in Welty's stories, the comedy of rigidity and the comedy of rebirth or transformation. The former thrives by exploring how people are comically imprisoned within stereotypes: Sister's family in "Why I Live at the P.O." is exemplary of this comic mode and raises the troubling question of why so often in such comedies ambitious women such as Sister seem the butt of Welty's humor. Welty's latter comic mode is well introduced by "*Women!!*" since it mocks how women's fashions, women's magazines, and even women's writings (especially when overindulging in italics) support absurd gender divisions within society. The sophisticated and ironic voice of the piece's anonymous female narrator contrasts strikingly with Sister's in "P.O." and well serves to allow a segue to the series of sophisticated later comedies from "The Wide Net" to "Moon Lake" and "Circe" about comic transformations: how people may be released from imprisoning gender roles by mocking and then revising them. Dividing Welty's comic stories into two groups becomes an especially interesting way of charting her development as a writer of comic stories because after doing so at least two hypotheses become apparent. First, Welty seems especially to have associated the comedy of rebirth with women, as shown by the frequent presence of women artist figures who act as mentors to younger heroines in these comic stories and, in *The Golden Apples,* by the way in which Virgie Rainey displaces King MacLain as the primary comic character in the story sequence as it evolves. Second, Welty may have first made a name for herself with comedies of rigidity, such as "P. O." and "Petrified Man," but beginning in 1942 and continuing through the 1950s she became increasingly interested in comedies of rebirth in her short fiction, though she did not abandon her earlier comic mode.

I realize that many stories discussed in these middle chapters, such as "Petrified Man," "June Recital," or "The Wanderers," are more tragicomic than either "tragic" or "comic" and that readers will be rightly skeptical that such portentous terms can capture the shifting tones that make Welty's stories so powerful and elusive. I can only reply that I recognize the problem and ask the reader to bear with me a little because I believe that such a way of organizing the book may ultimately help us think about "tragedy" and "comedy" in new and flexible ways. Certainly Welty's stories have done that for me.

The last chapter of this book analyzes how Welty's tales draw on earlier writing by American women, particularly sentimental romance novels, comedy, and "local color" short stories. Surprisingly, this topic has so far been little addressed in Welty criticism when it has discussed Welty's predecessors, partly because her relation to writers like Woolf or Faulkner is so compelling, and partly because her own critical comments from her earlier essays through *One Writer's Beginnings* have tended to ignore earlier American women writers, with the exception of Katherine Anne Porter and Willa Cather. It turns out that many earlier women writers explored most if not all of the issues discussed in the first three chapters, and that they can bring valuable light to bear on these topics by putting them in a wider historical context, making them part of a tradition. In some cases this involves a detailed discussion of relevant stories by earlier American writers such as Katherine Anne Porter, Willa Cather, or Sarah Orne Jewett whose names readers will not be surprised to find linked to Welty. In other cases, however—as with Augusta Evans Wilson, E.D.E.N. Southworth, Marietta Holley, and others, many of them southern— some surprises are in store. Such stress on American women writers who were Welty's predecessors is not meant to preclude discussion of other writers who were clearly important to Welty, such as William Faulkner or Virginia Woolf. But criticism has underestimated and oversimplified the importance of earlier American women writers for an understanding of Welty's writing, in my view. This book is just one of many examples of the renewed interest contemporary scholars have in earlier American women writers, many of whom for years were little read and less discussed. My book also marks one way a renewed per- spective on the past (including the canonical issues of who is read and who is not) can be stimulated by developments in contemporary fic- tion such as Welty's as well as by contemporary critical theory. The process works in reverse as well. Refreshed readings of earlier women authors and their tradition reinvigorate our reading of contemporary authors such as Welty who are sometimes rebellious heirs to that tradition.

I decided to focus primarily but not exclusively on Eudora Welty's stories for three reasons. The first has already been mentioned: Welty's stories are the most widely read of her works and the most frequently taught, and like many readers I feel they are the heart of her achieve- ment. The second reason is that several excellent books have been published giving equal attention to all of Welty's works, from her nov- els to her stories and essays. (I am especially thinking of Ruth Vande Kieft's *Eudora Welty*, surely one of the best guides to the work of a living author that has ever been published.) Yet another volume fo- cusing on Welty's writing as a whole hardly seemed necessary at this time, at least for me. I do, however, discuss Welty's longer fiction when it is directly relevant to issues raised by the stories, and when it will help me argue for the importance of a particular pattern of devel- opment in Welty's career as a whole. A final reason for restricting the

book's survey is that the average length of a discussion of an individual
story in many of the critical works on Welty rarely takes up more than
a half-dozen or dozen pages, sometimes much less. Of course, a discussion's length hardly guarantees high quality; this book's readers will
have to decide on their own whether its longer readings of stories
sustain themselves. But I found that as I let these stories' signals reg-
ister in my own Geiger counter, there were more and more messages
received that needed decoding. It took time, and it demanded space.
For similar reasons I chose not to try to discuss all of Welty's stories or
to organize the book in the most obvious way, with separate chapters
on *A Curtain of Green, The Wide Net, The Golden Apples, Innisfallen,*
and the 1960s stories in *The Collected Stories.* An earlier draft of this
book discussed more stories, but in revising I decided to sharpen my
focus on stories particularly central or especially challenging to my
lines of argument.

In consulting Welty's typescripts in Jackson, Mississippi, and Austin,
Texas, after I had completed a preliminary draft of the book, I found
hunches confirmed, some favorite beliefs demolished, and sudden
new ideas emerging unexpectedly. I do not attempt in these discussions of the stories to give a thorough accounting of all or even most
of the revisions Welty made, only those that either support or cause
difficulties for the particular reading I am making. I was particularly
interested in details that were present in her manuscripts from the
start, versus details that were added later. Collating her revisions with
the published stories has been a labor of love, and now that an invaluable guide to the manuscripts and other Welty materials is readily
available (Suzanne Marrs's *The Welty Collection*), I recommend a trip
to the archives to all interested readers. The Mississippi Department
of Archives and History in particular was a delight to work in, and
somewhat different (as I should have expected, but did not) from the
usual university library: as I read Welty's typescripts I was surrounded
by grandparents and parents and even a few teenagers doing family
genealogies. I could not help but think that my work was studying
family histories too. Seeing how carefully Welty typed, retyped, and
then re-retyped her stories, furthermore—sometimes affixing newly
typed passages to old with straight pins at the corners—gave me an

even deeper appreciation for the time these stories took to weave themselves, and the time they need to be read properly, or listened to. Silence and slow time: I imagined the new versions growing gradually on the page, the steady click of the typing machine, the pauses to cut and then carefully pin, with cicadas (perhaps) in the distance. Most of us are wedded to word processors now, where adding, deleting, and transposing is done at the speed of light. But the *process* that Welty's words required is something else again—more a procession, a light that moves as slowly and majestically as sunlight along the wall or a constellation or a galaxy through the sky.

My trip to Jackson (the first time I had been to Mississippi) taught me many unexpected things aside from what I learned in the archives. I suddenly realized how central the city is: all roads in Mississippi lead to it. It is not New York City (more power to it), but it is definitely the center of a thriving world. I felt a *circumference*, as Emily Dickinson would say. Government buildings, Confederate statues, governor's mansions, stores, the headquarters for the Foresters Union, and her father Christian Welty's impressive Lamar Life Insurance building all occupy the high ground above the Pearl River, while downhill to the east, barely more than a quarter mile from the archives building, lies the State Fair Grounds on the Pearl River's flood plain. Just north of town the Natchez Trace crosses on its way west and south toward the Mississippi. Living where she did, how could Welty not mix legends of the Natchez Trace with contemporary culture at its most shrill, or characters who think they represent the aristocracy with those who belong to the carnival, the side-show? It reminded me of my first visit to Concord, Massachusetts, when I discovered that the famous bridge at which the Minutemen made their stand was in the *backyard* of Hawthorne's Old Manse, or that a railroad embankment literally forms part of the very shore of Walden pond, so that to circumnavigate the lake you have to walk on the railroad's property as well as in the woods. No wonder Hawthorne was so obsessed with history, and Thoreau with machines in gardens. Other revelations in Jackson were sustaining too, especially after long days poring over manuscripts. Driving downtown to the archives each morning I passed the spacious new public library named in Eudora Welty's honor. A huge Rent-a-Sign on wheels was parked out by the front entrance, with the message "NEW WELTY HOURS." "Couldn't agree more," I thought to myself.

In a 1947 lecture entitled "Some Views on the Reading and Writing of Short Stories," written in the midst of working on *The Golden Apples,* Eudora Welty began and ended the lecture with what at first glance seem to be contradictory claims for her art. On the one hand, she said that "the great stories of the world are the ones that seem new to their readers besides their writers, on and on, always new because they keep their power of revealing something." Yet near the end of the lecture, she stated, "The fine story writers seem, have you noticed? to be obstructionists. They hold back their own best interests— or what would be in another writer their best interests. It's a strange illusion. For if we look to the source of the deepest pleasure we receive from a writer, how surprising it seems that this very source is the quondam obstruction. . . . [T]he story is held up forever, and through so delaying and through such refusal on the author's part, we enter the magical world of pure sense, of evocation."[2]

One of the goals of this book is to show that these two statements may be reconciled: they are really two versions of the same truth. Through the special delays, obstructions, refusals, and disguises of her art, Welty subverts what other writers—particularly women writers— were expected to do; she questions whether in life and in fiction the conventions that have been dictated to them are indeed in their own "best interest." Only after such refusals are made may new sources of power and evocation be revealed. The hidden subject of *The Heart of the Story* is how through a sibylline sleight-of-hand Welty's art merges disguise and revelation into one motion.

The Heart of the Story
Eudora Welty's Short Fiction

Chapter 1

The Anxieties of Authorship

Heroines and Women Artists in

A Curtain of Green

The woman writer . . . searches for a female model not because she wants dutifully to comply with male definitions of her "femininity" but because she must legitimize her own rebellious endeavors. . . . [F]or an "anxiety of influence" the woman writer substitutes what we have called an "anxiety of authorship," an anxiety built from complex and often only barely conscious fears of that authority which seems to the female artist to be by definition inappropriate to her sex.

—Gilbert and Gubar,
The Madwoman in the Attic

*that revolted cry
Is sobbed in thy women's voice forlorn, —
Thy woman's hair, my sister, all unshorn,
Floats back dishevelled strength in agony.*

—Elizabeth Barrett Browning,
"To George Sand—A Recognition"

The seventeen stories collected in Eudora Welty's first book, *A Curtain of Green*, are haunted by the sound of women crying, by images of dishevelled hair and hidden grimaces. The protagonist of the volume's title story, Mrs. Larkin, works in her hidden garden with her hair "streaming and tangled" (*Collected Stories* 107); the heroine of "Clytie" stares at an image of herself in water and sees "a wavering, inscrutable face," with a nose "ugly and discolored as if from weeping" and her dark hair "disreputable and wild" (90); Old Addie in "A Visit of Charity" curses and cries; and Sister in "Why I Live at the P.O." talks nonstop,

3

as if to keep from breaking down. Even tales with male protagonists such as "Old Mr. Marblehall" and "Powerhouse" have passages packed with enigmatic, highly charged figures of speech describing suffering women—the rage and despair of Mr. Marblehall's two wives, the moment when Powerhouse is turned into a Medusa, "an East Indian queen, implacable, divine, and full of snakes" (135).

A reader of the volume may also be struck by the fact that the stories are filled with descriptions of violent activity packed into hidden, claustrophobic spaces. Consider the following comment by Albert J. Devlin, for example: "Often Welty will endow objects and places with the pathos of restricted personal space—Keela's cage, Lily [Daw]'s hope chest, Ruby Fisher's imaginary coffin in 'A Piece of News,' the falling tree in the title story, a guitar box which focuses the random murder in 'The Hitch-Hikers,' the 'remote little station' in 'The Key,' Sister's 'little old window' . . . in 'Why I Live at the P.O.' and, most pathetically, the rain barrel from which Clytie's legs protrude 'like a pair of tongs' " (Chronicle 16).

To this list may be added Lily Daw's house "leaning steeply to one side" (5); Mrs. Larkin's "slanting, tangled garden" on a hill (107); Old Addie's cramped bedroom in a nursing home; the tiny purple booths and hair dryers at the beauty parlor in "Petrified Man"; Mrs. Marblehall's overstuffed parlor; and the run-down Gothic mansion in "Clytie."

These ghastly self-images are rarely presented in isolation. They are often paired with images of neat, "reputable" women, either singly or in groups. The violent Old Addie has a polite and gracious roommate; Mrs. Larkin has her women's-club neighbors spying on her from their second-story windows; Lily Daw must confront the respectable ladies of Victory; Mrs. Marblehall is paired with the violent Mrs. Bird; and Clytie must contend with her sister Octavia. Paired with women who represent the proper life a woman ought to lead in society, these heroines all experience the fate that awaits a woman who rebels.

Sandra M. Gilbert and Susan Gubar have remarked on the significance of such doubling in women's fiction:

> by projecting their rebellious impulses not into their heroines but into mad or monstrous women (who are suitably punished in the course of

the novel or poem), female authors dramatize their own self-division, their desire both to accept the strictures of patriarchal society and to reject them. What this means, however, is that the madwoman in literature by women is not merely, as she might be in male literature, an antagonist or foil to the heroine. Rather, she is usually in some sense the author's double, an image of her own anxiety and rage. Indeed, much of the poetry and fiction written by women conjures up this mad creature so that female authors can come to terms with their own uniquely female feelings of fragmentation, their own keen sense of the discrepancies between what they are and what they are supposed to be. . . . [W]omen writers in England and America, throughout the nineteenth century and on into the twentieth, have been especially concerned with assaulting and revising, deconstructing and reconstructing those images of women inherited from male literature, especially . . . the paradigmatic polarities of angel and monster. (*Madwoman* 78, 76)[1]

Anxious and guilty because both her life and her art challenge her society's definition of what a proper lady is, a woman writer's identification with her "mad" female characters may be both secretly sanctioned and also repressed. First the madwoman becomes the writer's alter ego, then she is "suitably punished" for her independence, becoming either a cautionary tale (if she persists in her errors unto death) or (if she repents) an example of the powers of reform.

There has been some debate as to whether the concept expressed in Gilbert and Gubar of an anxiety of authorship for women writers can possibly apply to southern women writers, who lack neither a tradition of women writers with which to identify nor (in many cases) family support for their work. Anne Goodwyn Jones, for example, has pointed out that between 1860 and 1870 two anthologies of southern women writers were published: southern women writers had become self-conscious of themselves as belonging to a tradition. Even before that, many of the most successful American novelists (like the audience for novels in general) were women, and many of those women were southern. Moreover, Jones argues that many southern women writers did not feel as sharp a division between their aspirations as writers and their duties to be mothers and "ladies" as other women writers may have: "with the help of southern traditions of family networks, [they] managed to live out a form of domesticity that gave them freedom to write yet kept them with their kin" (44).

Yet of course the fact that southern women writers thought of themselves as being part of a tradition does not necessarily mean that they cannot have felt an anxiety of authorship. There is a sharp difference between the proper role of "authorship" as it is defined by a particular society and the anxiety that may arise when a writer challenges those definitions of authorship. As Gilbert and Gubar use their concept of an anxiety of authorship, such ambivalence can just as well be felt by women writers working within a tradition of women writers as it can by women who feel essentially like isolated usurpers challenging a predominantly male tradition. This is particularly true if (as in the United States) that women's tradition proves unexpectedly constricting and conservative as well as empowering. Thus Anne Jones notes how often nineteenth-century American women's novels conclude in ways that are seriously at odds with their works' own inner development. The marriages that end many such novels are offered as a resolution of conflicts and anxieties that exfoliate throughout the novel's plot, but they tend to repress more than they resolve. Jones argues, for example, that the conclusion of Augusta Evans Wilson's *Beulah* (1859), a representative nineteenth-century American women's novel, "does not just turn the tables; it turns back the forward motion of the novel, denying the implications of the previous 450 pages rather than fulfilling them." Jones explains such an act as follows:

> Augusta Jane Evans [Wilson] found herself split between an inner vision and a desire to conform. The inner vision develops a female *Bildungsroman*, pioneering psychic integration and an inter-dependent relationship with one's community. But Evans' mask was that of the southern woman writer; the actual community for which and within which she wrote held strongly patriarchal values concerning religion, women, and the structure of society itself. Thus when Evans forces her *Bildungsroman* to fit the social expectations that it must, she has to convert her speculative protagonist to an All-Father God and shape her character into that of the child-wife who can serve as idol for a southern gentleman. . . . At the end . . . Beulah finds herself divided again, concealing her adult self behind the mask of a child. (57, 91)

Like Evans Wilson's character Beulah, the inheritance of southern women's fiction is divided against itself, filled with contrasts between its surfaces and its hidden interiors.

Eudora Welty is heir both to the popular tradition of southern women's fiction and to the ambivalence about that tradition and the social mores it underwrote shared by many of its participants. A full discussion of how Welty's fiction displays her debt to and rebellion against this tradition must wait for a later chapter, after Welty's stories have been closely attended to; for now, it will be sufficient to introduce the ways in which such ambivalence manifests itself in Welty's critical prose and her earlier short fiction.

"Ambivalence," admittedly, will probably not be the first word that comes to a reader's mind when reading Welty's comments on the craft of writing, and "anxiety" will most likely seem even less applicable. For Welty's critical prose from the 1940s through the 1960s brims with exuberance and confidence about the craft of fiction and the empowering examples earlier writers from Austen to Faulkner and Bowen have been to her. Moreover, she implies quite strongly that her work as a whole, like Chekhov's, is written not to protest but to praise: "Those who write with cruelty, and Lawrence is one, may not be lacking in compassion but stand in need to write in exorcisement. Chekhov was exorcising nothing, he simply showed it forth" (*Eye of the Story* 98). But other moments in Welty's critical prose suggest that a conception of the writer's gift that emphasizes only his or her drive "to praise, to love, to call up into view" (*Eye* 108) is simply not complex enough to capture an author's true sense of the relation between tradition and the individual talent. Intriguingly, several of the figures of speech Welty uses parallel those of Gilbert, Gubar, Spacks, Jones, and other contemporary women critics.

Welty's essays, for example, frequently return to the assertion that the art of criticism is essentially distinct from and foreign to the act of creation and may indeed be inimical to it if wielded irresponsibly. In 1949 she writes, "There is a Great Divide in the workings of the mind—shedding its energy in two directions—it creates in imagination, and it tears down in analysis" (*Short Stories* 8). Three later essays, "Words into Fiction," "Place in Fiction," and "Must the Novelist Crusade," among others, all touch on Welty's sense that the demands that readers make of an artist in the name of either literary tradition or social relevance—even when well-intentioned—often are misinformed, alienating, and oppressive. Her criticism is courteously stated but firm, and one senses underneath the surface of her strictures that she has been deeply hurt by some of the "careless" and "condescending" criticism her own work has sometimes received, especially early in her career (*Eye* 132; see also Devlin, *Chronicle* 3–15, 41–44, 82–85). Welty never defends her own work in her essays; rather she casts her defense as a defense of the best southern writing as a whole (especially in "Place in Fiction") or a defense of challenging, imaginative literature in general. What lingers in a reader's memory from these discussions of critics and criticism is principally how ambivalent Welty feels toward criticism: she is more than willing to concede criticism a place in cultural life but is strict about its proper limits and the damage it can do to writers when those limits are arrogantly transgressed. In particular, Welty seems especially apprehensive about which tradition she will be placed in and what standard she will be judged by; she seems driven by the knowledge that unless she defines her own tradition and her own criteria of judgment she will be defined by others. Similarly, in her interviews Welty has several times eloquently remembered the feelings of "exposure" and vulnerability she felt at the moment when her books were ready to be published and reviewed (Prenshaw, *Conversations* 27, 72, 76).

Even more revealing is the fact that when Welty claims a specific literary tradition for herself she *never* aligns herself with the tradition that we might expect, that of southern women's writing. Indeed, she seems to have gone out of her way not to mention in print any such precedents until the recent *One Writer's Beginnings*, as if she were anxious not to be associated with this tradition or judged by it. Welty's first extended essay on fiction, *Short Stories* (1949), mentions only two women writers, Katherine Mansfield and Virginia Woolf, while discussing over a dozen male writers. Since 1950 of course Welty has commented frequently on selected women writers in print and in interviews, but again the majority have not been American, much less southern, and when she was asked in interviews about earlier southern women writers, especially nineteenth-century ones, her disdain is palpable (Prenshaw, *Conversations* 8, 80). (Katherine Anne Porter and Flannery O'Connor are the two southern women writers whose work she is happy to acknowledge is exceptional.) Welty would no doubt protest against a reader raising her literary heritage as an issue in this way by saying that she is interested in exemplary artists regardless of their gender or nationality. But the fact that with a few crucial exceptions such role models for her have *not* been southern women suggests that she has found their example to be not especially empowering, that instead of criticizing their tradition directly she has gently steered her readers toward other authors with whom she feels she is more appropriately compared.

Welty's ambivalence toward earlier southern women writers demonstrates itself even more notably in certain references to hidden enclosures and dark recesses in her critical prose and her earliest stories. Consider the passage from *Short Stories* quoted in the preface, stressing that the best art achieves its power and mystery through the "obstruction," "delaying," and "refusal" of readers' expectations (50–51). She does not explain this cryptic declaration of independence further, but we can reasonably hypothesize that some of the literary conventions she has in mind to "obstruct" are those associated with popular women's sentimental romances, many of them by southerners. Or consider the following remarkable passage from "Words into Fiction":

> Fiction is not a cave; and human life, fiction's territory, merely contains caves. . . . Without the act of human understanding . . . experience is the worst kind of emptiness; it is obliteration, black or prismatic, as meaningless as was indeed that loveless cave [Mammoth Cave in Kentucky, described earlier in the essay]. Before there is meaning, there has to occur some personal act of vision. And it is this that is continuously projected as the novelist writes, and again as we, each to ourselves, read.
>
> If this makes fiction sound full of mystery, I think it's fuller than I know how to say. (*Eye of the Story* 136–37)

Welty begins this passage by implying that life has caves and cavities but fiction does not, but by the end of the paragraph and the beginning of the next she implies very clearly that fiction itself is mysterious and filled with hidden recesses. Later passages in the essay continue to link fiction and dark, hidden things: a writer has to "survive through some history or other if he is here to write at all"; he "has it to struggle with" and "may come on it by seeming accident, like falling over a chair in a dark room" (141); "the words follow the contours of some continuous relationship between what can be told and what cannot be told, to be in the silence of reading the lightest of the hammers that tap their way along this side of chaos" (143); and "the novelist took all he knew with him and made that leap in the dark" (145). Possibly influenced by the famous assertion of a novelist in Henry James's "The Middle Years" that "we work in the dark—we do what we can . . . the rest is the madness of art" (258), Welty's essay eloquently argues that praise is not the artist's only motive and that anxiety in the face of the task and the risks is central rather than peripheral. True, Welty to a large degree suggests that such a condition is *universally* felt by all ambitious artists regardless of place, time, or gender. But the difficulties of such a position must be doubly felt for an artist such as Welty whose primary tradition, that of other southern women novelists, bestows such a mixed inheritance upon her. Such an artist is doubly exposed and doubly threatened, particularly since she knows that the tradition she feels so ambivalent about is precisely the one against which she will often be measured. Hence it is hardly an accident that when the success of Welty's career was still problematic she did her utmost to disassociate herself from the southern women writer's tradition by mentioning as her models primarily European men and women, plus Faulkner. *Short Stories* suggests that fiction contains many mixed messages and hidden recesses, as indeed Welty's fiction, both long and short, proves to do. Surely we can also read her first extended essay on literary tradition and literary theory as a statement about how the "history" that an artist must "survive" includes not just her personal life but her relation to her literary predecessors.

Welty's early fiction, from *A Curtain of Green* through *The Golden Apples*, is even more revealing about the ambivalence and anxiety Welty felt about her southern literary heritage. It is to those early stories of a woman's and an artist's anxious and guilt-ridden inner life that we should now turn. This chapter first considers five early stories from *A Curtain of Green* in which some form of what Gilbert and Gubar ironically call being "suitably punished" (78) is exacted against a protagonist who creates either overt or covert challenges to an established order: "Lily Daw and the Three Ladies," "A Visit of Charity," "Old Mr. Marblehall," "A Curtain of Green," and "Clytie." Remarkably, the narrative voice in these stories (especially the last three) appears largely to side with the forces of conventionality, not the rebellious protagonists, and the allegedly omniscient narratives of these stories appear somewhat untrustworthy when read skeptically. Such mixed signals are in line with the special ambivalence toward their own art that Jones and Gilbert and Gubar associate with many women writers. The chapter then concludes with a discussion of three stories—"A Piece of News," "A Worn Path," and "Powerhouse"— whose more powerful protagonists escape any form of retribution and (especially in the last two stories) appear sharply to critique their society's mores.

*

Of all the stories in A *Curtain of Green,* "Lily Daw and the Three Ladies" represents most clearly the choice open to white southern women in Welty's early stories. (Perhaps it is for this reason that Welty chose it to open her first collection.) That choice is suggested by the story's title: a woman may be either a married and respectable lady, like Mrs. Carter and her friend Mrs. Watts, or she may be eccentric like the retarded girl Lily Daw, continually threatened by scandal, madness, and confinement.[2]

Lily grew up as a ward of the ladies of Victory, Mississippi, but now, in her teens, she has suddenly begun acting independently, talking back to her elders, sneaking away to circuses, and showing an interest in the opposite sex. The town's matriarchs first decide that confinement in an asylum can be the only remedy, but then, in a comic reversal caused partly by Lily's boyfriend's faithfulness and partly by the rebellion of one of their own members, Aimee Slocum, they decide that Lily's marrying her boyfriend must be accepted after all. By juxtaposing marriage and madness in such an exaggerated way, Welty's story comically subverts the ladies' authority. Their ideal of marriage comes to seem a kind of confining madness, whereas Lily's unconscious defiance of the community's standards becomes a liberating sanity, an escape and transformation. Yet even this twist is not the last the story has in store for us. Our euphoria over Lily's apparent victory over the ladies fades slightly when the story is reread: even as she is united with her lover we can see the ladies extending their control over her again. The story's acerbity and exuberance hardly suggest anxiety on Welty's part, yet its pointed linking of rebelliousness and madness provides an appropriate entry into the other, darker stories in A Curtain of Green about the potentially disastrous consequences of nonconformity.

Lily Daw's defection from the ladies' rule comes very suddenly; they hear that she went to a traveling circus the night before and became entranced with the red-headed boy playing the xylophone.

> "Oh, it was a very nice show," said the lady who had gone. "And Lily acted so nice. She was a perfect lady—just set in her seat and stared."
>
> "Oh, she can be a lady—she can be," said Mrs. Carson, shaking her head and turning her eyes up. "That's just what breaks your heart."
>
> "Yes'm, she kept her eyes on—what's that thing makes all the commotion?—the xylophone," said the lady. "Didn't turn her head to the right or to the left the whole time. Set in front of me."
>
> "The point is, what did she do after the show?" asked Mrs. Watts practically. "Lily has gotten so she is very mature for her age."
>
> "Oh, Etta!" protested Mrs. Carson, looking at her wildly for a moment.
>
> "And that's how come we are sending her to Ellisville," finished Mrs. Watts. (3–4)

Here, acting the part of a "perfect lady" means a careful suppression of what Mrs. Watts delicately calls "maturity." Mrs. Carson and her cohorts recognize that Lily's retardedness means that she will never learn to play the part of a lady well; she is too susceptible to "commotion"—to the excitement of music, the xylophone player's red hair and racy slang. When Mrs. Carson, Mrs. Watts, and Aimee Slocum hear about what happened at the circus, they realize that they have arranged just in time to entomb her permanently within propriety at the Institute for the Feeble-Minded at Ellisville: "Lily Daw's getting in at Ellisville," they whisper to the other women in the post office, as if she had graduated from high school and been accepted at the prestigious college of her choice.

Welty's portrayal of the three ladies in the story's opening scene shows how they have carefully repressed the sensual, "natural" Lily within themselves in order to construct their status as "ladies." Mrs. Carson is a prim, self-righteous Baptist minister's wife. Other women in the town are embarrassed even to mention the circus in her presence, but when they do, she unctuously replies, "'Don't mind me, I know there are such things in the world,' . . . looking down and fingering the tape measure which hung over her bosom" (3). Mrs. Watts, the most authoritative of the three, wears "widow's black, and the least thing made her hot" (4). The third woman in the group, a spinster named Aimee Slocum, has distinctly less success in turning herself into a lady. Not only is she addressed by her first name, as Lily is, but she works in the post office and is bumbling and ugly—even Lily can see that. She is the only one of the three ladies whom Lily dares to insult.

Welty deftly demonstrates the stature that these three women hold in the town by setting the first scene in the town's post office while the day's mail is being put up in everyone's boxes. The post office is a major gathering place in any small southern town (hence Sister's proud retreat to it in "Why I Live at the P.O."), and the hour that the mail is put up is naturally a social highlight of the day. During this time, Mrs. Carson and Mrs. Watts reign supreme. The ladies' power, however, is hardly absolute. It is dependent upon the institution of marriage; they could not achieve their eminence in society without it. This is why Mrs. Carson murmurs "praise the fathers" (8) when Lily finally consents to give up her plans to marry and go to Ellisville: she sees herself as defending the standards of God the Father and the male representatives of His authority on earth, including her husband. Thus the near absence of males in the story does not mean that the town is run by women, but rather that the women's power would be impossible unless sanctioned by the "fathers." The story is thus not a satire of women with too much power but of women self-righteously acting on behalf of the "fathers"—the patriarchal authority that defines "proper" roles for both men and women to play.

Throughout the narrative, the third-person narrator appears to side with the ladies' point of view towards the events, imitating their language and adopting their reasoning. The narrator takes their opinions and presents them as objective fact, as when it is said of one of the women in the town, "she never understood anything" (5). As the story develops and the women's tyrannization over Lily becomes more obvious, however, a reader cannot help but notice ironic parallels between their ideas of marriage and confinement in a madhouse. Lily's retardation means that the women can bribe her into going to Ellisville by offering to give her presents for her bridal "hope chest" and threatening to refuse to give her anything if she goes through with her plan to marry the xylophonist, but the fact that Lily and her lady's hope chest will be sent to Ellisville suggests an ironic link between getting married and getting institutionalized in an insane asylum. How different, in fact, is Mrs. Carson's and Mrs. Watts's position? After all, they are dependent on an institution for their status, possessions, power, and even their names. Welty's story raises this question, but her readers are the only ones who hear it asked; Mrs. Carson and Mrs. Watts certainly do not, nor do the townspeople. They greet the train that will carry Lily to Ellisville and even arrange for a band to play a comically inappropriate piece called the "Independence March" to honor Lily's departure.

The story of Lily Daw of course turns out differently from what the three ladies expect: the xylophonist shows up in the crowd at the last minute, just as the train is about to pull out of the station, and Aimee Slocum defects and decides to rescue Lily, eventually persuading her to give up her "gift" of the train ride to Ellisville. Lily's seeming passivity and shyness during this final scene should not mislead us: Lily's own earlier acts of rebellion in the story have apparently awakened Aimee's own dormant sense of independence, and she arranges a reunion that seems to force the ladies of Victory to accept Lily's marrying the man she loves as the "right" and "proper" ending. Even Mrs. Watts must smile and greet the musician cordially.

Yet Welty's story leaves several issues unresolved, repressed for the sake of the comic ending and the narrative's gentle mockery of the three ladies. The first is the fact of Lily's anger. It surfaces only once in the story, when Lily lashes out at Aimee Slocum's ugliness, but it is ever-present and powerful, just as male power is. We feel it in Lily's flight from the ladies and in her frenzied efforts to gather her belongings together when they finally catch up with her at her house and entrap her. We also sense it in Welty's description of Lily's house, the first of many Gothic portraits of decrepit and rambling houses of women in A *Curtain of Green*. The house lacks front steps, as if it, like Lily, will not easily accommodate visitors from the town, and it "leaned steeply to one side, toward the railroad," as if desiring to flee (5). (This latter detail was added when Welty revised the story, thus drawing its hidden undercurrents closer to the surface.)[3]

The second issue that the comic ending of the story does not confront is the question of why Mrs. Carson and Mrs. Watts suddenly capitulate to Aimee Slocum's demands and let Lily marry. They seem startled by the musician's presence and Aimee's unprecedented resoluteness, but why should they not simply override Aimee, as they often have before? One answer that suggests itself is that they are afraid that they may be sending a pregnant woman to Ellisville; once the musician appears they realize that marrying Lily off may very well be the safer course. Another is that they realize that their power over Lily once she is married may very well increase rather than diminish. Mrs. Carson's first comment when she sees Lily's future husband in the crowd, before they have agreed to let Lily get off the train ("Mercy! He's small, isn't he?" [11]), implies a victory for the ladies of Victory: Lily may yet be forced to conform to the standards of the "fathers" for being a lady. Despite her sometimes unconventional behavior and instinctive distrust of the three ladies, Lily has fully absorbed her society's standards for what a proper lady is: her treasured hope chest contains two bars of soap and a washcloth, and she is delighted when the ladies promise her other items associated with proper femininity, such as a Bible, hemstitched pillowcases, and a brassiere. The most revealing gift the women have bestowed on Lily is associated with mourning, not marriage: throughout the story Mrs. Watts wears "widow's black" (4), and the dress she gives Lily to cover up the petticoat Lily prefers wearing in public is "made out of part of Mrs. Watts's last summer's mourning" (9). Lily thus wears second-hand mourning to her wedding. There is something funereal about everything the three ladies do, in spite of their frantic energy, and the rite of marriage as they conceive it is more an act of entombment than of metamorphosis.

The complexities of the story's comic ending parallel the complexities of the story's narrative voice. Standard critical labels that may be used to define the narrative voice, such as "third-person" and "omniscient," are misleading. Recently the work of M. M. Bakhtin has advanced beyond Wayne Booth's classic *The Rhetoric of Fiction*, teaching us new ways of conceiving of the ironic play of meanings possible within a "third-person" voice. We must learn to notice the irony and the unspoken in Welty's narrative voices in *A Curtain of Green* and her later fiction; in Bakhtin's sense, these narrative voices are always dialogical, ironically quoting the language of social authority so that it can be questioned, can be engaged in dialogue rather than treated as a monologue. Apparent praise of the "fathers" (or of the ladies) is thus not necessarily praise. Just as importantly, we must learn to see how "omniscient" narrators in Welty always have blind spots and that the alleged unity of her "third-person" narrators is in practice fractured and multivocal. Indeed, Welty's third-person narrators are really no more unified than the "three ladies" in "Lily Daw": they may appear to speak in a single voice, but actually they are in perpetual contention with themselves and with opposing voices such as Lily's that they can so vividly imagine.

In *One Writer's Beginnings*, Welty notes that "it is not for nothing that an ominous feeling often attaches itself to a procession. . . . [W]e know to greet them with distrust and apprehension: their intent is still to be revealed. (Think what it was in 'My Kinsman, Major Molineux')" (37). Of all the stories in *A Curtain of Green*, "Lily Daw and the Three Ladies" has the largest and loudest procession—and, despite its exuberant tone and that straw hat thrown up into the telephone wires at the end (9), perhaps the most foreboding one. It is only in other stories in *A Curtain of Green* that Welty directly confronts the anger and claustrophobia that all her heroines feel.

"A Visit of Charity," for example, begins when two residents of a town's Old Ladies' Home are timorously visited by Marian, a young Campfire Girl hoping to earn points for a merit badge: "'any of them will do,' Marian stammered [to the receptionist]. With her free hand she pushed her hair behind her ears, as she did when it was time to study Science" (113). The Old Ladies' Home reminds Marian of a "robber's cave" (114) or "the interior of a clock" (113), and once she meets two of the inhabitants she finds that one has a hand like a "bird claw" grabbing at her and the other looks and sounds like a sheep. They both argue with each other in her presence and assault her with questions, startling her so severely that she forgets her name: "'I'm a Campfire Girl,' she said finally" (115).

When Marian cuts short the visit and runs out of the nursing home, she feels as if she is escaping becoming transformed into an animal and imprisoned. She grabs an apple she has hidden in the bushes outside the building and sprints to catch the bus home. "A Visit" is thus like a fairy tale in which a little girl becomes lost in a mysterious world and is in danger of becoming forever imprisoned. When Marian hops on the bus, takes a "big bite" out of her apple, and breathes a sigh of relief, it is as if her apple—unlike the apple that the witch gave Snow White—returns her to sunlight and sanity. The most important parallels between this girl's story and a fairy tale like "Snow White" are buried more deeply: if "Snow White" traces the links between opposed images of a woman's identity—an enraged Witch living alone and serene Perfection brought to life by a husband—"A Visit of Charity" also pairs images of a "normal" and "abnormal" women. Welty's portrait of the two old women whom Marian visits makes the same connection "Snow White" does between serenity and rage, a public acceptance of limited power and an inner sense of imprisonment and despair.[4]

There are two "witches" in the room that Marian visits, one a woman without a name who moves about the room and another who is confined to her bed and called "Old Addie." From the very beginning, the unnamed woman is the more sociable. Although she frightens Marian, she also accepts Marian's gift of flowers and asks, "Did you come to be our little girl for a while?" (114), and she politely explains to her that another girl "came out last month to see us" and "read to us out of the Bible." "We enjoyed it," she adds. She also mentions that she too once lived in the world and had an identity, not like now in the nursing home: "'When I was a little girl like you, I went to school and all,' said the old woman in the same intimate, menacing voice. 'Not here—another town'" (116). Old Addie, in contrast, speaks in non sequiturs and refuses to be polite, contradict-

ing everything and periodically exploding with rage. When her roommate praises Marian's flowers and says they enjoyed the last Campfire
Girl's visit, Addie says that the flowers were ugly "stinkweeds" and
that she hated the girl who brought them. Her roommate feels called
upon to explain away her rudeness: "'She's ailing today. . . . That's
only the contrary way she talks when you all come'" (115–16).

Part of Addie's angry refusal to be sociable is due to her resentment
at growing old and being confined to a bed. She is enraged when her
roommate tells Marian that it's her birthday today, then breaks down
and cries. The narrator's earlier comment that the Old Ladies' Home
smelled like "the interior of a clock" is relevant here: Addie feels
trapped by time itself, confined within her dying body. But Addie's
longest speech in the story shows that she is not enraged merely at the
natural event of aging. Suppressed resentments that have built up for
years when she lived in society now come boiling out whenever visitors bring that world back to her. When her companion mentions that
she too once lived in the world, Addie erupts:

> "Hush!" said the sick woman. "You never went to school. You never
> came and you never went. You never were anything— only here. You
> never were born! You don't know anything. Your head is empty, your
> heart and hands and your old black purse are all empty, even that little
> old box that you brought with you you brought empty—you showed it
> to me. And yet you talk, talk, talk, talk, talk all the time until I think
> I'm losing my mind! Who are you? You're a stranger—a perfect
> stranger! Don't you know you're a stranger? Is it possible that they have
> actually done a thing like this to anyone—sent them in a stranger to
> talk, and rock, and tell away her whole long rigmarole? Do they seri-
> ously suppose that I'll be able to keep it up, day in, day out, night in,
> night out, living in the same room with a terrible old woman—
> forever?" (116)

The obsessively repetitive rhythms of this long speech are frightening enough, as is its escalation from merely contradicting a fact
about her roommate's schooling to the anguished vision of eternal
insanity with which it ends. What is most disturbing about the monologue, however, is the fact that Addie is really talking about herself as
much as about her roommate, and in doing so she reveals sources for
her anger that go far deeper than her roommate's polite chattering to
visitors. Addie names all the things that give a woman an "identity"

in society—her body, her possessions, and her "talk," her ability to perform sociably—and then savagely empties all these things of the meanings that society gives them. Social graces and other forms of perfection and power are merely useless activity, "rigmarole," nonsensical signs of madness. (In the story's original draft, Welty wrote "display" rather than the more suggestive and mournful "tell away," and "run of emptiness" rather than "rigmarole.")[5]

This bitter truth may be called the story-inside-the-story in "A Visit of Charity," the mirror-image on its wall that reflects anger, not the fairest beauty in the land. As if to recognize that all women lead double lives, Welty's story contains two old women and two stories. The first is the more public story, the one belonging to the friendly but anonymous woman. It is represented by her every action and by the story that she begins to tell Marian: "When I was a little girl like you, I went to school and all." But that story is continually interrupted by Addie's story, which usually remains hidden like Addie under her counterpane: "you're a story," her companion says in frustration at one point (115). Addie's cry of despair is her version of the meaning of a woman's life, and, significantly, it is Old Addie who has a name and a "story," not her anonymous companion. Marian's bite from the apple and the supposedly "imperial" power (118) it gives her at the end of Welty's tale seems to resolve things and restore her to a world of light and freedom, but its real meaning is that it has given Marian her first knowledge of women's pain and powerlessness.

Another story in *A Curtain of Green*, "Old Mr. Marblehall," explores more fully than Addie can the cost of leading a double life. In that story there is also an old couple apparently made up of one well adjusted and one poorly adjusted member—Mrs. and Mr. Marblehall, respectively. In discussing the story, Welty's commentators have focused almost exclusively on Mr. Marblehall, approving his rebelliousness and noting how adroitly Welty raises the question of whether his double identity is actual or imagined.[6] But I would argue that the most interesting double life in the story is *Mrs.* Marblehall's. It is more necessary to her than her husband's and more hidden—until a crucial figure of speech used by the narrator near the end of the story gives it away.

The portrait of Mr. Marblehall and his secret second marriage (as

"Mr. Bird") seems to be of a social iconoclast who delights in appearing to conform to his society's standards while secretly flouting them. He often wakes up at night, "his old eyes watering and wild, imagining that if people knew about his double life, they'd die" (97). Mr. Marblehall is actually quite well adjusted to the mores of the town he appears to resent; he simply wants to lead two lives in society, not one. He greatly enjoys his public life as the eccentric and venerable aristocrat Old Mr. Marblehall, fathering children at sixty and wearing a "bit of snapdragon" from his garden in his lapel, just as he enjoys his other, country life as the lower-class owner of a bungalow with a whining screen door and zinneas in a row in front. His two wives, however, are another story. The narrator who tells us about their lives, admittedly, does not appear to recognize this, even though possessed of apparently omniscient knowledge of Mr. Marblehall's thoughts; the narrator seems to think that the tale is wholly about Mr. Marblehall.

Mrs. Marblehall appears at first to be eminently well adjusted to the life of the town's upper class, a tea-going member of the DAR and the United Daughters of the Confederacy, while Mrs. Bird spends her time screaming at her neighbors:

> She looks like funny furniture—an unornamented stair post in one of these little houses, with her small monotonous round stupid head—or sometimes like a woodcut of a Bavarian witch. forefinger pointing, with scratches in the air all around her. But she's so static she scarcely moves, from her thick shoulders down past her cylindered brown dress to her short, stubby house slippers. . . . But when she stands there on the porch screaming to the neighbors, she reminds [Mr. Marblehall] of those flares that charm him so, that they leave burning in the street at night—the dark solid ball, then, tongue-like, the wicked, yellow, continuous, enslaving blaze on the stem. (94–95)

The reasons for Mrs. Bird's anger are not made clear in the brief time that we see her; it is too excessive to be explained by any of the things that happen. Its sources, I think, are more clearly shown in Mrs. Marblehall's story: we may think of the women as doubles, like Addie and her roommate. When we do, we see that Mrs. Marblehall is not nearly so well adjusted as she first appears to be.

Welty's only paragraph describing Mrs. Marblehall is worth quoting at length; it is the most intriguing in the story. First, its opening: "His wife, back at home in the parlor standing up to think, is a large, elongated old woman with electric-looking hair and curly lips. She has spent her life trying to escape from the parlor-like jaws of self-consciousness. Her late marriage has set in upon her nerves like a retriever nosing and puffing through dead leaves out in the woods. When she walks around the room she looks remote and nebulous, out on the fringe of habitation, and rather as if she must have been cruelly trained—otherwise she couldn't do actual, immediate things, like answering a telephone or putting on a hat." This suggests that Mrs. Marblehall is even more hunted by her town's conservatism than her husband is, that she too has a secret self living like Mrs. Bird "on the fringes of habitation." The last half of the paragraph implies that under Mrs. Marblehall's polite submission to "training" lies a very unquiet voice, like Mrs. Bird's.

> She has a voice that dizzies other ladies like an organ note, and amuses men like a halloo down the well. It's full of a hollow wind and echo, winding out through the wavery hope of her mouth. Do people know of her perpetual amazement? Back in safety she wonders, her untidy head trembles in the domestic dark. She remembers how everyone in Natchez will suddenly grow quiet around her. Old Mrs. Marblehall, Mr. Marblehall's wife: she even goes out in the rain, which southern women despise above everything, in big neat biscuit-colored galoshes, for which she "ordered off." She is only looking around— servile, undelighted, sleepy, expensive, tortured Mrs. Marblehall, pinning her mind with a pin to her husband's diet. She wants to tempt him, she tells him. What would he like best, that he can have?
> (91–92)

As this passage progresses, ironically, the power of Mrs. Marblehall's hidden voice diminishes; instead of the "perpetual amazement" at the life she feels in private, we see her "pinning her mind" to the role of the proper wife in public. The last sound we hear from her is her wifely voice, not her own. Like Addie, however, Mrs. Marblehall's inner self knows that this social voice is a "stranger" to her own and seems to press against it.

In the last paragraphs of the story, the narrator notes that Mr. Marblehall "has multiplied his life by deception" and often dreams of "some glorious finish, a great explosion of revelations." He does this, apparently, to keep from dreaming that "he is a great blazing butterfly stitching up a net" (97). The narrator then comments that this dream "doesn't make sense." It does not, perhaps, if we take the protagonist of the story to be Mr. Marblehall, for his dream of a secret life has allowed him to fly in the face of the town's mores, but in fact he is never associated with either "blazing" or butterflies—his wives are. Mrs. Bird's anger is like the pitch-pot's "tongue-like . . . wicked, yellow, continuous enslaving blaze on the stem" (95), while Mrs. Marblehall, playing the role of the good wife in the passage just quoted, "pins" her mind to her husband's needs like a captured butterfly. More than her husband, *she* is the butterfly that, grotesquely, has been trained to stitch the net that captures it. The choice between a "great explosion of revelations" and self-destructiveness thus lies more with Mrs. Marblehall and Mrs. Bird than with their husband. Those revelations about Mrs. Marblehall's inner self show no prospect of being released in the story: her town cannot imagine what such a newly revealed woman would look like. Potentially, however, she is far more scandalous and threatening than Mr. Marblehall could ever be: she is so much more thoroughly hidden.

The story's strangely unreliable "omniscient" narrator may be said to be the collective "voice" of the town, especially its women. This voice defines its story conventionally, by associating it with men's rebellions and exploits. Welty thus deftly reveals how our assumptions about "omniscience" are also related to assumptions about authority and gender. Like the narrator, we too assume that the story is primarily "about" Mr. Marblehall, with his wives merely minor players, but this narrative really manages to tell another set of stories—the stories of the wives—within the narrative space that it has designated as "belonging" to the husband's story. Indeed, we may go even further on speculating on the significance of the hidden women's stories in this tale. The narrator clearly relishes the hidden rebellion of her male protagonist, especially the shock the town's more conventional citizens will feel when the "scandal" of Mr. Marblehall's double life finally is exposed. If we assume that the narrative voice to some degree represents the collective voice of the women in the town, and that the "real" story being told involves Mrs. Marblehall and Mrs. Bird, then this suggests that the narrator is even more involved in dreaming up "double" lives than Mr. Marblehall is. She has created two scandalous female alter egos for herself and then hidden them under the guise of telling a story about a man's alter ego. Such a reading implies that Mrs. Bird's and Mrs. Marblehall's rage is hidden in all women in the town, even the most respectable ones. The most scandalous secret of "Old Mr. Marblehall," therefore, is not Mr. Marblehall's double life but the unconscious desire of the narrative voice for an "explosion of revelations" (97) about the unknown lives of women.

[The woman's intellect] is . . . for sweet ordering, arrangement, and decision. . . . This is the true nature of home—it is the place of Peace; the shelter, not only from all injury, but from all terror, doubt, and division. . . . And wherever a true wife comes, this home is always round her. . . . [T]he woman is to be within her gates, as the center of order, the balm of distress, and the mirror of beauty.

—John Ruskin,
"Of Queens' Gardens"

Yet another story about a woman's anger and grief in *A Curtain of Green* is the title story, placed next to "A Visit of Charity" and one story away from "Old Mr. Marblehall." It has usually been read as a meditation on the leading female character's struggle with such feelings, ending with her heroic acceptance of the coexistence of death and life in nature. Such a reading is a seemingly convincing one, for the story's narrator shows us how angry Mrs. Larkin is but ends the story with a healing rainfall, as if the sources of Mrs. Larkin's anger have been washed away. This interpretation of "A Curtain of Green" ignores the true sources of the protagonist's anger, which are social rather than natural, and ignores as well the questions that the story's ending leaves unanswered. Generalizations about Mrs. Larkin's discovery of "wholeness" in nature obscure rather than illuminate the sources of the story's power.[7]

As a consequence of a freak accident in which Mrs. Larkin's husband is killed in front of his house by a falling tree, she has become moody and withdrawn, refusing to engage in the town's prescribed ritual of a widow's public mourning and choosing instead to shun society and become an obsessive gardener. As she watched the tree fall on his car as he was arriving home from work, "she had spoken in a soft voice to him, never so intimate as at that moment, 'you can't be hurt.' . . . It was accident that was incredible, when her love for her husband was keeping him safe" (109). Mrs. Larkin's gardening has the same mixture of innocence and arrogance, as if by releasing the garden's limitless productivity she will somehow compensate for her husband's absence: "the extreme fertility of her garden formed at once a preoccupation and a challenge to Mrs. Larkin. Only by ceaseless activity could she cope with the rich blackness of this soil" (108). This is one apparent meaning of the story's title: the garden in back of her house forms a dense "curtain of green" that hides her view of the front of the house, the site of her husband's death.

Despite Mrs. Larkin's efforts, however, she cannot keep that scene out of her mind, cannot substitute her vision of nature's fertility for her experience of its random destructiveness. In the narrator's words, it was as if her curtain of green kept being "jerked quite unceremoniously away" (109) to expose nature's blackness beyond. Thus one day after she is giddy from working too long in the sun she suddenly imagines murdering a black boy whom she has hired to be her helper, quite as if she were lopping off the head of a weed with her hoe: "such a head she could strike off, so deeply did she know, from the effect of a man's danger and death, its cause in oblivion" (110). If nature may punish randomly, so may she; in this moment of temptation, it is murder, not gardening, that seems to offer her the best compensation for her husband's death.

Mrs. Larkin's energy and anger seem too excessive, though, for us to accept the narrator's explanation that their cause lies in nature itself, "the workings of accident, of life and death, of unaccountability" (110). The awkward use of grandiose abstractions in this sentence, relatively rare in Welty's writing, suggests that it is an explanation that the narrator is straining to believe. The deepest sources of Mrs. Larkin's rage are not understood by the narrator at all and have little to do with talk about nature's "unaccountability." The story-within-a-story in "A Curtain of Green," like that of "A Visit of Charity," tells of a woman's rage against society for the restrictions it places on what she can and cannot do.

The fact that Mrs. Larkin's anger is initiated by her husband's death is revealing: the choice of activities open to her as a widow suddenly defines for her how differently she and her husband were expected to live. The small Mississippi town in which the story takes place is named "Larkin's Hill," after her husband's father (108), and when she remembers her husband's life she associates him with work, a "blue automobile," and the shady street in front of their house giving access to the outside world. In other words, he represents for her public power and freedom of movement. After her husband's death Mrs. Larkin realizes apparently for the first time that she cannot step into her husband's public role in the town; the only public roles available to her are associated with women's clubs, the kind of glorified domesticity that so oppressed Mrs. Marblehall. Mrs. Larkin's decision to retreat from society and grow an unruly garden is thus an embittered attack on the town's standards of women's behavior, which have their sources in the Victorian ideals of a woman's properly "private" sphere of spiritual and domestic labors—in Ruskin's terms, her "queen's garden" of order and grace. Welty's narrative voice subtly reflects the cultivated indignation of Mrs. Larkin's female neighbors at her willful violation of a woman's duty to concern herself with "sweet orderings," or what her neighbors think of as a required "effect of restfulness, or even harmony of color," in both a woman's garden and her influence on her family (108).

> Mrs. Larkin's garden was a large, densely grown plot running downhill behind the small white house where she lived alone . . . . Now the intense light like a tweezers picked out her clumsy, small figure in its old pair of men's overalls rolled up at the sleeves and trousers, separated it from the thick leaves, and made it look strange and yellow as she worked with a hoe—over-vigorous, disreputable, and heedless. Within its border of hedge, high like a wall, and visible only from the upstairs windows of the neighbors, this slanting, tangled garden, more and more over-abundant and confusing, must have become so familiar to Mrs. Larkin that quite possibly by now she was unable to conceive of any other place. . . . Every morning she might be observed walking slowly, almost timidly, out of the white house . . . often with her hair streaming and tangled where she had neglected to comb it. (107)

Mrs. Larkin works in a pair of her husband's overalls, "heedless" of what the neighbors will say, but her disreputable masculine energy can only remain a parody of the life her husband led; it must be private where his was public, scandalous where his was perfectly acceptable, self-destructive where his was self-fulfilling. Perhaps the most notable detail in the entire passage quoted above is the fact that the garden plot "runs downhill behind the small white house." Mr. Larkin's world belongs to the front of the house, the world of Larkin's Hill, whereas the only area in which his wife can imagine living is *behind* the house, slanting away almost obscured from view on the "other" or "back" side of the hill on which the town is founded. Mrs. Larkin thus cultivates a secret life on the other side of the town's public space, a subversive doubling and disfiguring that expresses both energy and despair, entrapping her even as it provides a form of release. This garden's "plot" must always be an untold story, the tangling and disfiguring of old forms in "protest" (111) but unable to become more than that.

The scene in which Mrs. Larkin plots the murder of her helper Jamey can in fact be read not as an arrogant assumption of nature's violence (as the narrator suggests) but as a recognition that her own labors are merely negative and solipsistic: she sees herself in Jamey and despairingly decides to destroy herself through him. Thus Jamey is said to be entrapped within a "ridiculous" dream of his own (110) and is treated by Mrs. Larkin as if he were a product of her garden. The dream that Mrs. Larkin wants to destroy is really her own, not Jamey's, but in imagining such an act she also sees that as a gesture of protest against the town it is wholly ineffectual: "a feeling of stricture, of a responding hopelessness almost approaching ferocity, grew with alarming quickness about her" (110). Here the narrator's diagnosis of Mrs. Larkin's plight is a good deal more accurate than elsewhere.

Just as Mrs. Larkin is about to strike Jamey down it suddenly begins to rain, causing Mrs. Larkin to faint and freeing her—as if by an act of grace—from succumbing to her anger and murdering an innocent child. The rain falls on her upturned face, and briefly her torments are "adjusted" and eased: "Slowly her lips began to part. She seemed to move slightly, in the sad adjustment of a sleeper" (112). But this sleeper is fated to dream again. The story's ending, moving as it is, is also incomplete, repressing rather than resolving the causes of Mrs. Larkin's frustration. Like Mrs. Larkin's garden plot, her plots against the town will continue to proliferate and then end in stricture and despair.

Of all the stories in A *Curtain of Green*, "Clytie" explores the double life of a woman most thoroughly. With "A Memory," "The Key," "The Whistle," and "A Curtain of Green," it is perhaps the least controlled of the volume's stories, at least in formal terms, for its language is sometimes inflated, its form is an unstable mix of melo-drama and baroque meditation, and its central conflict is left thor-oughly unresolved. Yet it is a fascinating story—especially when com-pared with the other stories in Welty's first collection. It gives us a glimpse of the tensions in Welty's own psychic life that she could not yet resolve at this early stage of her career—tensions that are created not only by the double life her characters are forced to live in society but also the double life a woman artist must lead. It thus prefigures the great stories about women artists that Welty was to write later in her career.[8]

Like Mrs. Marblehall and the three ladies in "Lily Daw," Clytie Farr and her sister Octavia in "Clytie" are part of their town's aristocracy. Indeed, the town, Farr's Gin, was named after one of their ancestors. As members of the upper class, however, they have recently lost their preeminent social position through a series of scandals; the Farrs' Gothic mansion at the edge of town has become run-down, and the family history has been rocked with suicide, alcoholism, disease, and the failure of the family's only two daughters to marry. (This compi-lation implies that on one level the story may be read as Welty's comic exaggeration of the plotting of southern Gothic fiction.) Of all the people in her family, Clytie lives in the widest world. Her father is confined to his room after a stroke; her sister Octavia "never came all the way downstairs for any reason" (83); and her brother Gerald oc-casionally comes downstairs dressed to go to work in a downtown store but soon loses heart and retreats upstairs to his bedroom to drink. A similar fate, the townspeople believe, awaits Clytie. She is shunned during her trips to town and ordered about by her sister when she is at home, forced to cook, clean, and keep shut all the house's windows and doors.

Despite outward appearances, Clytie has a lively inner life. As Clytie lights the fire to cook supper and gazes into the open door of the stove, the narrator gives us our first glimpses of it.

> Anyone could have told you that there were not more than 150 people in Farr's Gin, "counting Negroes." Yet the number of faces seemed to Clytie almost infinite. She knew now to look slowly and carefully at a face; she was convinced that it was impossible to see it all at once. The first thing she discovered about a face was always that she had never seen it before. When she began to look at people's actual countenances there was no more familiarity in the world for her. . . . Was it possible to comprehend the eyes and the mouths of other people, which concealed she knew not what, and secretly asked for still another unknown thing? (83)

By interrogating these faces, Clytie hopes to recover a vision she once had of a self she might become, but her dreaming is continually interrupted by the demands that Octavia and the rest of her family place upon her: "Their faces came between her face and another. It was their faces which had come pushing in between, long ago, to hide some face that had looked back at her. And now it was hard to remember the way it looked, or the time when she had seen it first" (85–86). Both the faces of Clytie's family and the face of the "other" who holds the key to Clytie's secret identity are contemplated as if Clytie is watching a face emerge in the mysterious depths of a very special mirror—a mirror in which the mirror's face determines what the watcher looks like, not the reverse. If the interruptions caused by Clytie's family and the townspeople permanently come between her dream face and her own, she fears, she will lose her inner life entirely and be perpetually measured against those people's standards for how the roles of servant or "lady" should be performed.

The paragraphs quoted so far suggest that Clytie's response to this threat is a rather passive resignation, but on the next page of the story we see a very different Clytie: "she would run back to the vegetable patch and begin to curse. The cursing was new, and she cursed softly, like a singer going over a song for the first time. But it was something she could not stop. Words which at first horrified Clytie poured in a full, light stream from her throat, which soon, nevertheless, felt strangely relaxed and rested" (89). Like Mrs. Larkin in her garden or Addie in her bed, Clytie's cursing is motivated by rage, and like theirs hers is largely impotent. Her outpouring of rage usually ends with her contemplating the face of her censorious sister staring down at her—ends, in other words, in guilt for being angry, not in a cure for her anger's causes.

The weird climax of "Clytie" occurs when the town barber, Mr. Bobo, arrives to shave Mr. Farr and Clytie decides to challenge her sister's authority more directly than she ever has, with disastrous consequences. She reaches out to touch the barber's face (rather than merely looking at it), but her touch and her glance terrify Mr. Bobo, who flees down the stairs while Clytie collapses against the stair railing, "pale as a ghost," sensing nothing but her sister's angry voice shouting down at her from above (89). Mr. Bobo's flight—plus the fact that, for the first time in the story, an outsider's face seems as terrifying to Clytie as the faces of her family—causes a crisis in Clytie's ability to believe in her inner visions of people's faces. Suddenly, she fears that her imaginative power is merely a sign of her madness and her monstrosity. When her sister orders her to shave her father, for the first time in the story Clytie acts like a servant with relief, not regret—as if by acting the part well enough she will escape having to think about what has just happened. She "move[s] obediently down the stairs" and goes to the rainbarrel outside to get the water necessary for shaving, but a face is reflected in the water—the face of what she takes to be her madness and narcissism. The difficult conclusion of the story follows:

> It was a wavering, inscrutable face. The brows were drawn together as if in pain. The eyes were large, intent, almost avid, the nose ugly and discolored as if from weeping, the mouth old and closed from any speech. On either side of the head dark hair hung down in a disreputable and wild fashion. Everything about the face frightened and shocked her with its signs of waiting, of suffering. . . .
>
> "Clytie! Clytie! The water! The water!" came Octavia's monumental voice.
>
> Clytie did the only thing she could think of to do. She bent her angular body further, and thrust her head into the barrel, under the water, through its glittering surface into the kind, featureless depth, and held it there.
>
> When Old Lethy found her, she had fallen forward into the barrel, with her poor ladylike black-stockinged legs up-ended and hung apart like a pair of tongs. (90)

As had been prophesied earlier in the story, the image of Clytie as a distraught maniac that she sees reflected back to her in the townspeople's (and her family's) faces appears in the barrel's water and overcomes her inner vision of herself. When the end comes for Clytie it is a relief, a Lethe greater than what even Old Lethy (the Farrs' servant) can give her; the water's "featureless" depths promise release from the image of herself as a madwoman that stares up at her from its surface.

The ending of "Clytie," disturbing as it is, becomes even more unsettling when the reader realizes that it seems to mark a reversal in the narrator's attitude toward Clytie. Earlier in the story, the narrator was markedly sympathetic towards Clytie's inner visions, often contrasting them with the stale mental confines of her sister or the women at the post office. Indeed, the sympathy with which Clytie's love for others is rendered recalls Clytie's namesake in Ovid, where she is a young woman whose love for the sun god remained unrequited. Eventually because of her steadfastness she was changed into a sunflower, whose face followed the sun in its path across the sky (Hamilton 291). But the story's last sentence (especially the simile comparing Clytie's legs to a pair of tongs) brutally reverses such suggestions; it upends and mocks Clytie's pretensions of achieving imaginative power. The last opening through which Clytie gazes is not a stove door and a fire (83) but a barrel of rainwater, implying that her visionary openings are merely mad, solipsistic worlds, proof of all her sister's and the townspeople's judgments of her. In terms of Ovid's story, Welty's heroine is uprooted and plunged headdown into water and compared to a pair of tongs, not turned into a sunflower.

The narrator's act of retribution against Clytie—no kinder phrase will do—is an interpretive crux. The third-person narrative voice of this story, like so many others in the volume, proves to be less than reliable and homogeneous, despite its seeming authority; the narrator literally gives voice both to Clytie's inner life and to the societal and familial voices seeking to repress that life. In "Clytie" Welty has imagined a heroine whose secret life is similar to Mrs. Larkin's, Lily Daw's, and Mrs. Marblehall's, but who rebels so strongly that neither a successful repression of that life nor a comic reconciliation with society is possible. Yet Clytie's rebelliousness, repressed anger, and potential solipsism apparently threatened as much as fascinated Welty. Given the ending of the story, she seems to have feared that Clytie's fate may be the fate of any woman of imagination, incurring the anger of her community and perhaps even the curse of insanity. Nevertheless, Welty's narrative shows that she also resented as strongly as Clytie does the "monumental" and "commanding" societal voice of Octavia and the ladies at the post office, and felt that having her character yield to them would also be a kind of madness and self-annihilation.

"Clytie" is powerful precisely to the degree that it teaches us to question the accommodations of other stories in *A Curtain of Green,* the compromises that they make in order to achieve their happy endings. "A Curtain of Green" ends through an act of grace, a supernatural erasure of Mrs. Larkin's anger. "Lily Daw" temporarily defuses the challenge that Lily represents by arranging a precarious truce with the forces of conventionality through an arranged wedding. "A Visit of Charity" allows the young girl to rejoin the "normal" world and repress the nightmare of Addie's despair. In "Clytie," however, and in "Why I Live at the P.O" (discussed in Chapter Three), Welty creates heroines whose drives toward independence cannot be completely contained; they upend the social roles that they are expected to play and feverishly try to envision a new form for a woman's selfhood. They release anger about the penalties that women must pay when they transgress the forms of authority and independence that society allows them, but also their actions inspire fears (represented in both the narrators' voices and the stories' use of mockery and drive toward closure) that such subversiveness may be merely narcissistic—not a quest for a new identity but merely a tantrum like Sister's, a delusion like Clytie's, or an irrational nihilism like Mrs. Larkin's. Must the "wavery, inscrutable face" Clytie sees in the water, discolored and speechless, be the only face a woman's Muse may have? The stories in *A Curtain of Green* discussed so far disturbingly suggest that it is.

*

Welty's apparent resolution of her feelings toward strong female characters comes in three other stories in *A Curtain of Green*—"A Piece of News," "A Worn Path," and "Powerhouse." In these works she at last finds a way to escape the either/or choice between conformity and madness that torment the other heroines in the volume. In each of the stories, moreover, the social forces that conspire to confine the protagonist are represented by a written "text" of some kind—a newspaper in "A Piece of News," a notecard in "A Worn Path," a telegram and the audience's notes to the bandleader in "Powerhouse"—whose authority is subverted during the course of the story. The heroines and heroes in those stories not only create an alternative self to replace the conventional and the mad selves that society would force them to choose between but also to varying degrees force others to acknowledge the reality of their newly made selves—something that Clytie and Mrs. Larkin could not do.

"A Piece of News," at first glance, may hardly seem to be a story about a woman who gains a new identity.[9] Its protagonist, Ruby Fisher, is a poorly educated country wife who appears thoroughly conventional. She keeps house and cooks for her husband, Clyde, serving herself dinner only after he has finished his. She seems to fear and admire him equally, even admiring him precisely because he makes her fear him. From the very first moment he walks in the door, it is clear that he is used to getting his way: "'What's keepin' supper?' he growled" (15). We can also be sure that he may beat her if he gets angry enough: "'Don't you talk back to me. You been hitchhikin' again, ain't you?. . . . Some day I'm goin' to smack the livin' devil outa you'" (15–16). Furthermore, the central incident of the story not only shows Ruby to have a thoroughly naive understanding of who she is but also demonstrates her husband's belief that he has a right to dictate how she should behave. Ruby reads an article in an out-of-state paper about a "Ruby Fisher" who was shot in the leg by her husband and immediately assumes that the article must be about her—about her future if not her present life. When she shows the article to her husband after he returns, he guffaws and explains that it is a Tennessee paper: "That wasn't none of you it wrote about" (16). Ruby's mistake is superb comedy—a country bumpkin's case of mistaken identity. But both her naive misreading of the article and her husband's worldly-wise "correction" of it reveal a good deal about how society assumes a woman's identity is changed by marriage. An audience that hears the story read aloud may sense the story's comedy more easily than one that reads it on the page without being able to imagine Welty's voice. In my experience (Washington, D.C., 1984), when Welty reads the story both the women and the men in the gathering—but especially the women—find it a wry and irreverent comedy about fixed gender roles; there was much laughter in the audience.

To begin with, Clyde corrects Ruby's naive egocentrism by showing her that her name is not unique: there are other Ruby Fishers in the world, and other states with newspapers than Mississippi. Her body may be unique, but her name is not; like any name, it is a more or less arbitrary marker, and may, coincidentally, be shared by more than one person. Secondly, Clyde's explaining that there are other Fishers in the world is implicitly an assertion of her dependence on his name: her last name is his, after all. Ruby may think she is unique, but her identity has now become inextricably wedded to her husband's. If her first name is not really hers alone, her last name is even less so. We laugh at Ruby's mistake, but we also ought to realize that the true "piece of news" that the story's title refers to is not only the article in the newspaper but the "news" that Clyde has for Ruby about how now her identity is tied to her husband's.

The narrator of the story appears to condone Clyde's assertion of male authority. Ruby's appearance, voice, and actions are all described in conventionally feminine terms, such as "fluttering" and "delicate and vulnerable." Clyde's appearance when he comes in from the rain for dinner, in contrast, is one of massive strength, and the most brusque assertions of his authority are invariably tempered by the narrator's references to his good humor, as if his wielding power lightly were a sign of his benevolence. "He almost chuckled," Welty says after Clyde grunts "Don't you talk back to me" (15), and later she notes, "He laughed, to show that he had been right all the time" (16). Even though Clyde has not shot his wife, he evidently thinks that such an act is hardly beyond a husband's right: he never says that the husband in the article should not have shot his wife, only that this husband has not—yet. If he has the right to beat her, he may, in a moment of anger, think he has the right to shoot her.

Such a reading of the story as a vindication of the rights of patriarchal authority, however, meets difficulties when Welty's portrayal of Ruby's and Clyde's characters is examined more closely and when the story's use of irony is taken into account. Although Clyde has very conventional notions about the absoluteness of male authority, for instance, the possibility that he might actually hurt his wife is new to him: "Rare and wavering, some possibility stood timidly like a stranger between them and made them hang their heads" (16). Violence is a "stranger" to their union, a foreign element intruding itself. When Clyde and Ruby burn the newspaper, their act suggests not only that they are rejecting violence but also that their tie together has a fire's warmth to it: when the paper catches fire, warmth and brightness flood the room, shutting out the thunderstorm.

Ruby Fisher's own actions also complicate the story's depiction of her naïveté and passivity: "When Clyde would make her blue, she would go out onto the road, some car would slow down, and if it had a Tennessee license, the lucky kind, the chances were that she would spend the afternoon in the shed of the empty gin" (14). Like Welty's other women, Ruby leads a double life, not because she does not love her husband but because she has more sexual energy than he is willing or able to deal with. Her shy dutifulness in his presence later in the story contrasts markedly with the story's opening scenes, filled with Ruby's singing, talking, and unself-conscious sensuality. The newspaper is also used in her own way, not in the more "correct" way that Clyde will later use it. "When she was still, there was a passivity about her, or a deception of passivity, that was not really passive at all. There was something in her that never stopped. At last she flung herself onto the floor, back across the newspaper, and looked at length into the fire. It might have been a mirror in the cabin, into which she could look deeper and deeper as she pulled her fingers through her hair" (13). Ruby's imagination is associated with the "natural" powers of rain and fire, not the artificial authority of written language. Lying on the text in front of the fire singing to herself, Ruby transforms the newsprint until it reflects her own powers back to her. Unlike the mirror images of themselves that Clytie and other failed heroines construct, this self-image of Ruby's celebrates power, not the loss of it: "There was something in her that never stopped."

The newspaper's authority remains potent, however; it is manufactured, male, and strange, and as soon as Ruby starts reading, the text's forces assert themselves. Welty pointedly shows how uncomfortable the print makes Ruby feel when she uses it for its "right" purpose, for reading rather than for lying on. She becomes suddenly self-conscious and tense, as if her husband has returned. This change is caused not merely by the fact that she sees her name in the paper but by the act of reading itself. "She did not merely look at [the text]—she watched it, as if it were unpredictable, like a young girl watching a baby. . . . Crouching tensely and patting the creases away with small cracked red fingers, she frowned now and then at the blotched drawing of something and big letters that spelled a word underneath. Her lips trembled, as if looking and spelling so slowly had stirred her heart" (12–13; my ellipses). When she suddenly sees her name, "an expression of utter timidity came over her flat blue eyes and her soft mouth. . . . 'That's me,' she said softly, with deference, very formally" (13). Texts and the complex tasks required to decipher them are clearly associated in Ruby's mind with her husband's ability to define her responsibilities as a vigilant mother and properly deferential wife.

Once Ruby deciphers the text she gives it unlimited authority over her life, much like the authority she concedes Clyde when he is present. Like him, it may even determine her future. Furthermore, this sudden reminder of absolute male power over her brings out her buried guilt for seeing a traveling salesman earlier that afternoon: "What eye in the world did she feel looking in on her?" (13). Ruby's fantasizing by the fire thus ends with a vision of herself laid out in a coffin: "At once she imagined herself dying. She would have a nightgown to lie in, and a bullet in her heart. Anyone could tell, to see her lying there with that deep expression about her mouth. . . . She lay silently for a moment, composing her face into a look which would be beautiful, desirable, and dead" (14). Welty's witty linking of those last three adjectives is crucial: in the dream inspired by the newspaper, the only proper form of power a woman may have is in perfect passivity, self-sacrifice, and martyrdom. She may make her husband feel "the tears of some repentance" for shooting her (15), but this form of power is dictated by and subordinate to the male power represented by the text: it is gained only through death, through conformity to conventional definitions of femininity rather than resistance to them. We laugh when we read or hear such phrases as "that deep expression about her mouth" because we see how comically inadequate her compensatory dream of frozen "perfection" in her husband's eyes is to her own inner energy.

At the end of the story, Clyde refuses to act out the role of the conventional angry husband. Instead, he parodies it in a way that seems to be his unarticulated recognition of Ruby's right to have a double life not defined solely by her marriage to him. He does not pursue questioning her, much less force her to admit her guilt; in fact, he mocks his own authority by saying that showing him the newspaper was a joke Ruby played on him. Ruby, similarly, intuitively under-stands that the newspaper is wrong about their marriage. For her, it seems to prove that given Clyde's limitations she has a right to have a double life without being punished. Her reinterpretation of the mean-ing of what she read in the newspaper (16) is partly inspired by the fact that when her husband returns she sees that at least for now he clearly loves her too much to hurt her. Ruby is hardly passive. She covertly celebrates her right to live a second life unknown to her hus-band and to call that life "Ruby Fisher's" as well. Thus the paper is described near the end of the story not in "male" terms but with figures of speech associated with Ruby's earlier fantasy life—her singing to herself, the soft "rustle" of the fire (16).

Welty's revisions to the story appear to confirm such a reading, for some of her changes reveal her adjusting the tone of her mockery of male authority. In its earlier form, the story consistently is more judg-mental of Clyde, as in the following deleted sentence: "There was something terrifying and blank in him, the way he looked out of his small eyes, and yet desirous of domination." Welty's changes make her description of the husband more ironic, replacing a phrase like "crashed down into the chair" with "sat down with dignity . . . mak-ing a little tumult of his rightful wetness and hunger" (15). There was also a suggestion, edited out, that Ruby's decision to show the news-paper to her husband is first made "petulantly," as if she does not really accept his authority to interpret it.[10]

As powerful and pleasurable as Ruby Fisher's double life is, how-ever, it must remain silent, never naming itself, and the threat of male retribution passes away only temporarily, like the storm at the end of the story. This fact is of central importance. "A Piece of News" is finally about the *opposite* of news—secrets and hidden meanings. Ruby and Clyde share much of their joy at the end of the story, of course, but he is not nearly as aware of all the reasons for Ruby's being joyful as she is, or we are. Ruby's energy and independence, like the fire in the room, is "something that never stops," and it secretly revises the texts that are dictated to it. Yet it is still dependent upon those texts in the first place, forced to work within them, giving secret meanings to the newspaper "item" but hardly changing the dominance of male authority in the society that the newspaper represents. It remains for characters in two other stories in *A Curtain of Green*, Phoenix Jackson in "A Worn Path" and Powerhouse in "Powerhouse," to demonstrate that such a revision of the texts of an individual's identity may at least partially be rewritten publicly, not secretly.

There has been much discussion about whether Phoenix Jackson's grandson in "A Worn Path" is dead and his grandmother senile, unable to face the fact that he died from swallowing lye several years before the story's action takes place.[11] Such inquiry fruitlessly draws us away from the story, however, because Welty has carefully written the story so that we cannot solve the question based on internal evidence. Phoenix Jackson thinks he is alive, but her failing eyesight, hallucinations, and lapses of memory mean that her word cannot be taken as infallible; if she is able, briefly, to forget why she came to the city after she finally arrives there (147), she very well may be capable of repressing the memory of her grandson's death. Conversely, we cannot discount her word that her grandson is alive. No evidence conclusively contradicts her, and she is able, when necessary, to distinguish clearly between her dream world and the outside world. Her grandson may very well be in the condition that she describes so precisely: "'No, missy, he not dead, he just the same. . . . [H]e sit up there in the house all wrapped up, waiting by himself,' Phoenix went on. 'We is the only two left in the world. He suffer and it don't seem to put him back at all. He got a sweet look. He going to last. He wear a little patch quilt and peep out holding his mouth open like a little bird. I remembers so plain now. . . . I could tell him from all the others in creation'" (148).

Since Welty has told the story in such a way that we cannot solve the mystery of the grandson's state of health, we ought to ask whether the story holds other, more important mysteries to ponder. To begin with, we should notice when the question of whether or not the grandson is dead is first raised. Significantly, this happens at the clinic

that Phoenix Jackson visits in her long journey to the city for throat
medicine. "'You mustn't take up our time this way, Aunt Phoenix,'
the nurse said. 'Tell us quickly about your grandson, and get it over.
He isn't dead, is he?'" (148). Far from being authoritative, this passage raises at least as many doubts about the nurse's understanding
of the matter as it does about Phoenix's. The nurse's comment is
prompted by her impatience and is just as much a wish-fulfillment as
any earlier vision of Phoenix Jackson's, but hers has the authority of a
text behind it: "she had a card with something written on it, a little
list" (148). To her, the child's death seems the natural conclusion to
her list of the facts of the case and the times of Phoenix's visits. That
text is incomplete, for the nurse isn't precisely sure when the accident
occurred; the office is apparently most concerned with noting the
dates of Phoenix's visits and the fact that she cannot pay for the medicine. In the city, however, the nurse's version of the events, incomplete as it is, has more authority than Phoenix's; it is supported by
written records, not oral memory. But Welty's depiction of the nurse
clearly emphasizes how subjective her judgments are. In doing so, she
not only contrasts Phoenix's strength and compassion with the nurse's
callousness but also questions the authority of the whites' educational
and medical institutions. Trying to "solve" the matter of the boy's
fate, ironically, thus puts the story's readers in the position of the
nurses. For Phoenix Jackson, conversely, remembering the boy is
closely associated with talking about him, not writing about him; he
becomes most alive to her when she describes him. "I could tell him
from all the others in creation" means that she can distinguish his face
but also that she can "tell" his story: his very identity is inseparable
from the words that name him, and the mere sound of the phrase "my
little grandson" is enough to set off a flood of memories in the present
tense, as if the boy is immediately before her.

Phoenix, admittedly, has great respect for written texts, despite (or
perhaps because of) being illiterate. When she arrives at the clinic's
office, she notices a medical diploma on the wall that represents the
clinic's special authority: "she saw nailed up on the wall the document
that had been stamped with the gold seal and framed in the gold
frame, which matched the dream that was hung in her head" (147).
The power conferred by this document is institutional and textual,

simply a fancier version of the notecards and case histories that the nurse wields so authoritatively. Phoenix's oral resources and her "dream" match these: her grandson lives in her mind, and she in turn lives by imagining him. No wonder Welty chose the name Phoenix for her. The memory of Phoenix Jackson's miraculous powers of re-birth stays longest in our memory, even though Welty ends the story on a more somber note, reminding us of the odds against her heroine: "her slow step began on the stairs, going down" (149).[12]

Like the other heroines discussed in this chapter, Phoenix Jackson is imprisoned within a world of much pain and isolation. She may be able to command the nurse's assistant to give her a nickel, or ask a white lady in town with an armful of Christmas packages to put them down and tie her shoes for her, but she essentially lives in a world of her own, unintelligible to the whites she meets. She is able to turn such isolation into the basis of her strength, however, because she never concedes that the whites have the right to judge her; she re-mains steadfastly oblivious to their scorn, condescension, and advice. Unlike Mrs. Marblehall or Mrs. Larkin or, most importantly, Sister, Addie, and Clytie, she dismisses the constraining judgments of others and lives within the world created by her own interior monologue. The white world may force her to lead a double life, to be both a "Phoenix" of mythical powers and an "Aunt," the racist and sexist generic name for black women, but unlike other tales in *A Curtain of Green*, the story of Phoenix's hidden life is told without becoming a cry of despair. Even more than with Ruby Fisher, there is something in Phoenix Jackson "that would never stop."

In one hand
I hold tragedy
And in the other
Comedy, —
Masks for the soul.
Laugh with me.
You would laugh!
Weep with me.
You would weep!
Tears are my laughter.
Laughter is my pain.

Cry at my grinning mouth,
If you will.
Laugh at my sorrow's reign.
I am the Black Jester,
The dumb clown of the world,
The booted, booted fool of silly men.
Once I was wise.
Shall I be wise again?
— Langston Hughes, "The Jester"

Like Lily Daw and her xylophone player, Powerhouse is associated with the power of music to overflow and undermine restrictive social barriers: its hero is a jazz musician modeled on Fats Waller.[13] Like "A Piece of News" and "A Worn Path," "Powerhouse" dramatizes the conflict between the threatening authority of a written text versus the evasive and transformative powers of oral speech. In "Powerhouse," the text that threatens is a telegram, not a newspaper or a notecard, but like the others it purportedly documents a disaster: Powerhouse's telegram reads, "Your wife is dead. Uranus Knockwood." As with Ruby Fisher's burning the newspaper and Phoenix's ignoring the nurse's notecard, however, Powerhouse teaches us to undermine this text's authority—and with it, the authority of the social institutions that oppress the story's protagonist.

"Powerhouse" also presents (in disguised form) the fullest resolution in *A Curtain of Green* of the anxieties of authorship that Welty dramatized in her stories about women. She achieves such a resolution by portraying a man, not a woman, but at certain crucial episodes in the story the narrator's figures of speech clearly describe a woman, not a man, as if a buried subtext for the story were temporarily surfacing. In order fully to resolve her anxieties of authorship, Welty apparently needed to displace and disguise them twice—first, by choosing a story of how an African American jazz artist deals with his own anxieties; second, by telling that story using one of her characteristically unreliable narrators.

The first three paragraphs of the story make it clear that we will not see Powerhouse directly but through the eyes of a member of Powerhouse's white audience in Alligator, Mississippi, who speaks to us in the second person as if we, too, were a member of that audience. The whites are simultaneously attracted to and repelled by the black performers. They are fascinated by their mugging, their call-and-response improvisations with the lyrics, and Powerhouse's "stride" piano playing, but they do not behave at all like an African American audience would: "It's a white dance, and nobody dances except for a few straggling jitterbugs and two elderly couples. Everybody just stands around the band and watches Powerhouse" (133). The blacks' antics seem "obscene" (a word used twice in the first page) and "monstrous" to them, as if they are watching a freak show. The narrator's voice pulses with the pleasantly scandalized excitement of examining a series of cultural "Others" that become progressively more different from the white middle-class "norm"—what is at first irrational and non-Western then becomes non-adult and finally (the monkey simile) nonhuman: "You can't tell what he is. 'Negro man'?—he looks more Asiatic, monkey, Jewish, Babylonian, Peruvian, fanatic, devil. . . . He's not coal black— beverage colored—looks like a preacher when his mouth is shut, but then it opens—vast and obscene. And his mouth is going every minute: like a monkey's when it looks for something. Improvising, coming on a light and childish melody—smootch—he loves it with his mouth" (131).

The narrator's second-person address, which Welty made much more consistent in revising the story, uncannily implicates us, the reader; we are assumed to share her racism too.[14] The white's claims of aesthetic enjoyment mask their power to control the blacks, to make them do their bidding. "Is it possible that he could be this! When you have him there performing for you, that's what you feel. You know people on a stage—and people of a darker race—so likely to be marvellous, frightening" (131). In Welty's two other stories dealing with stage performers in A *Curtain of Green*, the cruelty of the audience is exposed largely through their fascination with "freaks of nature"—with deformed limbs in "Petrified Man" or a "maiden" (who is really a Negro man) eating raw chickens in "Keela, the Outcast Indian Maiden." There are strong social determinants to how a society defines its freaks; it is hardly just a "natural" process. Thus Keela's grotesqueness is heightened by the fact that "she" is supposedly Indian and female; her identity as a social outcast is an important component of her fitness to be made into a spectacle. (That the spectacle is a charade for Welty merely emphasizes the artificiality of the social stereotypes the "freak show" capitalizes on.) "Powerhouse" unmistakably dramatizes this truth: we see the audience ogling "freaks" created by racism, not by "nature."

Just before intermission the band plays a song requested by the audience—*Pagan Love Song*, "the only waltz they will ever consent to play." (Presumably their white audiences are always asking for waltzes, not blues.) But the version of the song that Powerhouse plays is a blues song disguised as a waltz: it is built up through the traditional call-and-response techniques of the blues, and it often has a blues 4/4 rhythm superimposed over the waltz's 3/4 (133). After telling us that a "Uranus Knockwood" sent him a telegram that his wife is dead, Powerhouse cries out, "What the hell was she up to," then shudders and repeats the story again, with variations. This follows the traditional blues stanzaic structure AAB, in which the repetition allows the singer to shift the emphasis slightly and color even more strongly the emotions with which the lines are sung. Of course, Powerhouse's improvised song lines do not strictly conform to a three-line structure of the blues chorus, for his exchanges with the band are much longer. But his actions demonstrate the rich malleability of the blues: each verse may be almost infinitely expanded, yet each retelling of the story goes ever deeper into the sources of pain, anger, and black humor that inspired the song: "'You say you got a telegram.' This is Valentine, patient and sleepy, beginning again. Powerhouse is elaborate. 'Yas, the time I go out, go way downstairs along a cor-ri-dor to where they puts us: coming back along the cor-ri-dor: steps out and hands me a telegram: Your wife is dead'" (134). The story of Powerhouse receiving the telegram in an empty hotel corridor late at night reveals a side of the performer that his audience perhaps would prefer not to see, what their life offstage may be like. Such a rendition of *Pagan Love Song* is surely different from the one they were expecting.

Just before intermission begins, the audience gets another glimpse of what a black's face may look like under his performer's mask. Powerhouse

> draws the chorus to an end. He pulls a big Northern hotel towel out of the deep pocket in his vast, special-cut tux pants and pushes his forehead into it.

"If she went and killed herself!" he says with a hidden face. "If she up and jumped out that window!" He gets to his feet, turning vaguely, wearing the towel on his head.

"Ha, ha!"

"Sheik, sheik!"

"She wouldn't do that."

Little Brother sets down his clarinet like a precious vase, and speaks. He [Powerhouse wearing his towel like a turban] still looks like an East Indian queen, implacable, divine, and full of snakes. "You ain't going to expect people doing what they says over long distance."

"Come on!" roars Powerhouse. He is already at the back door, he has pulled it wide open, and with a wild, gathered-up face is smelling the terrible night. (135)

That hidden face represents an experience of pain and guilt that the whites can only guess at. Perhaps part of it is hidden from Powerhouse's fellow musicians as well, who quickly improvise another stage persona for him even after the song is over to try to temper his despair. Welty's intriguing description of the beturbaned Powerhouse as a Medusa figure "full of snakes" belies this interpretation, however; it suggests a Medusan mixture of terror, guilt, anger, and pain beneath the comfortably exotic stage clowning, "pagan" headdress and all. The whites must look away.

During intermission, Powerhouse and his band go to an African American cafe nearby. The songs Powerhouse asks to be played on the jukebox, *Sent for You Yesterday and Here You Come Today* and *Empty Bed Blues*, all sing of loneliness and misunderstanding, as *Pagan Love Song* did. The first is a standard of Count Basie's Orchestra, a contemporary of Fats Waller's, but the second is a blues song from the 1920s, not the 1930s, and even though it is by one of the greatest black artists of all time, Bessie Smith, it is not on the jukebox. Welty's subtly made point is that Powerhouse is to some degree as isolated from this black audience as he is from the white one: they have already forgotten a part of their heritage that he most values. One of Powerhouse's musicians makes up a title for a blues song that captures their frustration: "White dance, week night, raining, Alligator, Mississippi, long ways from home" (136).

As word gets out that Powerhouse is in the cafe, the blacks crowd around expecting a performance, and Powerhouse starts yet another chorus of *Pagan Love Song,* trying once again to interpret the cold words of the telegram. Now Uranus Knockwood occupies an even more prominent place in the song. Powerhouse has personified all of the musicians' fears and guilt for leaving lovers behind in the figure of Uranus Knockwood, who may or may not be invented; each time the song is sung, those emotions come closer to the surface:

> "Uranus Knockwood!" [they sing.]
> "Yeahhh!"
> "He take our wives when we gone!"
> "He come in when we goes out!"
> "Uh-huh!"
> "He go out when we comes in!"
> "Yeahhh!"
> "He standing behind the door!"
> "Old Uranus Knockwood." (138)

Powerhouse teases his audience, who at first think he's merely making up a story. But then he pushes his tale to the very edge of tragedy, where tall tale becomes confession and laughter turns into pain:

> "Gypsy say," Powerhouse rumbles gently again, looking at them, "'What is the use? I'm gonna jump out so far—so far . . . .' Ssssst—!"
> "Don't, boss, don't do it agin," says Little Brother.
> "It's awful," says the waitress. "I hates that Mr. Knockwoods. All that the truth?"
> "Want to see the telegram I got from him?" Powerhouse's hand goes to the vast pocket.
> "Now wait, now wait, boss." They all watch him.
> "It must be the real truth," says the waitress, sucking in her lower lip. (139)

Has Powerhouse really received such a telegram? The drummer never quite fits into the routines of the band either on or off stage, and as the musicians are leaving to go back to the concert he clumsily breaks up the story that Powerhouse has been building and gives us a hint when he asks him, "'But ain't you going back there to call up Gypsy long distance, the way you did last night in that other place? I seen a telephone . . . . Just to see if she there at home?'" (140). This comment implies that Powerhouse could not have gotten the telegram he says he did last night because he talked to his wife on the phone that very night. Powerhouse's version does not make it clear when he got the telegram: he could have spoken to his wife earlier and then received it several hours later. No firm answer is possible. The important point is what Powerhouse does with his story, not whether it is "true" or not. He uses it as he uses his music, to wrestle with his emotions until he gets them under control. Pain is brought up to the surface and transformed—by brute effort—into a thing of beauty, a song with a pulse. The following superb passage was added late to the story, in revision: "Then he took hold of the piano, as if he saw it for the first time in his life, and tested it for strength, hit it down in the bass, played an octave with his elbow, lifted the top, looked inside, and leaned against it with all his might. He sat down and played it for a few minutes with outrageous force and got it under his power—a bass deep and coarse as a sea net—then produced something glimmering and fragile, and smiled" (140–41).

During the course of the story, Welty quietly shifts the voice of the narrator so that it is not so garrulously and embarrassingly that of a white person at the dance. The "white" narrator who addresses readers in the second person at the opening of the story is dropped for a more objective third-person narrator when the musicians go to Negrotown, and when Powerhouse's band returns to the stage after intermission the narrator's point of view seems to have transcended that of either a white or a black person. Even more importantly, when Welty revised the story she changed the ending from the narrator's discussing Powerhouse in the third person to Powerhouse directly addressing us, the audience, in the second person.[15] This change is significant; the second-person address that dramatized the narrator's condescending distance from Powerhouse in the first part of the story now demonstrates Powerhouse's closeness to the audience and the power he has gained: he addresses them, not the narrator. Powerhouse thus forces the whites to see and accept his act as much more than mere entertainment. For a moment at least, they cannot look away or merely ask for waltzes; they must gaze at his Medusa's face—the face of his anger and suffering—and recognize that "'Somebody loves me! . . . Maybe it's you!'" (141).

Powerhouse's transfiguration of the narrator's voice in the story is complemented by another, less obvious change: his revision of texts through the power of an oral art. Such a power is especially important because for black musicians the written word and the written musical sign are associated with the power of white culture: in Powerhouse's time in the 1930s white popular music was usually written down and published, black music improvised. Hence in "Powerhouse" each time a text is mentioned it is a threatening text. His white audience always hands him written requests for songs, for example, making it clear that this act is symbolic of the power that his white audience feels it can exercise over him as its entertainer: "Powerhouse has as much as possible done by signals. Everybody, laughing as if to hide a weakness, will sooner or later hand him up a written request. Powerhouse reads each one, studying with a secret face: that is the face which looks like a mask—anybody's; there is a moment when he makes a decision. Then a light slides under his eyelids, and he says, '92!' or some combination of figures—never a name" (132).

Powerhouse thus counters written requests with his own oral language, a system of signals, code words, and numbers signifying musical "numbers" or songs. Significantly, this system has the crucial function of disguising whether or not he has actually followed all of his audience's requests. Such a "mask" is important for maintaining a degree of freedom and dignity: over the course of the evening he may very well have played what he wanted to play, as well as what the audience wanted.

The other piece of writing in the story, the telegram, of course threatens Powerhouse much more directly. It too is transformed and partially evaded, as Powerhouse improvises different versions of what happened and, in the end, hints that the telegram may not exist: "'No, babe, it ain't the truth.' His eyebrows fly up . . . 'Truth is something worse, I ain't said what, yet. It's something hasn't come to me, but I ain't saying it won't'" (139). The fact that the telegram may have been "written" by a black (either Uranus or Powerhouse) does not diminish its link to white culture. Although all musicians have to confront fear and loneliness on the road, Jim Crow laws in the North and South in Powerhouse's time made the black musician's plight on the road more frustrating. The telegram symbolizes that truth. Powerhouse's improvising his blues choruses around the telegram's brutal four words, "your wife is dead," consequently stands as his protest against it. It is surely not a coincidence, moreover, that Powerhouse chooses the waltz number to begin that protest. He takes a form associated with his white audience and then turns it into blues, overlaying 4/4 on 3/4 rhythms and translating the original lyrics into a series of blues choruses. In the process, he forces his unexpecting audience to see the pain as well as the power of his art.

If blacks such as Powerhouse and Phoenix Jackson to varying degrees may revise the roles that white society writes for them, so may white women; the conditions of their oppression, while hardly identical, are analogous. With the exception of Ruby Fisher and Phoenix, the women in *A Curtain of Green* do not find a way to alter the cultural scripts that were given to them. The price that they pay is to become secret Medusa figures, full of rage that cannot express itself. The Medusa head that rears upward briefly in the midst of "Powerhouse" near the end of *A Curtain of Green* ("he still looks like an East Indian queen, implacable, divine, and full of snakes" [135]) is the last in a series of portraits of grief-distorted, wild, and threatening women's faces in that volume. Significantly, these portraits are also associated with frustrated oral energy, the repressed voices of their inner feelings clamoring to get out: Mrs. Larkin's obsessive interior monologue is complemented by Addie's shouting down her roommate's polite conversation; Mrs. Marblehall's possessing "a voice that dizzies other ladies . . . full of hollow wind and echo, winding through the wavery hope of her mouth" (92); Mrs. Bird's "screaming," a "wicked, yellow, continuous, enslaving blaze" (95); and Clytie's uncontrollable cursing. The end result of such an impotent release of energy is silence: the face that greets Clytie in the water just before she drowns herself has a mouth "old and closed from any speech" (90). With Powerhouse, however, Welty imagines a Medusa figure whose speech not only controls its audience but also carefully evades or rewrites the cultural texts she is "requested" to perform. In "Powerhouse" an image of emptiness and imprisonment that has tormented many of Welty's characters—the abandoned house that Lily Daw lives in, the "mad-houses" of Addie, Sister, and Clytie—becomes a *power*house. Power-house not only shows his audience his Medusa-like grimace, emblem of the price his psyche pays for their treating him as a monster, but he presents himself as a sibyl, an interpreter and controller of texts: "Then all quietly [Powerhouse] lays his finger on a key with the prom-ise and serenity of a sibyl touching the book" (131). (Note that Welty says "the" book, not "a" book, to make the sibyl's power more inclu-sive. This crucial sentence was not added to the story until its final version.) [16] Such a vision lasts only briefly, of course, but Welty's im-age of Powerhouse as a sibyl altering her culture's texts is the single most powerful instance in *A Curtain of Green* of what she expects a heroine (and an artist) to be.

"Powerhouse" thus provides a fine introduction to those stories dis-cussed in Chapter Three, all concerned with women whose indepen-dence does not cost them their sanity or their place in society. Inter-estingly enough, those women are often inspired by a musician figure, but in those later stories it is usually a female musician, not unlike the figure of Powerhouse-as-sibyl who briefly appears in "Powerhouse." Like the sibyl, such figures fuse the powers of oral and written art with an authority that is unavailable to any of the characters in *A Curtain of Green*, male or female. With these heroines is Welty finally able to transform the nightmare of the artist-as-Medusa into a vision of the artist-as-sibyl, as heroine.

The hidden power that the Medusa's face had for Eudora Welty's imagination, however, continues in the later stories she wrote. These include portraits of men who fear and hate women, as well as tales about tragic heroines who succumb to the Medusan images that their society projects onto them. In *A Curtain of Green*, Welty's tragic art has not yet matured; her tragic protagonists are striking but also rather two-dimensional and grotesque, without a past. In her mature tragic stories, many of which are discussed in the next chapter, her central characters have a complexly imagined past and present, and Welty is even clearer than she is in *A Curtain of Green* that their tragic fates are caused not by the stars but by ourselves—by confining cultural texts prescribing how men and women ought to behave.

CHAPTER 2

Misogyny and the Medusa's Gaze

Welty's Tragic Stories

From the very beginning of her career as a story writer, Welty tried her hand at writing tragedy. The earliest tragic story of those included in *The Collected Stories* is "Death of a Traveling Salesman" (1936), the first of a series of stories about troubled male wanderers; the most recent stories in the same collection, "Where Is the Voice Coming From?" (1963) and "The Demonstrators" (1966), depict an entire society that seems tragically to have lost its bearings. Reynolds Price has argued that at the beginning of Welty's career she kept her tragic stories strictly separate from her comic ones, whereas later she did not: "In [Welty's] early work—till 1955—she tended to separate [tragedy and comedy] as firmly as a Greek dramatist. There is some tentative mingling in the larger works, *Delta Wedding* and the linked stories of *The Golden Apples;* but by far the greater number of the early stories divide cleanly—into rural comedy or farce, pathos or tragic lament, romance or lyric celebration, lethal satire" ("The Onlooker Smiling" [1986], 76). Price's point is sound in many ways: in *A Curtain of Green* the techniques of "A Memory" are markedly different from "Why I Live at the P.O.," and the genius of both *Losing Battles* and *The Optimist's Daughter,* two later works, is their constantly shifting mixture

of tragedy and comedy. But I believe Price's comment is also somewhat overstated, false to *The Golden Apples,* in which Welty's mix of
comedy and tragedy is hardly "tentative," tending to draw our attention away from those early stories such as "Petrified Man" or "A Worn
Path" that do attempt to intertwine tragedy and comedy or satire.
Welty's experiments with mixing tragedy and comedy begin in earnest
not in 1955, with *The Bride of the Innisfallen,* as Price implies, but over
a decade earlier. It indeed appears that from the beginning it was
Welty's instinct as an artist—like Shakespeare, Chekhov, Woolf, and
other writers she admires—to *mix* her genres as thoroughly as possible.
The more "tragic" a story is in outline the more carnivalesque Welty's
narrative method tends to become, and, conversely, the more "comic"
and farcical a story's surface the darker and more disturbing its inner
heart. ("Keela, the Outcast Indian Maiden" and "June Recital" are
examples of the former case; "Why I Live at the P.O." and "Petrified
Man" of the latter. See also Welty's comments on tragicomedy in
Prenshaw, *Conversations,* 189.) Certainly this is true of Welty's best
stories, whereas stories like "The Key" or "Clytie" or "Asphodel" seem
to be more minor tales in comparison precisely because they lack such
a controlled tension between their form and their content.

Other readers, including Robert Penn Warren, Ruth Vande Kieft,
and Michael Kreyling, have stressed the continuities in Welty's work
over four decades, noting that one of the most frequent motifs in Welty's stories throughout her career is the tragedy of isolation—what
Robert Penn Warren aptly called stories of "love and separateness."
Following Warren, Kreyling argues that motifs of physical and spiritual
pilgrimage as well as separateness interlace all of Welty's short-story
collections, especially *The Golden Apples* and *The Bride of the Innisfallen:* "passages toward fulfillment of dream, lonely souls in need of response, calls sent out in hope of connecting with other lonely hearts
(128–29). Vande Kieft notes further how often in *The Bride of the
Innisfallen* this tragically unanswered call is a woman's:

> Except in "Kin," where the pleading call is that of an old man remem-
> bering, the call is a woman's, as in "Ladies in Spring"—secret, plain-
> tive, unanswered. A small boy named Dewey, "playing hooky" and
> gone fishing with his father Blackie, hears him called and feels intui-
> tively the desolation of that lonely girl's cry. Each of the heroines is

abandoned by her potential or actual lover: even the powerful Circe, semideity that she is, must endure the departure of the mortal Ulysses. Yet each of the love-burdened heroines retains the virtues of openness to life, the capacity to love, to renew hope and joy, to achieve an inner poise, steadiness, or stillness. (133)

In Welty's three earlier collections of stories there seem to be an equal number of male and female wanderer figures, unlike in *The Bride of the Innisfallen,* where they are predominately women. (The same holds true for her early longer fiction, as shown by Jamie Lockhart and Rosamond Musgrove in *The Robber Bridegroom* and George Fairchild and Laura McRaven in *Delta Wedding.*) There are portraits of men who feel oppressed by their relations with women, from "The Hitch-Hikers" and "Old Mr. Marblehall" and "Flowers for Marjorie" (in *A Curtain of Green*) to the stories featuring King, Ran, and Eugene MacLain in *The Golden Apples.* But disappointment haunts many of Welty's earlier heroines as well, some of whom are rescued (or rescue themselves) and some of whom are not: Livvie from "Livvie" and Jenny from "At the Landing" are just two examples from *The Wide Net,* and *The Golden Apples* has a host of major and minor women characters of this type, from Miss Eckhart, Virgie Rainey, and Cassie Morrison to Mrs. Rainey, Mrs. Morrison, and Miss Snowdie MacLain. Miss Eckhart's tragic story is the best known in Morgana, the fictional Mississippi town in which all but one of the stories in *The Golden Apples* is set, but the tragic story of a minor female character like Mrs. Morrison can become equally poignant. We meet Mrs. Morrison first at the edge of the action in "June Recital," the story focusing on Miss Eckhart, but by the end of the collection we learn in an aside that she has committed suicide—her reasons unknown, the story of her hopes and her pain largely untold (449).

Most of these and other tragic stories, like those described by Kreyling and Vande Kieft in *The Bride of the Innisfallen,* turn on abandonment: a character's love for another is expressed and then ignored or misunderstood, or remains unexpressed and unknown. About the same number of the characters who figure in these stories are male as are female, suggesting, at first glance at least, that for Welty tragedy transcends time, place, gender, and race and occurs whenever a human being is unable to make life-sustaining contact with another. As she has stressed in her interviews, her tragic characters tend not just to lack love but to be "separate," cut adrift from identity-grounding forces rooted in a particular place and time. Their great "affliction" is to live without memory: "They have nothing to draw on. They don't understand their own experience" (Prenshaw, *Conversations* 335–36).

A closer look at Welty's stories, however, reveals very interesting differences along gender lines among Welty's tragic protagonists. All of Welty's tragic characters, whether male or female, tend to be displaced wanderers restlessly looking for connection with others that will satisfy their craving for respect and love. Her male characters either tend to be looking for a lost maternal bond they cannot recover (as in her first published story, "Death of a Traveling Salesman") or, more frequently, they flee from one maternal bond to another, seeking to satisfy both their craving for unquestioned affection and their desire for "masculine" independence (as in "Flowers for Marjorie" and "The Whole World Knows"). Some of Welty's best stories of tragically isolated male characters feature wanderers whose responses to women range from distrust to outright misogyny, whereas the tragic heroines in her short fiction tend to be confined within a domestic sphere of some sort and are unable to wander, blocked not only by social restrictions but also by what this chapter will call the "Medusa's gaze," their view of themselves as monstrous. The forms of violence at the heart of these tragic stories also differ. The most frequent motif in Welty's tragic stories with a male protagonist is that of a husband stabbing or shooting a wife near the breasts (or imagining doing so): this is the act of violence buried at the center of "Flowers for Marjorie," "The Purple Hat," "The Whole World Knows," and "The Demonstrators." Other stories that focus on martial discord, from the early "Acrobats in the Park" to the later "Music from Spain" and "No Place for You, My Love," feature less violent mistreatment of women, but they are not really less disturbing for that. (The female protagonist in "No Place for You," for example, has a bruise on her face—possibly from her lover—and is mistreated by the story's other main character, a businessman, in a way that psychically bruises her a second time.) If the men in Welty's tragic stories often direct their violence towards others, however, Welty's female tragic figures tend to direct their violence against *themselves*: "Clytie" is the paradigmatic case in *A Cur-*

tain of Green, and in *The Golden Apples* Maideen Sumrall and Mrs. Morrison are suicides, and Miss Eckhart attempts suicide. No male character in any of Welty's stories commits suicide, though one, Ran MacLain, attempts to shoot himself, and another, Ran's father, leaves clues to make it seem that he has drowned. If this pattern of gender difference within tragedies of love and separateness is indeed in Welty's stories, several questions immediately arise. Why is this difference present, and what does it mean? What can these stories tell us about the causes of these differences? Is it simply fate or nature or chance, or is it social history?

Welty criticism has just begun to face such questions, much less answer them, but a discussion of them will be central as Welty's work is read and discussed in the next decades. (Indeed, in the 1980s such topics have emerged as central to the fields of literary history and theory in general.) In the interest of contributing to such a debate, the rest of this chapter and the next chapter on comedy will focus on those Welty stories that raise most provocatively the issues of gender difference in tragedy and comedy. Hence this chapter will not be an overview of all tragic motifs in Welty's stories—Welty's treatment of the tragic theme of love and separateness has already been well discussed by Warren, Vande Kieft, Kreyling, and others. Instead, the chapter will concentrate first on several of Welty's stories that specifically link tragedy to a man's fear of women, particularly "Flowers for Marjorie," "The Whole World Knows," and "Music from Spain," and then will conclude with close readings of "Petrified Man" and "June Recital," two stories in which Welty reinterprets the story of Perseus and the Medusa to investigate why women inflict violence on themselves. Concentrating on issues linking misogyny, the Medusa's gaze, and tragedy in Welty's fiction does not refute the insights of earlier definitions of Welty's tragic mode, but it adds what may be a significant and provocative new angle to discussion of this topic. Such a focus also demonstrates that much is to be gained by bringing together Welty's stories and contemporary developments in feminist criticism.

Of all the stories in *A Curtain of Green*, "Flowers for Marjorie" is the one in which we are made most conscious of the presence of male fears of women. The story is set in New York City during the depres-

sion, and Welty's original draft indicates that the opening scene occurs in "the park at Union Square."[1] From the very beginning of the
story, Welty contrasts the husband Howard's character with his wife
Marjorie's. His sense of time, for instance, is artificial, while hers is
associated with her body's biorhythms. "'Oh, Howard, can't you keep
track of the time?'" she says when he asks her for the umpteenth time
when their baby will be born. "'Those things always happen when
they're supposed to. Nothing can stop me from having the baby, that's
sure . . . even if you don't want it'" (100). When Howard sits next
to her he smells clover, reminding him that it is springtime, and he
also associates her with the "large curves of a mountain on the horizon
of a desert" (99)—as if for him she is Nature herself. Howard's sense
of time, in contrast, is derived solely from man-made things, and he
both yearns for and is threatened by his wife's difference from him.
"The ticks of the cheap alarm clock grew louder and louder as he
buried his face against her, feeling new desperation every moment in
the time-marked softness and the pulse of her sheltering body" (100).
Here Howard both seeks shelter and rebels against that shelter, listening to the clock's ticks even as he also feels her body's pulse. His
obsession with the clock is symptomatic of how his entire sense of time
and identity is dependent upon man-made things—upon clocks and
work-week calendars. Time for him means living in history, in New
York City during the depression. Each tick of the clock represents
another second in which he remains unemployed, unable to fulfill his
designated role of breadwinner for his family. He tries to show Marjorie that his sense of time is the correct and "responsible" one,
not hers:

> "Just because you're going to have a baby . . . doesn't mean every-
> thing else is going to happen and change! . . . That doesn't mean I will
> find work! It doesn't mean we aren't starving to death. . . ." In some
> gesture of his despair he had brought his little leather purse from his
> pocket, and was swinging it violently back and forth. "You might not
> know it, but you're the only thing left in the world that hasn't
> stopped!"
> The purse, like a little pendulum, slowed down in his hand. He
> stared at her intently, and then his working mouth drooped, and he
> stood there holding the purse as still as possible in his palms. (101)

The pendulum that governs Howard's world is an empty purse, as if money and a job are necessary to give time meaning. His purse's flaccid emptiness contrasts provocatively with Marjorie's swelling womb: the more he stares at her, the more threatened he is. A few paragraphs later, he suddenly stabs her just above the womb, killing her instantly.

Afterwards, he coldly views her body as a pendulum that he has stopped: "it was a perfect balance, Howard thought, starting at her arm. That was why Marjorie's arm did not fall" (102). He then flees to the crowds in the street seeking to lose himself, and we discover that this sense of time is not merely clock time but *commercial* time—a world of instant gratification and miraculous rather than natural growth. Welty's catalogue of the things that catch Howard's eye in the store window displays is not merely a wry parody of advertising but an analysis of how advertising shapes our thinking. Welty is particularly qualified to give such an analysis of commercial culture because she studied advertising in New York City at the Columbia School of Business in the late 1920s and early 1930s and wrote and sold advertisements on the side (Vande Kieft 5). In a 1942 interview she stressed that "I quit advertising because it was too much like sticking pins into people to make them buy things that they didn't need or really much want" (Van Gelder 5). Welty's analogy between voodoo and advertising's psychology of suggestion is demonstrated in "Flowers for Marjorie": advertising stereotypes condition Howard without his knowledge.

Howard's self-indulgent despair at not being able to get a job is linked to a belief that money will miraculously give him whatever he needs, even the perfect marriage. "He reached a crowd of people who were watching a machine behind a window; it made doughnuts very slowly. He went to the next door, where he saw another window full of colored prints of the Virgin Mary and nearly all kinds of birds and animals, and down below these a shelf of little gray pasteboard boxes in which were miniature toilets and night jars to be used in playing jokes, and in the middle box a bulb attached to a long tube, with a penciled sign, 'Palpitator—the Imitation Heart. Show her you Love her'" (102).

In these and other window displays and advertisements, commercial products are treated as sacred objects capable of creating endless riches or instantaneous, permanent love. Later, however, Welty's description of Howard's winning the jackpot at a slot machine becomes a scatalogical parody of a woman's giving birth, in tune with the toilet humor of the window display: "The many nickels that poured spurting and clanging out of the hole sickened him; they fell all over his legs, and he backed up against the dusty red curtain" (103). After killing Marjorie, therefore, Howard tries to replace her with an alternative source of happiness, one that will instantaneously and repeatedly gratify his desires and free him from poverty—as Marjorie would not. Marjorie means work, self-sacrifice; the city's commercial culture for Howard signifies play and unlimited self-indulgence. Only Howard's fright when the money comes cascading down betrays his hidden guilt for wanting to trade a woman for a money machine.

Later in the story Howard's wish for instant wealth is granted, when merely by coincidence he happens to be the ten millionth person to enter Radio City Music Hall. He is given roses and "the key to the city" by "a large woman with feathery furs and a small brown wire over one tooth" (104–5). This strange woman, half mother and half machine, represents the culmination of Howard's demands for instant gratification. Radio City Music Hall is a kind of gargantuan slot machine, and she its personification. Through her, Welty shows that Howard's demands are identical to an infant's demands that his mother instantly satisfy his every desire. After killing the woman who has asked that he act like an adult, Howard has regressed with the help of commercial culture to fantasizing about automatons that eternally gratify his every demand. Yet such a fantasy also makes him feel guilty, as he did in front of the slot machine, and when the Radio City woman comes close to him to give him his prize, he suddenly is terrified and flees; she seems a mechanized monster with a wire over her tooth advancing to consume him. His contradictory fantasies betray his contradictory feelings toward women: he asks that they shelter him, yet he also recoils from them as if their sheltering will destroy his manhood.

Welty's several references to flowers in the story highlight Howard's conflict between commercialized and more humane visions of maternity. When Howard first returns to the apartment after a day of sitting on benches when he was supposed to be looking for a job, he notices that a walk that Marjorie took that day was much more fruitful: "there lay Marjorie's coat with a flower stuck in the buttonhole. . . . She had only found it, Howard thought, but he winced inwardly, as though she had displayed some power of the spirit" (99). That "power" is the force of Marjorie's self-reliance, her faith in natural rather than commercial time. As he stares at the flower, he suddenly hallucinates not just the vision of desert mountains quoted earlier, but a profoundly threatening vision of the female body—especially its genitalia—as a devouring landscape. The pansy began in "Howard's anxious sight to lose its identity of flower-size and assume the gradual and large curves of a mountain on the horizon of a desert, the veins becoming crevasses, the delicate edges the giant worn lips of a sleeping crater. His heart jumped to his mouth" (99). All of Howard's fears of the rightful demands that Marjorie will make upon him as a husband and father are expressed in this vision, as is his guilt for being afraid. His assault upon her with a kitchen knife tries to put a stop to this bewildering power, this "excess of life."

The other flowers that figure prominently in the story are the flowers of the title. They refer to the roses Howard receives from the Radio City lady and then unconsciously takes homeward when he flees. Unlike Marjorie's buttonhole flower, these flowers are figures for Howard's infantile demands and fantasies of power. Welty's title, moreover, ironically stresses the *link* between male desires to treat women as objects of male chivalry and as objects to be controlled. "Flowers for Marjorie" alludes to a conventional act of chivalry, the very sort of act that might appear in the ads that Howard sees using images of happy couples to sell their products, but the story's narrative displaces that chivalrous image with another, an emblem of Howard's secret fear of women and its result.

By juxtaposing Howard's impulsive act of murder with his flight into a commercial fantasy-land, Welty is able to demonstrate far more complex causes for Marjorie's murder than may first be apparent. The story gives us several superficial motives, from Howard's sense of shame from unemployment to the hallucinations that he experiences because of a lack of food. But Howard's hallucinations are hardly private; they merge with and are corroborated by the collective fantasies promoted by advertising. It is Howard's vision of success, not his fear of failure, that is at fault, and Marjorie is ultimately the victim not of her husband's knife but of his infantile ideal of male-gratifying women and of the mass culture that sustains that ideal.

"Flowers for Marjorie" contrasts strikingly with other portraits of married couples in *A Curtain of Green*, "The Key" and "The Whistle," that portray an older husband whose love for his wife is undiminished by poverty. "Flowers for Marjorie" contrasts as well with Welty's first published story, "Death of a Traveling Salesman," whose protagonist longs for a homelife rather than being threatened by it. The issues "Flowers for Marjorie" explores align it with two other stories in *A Curtain of Green*, "The Hitch-Hikers" and "Petrified Man." "Flowers for Marjorie" does not explore the reasons that women are so threatening to men like Howard, beyond suggesting that their "excess of life" (which the story codifies as being associated with "nature") refuses to be confined within the forced stereotypes of men. Tom Harris in "The Hitch-Hikers," similarly, is threatened by women—he "remembered the girl dropping money into her heart-shaped pocket, and remembered a disturbing possessiveness, which meant nothing, Ruth leaning on her hands. He knew he would not be held by any of it" (72)—but the causes for his problems are not really explored by the story, except insofar as it links them to other more obvious forms of cruelty, such as the tramp's murder of his companion. "Petrified Man," however, does explore the link between sexual fears and violence toward women. It is a complex and justly famous critique of the power of advertising and modern American commercial culture, and will be discussed later in this chapter. For now it makes sense to turn to two later stories that seem to be direct descendants of "Flowers for Marjorie"—"The Whole World Knows" and "Music from Spain" in *The Golden Apples*.

🍂

The Golden Apples includes a total of seven stories, all but one set in the imaginary town of Morgana, Mississippi, near the Big Black River about nineteen miles from Vicksburg (387). They are arranged in chronological order and cover a time span of approximately forty-five years, from 1900 to the late 1940s. (In typescript, Welty dated the final story in the collection, which she wrote in 1949, as taking place in "present time.")[2] The stories share many of the same characters and turn on dramatic confrontations between heroic, iconoclastic wanderer figures and more conventional characters who represent Morgana's social mores. As Welty has said, "What had drawn the characters together there was one strong strand in them all: they lived in one way or another in a dream or in romantic aspiration, or under an illusion of what their lives were coming to" (*One Writer's Beginnings* 99).

The first tale, "Shower of Gold," introduces King MacLain, a Zeus-like figure who impregnates his wife with twins and then leaves Mississippi to wander west, coming home to visit Morgana only for brief periods until the very end of his life, when he returns to stay. Each of the succeeding stories turns on a comic or tragic encounter between that story's wanderer figure(s) and Morgana's more proper characters. "June Recital" is the tragic story of how the town's unconventional music teacher, Miss Eckhart, is driven mad. "Sir Rabbit" tells of King's sexual intercourse with a local woman he finds on a hunting expedition with her new husband in the Morgana woods just outside of town. "Moon Lake" presents the comic adventures of two younger wanderer figures at summer camp: an orphan girl named Easter and Loch Morrison, the camp's Boy Scout and life-guard. It appears to be the only story in *The Golden Apples* in which King does not directly figure, but there is evidence to suggest that both Easter and Loch may be children of King's, among the numerous progeny of his that live in the County Orphans' Home and elsewhere throughout MacLain county, "known and unknown, scattered-like" (264). If they are not actually fathered by him, they are certainly spiritually kin to him in many ways. "The Whole World Knows" (set in Morgana) and "Music in Spain" (set in San Francisco) are filled with allusions to King MacLain's wandering and Miss Eckhart's madness; they chronicle the failed marriages of King MacLain's two sons, Ran and Eugene, now in their forties. "The Wanderers" concludes *The Golden Apples* with an account of the death and funeral of the narrator of "Shower of Gold," Mrs. Katie Rainey, told from the point of view of her daughter, Virgie, the story's heroine and Miss Eckhart's star music student.

King MacLain's symbolic and possibly biological ties to the book's wanderer figures are stressed both through the imagery with which Welty describes them and through a series of coincidences in the sto-

ries' plots that allow their paths to cross with his. In "June Recital,"
for example, King shows up during the climactic scene in which Miss
Eckhart is led away from the house that she has tried to burn down.
He is present in part of "Sir Rabbit," addressed directly in his son
Ran's interior monologue ("The Whole World Knows"), and attends
the funeral in "The Wanderers," where Virgie Rainey feels a special
kinship with his disdain for the staid funeral ceremony and the hypoc-
risy of some of the mourners. All of the book's most attractive heroes
and heroines have unruly hair and an ungovernable restlessness and
wildness in their souls. Easter's hair is a "withstanding gold" (346),
recalling the gold light associated with King in "Shower of Gold";
Virgie's hair is dark and often uncombed, and she once literally butted
her head against a wall, something that, figuratively speaking, King
did all his life (291, 452); Miss Eckhart's hair catches fire. Another
detail of note is that Loch Morrison's mother inquires mournfully after
King in "June Recital," implying that Loch's father may be King, not
Wilbur Morrison (326–27).[3]

The dominant school of criticism in Welty scholarship in the 1960s
and 1970s has been archetypal or myth criticism. The majority of
commentators who have discussed King's role in The Golden Apples
have generally presented him as the heroic embodiment of "mythical"
as opposed to narrowly "historical" thinking. King and the book's
other wanderers are associated with natural cycles, sexuality, disguise
and metamorphosis, wandering, and occasionally madness, whereas
the representatives of proper Morgana society—usually women—are
linked with social restrictions, possessiveness, a repression of sexuality, and a provincial belief that Morgana is the center of the universe. Occasionally a character such as Miss Eckhart will embody both
mythical and historical points of view—she represents both rebellion
and restriction, music's freedom and metronomic regularity. More frequently the stories in The Golden Apples are said to chronicle what
appears to be a confrontation between independence and conventionality, a King and a Mrs. Rainey, an Easter and a Jinny Love Stark.
Such conflicts are dramatized by Welty's many allusions to similar conflicts in mythology, so that the heroic wanderer figures are compared
to Zeus ("Shower of Gold"), Hercules ("The Whole World Knows"),
or Perseus ("Music From Spain").

Whatever the undeniable virtues of the many archetypal readings of Welty's stories that have been published—and they have produced richly nuanced readings of the stories—many of them share certain troubling biases. The first is that any "mythic" vision described in *The Golden Apples* must necessarily be superior to the so-called "historical" and regional points of view represented by other citizens in Morgana—superior because it does not seek to stop time, own possessions, or maintain social status. Even when characters as seriously troubled as Ran and Eugene MacLain abuse their wives, critics tend to describe their neuroses in terms of their "mythic" vision and to assume that all such visions must necessarily be restorative, at least in the long run. Such an assumption means that not enough allowance can be made for irony in *The Golden Apples:* when mythic imagery appears, it is often made to be on the side of supposedly "natural" freedom versus social restrictiveness and emotional immaturity.

A second unstated bias of some myth criticism on *The Golden Apples* is, frankly, sexist. For such criticism invariably pits the "male" virtues of King and his followers (including "unfeminine" women such as Miss Eckhart, Easter, and Virgie) against the "female" representatives of Morgana conventionality—Mrs. Rainey and King's wife, Snowdie MacLain, in "Shower of Gold"; Ran's and Eugene's rather shallow wives in "The Whole World Knows" and "Music from Spain"; and Mrs. Stark and the other Morgana matriarchs in "The Wanderers," for example. This bias is particularly notable in the many readings of "The Whole World Knows" and "Music from Spain," which fall into the trap of blaming the victims—Ran and Eugene's wives—for their husbands' behavior, and then excusing the husbands' actions by making reference to all kinds of mythological or existentialist imperatives. Such criticism of course hardly denies that men may act conventionally or women rebelliously, and its depiction of the limitations of women such as Jinny Love Stark or Perdita Mayo or even Miss Snowdie MacLain has often been well argued, but like King MacLain himself it tends to assume that male energies are predominately creative and individualistic, female energies possessive and conventional. Miss Eckhart, Virgie Rainey, and Easter are marked as the exceptions among the women of Morgana.

In recent criticism on *The Golden Apples*—especially pieces written by women—these emphases are gradually being revised. There is a much stronger stress on King as a mock epic figure who is frequently satirized, and a discussion of the disparity between how men and women are treated in Morgana story-telling and the social divisions those disparities represent. Carol Manning's comments on this latter point are exemplary:

> The society's values preclude . . . females from being the objects of its hero-worship. Though individual females are subjects of single, scattered tales, none of these inspires a general mythology, as do Don McInnis, Denis Fairchild, George Fairchild, King MacLain, Daniel Ponder, Sam Dale Beecham, and Jack Renfro. On the contrary, females who become frequent subjects of tales are likely to be presented by the narrators as villains or unpopular strangers: Miss Sabina ("Asphodel"), Miss Eckhart (GA), Miss Julia Mortimer (LB) . . . .
> The basis for the absence of mythicized females is traceable to the double standard, which is an accepted fact of life in the South of Welty's fiction. As their heroes the people select individuals whom they interpret as sensuous nonconformists or as strong, capable protectors of the family, and these roles, in the conventional society, are generally reserved for men. (192)

A particular strength of recent criticism is that it makes such new points without going to the other extreme and overly heroizing the women of Morgana or treating them as martyrs to patriarchy. Ruth Vande Kieft, to pick just one example, is as incisive in discussing the limitations of women such as Jinny Love Stark or Perdita Mayo as she is in discussing how King is satirized in "Sir Rabbit" (104–5, 91–92).

Building on this recent work, in the next two chapters I will argue that conventionalism in Morgana and Welty's other imaginary towns is represented as thoroughly by male figures as by female ones, and that it is often *disguised* as mythological experience. Far from being exempt from historical prejudices, for example, the tales of King's Zeus-like "heroism" in "Shower of Gold" and elsewhere embody his society's most ingrained stereotypes about proper male and female behavior. Conversely, when truly heroic wanderer figures appear in the book, they tend to be female, not male, and they become heroic not because they simply appropriate male definitions of heroism but because they radically revise our ideas of what heroism may involve. To make such an argument is not to denigrate King MacLain as a heroic figure: he is as fascinating to me as he has been to Welty's other readers, and to citizens of Morgana like Katie Rainey. But such a reading does enjoin us to question what our standards for "heroism" are and asks whether other characters such as Miss Eckhart or Virgie Rainey do not in the long run have a better and different claim to heroism than King does.

As Thomas McHaney has shown, Perseus emerges as the most important quester figure in *The Golden Apples;* he was fathered when Zeus appeared to Danaë in a "shower of gold." But the true Perseus figures in *The Golden Apples* are not the logical choices, the twins Ran and Eugene whom King fathered in "Shower of Gold"; rather, King's twin sons are tragic distortions of the Perseus figure, men whose narcissism and misogyny are disguised as a heroically "Persean" attack on what they take to be monstrous, Medusa-like women. Better candidates for Perseus in *The Golden Apples* are Miss Eckhart, Virgie Rainey, and Loch Morrison. Miss Eckhart may be thought of as a Perseus figure who fails to slay Medusa: Morgana's image of her as an eccentric monster takes over her imagination and drives her mad. Virgie, on the other hand, is a successful Perseus who during the course of "The Wanderers" learns the meaning of both Perseus' heroism and Medusa's rage. By making the majority of her Perseus figures women, Welty thus revises how we read the myths that she alludes to—revises them in ways that are more complicated, I think, than acknowledged by the mythological readings that *The Golden Apples* has so far received.[4]

The Golden Apples contains three stories about male violence towards women: "Sir Rabbit," "The Whole World Knows," and "Music from Spain." In "Music from Spain," the main character, Eugene MacLain, slaps his wife's face at the breakfast table on the day after she has stopped wearing mourning for a dead child of theirs. He then rushes from the house and begins a day's wandering through the streets of San Francisco, in imitation of his father. In "The Whole World Knows," the parallel is not as easy to see, for the story begins in mid-wandering, so to speak, after the act that initiated the wandering has taken place. This act is Ran MacLain's leaving his wife, Jinny, whom he accuses of adultery, to move into a one-room apartment in what used to be his family's house, now owned by others and filled with renters. Like Howard in "Flowers for Marjorie," Ran and Eugene substitute fantasies of an ideal woman for their memories of their actual wives, only to have their acts of wish-fulfillment collapse as the repressed fear and guilt for what they have done to their wives resurfaces during the stories' climactic scenes. That is, just as Howard's commercialized success fantasies turned into a vision of an avenging female automaton, the Radio City lady, so do Ran and Eugene try to substitute idealized women for real ones, only to have their fantasies become nightmarish.

A structural comparison of "Flowers for Marjorie," "The Whole World Knows," and "Music from Spain" indicates that as Welty evolved her understanding of the tragedy of male misogyny during the 1940s she moved away from concentrating on the larger social causes of her protagonists' difficulties (depression unemployment and the marketing of masculine and feminine stereotypes by advertising and mass media, as shown in "Flowers for Marjorie"), to explore in greater detail how children's concepts of gender roles are shaped by their parents. Both "The Whole World Knows" and "Music from Spain" contain much family history, something that was largely excluded from "Flowers," and together these two stories represent Welty's fullest depiction of how the sex roles that parents play are influenced by sometimes dangerous cultural stereotypes for proper masculine and feminine behavior.

Another way to make this point is to say that Welty in these three stories moves from depicting gender stereotypes in mass culture to a careful analysis of the *process* by which children inculcate those stereotypes. The fact that Ran and Eugene are twins makes the evidence for their psychological problems even more intriguing. For although as adults they are now living apart from each other, one in a small town in Mississippi and the other in the most cosmopolitan city in California, they experience many of the same neuroses, implying that the deepest causes of their problems indeed lie in their childhood. Published in 1947, Welty's portraits of Ran's and Eugene's problems also confirm and in some cases anticipate the insights of some recent psychoanalysts and sociologists, especially Melanie Klein, Karen Horney, D. W. Winnicott, and Nancy Chodorow, in their revisions of

Freud's ground-breaking speculations on the Oedipus complex, infantilism, narcissism, and male fears of women.[5] Although these analysts have tended to focus on the so-called "nuclear" family where the father works away from home and the mother becomes the dominant nurturer, their results appear to be very relevant to cases like that of Welty's MacLains, where the father quit his regular job (as a traveling salesman) and was absent for even more extended periods of time, so that his children hardly ever met him, only heard stories about his sexual exploits and endless travels.

Ran's and Eugene's relations with women are dominated by infantilism. On the one hand, they have an uncontrollable nostalgia for what Welty portrays as a pre-Oedipal state in which their mother's breast and the absolute security and oral satisfaction it could give them seemed eternally present. Such a fantasy is ultimately a fantasy of returning to the womb, but without any recognition that it is another's interior space one desires to return to; rather, through the fantasy the mother becomes a projection of the child's own needs, entirely subservient to gratifying them—an extension of the child itself, not a separate entity. In this state, the baby experiences itself as the entire universe; no concept of the mother or any other persona as an "Other," a separate human being, is imaginable. Ran and Eugene make such demands of all the women in their lives (especially their wives), treating them as potential substitutes for an eternally satisfying mother figure whom they have lost. Outside of the womb such an infantile world is unsustainable, of course, either when it is first lived by the infant, who finds that the breast is not always present, or later when it is reexperienced through regressive fantasy, as Ran and Eugene try to do. When the fantasy fails, two things happen. First, Ran and Eugene try to destroy the women. Welty portrays these fantasies using remarkable language that makes their destructive, hallucinatory violence quite vivid and frightening. Second, Ran and Eugene then guiltily imagine the women turning on them and treating *them* as something to feed upon and destroy. These nightmarish fantasies, as Welty depicts them, are marked by sexual imagery and sexual phobias, suggesting that the obverse of an infantile fantasy of women as an eternal breast is of women as a sexual vampire, smothering the male and draining him of vital fluids rather than providing him with them.

Complicating Ran's and Eugene's relation to their mother is their relation to their father. Masculinity, especially for Ran, becomes identified with physical aggression, fast and frequent travel, sexual competition with his father, and, above all, a fear of being allied with anything that he thinks is domestic and feminine. For Ran and Eugene, such an inheritance is traumatic, mixing fears that women will destroy their independence with uncontrollable nostalgia for a pre-Oedipal state in which their mother's breast is inseparable from them. Everything the boys have learned from their father about defining masculinity tells them that their need for their mother is an unmanly desire for a return to childhood. Yet even if they try to compete with their father on his own terms, his legendary stature makes him seem superior to them. The stories about him report his experiencing no nostalgia for the womb, as they guiltily do, and his sexual conquests and wandering far outdo whatever the boys try to accomplish. Both "The Whole World Knows" and "Music from Spain" reveal that underneath Ran's and Eugene's idealization of their father is a volatile mixture of repressed emotions toward him—guilt for not measuring up to his standards of masculinity and deep anger toward him for abandoning them and making their relations with women so troubled. Together, the stories give us a twinned portrait of a boy's Oedipus complex and its causes. By stressing the trauma that King MacLain's absence causes his sons, moreover, Welty is not implying that the mere presence of the father in the MacLain household would have prevented Ran's and Eugene's problems. Rather, her stories suggest that it is King's compulsion to enact stereotypes of "male" behavior that destroys any possibility for fluid and nonsexist role-playing for both the parents and their children. The mother becomes condemned simply to play the role of servile nurturer, while the father becomes a facile and illusory "heroic" example of male aggressiveness and freedom. The devastating effects of such sexual stereotyping on the MacLain boys are thus the true subject of "The Whole World Knows" and "Music from Spain."[6]

"The Whole World Knows" is narrated in the first person by Ran MacLain. He is a clerk in the Morgana bank and recently married one of the most eligible girls in town, Jinny Love Stark, who is more than ten years younger than he is. They have just separated because of

Ran's mistreatment of her and the fact that, in retaliation, Jinny has had an affair with Woody Spights, an employee of the same bank in which Ran works. Ran can express his anger against Jinny Love only indirectly and ineffectually. He leaves her and moves into a room in his family's former home in Morgana, now owned by a woman who has divided it up into apartments for rent. (Ran's mother has moved back to her family's home in MacLain's Courthouse, seven miles outside of town, and implores Ran to move in with her.) He also fantasizes taking revenge against Jinny Love and Woody Spights. Inspired by the chance comment during a game of croquet that he is "dead on Woody" (i.e., on Woody's croquet ball), Ran suddenly hallucinates beating his wife's lover with his mallet (382). Even more disturbingly, in response to Jinny's mother's and a servant's criticism of him during a visit ("Of course I see what Jinny's doing, the fool, but you ailed first. You got her answer to it, Ran," her mother says [385]), Ran imagines shooting his wife. This crucial episode in the story is worth quoting, for it gives us an exemplary instance of how Ran's solipsistic fantasizing both soothes and accentuates his pain, and it will demonstrate how the stories in *The Golden Apples* of husbands' violence toward their wives are more sophisticated in their portrayal of its causes than "Flowers for Marjorie." Upon first reading, the following passage is difficult to decipher, for Ran's point of view has trouble distinguishing between his own hallucinations and what actually happens:

Jinny looked at me and didn't mind. I minded. I fired point-blank at Jinny—more than once. It was close range—there was barely room between us suddenly for the pistol to come up. And she only stood frowning at the needle I had forgotten the reason for. Her hand never deviated, never shook from the noise. The dim clock on the mantel was striking—the pistol hadn't drowned that out. I was watching Jinny and I saw her pouting childish breasts, excuses for breasts, sprung full of bright holes where my bullets had gone. But Jinny didn't feel it. She threaded her needle. She made her little face of success. Her thread always went straight in the eye.
"Will you hold still."
She far from acknowledged pain—anything but sorrow and pain. When I couldn't give her something she wanted she would hum a little tune. In our room, her voice would go low and soft to complete dispar-

agement. Then I loved her a lot. The little cheat. I waited on, while she darted the needle and pulled at my sleeve, the sleeve to my helpless hand. It was like counting breaths. I let out my fury and breathed the pure disappointment in: that she was not dead on earth. She bit the thread—magnificently. When she took her mouth away I nearly fell. The cheat. (385)

Ran cannot admit that he has not fired the gun, and he cannot face the reasons for wanting to shoot his wife, so he transforms his own failure into the failure of others. In his eyes Jinny refuses to acknowledge that she has been mortally shot or that she is in the wrong; she merely keeps on sewing. Ran's fantasy then turns dark with resentment and self-pity and guilt. Not only is Jinny's "aim" better than his, but "[h]er thread always went straight in the eye." The sorrow and pain that Ran claims she refuses to acknowledge is of course *his* sorrow and pain, not hers; he wants his acknowledged by her, even as he refuses to admit that he bears much of the responsibility for their marital problems.

Ran's fantasy also demonstrates how he unconsciously wants a woman who will unquestioningly be a mother to his every need, not an equal partner in marriage. Welty emphasizes how infantile Ran's demands are by having him stare at his wife's breasts—"excuses for breasts," he calls them—as he imagines shooting her. He is like a child who is enraged at his mother for not feeding him and imagines destroying her. As his fantasy-tantrum proceeds, it becomes more and more infantile and oral: "I waited on. . . . It was like counting my breaths. I let out my fury and breathed the pure disappointment in: that she was not dead on earth. She bit the thread—magnificently. When she took her mouth away I nearly fell. The cheat" (385). This passage ought to be read as freely as if it were a dream, allowing multiple meanings for each action and treating seemingly external events as projections of the fantasies of the dreamer. Jinny's sewing, for Ran, is in part a "magnificent" and threatening assertion of her own independence from him, breaking the thread with her teeth seems to his diseased imagination to be the equivalent of severing a life-giving (perhaps umbilical) tie: thus his melodramatic phrase, "I almost fell." (The irony here is increased by the fact that Jinny is sewing a button back on Ran's shirt; even as he has asserted his "right" to ask wifely favors of her he knows that such ploys will not work; her obliging him hardly is an agreement to live with him again.) Yet Jinny's biting the thread may perhaps also be read as a disguised version of what Ran in his infantile rage wants to do to her—to bite and tear her for "cheating" and taking her breast away. His imagined shooting of her in the chest performs the same function: "I saw her pouting, childish breasts, excuses for breasts, sprung full of bright holes where my bullets had gone" (385). The result of this infantilism, apparently, is that Ran is now impotent with Jinny: "When I couldn't give her something she wanted she would hum a little tune. In our room, her voice would go low and soft to complete disparagement" (385).[7] Ran also treats the pistol he imagines having as if it were a penis ("there was barely room between us suddenly for the pistol to come up"), so his sexual potency is linked to violence.

The very first paragraph of "The Whole World Knows," when re-read in light of its later action, can be shown to link Ran's rage at his wife with his disturbed feelings towards his mother and father. "Father, I wish I could talk to you, wherever you are right now. Mother said, *Where have you been, son?*—Nowhere, Mother.—*I wish you wouldn't sound so unhappy, son. You could come back to MacLain and live with me now.*—I can't do that, Mother. You know I have to stay in Morgana. . . . *I can tell you're all peaked. And you keep things from me, I don't understand. You're as bad as Eugene Hudson. Now I have two sons keeping things from me*" (375). His mother's voice keeps invading Ran's monologue to his father because despite himself Ran longs for the security his mother once gave him and then immediately feels ashamed for desiring her presence so strongly. She offers to let him move back in with her, yet to Ran she also seems to him to be intent on entirely dominating his identity: he specifically remembers that she calls his brother Eugene *Hudson* rather than Eugene MacLain, taking revenge against her irresponsible husband and his family name by calling her son by his middle name, her family's name.

Ran, however, elects to retreat to the house in Morgana that his mother and father once shared, not the Hudson home in MacLain's Courthouse. Still stored in the room that Ran rents are some of his mother's possessions that she angrily left behind when she moved back to MacLain—a trunk with some of her quilts and her wedding dress (381). The MacLain house in Morgana thus appears to be a kind of half-way house for Ran, allowing a strategic withdrawal that may give him all the security of retreating into his mother's presence while still allowing himself the illusion of manly independence and respect for his father's memory. But such a solution fails, as the scenes with Ran and Jinny prove. Ran tries to assert his masculine independence, but he senses that his demands on women remain thoroughly infantile. Some of the most moving moments in the story come when Ran punctuates his monologue with pleas to his father to let him be able to move back in with Jinny and live a normal life: "Father, I wished I could go back" (378); "Father! You didn't listen" (379).

Both Ran and Eugene also attempt to substitute acquaintances they meet for their threatening wives. In Ran's case, this is Maideen Sumrall, a grocery-store clerk who is flattered by Ran's attentions and apparently hopes to inspire him to divorce Jinny and marry her. For Eugene, this substitute proves to be the androgynous figure of a chance acquaintance, a Spanish guitar player named Bartolome Montalbano, who combines a feminine appearance (he has long hair and red fingernails) with what Eugene thinks of as an enviably masculine life free from all family ties.

Ran wants to turn Maideen into the wife that he has lost, forcing her to return to the Starks' house as if it were her house and to visit the Stark family as if she were their daughter and his wife. His motives for doing this are complex: he seeks to humiliate and mock both Maideen and Jinny yet also seeks to convince himself that nothing has happened, that Jinny still loves him, will be jealous of Maideen, and will take him back. Thus when a woman does not live up to his ideal of perfect subservience, he tries to replace her with another woman who will. After Ran's and Maideen's visit to the Starks' ends with his failed vision of shooting Jinny, he decides that what he really wants to do with Maideen is to drive up to Vicksburg's nightspots and motels with her. The trip ends in disaster. After Ran and Maideen return drunk to a motel room and pass out wearing their clothes, Maideen wakes and turns out a light they left on. Ran suddenly wakens to see her take off her dress and approach their bed wearing only her slip.

His reaction is the most frightening instance of male fear of women in all of Welty's stories:

> I saw Maideen taking her dress off. She bent over all tender toward it, smoothing its skirt and shaking it and laying it, at last, on the room's chair; and tenderly like it was any chair, not that one. I propped myself up against the rods of the bed with my back pressing them. I was sighing—deep sigh after deep sigh. I heard myself. When she turned back to the bed, I said, "Don't come close to me."
>
> And I showed I had the pistol. I said, "I want the whole bed." I told her she hadn't needed to be here. I got down in the bed and pointed the pistol at her, without much hope, the way I used to lie cherishing a dream in the morning, and she the way Jinny would come pull me out of it.
>
> Maideen came into the space before my eyes, plain in the lighted night. She held her bare arms. She was disarrayed. There was blood on her, blood and disgrace. Or perhaps there wasn't. For a minute I saw her double. But I pointed the gun at her the best I could. (391)

Even though all of Maideen's actions in this scene seem quite innocent, Ran is threatened by them. Maideen's treating the room's furniture "tenderly," as if it were her own rather than the motel's,[8] is taken by Ran to signify her possessive domesticity, and her undressing is even more frightening for him. Ran is terrified by independent, adult female sexuality; it suggests "blood and disgrace," menstruation, "disarray," violence, adultery. He recoils from her presence as if from an attempt to capture and devour him.

After demanding that Maideen stay away from him, Ran then suddenly turns the gun on himself: "I drew back the pistol, and turned it. I put the pistol's mouth to my own. My instinct is always quick and ardent and hungry and doesn't lose any time. There was Maideen still, coming, coming in her petticoat" (392). Once again, an attempt to act "masculinely" collapses into infantilism, a nostalgic hunger for that moment in his life when women existed only to nurse him. Welty makes this explicit by carefully using language that suggests a baby's instinctive response to hunger: "quick and ardent and hungry," but, horrifyingly, it is the barrel of his father's *gun* that Ran puts in his mouth. Such a contradictory image—the gun as a symbol of his father's independence and of Ran's need for sucking, for *dependence*—is

Welty's version of the "condensation" of images Freud argued was a defining element of fantasy and dream-work ("The Dream-Work," 170–83). Furthermore, the fact that Ran's oral fantasy in the motel room involves suicide shows that guilt is irrevocably intertwined with his fantasies of nursing. Earlier in the story, Ran remembers his mother's worrying about his having his father's gun, as if he were not man enough to handle it (375), and because Ran feels that he has failed to use it "heroically," he now sentences himself to die, castrating himself in the name of his father.

When the gun misfires, Ran's anger returns as a defense against the sexual shame engendered by the misfiring. Instead of threatening to shoot Maideen, he turns on her and rapes her. "In a minute she put her hand out again, differently, and laid it cold on my shoulder. And I had her so quick" (392). The context of this passage and the adjective "cold" make it clear that Maideen's gesture is not a sexual overture but an act of pity. (She expected to have sex when she started the trip with him, but she is hardly making an overture now. We can only assume that she does not resist the rape because she is too frightened.) Ran is even more threatened by Maideen's pity than he was by her undressing. Shared, mature sexuality intimidates him, as does maternal consolation, but rape is restorative: it reaffirms his deflated manhood and reasserts his right to turn women simply into objects of his desire. In this scene Welty thus shows rape to be the ultimate form of misogyny and links it with pre-Oedipal rage and Oedipal self-hatred. Such an analysis of the causes of rape, done in the mid-1940s, to some extent anticipates the conclusions made by contemporary social scientists such as Susan Brownmiller and Nicholas Groth.

In "Music from Spain" Ran's brother Eugene has moved from Morgana to San Francisco. Although his brother thinks he is "safe in California" (375), he is as threatened by women as Ran, perhaps even more so, and his personality is just as volatile a mix of guilt, anger, fear, and narcissism as his brother's.

The story opens with Eugene slapping his wife's face at the breakfast table, "without the least idea of why he did it" (393). Eugene then spends the day wandering through San Francisco, much of the time accompanying a chance acquaintance, the guitarist Montalbano. During the day's wandering, Eugene's imagination turns his unsuspecting companion into an idealized version of both his parents, a model of both "male" romantic independence and "female" self-sacrificial nurturing. Such a vision is impossible to sustain for long, but while Eugene can do so, many infantile fantasies about both his parents are secretly acted out.

To Eugene, Montalbano is living proof that the feminine world may be escaped. "The formidable artist was free," Eugene assures himself simplistically; "there was no one he loved, to tell him anything, to lay down the law" (406). Like Eugene's father, Montalbano seems a law unto himself. When Eugene offers to guide him around the city, though, Welty makes it evident that his attraction to him is not merely theoretical. After staring at the performer's red fingernails, Eugene "felt a lapse of all knowledge of Emma as his wife. . . . The lapse must have endured for a solid minute or two, and afterwards he could recollect it. It was as positively there as a spot or stain, and it affected him like a secret" (403). The full meaning of this sexually charged moment of secret sharing emerges only near the end of the story, after a day in which Eugene and the musician have wandered through the city as if they were illicit lovers. As they stand on the cliffs overlooking the Pacific, Eugene suddenly gives Montalbano a bear hug: "Eugene clung to the Spaniard now, almost as if he had waited for him a long time with longing, almost as if he loved him, and had found a lasting refuge. He could have caressed the side of the massive face with the great pores in the loose, hanging cheek. The Spaniard closed his eyes" (421). In Eugene's imagination, the Spaniard's jowls are transformed into a woman's breast whose open pores promise "refuge" and sustenance. Eugene thus unconsciously seeks to substitute his wife's threatening heterosexuality with what seems like a homoerotic vision of a man as nurturing mother who will not deny or smother him. As the embrace continues, the Spaniard, frightened, grabs Eugene and whirls him around and around in the air. As he does this, Eugene suddenly imagines returning home and being devoured by his wife:

Pillowed on great strength, [Eugene] was turned in the air. It was greatest comfort. It was too bad the daylong foreboding had to return, that he had yet to open the door and climb the stairs to Emma. There she waited in the front room, shedding her tears standing up, like a bride, with the white curtains of the bay window hanging heavy all around her.

When his body was wheeled another turn, the foreboding like a spinning ball was caught again. This time the vision was Emma MacLain turning around and coming part way to meet him on the stairs. . . . She lifted both arms in the wide, aroused sleeves and brought them together around him. He had to sink upon the frail hall chair intended for the coats and hats. And she was sinking upon him and on his mouth putting kisses like blows, returning him awesome favors in full vigor. (423)

Welty's commentators have tended to read this vision as a regenerative one, a vision of the renewal of love between Eugene and his wife Emma. The next two paragraphs of the passage (not quoted above) provide them with their strongest evidence, for Eugene decides that "it was out of such relentlessness, not out of the gush of tears, that there would be a child again" (423). (Eugene and Emma have recently lost their only child, for which Emma blames her husband while her husband blames her [413].) Nevertheless, the entire passage is prefaced by the word "foreboding," and crucial phrases in the fantasy itself (as opposed to Eugene's reflections on the fantasy) are quite threatening to him: "wide aroused sleeves . . . around him," "he had to sink," and "kisses like blows." If Eugene projects his fantasies of an unthreatening female onto the Spaniard, he also cannot help but project his fear of women onto him too. At first the physical contact with him is comforting, even exhilarating, but then it brings out all his sexual fears as "pillowed in great strength" modulates into images that he associates with women—heavy curtains and "wide, aroused sleeves" surrounding and smothering him. Eugene MacLain as well as the story's readers may consider this fantasy to be a healing one, but they do so only by repressing much of the dream's content.[9]

Earlier visions Eugene has of his wife are similarly troubling. When he slaps his wife, the baroque metaphors Welty uses to depict his reaction stress his association of her with domesticity, sweetness, and claustrophobia: "her stiffening and wifely glaze running sweet and fine-spun as sugar threads over her" (393). Later, like Howard in "Flowers for Marjorie," Eugene visits a street fair and sees another threatening female icon. One of the side-show monstrosities is named Emma (like Eugene's wife)—a coincidence that Eugene thinks is highly significant. His vision of this side-show character is hard to interpret, it is so grotesque: "her small features bunched like a paper of violets in the center of her face. But in the crushed, pushed-together countenance there was a book; it was accusation, of course. . . . The photograph showed [the side-show] Emma as wearing lace panties, and opposite it a real pair of panties—faded red with no lace—was exhibited hung up by clothespins, vast and sagging" (405). Given the extravagance of this passage's metaphors, we ought to read extravagantly as well: like Howard in "Flowers for Marjorie," Eugene MacLain here imagines women as a monstrosity, an enlarged vagina threatening to crush him.

Both Eugene and Ran indirectly blame their father for their fears of women. Eugene's vision of the Spaniard is not only a vision of an ideal or a threatening lover, but also of his shadow self, his madness. Earlier in the story Eugene often addresses the Spaniard as if he were addressing himself: he turns him into the living image of his father's influence on him. (Montalbano does not understand English and thus for Eugene's purposes makes a perfect companion.) "You know what you did," Eugene shouts at him at one point, "You assaulted your wife" (419). Another moment of self-reflection in the story does not directly involve Montalbano, but it is even more revealing of why Eugene's idealization of wanderers like Montalbano and his father hides great resentment toward them: "Eugene saw himself for a moment as the kneeling Man in the Wilderness in the engraving in his father's remnant geography book, who hacked once at the Traveler's Tree, opened his mouth, and the water came pouring in. What did Eugene MacLain really care about the life of an artist, or a foreigner, or a wanderer, all the same thing—to have it all brought upon him now? That engraving itself, he had once believed, represented his father, King MacLain, in the flesh, the one who had never seen him or wanted to see him" (409).

It is not enough, I think, to read this passage merely as Eugene's rather envious tribute to Montalbano's artistic heroism or his father's wandering. For in Eugene's vision, the kneeling Man in the Wilderness seeks merely infantile love, a lover either male or female who like the Traveler's Tree will endlessly supply his needs yet also allow him the illusion of his freedom to travel further. As the shift in tone from wonder to anger in the passage suggests, moreover, Eugene secretly is upset by the fact that his father gave him no example of love other than infantile narcissism. Whatever sustenance his father gave him, Eugene finds that he is also responsible for making him *thirsty:* it is his absence that has made both his childhood and his adult life a wilderness.[10]

Eugene's brother Ran in "The Whole World Knows" also simultaneously idolizes his father and blames him for his madness, but his relationship with him is more easily seen because he often addresses him directly, as Eugene does not. Ran frequently calls out his father's name just when he feels most entrapped by women, as if to give himself his father's courage, but he also does so when he is feeling most resentful toward him. In the following example, occurring immediately after Ran imagines shooting Jinny as she sews for him, admiration and hatred are equally mixed: "Father! Dear God wipe it clean. Wipe it clean, wipe it out. Don't let it be" (386). The pronoun "it" may be read as referring to Ran's troubles with Jinny and Maideen, thus making the passage a plea for escape and independence from women, but it may also be taken to refer to Ran's own misogyny and infantilism. Even the conjunction of "Father!" and "Dear God" is turbulent. We may interpret it as reverential, a plea to his father, or as condemnatory, as a plea to God to cleanse what his father has wrought in him.

Another clue that Welty has buried in "The Whole World Knows" suggests yet one more approach to understanding Ran's anger toward his father. Alfred Appel has pointed out how violently Ran reacts when he learns from Maideen that her mother's maiden name is Sojourner: "And now I was told her mother's maiden name. God help me, the name Sojourner was laid on my head like the top teetering crown of a pile of things to remember. Not to forget, never to forget the name of Sojourner" (386; Appel 223–24). This comment is part of a diatribe against all the things that Maideen told him about herself, but Ran's anger is so vehement that Appel believes Welty may be hinting that Maideen is in fact the child engendered by King when he accosted Mattie Will Sojourner in "Sir Rabbit" earlier in *The Gol-*

den Apples. If this is true, then when Ran rapes Maideen at the end of "The Whole World Knows" he knowingly commits incest with his half-sister. Appel does not speculate on how Ran learns that his father had sex with Maideen's mother, nor does he admit that for his suggestion to be true we must make three rather large assumptions: (1) that Maideen's mother is Mattie Will, rather than another female Sojourner (we never learn for certain); (2) that Maideen's last name is now Sumrall because her mother for an unknown reason remarried in the two decades that separate "Sir Rabbit" and "The Whole World Knows"; and (3) that Ran somehow found out about his father's encounter with Mattie Will, probably through gossip that "the whole world knows."[11] If the evidence in support of Appel's hypothesis is circumstantial and tenuous, however, it is certainly intriguing. Ran and Maideen are the correct ages, about twenty years apart. Adding incest with his half-sister to the other problems Ran has certainly makes "The Whole World Knows" an even darker story. Welty leaves such a possibility open but does not give us enough evidence to prove or disprove it. We should not focus on such speculation at the expense of the central issue, which is why Ran is so oppressed by learning that Maideen's mother's maiden name is Sojourner. The one thing that is certain is that when Ran protests against the name of Sojourner he is showing that he resents being forced to measure his exploits with the Sojourners against his father's. ("Sir Rabbit," revealingly, contains another example of such competition between son and father: in the first half of the story Ran and Eugene sensuously wrestle with Mattie Will in the Morgana Woods when she is fifteen; in the second half, occurring later, King rapes her.) Ran's rape of Maideen Sumrall may or may not be incest, but Oedipal guilt and anger it certainly is, forever caught in a losing struggle with his father.

Ran's monologue in "The Whole World Knows" ends in utter despair and isolation: "Father, Eugene! What you went and found, was it better than this? And where's Jinny?" (392). His voice echoes within the empty rooms and endless corridors of his compulsions much more frighteningly than Sister's boast echoes at the end of "Why I Live at the P.O.": unlike her, Ran has the power to harm others. In the concluding story in *The Golden Apples*, "The Wanderers," we learn that Maideen commits suicide after the night she was humiliated by Ran (433). Ran's interior monologue is thus "spoken" *after* Maideen's suicide: "How was I to know she would go and hurt herself," he pleads guiltily and then, in a paroxysm of selfish anger, adds: "She cheated, she cheated too" (392). Eugene's story, in contrast, ends with an act of silent disdain: he returns home and coldly watches his wife and her best female friend in the kitchen after dinner. Eugene's violence and wandering may seem to have temporarily been spent, but actually his misogyny has only taken a more disguised (i.e., latent) form; he remains obsessed with women as devourers: "Eugene tilted back on his chair and watched Emma pop the grapes in" (426).

Such a somber analysis of the tragedy of Ran's and Eugene's misogyny need not assume that the women in these stories are paragons of virtue. Indeed, both Jinny Love and Emma MacLain are two of the most callous women in all of *The Golden Apples*. Jinny quickly takes a new lover rather than trying to help Ran overcome his fear of women, and Eugene's charges that Emma is neglectful, conceited, and hypocritical appear to be at least partially correct. Welty's manuscripts, however, reveal that she revised the beginning and the ending of "Music from Spain"—the two scenes in which Eugene's wife Emma is present—in ways that make it easier for us to question Eugene's view of her as a monster. In the opening scene, Welty's revisions added the detail about the "wounded cry" Emma makes when, upset by her husband's cruel behavior toward her, she burns herself on a toast pan (393); and the concluding scene involving Mrs. Herring, Emma, and Eugene includes more details in the later version that stress the friendship between the two women (425–26). These revisions make Emma seem a more sympathetic character, and Eugene's views of her more irrational.

One final note on these two stories. As interesting as "The Whole World Knows" and "Music from Spain" are, they are not on a par with each other artistically. Only "The Whole World Knows" has the power and compression necessary for tragedy. "Music from Spain" often seems awkwardly written and too slowly paced in comparison with its companion tale; the following sentence, for example, is unintentionally comic: "Eugene, unaccustomed to visions of people as they were not, as unaccustomed as he was to the presence of the Spaniard as he was, choked abruptly on his crust" (408). Furthermore, the character of the guitar player is ultimately intelligible only as a projection of Eugene's fantasies, not as an identity in his own right—an awkward flaw in a story told using a third-person narrative. The characters who speak to Ran in his monologue, in contrast, are both powerfully rendered independent figures and projections of his own fantasies and fears. Consequently, "Music from Spain" has neither the economy nor the tragic tension between fantasy and fact that gives "The Whole World Knows" its impact. One is not surprised to learn that "Music from Spain" was the last story written in *The Golden Apples* sequence and that Welty herself has had doubts about its success (Prenshaw, *Conversations* 285–86, 332–33). Yet the twinned psychological terrain explored by "The Whole World Knows" and "Music from Spain" is as rich as it is frightening, and the two stories should be read together as Welty's most daring exploration of the tragic causes and consequences of male misogyny.

🦋

> To play with mimesis is thus, for a woman, to try to recover the place of her exploitation by discourse, without allowing herself to be simply reduced to it. It means to resubmit herself . . . to "ideas" . . . that are elaborated in/by a masculine logic, but so as to make "visible," by an effect of playful repetition, what was supposed to remain invisible: the cover-up of a possible operation of the feminine in language. It also means "to unveil" the fact that, if women are such good mimics, it is because they are not simply reabsorbed in this function. They also remain elsewhere. . . .
>
> — Luce Irigaray,
> *This Sex Which Is Not One*

Of all of Welty's early stories exploring the way in which women do violence to themselves, none is more incisive than "Petrified Man," and it provides an especially revealing introduction to a discussion of what happens in Welty's tragic stories when a woman rather than a man is the central character. The story seems in part inspired by circuses that came to the Jackson fairgrounds in the late 1930s; Welty photographed them assiduously—including a side-show poster touting an "Ossified Man" (Marrs 103–04, 113–14). Not coincidentally,

"Petrified Man" is also Welty's first intensive investigation of the meaning of the Greek myths associated with Medusa, the only mortal Gorgon, dragon-like creatures with wings, human heads, snakes for hair, and a gaze that would turn human beings to stone. From the first appearance of Medusa motifs in Welty's stories, Welty seems to have understood that she could use Medusa's story as a means of investigating the dilemmas facing modern American women. A brief reading of the role played by the Medusan gaze in "Petrified Man" may serve as an introduction to "June Recital."

Welty's critics have greatly praised "Petrified Man," but the readings they have given it are somewhat odd, for they are unanimous in blaming the women in the story for the perversions of sexuality that it satirizes. It is rather as if the story's Medusan gaze were so disturbing that its commentators—both male and female—have rushed to cast themselves in Perseus' role and wield righteous swords against the women whom they take to be the story's villains. Most commonly, this takes the form of arguing that the women have assumed the role of men, stripping men of their masculinity and perverting "natural" gender distinctions. In this view, the women are modern Medusas, women who turn to stone the men who come in contact with them. Astonishingly, however, no commentator has fully confronted what it means to have the central male figure in the story be a rapist or explored the connections that the story draws between representations of women in advertising and violence toward women in society. The women may be Gorgons to their men, but the true Gorgon in the story is the world of mass culture, a Medusan world whose uncanny power consists in its ability to make women see themselves only through an essentially male point of view, both idealizing them and treating them as objects of rage and violence. Welty plays a better Perseus than her critics, for she knows how to spot the real villain and decode its dangerous gaze—and all this in 1941, years before the recent developments in feminist criticism and theory that it anticipates. [12]

"Petrified Man" is told entirely through two conversations that take place between Mrs. Fletcher and Leota while Mrs. Fletcher is getting her hair done on 9 March and again on 16 March 1941, in Leota's beauty parlor. The subplot of "Petrified Man" is concerned with lurid crimes and traveling freak-show exhibitions, whereas the main plot depicts the commonplace violence against women that occurs in a beauty parlor. In the subplot, a rapist joins a freak show and disguises himself as "Mr. Petrie" the Petrified Man, realizing that a man whose body supposedly turns everything he eats into stone will be the perfect cover for his brutal appetites as a rapist. In the main plot, Mrs. Fletcher seeks to disguise the fact of her pregnancy—the fact that her body will change its shape and use its food to nourish another life—with a petrified disguise of her own, a "permanent" hair-do and "fixed" smile that conform to her conception of the eternal forms of feminine beauty. A newcomer to town named Mrs. Pike is the only character in the story who figures in both plots. She first notices that Mrs. Fletcher is pregnant and that Mr. Petrie is the same man as the one pictured in an old copy of *Startling G-Man Tales* with a $500 reward on his head for rape.

Welty's story is less concerned with Mr. Petrie's private motives for rape than it is with unmasking the cultural connections between the marketing of idealized images of female beauty and the hidden rage and violence against women that underlie those supposedly pure images. For Leota and Mrs. Fletcher have been conditioned to see what is done to their bodies in the beauty parlor not as acts of violence but as acts of love—techniques that affirm their beauty, independence, and importance as women. Such thorough conditioning may be their culture's most disturbing act of violence against women, for unlike the crime of rape the beauty parlor's ideal is universal and disguised as its opposite, as something indispensable to a woman's self-esteem, and it affects more women than all the rapists in the country.

Leota's beauty parlor is an elegantly appointed torture chamber with the female body as its victim. In order to achieve the physical standards that society sets for beauty, an array of tools and machines in Leota's shop remake nature. References to the high technology of the beauty industry are frequent, from the "aluminum wave pinchers" used to make curls to the hair-drying machines that "cook" their occupants (18). The inborn shape of one's hair is given a new "body," and called a "permanent"; one's smile is no longer natural but "fixed" (28) by face powder and lipstick. If the parlor's creations are not truly "permanent"—Welty notes ironically that Mrs. Fletcher speaks of her "last permanent"—nevertheless the body's new shapes aspire to the permanent and "ideal" standards that the beauty parlor's machinery represents. Even more importantly, Welty shows that the beauty parlor's standards of beauty are themselves created by a larger machine, the mass marketing apparatus of popular culture. Several times she mentions popular reading materials in the story, which vary from the purportedly high-class "rental library" (where Mrs. Fletcher primly says that she first met her husband) to the "drugstore rental" library supplying the cheap novels and some of the periodicals with names like *Life is Like That* and *Screen Secrets* that entertain the parlor's customers while their hair is being dried. As the title *Screen Secrets* suggests, the standards of beauty that the parlor sells are created by the motion picture and advertising industries. Those mass cultural images of perfection become molds that may create endless reproductions of their products in the women and men who are influenced by them. And although pop cultural icons purport to portray healthy images of women as wives and mothers, they in fact teach the women to treat their sexuality as threatening and scandalous—an affront to the static image of proper beauty that the beauty parlor mass-produces.

Welty first alerts us to this fact when she describes the women at the parlor as "customers" who are being "gratified in [their] booths" (17)—a striking verb that suggests sexual pleasure perversely displaced not merely onto consumer objects but onto the narcissistic contemplation of a constructed image that is sold with those products. When sexual relations do occur in the story, they threaten ideal standards of beauty by causing everything from dandruff to pregnancy. "I couldn't of caught a thing like that [dandruff] from Mr. Fletcher, could I," Mrs. Fletcher whines early in the story (18), and Leota on the same page gingerly spells the first four letters of the word "pregnant" (as if it were something that must never be named aloud) and then asks, "how far gone are you?" implying that Mrs. Fletcher's pregnancy is a kind of dying. The women's belief that both sexuality and pregnancy are grotesque rather than beautiful is shown most clearly in their discussion of the traveling freak show that comes to town. Significantly, it occupies "the vacant store next door" to the beauty parlor (20): businesses selling beauty and ugliness are adjacent, as if they were mirror images of each other. Indeed, as the women's conversations show, they need to have a sense of the grotesque in order to enforce a sense of their own normality, but the more they try to separate what is normal from what is monstrous, the more the two threaten to merge. Welty adroitly shows this largely unconscious connection in their minds by having Mrs. Fletcher's and Leota's conversation about the freak show continually stray from discussing the freaks to discussing their own lives. The show is first mentioned almost in the same breath as Mrs. Fletcher's newly revealed pregnancy; it is as if Mrs. Pike has as keen an eye for the spectacle that Mrs. Fletcher makes as she does for the freaks. As Leota says, "Well, honey, talkin' about bein' pregnant an' all, you ought to see those [Siamese] twins in a bottle, you really owe it to yourself" (20). Part of the women's horror and fascination with this display is that it seems not only to be an example of the frightening disorder of nature (creating two babies instead of one) but also of what they take to be the sickening and unnatural union of mother and child: "they had these two heads an' two faces an' four arms an' four legs, all kind of joined *here*. See, this face looked this-a-way, and the other face looked that-a-way, over their shoulder, see. Kinda pathetic. 'Glah!' said Mrs. Fletcher disapprovingly" (21).

If the beauty parlor and the freak show next door are the arbiters of the beautiful and the ugly, then, the lines that they draw are not nearly so sharp as implied by the architectural lines dividing the two buildings. The mirrors on the wall of the beauty parlor (perhaps on the very wall that separates the parlor from the freak show) play a crucial role in "Petrified Man": they give us lucid glimpses of the many ways in which society defines beauty and ugliness as mirror opposites. More powerfully than any other piece of equipment in the parlor, the mirror presents a standard of beauty and measures the women against it. When they view themselves in the mirror, they view not only their own image but the ideal image of what they wish to be. The mirror (like a movie screen) holds the spectacle of infinite examples of Beauty itself yet also cruelly presents an (also infinite) spectacle of monstrous failure: "[Mrs. Fletcher] stared in a discouraged way into the mirror. 'You can tell it when I'm sitting down, all right,' she said" (23). Beauty and the Medusa are twinned images, each the "negative" of the other.

The parlor's mirror does not hold an image, of course, so much as reflect one that is projected upon it. In Mrs. Fletcher's case, Welty shows, she projects that ideal image from her own imagination, which is in turn projected (much like a movie) by the powerful and subtle machinery of popular culture that has invented those beautiful images and then imprinted them in the women's minds. Here lies the subtlety of Welty's diagnosis of how commercial culture may corrupt. The women are dependent upon market images for their sense of beauty and normality, yet they do not realize this; rather, they take those very images as sign of their own independence and power, the irrefutable proof of respectability that they themselves have earned. The most powerful allure of mass culture in Welty's view is not that it sells the comforts of conformity but that it promotes them as their opposite—as heroic examples of an individual's independence and power. The function of the beauty parlor mirror is to show how this hidden process works. Looking into the mirror as she receives her shampoo and set, Mrs. Fletcher proudly boasts: "Women have to stand up for themselves, or there's just no telling. But now you take me—I ask Mr. Fletcher's advice now and then, and he appreciates it, especially on something important, like is it time for a permanent—not that I've told him about the baby. He says, 'Why, dear, go ahead! Just ask their advice' " (25).

The beauty parlor is an all-female domain where they can mock the men and assert their own power over them; this surely "gratifies" them (17) as much as the beauty treatments. But like the beauty treatments, the sense of power that the parlor gives them—power over their husbands, over each other, and over their own bodies—is a dangerous illusion; it is not at all the kind of power it seems. The parlor's images of perfection dictate the terms by which Mrs. Fletcher must define her "independence," and all of those make her dependent upon mass cultural images of perfection that are marketed by men (Marchand 1–51, 66–69). Welty subtly enforces this irony by having Mrs. Fletcher *sitting down* in one of the parlor's chairs staring at the mirror even as she speaks about women "standing up for themselves."[13]

If there is a Medusa in "Petrified Man" who turns all who gaze on her to stone, therefore, it is the world of commercial culture, not the women who are its victims, and it has done its work not by petrifying its victims with a vision of ugliness but by hypnotizing them with a vision of false beauty. The presence of a rapist on the other side of the beauty parlor's mirror, moreover, exposes the connection between commercial culture's images of women as beautiful objects and its treatment of them as perverted monsters. The same advertising world that reproduces endless images of idealized women for women to copy also treats women as sex objects for men like Mr. Petrie to possess and desecrate: sexual relations are perverted into either utter passivity (as with Leota's and Mrs. Fletcher's husbands) or violent aggression (as with Mr. Petrie).

Who is Perseus in this retelling of the myth of Medusa? Welty, of course. Like Perseus, she uses her art to allow us to see how the Gorgon's gaze is directed at us without letting us succumb to its power. The story's meticulous commercial details of the parlor's decor and the women's slang may be thought of in traditionally mimetic terms, as a mirror. In Welty's hands, however, this mirror functions differently from the mirror in the beauty parlor or the screen in the movie house: it does not present these images under the guise of the "natural," but reveals them to be representations, a set of artifices and disguises. In doing so, Welty's story exposes the hidden, demonic *source* of the images that are projected onto its mimetic reflective surface and uncovers how those representations acquire authority until their naive consumers believe, as the title of one of their favorite pulp novels puts it, that "life is like that." Such an understanding of culture is the true "screen secret" of "Petrified Man," allowing us to decode the sexual politics involved in making some forms of representation become accepted as "natural" in mass culture while other ones are excluded. These revelations are the reward Welty reserves for us if we read even more carefully than Mrs. Pike.

"Petrified Man" is one of Welty's greatest comic stories, of course, because of its brilliant imitation of how commercial culture corrupts language and personal relations, but I have found when teaching the story that my students are as disturbed as they are amused by it; in fact, some of them find it very hard to laugh, so uneasy do they feel. Ruth Vande Kieft's comment on the story is most apt: "We can say of this story what a critic has said of the comic spirit of Jonathan Swift: it 'frightens us out of laughter into dismay'" (Vande Kieft 65; see also Sypher 235). The story has generally been praised as an example of mimesis, the artist holding a mirror up to her culture and stunning us with the image of ourselves that we see. But the story should also be understood as a darkly comic analysis of mimesis as a *Persean* mirror/ shield that may either paralyze or protect, depending on how it is used. Welty's gift to us, in effect, should be thought of like Athena's gift to Perseus: it allows us to "see" the paralyzing gaze of popular culture's gender stereotypes without being overcome by it. In Luce Irigaray's terms quoted in the epigraph to this section, Welty uses her skill at mimicry to unveil to us not just the beauty parlor but "the place of women's exploitation by discourse." Like Perseus she remains "elsewhere," her heroic critical energy distanced from such a petrifying language.

And in her lurid eyes there shone
The dying flame of life's desire,
Made mad because its hope was gone,
And kindled at the leaping fire
Of jealousy, and fierce revenge,
And strength that could not change nor tire.

Shade of a shadow in the glass,
O set the crystal surface free!
Pass—as the fairer visions pass—
Nor ever more return, to be
The ghost of a distracted hour,
That heard me whisper:—"I am she!"
— Mary Elizabeth Coleridge,
"The Other Side of a Mirror"

"June Recital" marks the highest achievement of Welty's tragic art in the short story form. Counterbalancing the stories of the MacLain twins in the *Golden Apples* sequence (it is second and they are penultimate), this story of the downfall of Miss Eckhart, Morgana's music teacher, brings into focus as none of Welty's other stories do the social pressures that ostracize a woman, forcing her to choose between marriage and monstrosity, being a lady in the parlor or a madwoman in the attic, and it allows us to define the ways in which the story of Welty's tragic heroines differs significantly from that of her male tragic protagonists.[14]

This feature alone would single out the story in importance, but the tale is also one in which Welty makes her most daring experiments in narrative form, especially in structure and point of view. In contrast to her approach with the MacLain twins, she chooses to tell Miss Eckhart's story from the point of view of two children, Loch and Cassie Morrison, who live next door to the MacLain house that Miss Eckhart called home for many of her years in Morgana. Cassie was one of her piano students (as was Ran MacLain, her only boy pupil), while Loch knows her from the stories Cassie has told and the town gossip he has heard. It is important to ask why Welty chose two distant points of view to present Miss Eckhart's story, rather than the more intimate method she used for the two male tragic protagonists in *The Golden Apples*, and I will confront this question later in this chapter.

The structure of "June Recital" is equally daring. Part I is told from Loch's point of view, first as he observes the action from a bedroom window, and then as he climbs out onto a nearby tree. Part II is told from Cassie's point of view, and focuses not on what she sees but on a strain of music she hears coming from Miss Eckhart's old piano and the flood of memories it releases for her. Part III returns to Loch in his tree; much of the action in this section is viewed upside down, as Loch hangs from a branch. Part IV begins from Cassie's point of view, as she sees Miss Eckhart and joins Loch outside of the house to identify her; then reverts briefly to Loch's point of view; then ends much later in the evening with Cassie in bed, following her thoughts just before and then *after* she has fallen asleep and begun dreaming. Structurally, the story moves simultaneously backward and forward in time. We first see Miss Eckhart in the "present" (the 1920s), as she returns after an absence of about half a dozen years to the site of her abandoned music studio in the MacLain house and, driven insane by what she has lost, tries to burn the house down. Her one-time star pupil, Virgie Rainey, has been in the abandoned house with her boyfriend and has played a tune on the downstairs piano that Miss Eckhart particularly associated with her. Miss Eckhart may or may not have heard Virgie play this tune (the narrative is ambiguous on this point [280–82], just as it is ambiguous as to whether Miss Eckhart knows Virgie is in the house upstairs [282]).[15] But Miss Eckhart's memories of the tune are surely running powerfully through her head as she prepares her fire. Part II begins a chronicle of Miss Eckhart's history in Cassie's memory, progressing from a retelling of the town's opinions about her and the various "scandalous" events associated with her that helped drive her into exile; to a recounting of her music lessons and her rite of an annual recital in June for her pupils; to a detailed account of the single most important June recital she ever staged, in which she "graduated" and said goodbye to Virgie Rainey, who had just turned thirteen years old. Part III returns to the present and is the story's most comic section (thus Welty's use of Loch's topsy-turvy point of view.) It catalogues the slapstick attempts of two Morgana bumpkins, Old Man Moody and Fatty Bowles, to put out the fire Miss Eckhart has set. These events owe not a little to the comic interludes in Shakespearean tragedy (and to scenes such as Dogberry's in *Much Ado About Nothing*), and even more to the silent movie comedies Welty and her brothers loved as children, especially those with Charlie Chaplin and the Keystone Kops (*One Writer's Beginnings* 36). Part IV involves Miss Eckhart and Virgie, both once again targets of the town's censure as Virgie emerges from the house with her lover and Miss Eckhart is prepared to be taken away to an insane asylum in Jackson. Welty's narrative thus juxtaposes a recounting of Miss Eckhart's descent into madness with the story of her ascent to the one great moment in her life in Morgana, the June recital featuring Virgie Rainey's last concert, in which she came close to being integrated into the Morgana community. This contrapuntal interweaving of various narratives and points of view makes "June Recital" formally the most ambitious (as well as the longest) of all Welty's stories.

As Part II chronicles Miss Eckhart's history through Cassie's memories of her, it focuses primarily on the town's view of her and the scandals surrounding her, for Cassie has been much influenced by the town's (and her own parents') judgment of her former music teacher. Their list of grievances against Miss Eckhart is long. Not only is she of German descent, middle-aged and single, and living with her near-senile mother, but she is also from the North and comes to Mississippi determined not just to make her living by teaching piano but to show the status-conscious citizens of Morgana that they are really quite provincial, with little knowledge of sophisticated Old World culture, including music. Several sexual scandals associated with Miss Eckhart serve further to stigmatize her, even though she is responsible for only one of them. One evening she is assaulted by "a crazy Negro" (301), but instead of considering moving to another town or accepting the town's condolences she insists on acting as if nothing has happened. Miss Eckhart also has a romance with Mr. Sissum, the local shoe-store salesman who plays the cello, and after he is accidentally drowned she breaks free from the circle of mourners at his funeral and tries to throw herself into his grave. Finally, another roomer at Mrs. MacLain's, Mr. Voight, begins protesting the noise the music lessons make by appearing at the end of the hall during a lesson and exposing himself, bathrobe opened and face violently grimacing. Miss Eckhart threatens her pupils so they will not tell their parents, but eventually word leaks out. Miss Eckhart thus not only affronts the town's standards of proper behavior by proudly following her own private ideals of what a lady may be, but she also becomes associated with ungovernable passions, the very thing that a "lady" must avoid.

Throughout all of these scandals, the town tolerated Miss Eckhart because she had one skill that was deemed indispensable to them: she could teach their daughters the proper social skill of playing the piano. With the eruption of World War I, however, those lessons suddenly became a luxury. The war caused a crash in cotton prices throughout the South because 60 percent of its cotton was exported, primarily to Europe. With that crash came an economic crisis for at least some of Morgana's aristocratic families. Miss Eckhart loses all the pupils that she has not already lost because of earlier scandals and, to make matters worse, is suspected of sympathizing with the Germans. Simultaneously, Mrs. MacLain decides that she can no longer afford to live in the big MacLain house in town, even with the help of rent from her roomers; she moves back to her family's home in MacLain's Courthouse after selling the house to an owner who does not put up with Miss Eckhart's falling behind on her rent. Miss Eckhart thus loses her apartment and her piano studio as well as her students and is forced to move into a rundown, one-room apartment in the Holifield's on the outskirts of town. An early draft of the story has this apartment located "down near the edge of nigger-town," stressing even more strongly Miss Eckhart's ostracism in the eyes of the town's whites. The same draft makes the circumstances of Miss Eckhart's move even more clearly sordid in the townspeople's eyes: "Miss Eckhart was put out of the house and her piano and many of her possessions kept behind to pay for a whole year's rent she owed." The published version's account is slightly less harsh (307). [16]

Even at the height of her power in Morgana, the very name by which Miss Eckhart is known proclaims her foreignness. Married women from the best families in Morgana are still properly addressed using *their first name and their maiden name,* as with Miss Snowdie Hudson (Mrs. King MacLain) or Miss Billy Texas (Mrs. Felix Spights). Such a custom both acknowledges their status as married women yet preserves their earlier position as leading members of some of the town's most important families—a position that they are expected to preserve after their marriage. The practice pays homage to the belief that a woman from the town's aristocracy gives up none of the power and prerogatives that she had as an eligible daughter when she marries. Yet though this practice can properly be called "matriarchal" because it proclaims the importance of original family ties and the network of friendships that women have established among themselves in Morgana, it also concedes that their groups remain subordinate to the male institutions of marriage and the church: the courtesy title "Miss," their first names, and their "maiden" names belong to the women, so to speak, and are used when they address each other, but their last names remain their husbands' and are used in those situations where their husbands' power must be acknowledged. (Women with decidedly lower social status, such as Maideen Sumrall of "The Whole World Knows," are apparently never addressed as "Miss" and will lose their maiden names altogether upon marrying, as if their families' names were not important enough to preserve.)

Miss Eckhart, in contrast, is called "Miss" simply because she has not married, and this is always coupled, at her own request, with her *last* name, never her first name. Such a procedure immortalizes her foreignness and her spinsterhood, and it also signifies her permanent social exile: she must always be addressed formally, never intimately. Although one of the story's characters, Missie Spights, argues that this formality became the custom at Miss Eckhart's own insistence, her words show that Miss Eckhart's isolation was not solely of her own making: "if Miss Eckhart had allowed herself to be called by her first name, then she would have been like other ladies. Or if Miss Eckhart had belonged to a church that had ever been heard of [she is Lutheran, the rest either Presbyterian or Baptist or Methodist], and the ladies would have had something to invite her to belong to. . . . Or if she had been married to anybody at all, just the awfullest man—like Miss Snowdie MacLain, that everybody could feel sorry for" (308). The town would be willing to accept a newcomer as a proper lady or as a martyr who will accept their pity, but it must be on *their* terms, not hers, and Miss Eckhart will not accommodate them. Her name, like her church, is "unheard of" in Morgana; it represents as much a violation of the town's rules of speech as her life does its rules of good behavior.

What makes Miss Eckhart's name intolerable for the women of Morgana is not that she does not allow her first name to be used but that her name forces the other aristocratic women of the town to feel very strongly the contradictions commemorated by their own custom of compromise linking matriarchal lineage and power ("Miss Snowdie") with patriarchal power ("Miss Snowdie *MacLain*"). Most of the time (and always when they are together), the women act as if matriarchal power is dominant, speaking of themselves using the first name and "Miss," the sign of aristocratic standing. It is only when they must concede that this separate women's sphere is bounded by a patriarchal one that they introduce the woman's "married" name to which their matriarchal names must be subordinate. (Thus Miss Snowdie is called Miss Snowdie MacLain in the above comment of Missie Spights, which alludes to the ways she has suffered because of her husband King MacLain.) Hence Miss Eckhart's name for herself does not merely reject Morgana's naming customs for women—it exposes the contradictions at their heart. Miss Eckhart refuses to use her first name, the heart of where matriarchal signifying power resides, and she taints the honorary title "Miss" with suggestions of spinsterhood, eccentricity, and poverty. Just as badly, she uses her last name to signify her special status in the town, her aristocratic "difference." Morgana's ladies find such a transgression of their naming system unforgivable and threatening.

Also "unheard of" and threatening is the fact that Miss Eckhart picks up "associates" or her "people" (308) only through her work. The unwritten social rules of the town dictate that women's socializing should not occur except through events centered around gatherings such as parlor parties, church going, political speeches, concerts, family gatherings, marriages, and funerals. Miss Eckhart's social contacts are arranged by her alone, without the supervision of either the matriarchal or patriarchal power structures in the town, and she has the gall to appear to want no relationships other than those with her pupils, especially her star student, Virgie Rainey. When such independence is coupled with the fact that she is unmarried, her close contact with her female pupils becomes vaguely ominous—as much an affront to proper womanhood as the sexual scandals surrounding her. This comes to be true even though she is teaching her girls the eminently ladylike art of piano playing: her relations with her students are too intense and too unsupervised.

It is Miss Eckhart's relationship with Virgie that makes these "unheard of" fears heard and spoken repeatedly in the town's gossip. Everything that must be repressed in her public life in town is channeled into her friendship with Virgie. Virgie both courts and resists Miss Eckhart's attention. She is honored by it but also threatened by it, for Miss Eckhart's standards seem so different and so much more exacting than those she is used to, and they tempt her into thinking that what the other women of the town believe is important is not important at all. She willfully breaks rules that Miss Eckhart has laid down for her students, arriving late for lessons, banging her bicycle against the porch, rolling up her music instead of carrying it in a portfolio, and, one day, refusing to play another note with that "thing"—Miss Eckhart's prized metronome—in front of her face (293). As passionate and independent as her teacher, Virgie quickly finds that she can exploit Miss Eckhart's devotion to her. Showing her "weak place" (293) to the other girls gives Virgie something she cannot get any other way. She may be the daughter of one of the town's poorer families, but by exhibiting her ability to flout Miss Eckhart's rules she gains a measure of status that even her superior piano playing can never give her: she becomes a leader for all the girls, even those from the best families.

The town christens Virgie with a special name that is as "unheard of" as her teacher's—and, like hers, it reflects their uneasiness as well as their sense of superiority. Miss Eckhart always praises Virgie's skill in playing by saying "Virgie Rainey *Danke schoen*" ["thank you"]. This compliment perfectly captures the special nature of her tribute. By using her native tongue, Miss Eckhart hints that Virgie is the only student whom she will ever allow to share a part of her life and language, the skill and passion of her art. The poignant, old-fashioned formality of the phrase suggests that in none of her other relations with the townspeople of Morgana has she received something for which she is as grateful as Virgie's gift. All her other daily "thank you's" to merchants and acquaintances are mere commonplaces compared with the passion of her compliment to Virgie. It is as if Virgie has given her a reason for living—has made worthwhile all the drudgery and disillusionment of teaching classical music in a small provincial southern town.

Morgana's children and adults know of Miss Eckhart's compliments to Virgie and, in mock tribute, call Virgie by the new nickname whenever she acts unconventionally: "they just added that onto Virgie's name in the school yard. She was Virgie Rainey *Danke schoen* when she jumped hot pepper or fought the boys, when she had to sit down the very first one in the spelling match for saying, 'E-a-r, ear, r-a-k-e, rake, ear-ache' (291). The townspeople's adoption of Miss Eckhart's name for Virgie, ironic as it is, shows more than mere disdain for her standards. Miss Eckhart's compliment to Virgie (like the women's custom of calling married women "Miss") commemorates the importance of friendships between women. Unlike the ladies' practice, Miss Eckhart's does not even provisionally make itself subordinate to anything; it is a potentially revolutionary form of naming, a passionate proclamation of the importance of bonds between women *in spite of* their obligations to be ladies, wives, and mothers. When Miss Eckhart compliments Virgie in her frighteningly "foreign" voice, she is implicitly naming other "unheard of" things—the existence of women's repressed voices, hidden identities, and potential power. She intends to teach Virgie to discover such a voice for herself, to make the unheard heard. "Virgie would be heard from in the world, playing that [piano piece], Miss Eckhart said, revealing to children with one ardent cry her lack of knowledge of the world. How could Virgie be

heard from, in the world? And 'the world'! Where did Miss Eckhart
think she was now? Virgie Rainey, she repeated over and over, had a
gift, and she must go away from Morgana" (303).

A passage on this matter cut from a draft of "June Recital" is even
more explicit: "There had been without anyone's expecting it almost
an equality between Virgie Rainey and Miss Eckhart that made look-
ing-down-on and looking-up-to impossible. Maybe from the start,
there had been nothing to disavow their equality, and leniency, and
love, except the thanking. When Miss Eckhart had said, 'Virgie
Rainey, *danke schoen*,' she held apart and kept at bay the fiercest
spirits . . . the fiercest Sally [Cassie] knew." When Virgie torments
Miss Eckhart, she does so partly because, like the townspeople alluded
to in these passages, she mocks Miss Eckhart's pretensions. But she
also does so because she fears the consequences of discovering such a
voice and "fierce spirit" within herself—fears that such hidden powers
may bring estrangement and unhappiness to her as they did to her
music teacher. Like the phrase "Miss Snowdie MacLain," the phrase
"Virgie Rainey *Danke schoen*" expresses strong tension among its parts
and points to intolerable contradictions within girls' and women's
identities as they are defined in Morgana.

Miss Eckhart has created one event in which the town must concede her some public form of power: the annual recital in June that
her pupils give in her cramped studio in the MacLain house. It is the
one time in which the rest of the town may enter her private world,
the one time when her authority is recognized and even celebrated.
In revising the story, Welty made many of her changes in the section
describing the concerts, especially Virgie's climactic one; she added
detail after detail, greatly increasing the scene's length and prominence (308–15). In the month leading up to the concert, Miss Eckhart seems to be the schoolmistress of the entire town, defining the
rules and instructing all on their proper behavior. In fact, she has all
the authority of a bride who is planning the arrangements before she
is married. But Miss Eckhart's authority is temporary and special,
something given to her in May and June as if to compensate for her
powerlessness during the other months, and the importance of the
event for the townspeople is predominantly social, not artistic. It has
nothing to do with Miss Eckhart's desire to make a student like Virgie
be "heard from" but merely with the townspeople's desire to display

what new social skills and formal dresses their daughters have acquired during the past year. "Miss Eckhart decided early in the spring what color each child should wear, with what color sash and hair ribbon, and sent written word to the mother . . . . And it could seldom be worn again; certainly not to another recital—by then an 'old' dress. A recital dress was fuller and had more trimming than a Sunday dress. It was like a flower girl's dress in a wedding" (309). The women of the town feel comfortable giving Miss Eckhart "special dispensation" (309) because the form of the recital really commemorates their power, not hers. Not only is she dependent upon the other women to make the dresses, but she is now expressing herself in a "language" that is no longer unheard of: "this was the kind of thing that both Miss Perdita and most mothers understood immediately" (309). Thus even though the mothers speak of being scared by Miss Eckhart in May and June, they also trust that they are more in control of Miss Eckhart then than at any other time.

There is another reason that the authority Miss Eckhart has during her June recitals is unthreatening: she publicly concedes that her authority over her girls ceases once they enter adolescence. Virgie's last recital, Welty pointedly notes, comes when she is thirteen (313). After that, an unwritten rule says that all girls must break their ties with Miss Eckhart and enter fully into the adult world of womanhood defined by Morgana society—the matriarchal world of parlors and church socials that exists carefully subordinate to the more powerful patriarchal institutions of family and church and jobs and schools of higher learning.

Welty's chronicling of how Cassie Morrison wins a music scholarship illustrates how this process works. Miss Eckhart's star pupil continues to play piano after "graduating" from Miss Eckhart's school, but instead of making her special or giving her a voice (as Miss Eckhart hoped it would) her employment merely signifies that she has fallen in status in her classmates' eyes: "Virgie Rainey worked. Not at teaching. She played the piano for the picture show, both shows every night, and got six dollars a week, and was not popular any more" (286). She receives no scholarship to college; her church (Methodist) does not offer one. The less talented Cassie Morrison, on the other hand, belongs to the most prestigious church in Morgana, the Presbyterian, and their church deacons do give music scholarships. (Miss

Eckhart, in revenge, gives Virgie an emblem of their private bond, a silver brooch shaped like a butterfly, to commemorate her leaving.) Miss Eckhart's "graduation ceremony" of the June recital therefore marks the moment when her pupils pass from the control of their private music teacher, a surrogate mother-figure, into the supervision of institutions that are public and patriarchal—the churches and schools that will "complete" their initiation into adulthood. Such a rite of passage thus anticipates the later, most crucial one that they will make when they leave the woman's sphere of their adolescence (represented by their bridesmaids' dresses at the music recitals) to take a husband's name and accept his authority.

Of course, each girl is not the "bride" in the June recital, Miss Eckhart is: she is the one who orders all the "bride's-maids'" dresses. There are several possible ways to interpret this. The townspeople surely see it as another example of Miss Eckhart's self-delusion: a pathetically comic attempt to give her "graduations" the importance of a marriage and thus an attempt to recoup some of the status and power that derives from marrying well. The town tolerates such displays of her ego because the very form they allow her defines the limits of her power. For Miss Eckhart, however, her June ceremony has as many hidden meanings as her phrase "Virgie Rainey, *Danke schoen*"— meanings that subvert those that the town allows her. She treats the event as if she really is "married" to the role of music teacher. Such seriousness is troubling because it does not seem entirely to recognize a higher, patriarchal authority. Even in the midst of the social spectacle of the June recital, Miss Eckhart's demeanor proclaims the self-sufficiency of her bond with her students and the fact that she feels bound to teach her best students not just social skills but the ability to discover a decidedly individual, independent, and "unheard of" voice—at whatever cost. As an informal institution, therefore, Miss Eckhart's June recital has precisely the same kind of tension that exists in the ladies' conventions for naming themselves. It should be understood to function both as a concession to superior patriarchal power and as a matriarchal bond that (potentially at least) may subvert the status quo rather than signify subordination to it.

Such possibly subversive readings of the marriage symbolism in Miss Eckhart's June recital are duplicated by a secret ritual that Miss Eckhart and Virgie invent for themselves. On the top of the piano during the public recital would always stand the sign of Miss Eckhart's authority, her metronome, closed and locked. After each pupil's playing, she would be given a florist's bouquet by her teacher, hold it "for a count of three," and then return it to Miss Eckhart, who would place it on the floor to one side, gradually forming a crescent moon design (310). In Virgie's private lessons before she orders her teacher to hide the metronome, however, Virgie and Miss Eckhart spontaneously invent a ritual that can be interpreted as a kind of *counter*-marriage ceremony, a secret enactment expressing just the sort of passionate bonding that makes Morgana uneasy. Virgie often brings Miss Eckhart a bouquet of stolen magnolia flowers and leaves, not a florist's bouquet, and Miss Eckhart would arrange it around the base of the metronome on top of the piano (283, 290, 321). The metronome's obelisk signifies the absolute authority that Miss Eckhart wields over her girls during the privacy of their lessons; both its shape and its function make it rather phallic. The magnolia flower and leaves, in contrast, seem "feminine" and are arranged so that the obelisk penetrates their center. But pondering the possible sexual connotations of this arrangement may be less fruitful than considering its social meanings. As a private variation of the recital's public ritual, it celebrates all the "unheard of" things a bond between women may discover. It recognizes no boundaries to a woman's authority, no patriarchal supervision.

After Miss Eckhart loses her pupils and is forced to move to the edge of town, she "would be seen from time to time walking into Morgana, up one side of the street and down the other and home" (307). On each trip she passes the MacLain house, trying to relive the time when she taught there. On one of those visits, coincidentally, she apparently passes by just as Virgie is playing Beethoven's *Für Elise* again on the abandoned piano in the old studio. (It is a piece that Miss Eckhart and the other pupils particularly associate with Virgie.) Virgie has secretly sneaked back into the house with her boyfriend in order to show the place to him and make love on an old broken bed directly upstairs from Miss Eckhart's abandoned music studio. Miss Eckhart turns and enters the house (Virgie and her boyfriend have gone upstairs again by this time) and feverishly begins to gather old newspapers to decorate the studio as if for another triumphant recital. She tears up the newspapers and hangs a series of streamers from the central chandelier—just as she did during her June recitals. "As Loch leaned his chin in his palm at the window and watched, it seemed strangely as if he had seen this whole thing before. The old woman was decorating the piano until it rayed out like a Christmas tree or a Maypole. Maypole ribbons of newspaper and tissue paper streamed and crossed each other from the piano to the chandelier and festooned again to the four corners of the room, looped to the backs of chairs here and there" (283).

It is not certain that Miss Eckhart in her derangement actually realizes that Virgie is in the house, but it is hard to believe that she can be oblivious to Virgie's presence: Virgie and her boyfriend are described as dancing and laughing just one floor above the very room in which Miss Eckhart is working [282].) Miss Eckhart's arrangement of newspapers at first is described as if it were festive, like a "Christmas tree or a Maypole" (283). She even improvises a Maypole crown out of a magnolia branch and places it on the piano around the metronome. This special decoration of the metronome did not occur in the public June recitals (312), and thus *for the first time* Miss Eckhart is merging her public June recital rituals with her private magnolia ritual for Virgie: it is a desperate attempt to relive the most significant private and public moments of her life in Morgana.

The lines from Yeats's poem "The Song of Wandering Aengus" that figure so prominently in the story commemorate Miss Eckhart's love for Virgie:

> Though I am old with wandering
> Through hollow lands and hilly lands,
> I will find out where she has gone,
> And kiss her lips and take her hands;
> And walk among long dappled grass,
> And pluck till time and times are done
> The silver apples of the moon,
> The golden apples of the sun. (57–58)

Virgie's fellow pupil Cassie recalls these lines when she hears Virgie playing *Für Elise* on the old piano next door near the moment when Miss Eckhart is passing by the house. Cassie remembers them because their tender melancholy is shared by Beethoven's piece, but the lines describe Miss Eckhart's passion for Virgie as well. Like Aengus, she also near the end of her life tries to recapture a girl—one who has vanished into adulthood, not into Yeats's brightening air. And like Aengus she is trapped in time while desperately trying to transcend it. The syntax of Yeats's last sentence moves from a present tense in which the speaker concedes his age ("Though I am old") to the future tense ("I will find out") to a clause in which the speaker wills the illusion of living in an eternal present: "And pluck till time and times are done." By returning to the house and recreating her private and public recital rituals as if on cue from *Für Elise*, Miss Eckhart seeks to do the same thing. But in the face of evidence that her pupil has grown up, left her, and renounced her art—the dilapidated house, abandoned piano, and the sounds of Virgie romping upstairs with her boyfriend—she can only give in to her anger and despair.

Another line in the poem that Cassie Morrison does not remember right away is relevant: "Because a fire was in my head." In the Yeats poem it initiates and continues the action; it drives Aengus out into the night even before he meets the faery girl, and it inspires him afterwards on his lifelong quest to find her again. In Welty's story, in contrast, the line alludes to Miss Eckhart catching her hair on fire, her tragic decision to destroy what she cannot keep by burning down the house. In despair, she wants to turn the one golden apple in her life—her bond with Virgie—into ashes. An early draft of the story's end reveals that Welty originally had Cassie remembering and quoting the entire last stanza of Yeats's poem (quoted above). She then changed this to Cassie's quoting the earlier line in the poem about fire, to emphasize Miss Eckhart's passion and self-destructiveness.

By imbedding Yeats's poem within a story about the social and historical context that constrains Miss Eckhart's dream, Welty gives Aengus' quest meanings that it does not have in Yeats's poem. She makes it clear that we should not read Miss Eckhart's actions merely as a deranged and arrogant protest against nature—against Virgie's growing up. For her pyromania is also fired by anger against the society that has ostracized her. Her reenactment of her June recital seeks revenge against the social standards of Morgana that were threatened by her independence and her desire to give her girls an independent voice. In her delusion she tries to attack the town's entire social structure, to burn down the house of one of Morgana's best families and (symbolically) all of Morgana itself.

Miss Eckhart is not just attacking Morgana, admittedly; she is also attempting suicide. The final target of her anger is thus not Virgie or Morgana, but herself. Like the heroine in Welty's story "Clytie" from *A Curtain of Green,* but much more complexly, Miss Eckhart has so absorbed her society's judgments against her that she guiltily directs her anger inwards as well as outwards: she rages not only at others but at her own rage. For this reason, several crucial images in "June Recital" and *The Golden Apples* make it clear that the stories of Fata Morgana and the Medusa are as relevant to Miss Eckhart's life as the Gaelic or Greek myths about the golden apples. Like Clytie's suicidal despair, Miss Eckhart's is caused because despite all her efforts she has absorbed Morgana's image of herself as a monstrous enchantress of their children, a Fata Morgana. Welty has said that one of the reasons she picked the name "Morgana" for her imaginary town in *The Golden Apples* was because it reminded her of Fata Morgana or "mirage"— thus implying that Morgana's carefully ordered social world, powerful as it is, is illusory.[17] The phrase is also associated with dangerous female supernatural beings such as Fata Morgana in Ariosto, Morgan le Fay in English legends, and (because Morgana was said to be in league with the infernal deity Demogorgon) the three Gorgons, including Medusa. Of all the women in Morgana, only Miss Eckhart has enough isolation and power to qualify her to be compared with such demonic figures. Cassie Morrison's mother describes her studio as being like the witch's house in Hansel and Gretel, "including the witch" (288), but because of the prominence of the Perseus myth in *The Golden Apples* (especially in "The Wanderers"), Medusa's story is the most germane of all. Miss Eckhart's unmarried and isolated life, her unfashionable and sometimes frightening appearance, her temper, and her dangerous powers all make Morgana's other women think of her as if she were their resident Gorgon.

One scene in "June Recital" illustrates with particular poignancy how Morgana links Miss Eckhart and Medusa. Ironically, this linkage is perpetrated by Virgie herself—an act of mockery and rebellion prompted by her own fears that when she grows up her rebelliousness may make her a Gorgon as well. The incident occurs when Virgie is still Miss Eckhart's pupil, during an outdoor summer evening concert in the Starks' yard in which Mr. Sissum plays the cello while Miss Eckhart watches in the audience. Virgie has discovered that Miss Eckhart is "sweet" on him (296), but her preternatural intelligence also guesses correctly that it will be a doomed love affair. She performs a mock Maypole ritual at Miss Eckhart's expense—and in the process parodies her own magnolia ritual as well.

> Virgie put a loop of clover chain down over Miss Eckhart's head, her hat—her one hat—and all. She hung Miss Eckhart with flowers, while Mr. Sissum plucked the strings up above her. Miss Eckhart sat on, perfectly still and submissive. She gave no sign. She let the clover chain come down and lie on her breast.
> Virgie laughed delightedly and with her long chain in her hand ran around and around her, binding her up with clovers. Miss Eckhart let her head roll back, and then Cassie felt that the teacher was filled with terror, perhaps with pain. She found it so easy—ever since Virgie showed her—to feel terror and pain in an outsider; in someone you did not know at all well, pain made you wonderfully sorry. It was not so easy to be sorry about it in the people close to you. (298)

It is hard to know how to interpret this scene, since Virgie's actions seem such a mixture of tenderness and aggressive mockery, but Cassie's intimation that something in Virgie's gesture fills Miss Eckhart with terror and pain is crucial. Like Morgana's attempts to pity Miss Eckhart, this one succeeds in freezing her into the image of a grotesque "outsider," a pathetic, fat old maid with only "one hat," wilting flowers on her breast, and only a failed love affair and scandal to her name. Virgie's act is unconsciously rather than consciously cruel, but it nonetheless transforms her teacher into something pathetic, a scapegoat for Virgie's own fears that any woman who discovers an "unheard of" voice within herself will be ostracized. By doing so, Virgie's seemingly innocent ritual acts out what Morgana has been doing to Miss Eckhart over many years and would continue with even more intensity once Miss Eckhart loses her pupils and her livelihood: Virgie freezes her into an image of Medusa's terror, pain, and monstrosity.

Such a reading of the scene may seem too somber and too negative regarding Virgie's motives, but readers who are skeptical should consider the way in which Welty has framed this episode. Near its beginning is a reference to a statue of a "goddess" (possibly Venus) on the Starks' lawn near Miss Eckhart (297). This detail was added only during a late stage of revision (the statue was originally of a Confederate soldier) and serves to heighten the contrast between ideal images of women and Miss Eckhart. The scene is closed by recounting the story of Mr. Sissum's giving Miss Eckhart a funny, ugly "Billikin" doll that made her laugh in a "distorted" way until she began crying (298–99). Miss Eckhart clearly responds to the doll this way because she identifies it with her own "funny and ugly"—and monstrous—image in the eyes of Morgana. A later passage in the story that is also about Miss Eckhart's self-image supports such a reading: the narrator says that Miss Eckhart at her recitals "called up the pictures on those little square party invitations, the brown bear in a frill and the black poodle standing on a chair to shave at a mirror" (311). This sentence, like the phrase about the "goddess" statue, was added in revision to clarify how Morgana judges Miss Eckhart's appearance. Both this passage and the Billikin one treat Miss Eckhart as a circus act, a sideshow grotesque, half-human and half-animal. When Miss Eckhart tries to burn herself to death, therefore, she appears to be trying to find peace by destroying the monstrous half-animal self—the Fata Morgana or Medusa—that Morgana has made her believe she has become.

Unlike the other stories about madness in The Golden Apples, "The Whole World Knows" and "Music from Spain," "June Recital" is not written from the point of view of its principal character. Miss Eckhart's plight is instead presented through the eyes of two children, Loch and Cassie Morrison, who unwittingly represent society's view of her. The result is to distance us from her inner life; we must work our way through society's view of her as a rather comically demented creature before we can come to know her on her own terms.

Cassie and Loch Morrison are privileged observers because they both happen to be in their bedrooms in their house next door the night Miss Eckhart tries to burn the MacLain house down. Loch treats the events merely as an exciting adventure that he may spy on using his father's telescope from his bedroom window. He laughs at Miss Eckhart's incompetence when trying to start a fire and at the bumbling rescue attempts staged by two men who wander on the scene. In the end, as she is being taken away, her hair scorched by the fire and her mind incoherent, Loch is largely oblivious to all that has happened. Instead, he is deliriously happy because he has gotten Miss Eckhart's metronome, which he thinks is a mysterious new kind of bomb. Loch's point of view here is hardly censured by Welty; rather, it is presented as the natural kind of interest that a young boy would have in a house burning, but the comical way in which Loch regards Miss Eckhart as a freak is in fact not unrelated to the townspeople's view of her; it just represents this view in an exaggerated form. (In fact, when Loch climbs out onto a tree to hang upside down to view the happenings in the house next door, Welty seems to be wryly implying that the town's seemingly mature and reasonable opinions of Miss Eckhart's eccentricities may be as skewed a view of her as Loch's).[18]

Cassie Morrison's memories of Miss Eckhart are even more closely associated with the views of Morgana society. The point of view of "June Recital" shifts from Loch's to hers as soon as Virgie begins to play Für Elise (285), for Cassie was a student with Virgie and the melody brings back memories of Miss Eckhart that Loch cannot have. Through Cassie's recollections and a series of flashbacks, Miss Eckhart's history is presented even as (unknown to Cassie, who is not watching the events as her brother is) she is preparing to set the house on fire. The effect is a heart-wrenching juxtaposition between past and present—Cassie's remembering Miss Eckhart at the height of her power during her June recitals while Loch is seeing her inverted, in the depths of her madness. Cassie is rather frightened by the intensity of the memories that Für Elise recalls, for she principally remembers Miss Eckhart as an unfashionable and slightly demonic woman, someone for a proper girl to keep at a distance, not to use as a role model: "There could have been for Miss Eckhart a little opening wedge—a crack in the door. . . . But if I had been the one to see it open, [Cassie] thought slowly, I might have slammed it tight for ever. I might" (308).

When Cassie first hears Virgie playing Für Elise, she is trying on different kinds of make-up and tie-dyeing a scarf in preparation for a date, and also thinking of what clothes she will take to college with her music scholarship in the fall. She instinctively seeks to place as much distance as possible between her success and the unfashionable nonconformity of Miss Eckhart and Virgie: "Cassie edged back to the window, while her heart sank, praying that she would not catch sight of Virgie Rainey or, especially, that Virgie Rainey would not catch sight of her" (286). When Cassie finally goes to the window at the end of the story and sees Miss Eckhart being dragged away, she recognizes her only by her slim ankles, the one conventionally "feminine" and fashionable feature about her that had always been praised (324). At that moment she also sympathizes with her plight and blames herself, Virgie, and all Morgana for forcing her into being a Medusa. Cassie calls it cruelly "placing" her: "People saw things like this as they saw Mr. MacLain come and go. They only hoped to place them, in their hour or their street or the name of their mothers' people. Then Morgana could hold them, and at last they were this and they were that" (325).[19]

Even though "June Recital" is narrated using a third-person, "omniscient" voice, that voice, like Cassie herself, actually contains multiple intonations and inflections; it hardly represents a single perspective. We need only listen carefully to the story's narration to discern its hidden dissonances—the same kind of dissonances that are present in phrases like "Miss Snowdie MacLain" and "Virgie Rainey, *Danke schoen.*" On one level, we can pick out the self-satisfied voice of Morgana (and Cassie at her most conventional) through the narrator's purported omniscience: "Perhaps nobody wanted Virgie Rainey to be anything in Morgana any more than they wanted Miss Eckhart to be, and they were the two of them still linked together by people's saying that. How much might depend on people's being linked together? Even Miss Snowdie [MacLain] had a little harder time than she had had already with Ran and Scooter, her bad boys, by being linked with roomers and music lessons and Germans" (306).

On another level, this passage reveals that even Cassie herself is fascinated with what social ostracism may bring, largely against her will: in asking "how much might depend on people's being linked together?" she reluctantly takes the first steps towards questioning Morgana's self-righteous judgments. The tone of such a question (not to mention its dangerous implications) stands in dissonant contrast to the more self-righteous inflection of the next sentence, pursing its lips in disdain over "roomers and music lessons and Germans." The narrator's voice throughout "June Recital" thus functions as a kind of tragic (or tragicomic) chorus, commenting upon the tragic protagonist's story from the periphery and acting as a spokesperson for society's most widely shared points of view. As in Greek tragedy it is the tragic protagonist's fate to expose the threatening divisions and dissonances—what Bakhtin calls "heteroglossia"—within the supposedly unified voice of the chorus.[20]

Is it merely a coincidence that the tragic stories of Ran and Eugene in *The Golden Apples* are presented "directly," focusing on their points of view, whereas Miss Eckhart's is not? Welty of course had presented directly the story of a woman's inner torment before, using a guilty monologue in a story like "Why I Live at the P.O." and a third person narrator who restricted herself to the point of view of the protagonist in "Clytie." Welty surely could intend the elaborate distancing techniques of "June Recital" merely to contrast with the stream-of-consciousness in Ran's and Eugene's narratives—such variety works well for the balance of *The Golden Apples* as a whole, after all. Yet her decision to create an "outside" rather than "inside" narrative underlines the contrasting patterns of behavior in her male and female tragic characters: men wander, women are confined. Ran MacLain and Tom Harris ("The Hitch-Hikers") try to flee a society that they see as being governed by oppressive maternal presences, whereas Welty's tragic heroines from Clytie to Old Addie to Miss Eckhart are imprisoned within the walls of their society's expectations, able to subvert them secretly, perhaps, but still forced to remain their prisoner. Such dramatically different fates conform to the different stereotypes that govern the society that Welty depicts. Men are expected to be independent, even though such "freedom" may be achieved merely by negating all forms of human sympathy, while women are expected to sacrifice themselves for others, even though such a form of responsibility may result in imprisoning the self entirely within conventional roles. The stereotypes of male self-indulgence and female self-sacrifice are ultimately just as constricting, admittedly; Tom Harris or Ran MacLain in their motel rooms are no less prisoners of their psyches than Miss Eckhart is when she shuts herself up in her "airless" (285) studio with her piano to burn the house down. Yet the dramatic ironies of these confinements are not equivalent and portray the distinct ways in which male and female stereotypes wound Welty's tragic characters. If both Welty's male and female tragic heroes are imprisoned, therefore, her men are trapped within the illusion of their freedom, their belief that they may erase their identities and start over, whereas her women are trapped within the illusion of their guilt, their belief that their inner as well as outer selves are monstrous. The different forms of third-person narrative and first-person monologue that Welty chose for "June Recital" and "The Whole World Knows" ably dramatize the gender difference she perceives in the genre of tragedy.

One element does unite Welty's male and female tragic heroes: they experience no recognition scene, at least in the classic sense. Unlike, say, the recognition by Oedipus that the entire identity that he has constructed as Oedipus the King is a delusion, no such moment of self-knowledge is experienced by Miss Eckhart, Ran MacLain, Clytie, Howard, or Tom Harris. They remain caught within their delusions and their hubris—just on the verge of uncovering the sources of their torment, but never doing so. Her tragic characters are forced to endure forever the "wandering" of their souls that leads them into the darkest parts of their psyches. Their experience is analogous to Oedipus' first inkling that he may be guilty:

> O dear Jocasta,
> as I hear this from you, there comes upon me
> a wandering of the soul—I could run mad. (ll. 725–27)

Unlike Oedipus, they are never able to "bear witness" (l. 1384) against themselves or against their society. The blinding insight of the recognition scene is experienced not by the hero and only partially by the "chorus." The burden of its meanings lies predominantly on us, the audience. Only we are able to bear witness to the tragedy's causes.

"June Recital" brings to a culmination all of Welty's earlier stories about women who become mad. Like Mrs. Larkin, Mrs. Marblehall, Clytie, and the two women in "A Visit of Charity," Miss Eckhart has had to imprison an inner self that society has refused to accommodate. The many earlier descriptions of obsessive activity within enclosed spaces, of anger, fire, hidden voices, and the terrifying face of madness, all resurface to stunning effect in "June Recital." Of all the stories that analyze the social causes of these nightmares, "June Recital" is by far the most detailed and ambitious. We see her despair grow with heartbreaking clarity, are forced to trace its sources and consider how its example influences the next generation of women in Morgana—the Cassie Morrisons and Virgie Raineys. Above all, in "June Recital" we hear that woman's potentially subversive inner voice in all its power.

> One summer morning, a sudden storm had rolled up. . . .
>
> Miss Eckhart, without saying what she was going to do, poked her finger solidly along the pile of music on top of the piano, pulled out a piece [a sonata by Beethoven], and sat down on her own stool. . . .
>
> The piece was so hard that she made mistakes and repeated to correct them, so long and stirring that it soon seemed longer than the day itself had been, and in playing it Miss Eckhart assumed an entirely different face.
>
> . . . The face could have belonged to someone else—not even to a woman necessarily. It was the face a mountain could have, or what might be seen behind the veil of a waterfall. There in the rainy light it was a sightless face, one for music only. . . . And if the sonata had an origin in a place on earth, it was the place where Virgie, even, had never been and was not likely ever to go. (300–1) [21]

Miss Eckhart's—and Morgana's—tragedies are that such inner energy must remain "veiled"; its restless authority frightens her students, the townspeople, and even herself.

Miss Eckhart's former pupil Cassie Morrison may for the most part see her stereotypically in "June Recital," but she does have moments in the story when she understands her inner life and feels the attraction of its power. When she returns from a date later that night after the fire has been put out and Miss Eckhart taken away to the insane asylum, she has a vision of Miss Eckhart's face rising before her in the window, watching her. The last sentences of the story move from Cassie's conscious thoughts of Miss Eckhart's to her unconscious ones: "She slept, but sat up in bed once and said aloud, '*Because a fire was in my head.*' Then she fell back unresisting. She did not see except in dreams that a face looked in; that it was the grave, unappeased, and radiant face, once more and always, the face that was in the poem" (330). Like the face of the faery that captures Aengus' heart in the Yeats poem, this face forever haunts the viewer after it is seen, but it is monstrous as well as beautiful, "unappeased" and mad. Its radiance suggests inner power but also inner torment—the face of Miss Eckhart inside the burning house with her hair on fire (322). (Compare the Mary Elizabeth Coleridge poem on a similar subject, used as an epigraph to this section.) The disturbing memory of Miss Eckhart is thus buried within her female pupils and may surface even when they are acting most conventionally, as Cassie is through most of the story. It is also not merely a memory of their teacher but, even more disturbingly, of another "voice" that Miss Eckhart tried to teach them to have, a voice that they have all partially or wholly suppressed in order to blend their voices into the chorus of their society.

In the stories considered in the next chapter, the heroines at last are able to come to terms with the veiled image of the Medusa that has haunted so many of Welty's strong heroines. They become Perseus figures as well as Medusa figures: that is, they learn to control or limit society's ability to cast a rebellious woman as a Medusa. Comedies rather than tragedies, these stories do feature recognition scenes, but unlike the recognition scenes of tragedy, they reveal sources for a new identity rather than the causes that destroyed the old. Their rebellious protagonists are at least partially accepted as role models for their communities, not treated as monsters or scapegoats. Thus they begin to build with their own force of will and imagination "a place on earth" where power such as Miss Eckhart's can survive.

CHAPTER 3

Rigidity and Rebirth
Eudora Welty and Women's Comedy

In 1941 Welty published two exuberant pieces that will be excellent springboards to launching a discussion of the development of her comic stories. The first, "Why I Live at the P.O.," became perhaps her single most famous piece of fiction; certainly it is her most well-known comic story. The second piece, "*Women!!* Make Turban in Own Home!" appeared in the *Junior League Magazine* in November 1941 complete with illustrations and the byline "Eudora Welty, Jackson"; it remains largely unknown.[1] It is a witty piece of journalism rather than a story, but when paired with "Why I Live at the P.O." it allows us to approach "P.O." (a perhaps too familiar story) from an unusual angle and see links between Welty's comic sensibility and her interest in issues of gender differences and power.

"*Women!!* Make Turban in Own Home!" achieves much of its comic edge through incongruity, imitating the voice of a mechanically incompetent woman who inspired by reading too many issues of *Popular Mechanics* tries to build her own version of the latest rage in women's fashion in 1941, a "Hedy Lamarr turban." As the title of the article suggests with its use of italics and its three exclamation points, this woman is breathy and excited about her project, gallantly admitting her mechanical ineptitude but consoling herself with the fact that her best energies are no doubt mental: "Of course," she admits, after reading all those *Popular Mechanics*, "I never made a thing. As a matter of fact, I am singularly inept at all mechanical tasks. To me, all *things* are motivated and active enemies, and a stuck table drawer will always be more cunning than I am. But throughout my childhood, I was a constant mental handy-man. I could have fixed anything, and if I had ever wanted to, I could have made anything. I could have changed everything in the household into something else if I had wanted to, just like a witch. But I never did."

Being proud of her mechanical ineptitude is proper for a southern lady, of course: "We Southern women would not think of having a washing machine installed in the home, but we may at any moment descend (or ascend) to some form of heinous physical drudgery, emerging only to declare our prowess before falling flat. I don't know what causes this. We all do it. We are so proud of being able to do anything you might name." But the narrator nonetheless is fascinated with the magazine's "Yankee" bustle and gospel of self-improvement:

> The true message of *Popular Mechanics* is: "You want something? You've got it." And that's like having a finger pointed at you. There's a feeling of guilt there somewhere; I still don't think it's a good idea to read things like that unless you have poison ivy. You haven't got this thing you want, such as a high dive for that home-made pool of yours, in its ultimate form, of course: it's your old fireless cooker. But in its lesser state, that high dive is right there looking at you, staring at you. In one more minute you are going to open a box of as horrible a set of tools as I have ever seen outside "The Return of Frankenstein," and work your head off.

As a child, our heroine the narrator did have a very practical interest in reading the magazine: although she could not imagine herself building the contraptions depicted, she did see how the magazine could contribute to a proper girl's activity, her paper-doll collection. She had plenty of mothers and children in paper cutouts (presumably from ransacking women's magazines), but she lacked *fathers*. Fortunately, *Popular Mechanics* was filled with images of men. "The only men in the mail-order catalogue wore long underwear, smiled, and carried another pair. I think they still do. My choice was the man under water. In *Popular Mechanics,* besides these undersea men at 45-degree angles, and frowning inventors with spangled headlights on their foreheads, you could get standing-up men like Lionel Strongfort and Charles Atlas for fathers of your families. They had their measurements, with fractions, printed on dotted lines across them, I remember. They very nicely matched the mothers with pricemarks on their upper arms." Welty's deadpan humor here works superbly, contrasting the girl's enthusiasm with a very knowing eye for the comically artificial costumes and poses differentiating the sexes and turning all into commodities to be purchased on the market.

Later, when the subject turns to making a turban, the piece's wry mixture of buoyancy and skepticism continues. The Austrian-born actress Hedy Lamarr made her first American movie, *Algiers,* in 1938, as a femme fatale who lured a criminal played by Charles Boyer out of the Casbah, the native quarter in Algiers, to his death. Several scenes in that movie in which she wears a turban inspired women all over America to try out turbans for the next few years. In Lamarr's words,

> I was "Gaby," a romantic figure, set off against a romantic North African background . . . .
> My big break came of all places in wardrobe. The wardrobe mistress wanted to add a touch of sophistication to my dress, something that would lend mystery yet dignity. We experimented, but nothing seemed to do it. Finally I suggested varying the headgear. In a bit of mad inspiration I shaped up a white turban. [Actually, it is a darker color in *Algiers.*] It was just the touch we needed.
> . . . Turbans came into style as a direct result of Gaby. . . .
> All the actresses were going brunette and sultry, which motion picture columnists said was my influence. Joan Bennett, Claudette Colbert, Joan Crawford, and Kay Francis, just to name a few, soon looked like Gaby from *Algiers,* and the line, "Hay-dee darling, come wiz me to the Casbah," with [sic: was] the schtik of every night club comic. (63, 70)

This fever for turbans also infects the narrator, who feels that one will be the perfect thing to contain her hair, which "with much brushing, extended through absent-mindedness and brooding," was "growing longer and longer."

> With the [department store] clerk's sympathy, I finally had to buy
> one to take home and study by myself. She explained that she was
> wrapping up a blouse with the turban, made of the same material and
> attached to it. I had thought it a part of the turban's tail, and that had
> added to my confusion.
>
> "Comes with it, hon," said the clerk. "It's an inducement." She
> pointed to where you could break a thread and separate the things; but
> she said that I would have to be the one to do it. It was the religion of
> the store.

Our heroine then tries to use the store-bought turban as a model for
one of her own concoctions, out of a piece of maroon silk filled "with
a design of little keys" that originally was part of a dress bought at
Lord & Taylor's Budget Shop. The result is hardly up to Gaby's high
standards: "It had ears. When I brushed my hair and put it on, I looked
like a lady in *Popular Mechanics*, ready for goggles and a rocket ship."

"*Women!!* Make Turban in Own Home!" reverberates with echoes
from stories Welty published in *A Curtain of Green* the same year,
especially "Clytie," in which a woman's "disreputable and wild" hair
(90) is linked to even more rebellious thoughts and actions.[2] But this
little piece of journalism gives it all a farcical twist, deftly skewering
women's fashions and the elaborate and absolute gender distinctions
drawn in American popular culture. In this piece, gender is literally
a construction, a mechanical contraption of misaligned, jerry-rigged
parts and contradictory social codes as comic and confining as the
suits those undersea men had to wear in *Popular Mechanics*. Welty
also dryly notes that these distinctions apply to popular writing: "I
even thought of writing a little article to send *Popular Mechanics* on
how to make a turban," she says, but then reflecting that girls are not
supposed to read the magazine, much less write for it, she ends the
fantasy abruptly: "but this is it"—publication in the *Junior League
Magazine* for girls and women only.

꒰

One way to think of the Rondo family in "Why I Live at the P. O."
is as an exceptionally noisy family of paper cutouts. Certainly the
characters are as delightfully two-dimensional, and as farcically posed,
as the cutouts described in "*Women!!*" but the story is also a comedy
about fashion, gender differences, and power.

"Why I Live at the P.O." is set in China Grove, Mississippi, and features Sister as the narrator, Stella-Rondo (her younger sister), Papa-Daddy (Sister's grandfather), Mama (Sister's mother), Uncle Rondo, Stella-Rondo's two-year-old daughter Shirley-T., and (briefly) a dying woman named Old Jep Patterson. In the beginning of Sister's monologue, most readers tend to share Sister's view of the absurdity of her family members. Sister's main tactic is to show how false their language is. Stella-Rondo, Shirley-T., Mama, Papa-Daddy, and Uncle Rondo all speak an inflated language filled with euphemisms and the brand names of fashionable commercial products. When Stella-Rondo displays the clothes she has brought home, for example, she shows her sister something she has never seen before—a kimono that "happens to be part of my trousseau, and Mr. Whitaker took several dozen photographs of me in it" (49). By replacing her sister's ignorance with exotic and fashionable words such as "kimono" and "trousseau," Stella-Rondo reminds Sister that although she may be older and have a job at the P.O., it is her younger sister Stella-Rondo who married the man they both dated and who escaped to live in the wide world. Thus she plays the sophisticated, well-traveled belle, full of polite condescension and a histrionic sense of martyrdom. In retelling her versions of these events, however, it is Sister and not Stella-Rondo who has the last word: the kimono becomes "a terrible-looking flesh-colored contraption I wouldn't be found dead in." Sister uses a similar tactic when relaying Papa-Daddy's speech to us. "This is the beard I started growing on the Coast when I was fifteen years old," Papa-Daddy boasts, but Sister deflates this boast with the comment, "he would have gone on till nightfall if Shirley-T. hadn't lost the Milky Way she ate in Cairo" (47). All these examples are insults made after the fact, private acts of revenge taken during the retelling of the events to make up for her not being able to have her say earlier. Many of the most delightfully vulgar commercial references in the story, such as Shirley-T.'s Milky Way and the Add-a-Pearl necklace, furthermore, were not in Welty's early draft of the story; neither was fancy vocabulary like "disport" and "trousseau" (originally, merely "eat" and "underwear"). In revising, Welty carefully highlighted the story's comic contrasts of diction.[3]

In Sister's war of words with her family, she continually seeks to draw our attention to the fact that their versions of the events are supposedly much less reasonable. Instead of admitting that her marriage to Mr. Whitaker has failed and that she has had to return to her family home with her two-year-old child, for instance, Stella-Rondo steadfastly maintains that the girl is adopted. Stella-Rondo's "proof" consists of nothing more than repeating her assertions more and more loudly—something that seems to work especially well in the Rondo family. Our sympathy for the narrator increases even further when Stella-Rondo lies about what her sister said about her grandfather's beard (46) to turn her grandfather against her: " 'Papa-Daddy,' she says. . . . 'Papa-Daddy, Sister says she fails to understand why you don't cut off your beard' " (47). The narrator's anger at her sister's airs becomes understandable after a few such scenes, and we begin to relish the ways in which Sister gives others their comeuppance, both in her original retorts and again, even more successfully, in her later storytelling. The victories she gains through storytelling are especially sweet because at last she seems to have an audience who sides with her, not with her sister. As she says triumphantly to her imagined listeners at one point, when she relates how her sister accuses her of calling Uncle Rondo a fool in his kimono: "Do you remember who it was really said that?" (52). Welty's witty last name for this family denotes a musical form that has a refrain occurring at least three times between contrasting couplets. In the Rondo family, however, repetition and contrast produces only discord and disorder.

As "Why I Live at the P.O." progresses, the reader cannot but begin to notice that the narrator has many of the same family traits that she so despises in others. This is especially true of the way she talks and the way in which she deals with inconsistencies in her account of the events. Sister's vanity infects her language as thoroughly as that of the other characters infects theirs. At the beginning of the story we may not notice it as readily because Sister has so carefully placed the other characters and their foolish actions at the center of our attention. But as her story approaches the tale of her climactic break with her family, her own pretensions become more prominent. When she describes her Uncle Rondo's throwing firecrackers into her room at 6:30 A.M., for instance, her language is as comically inflated as anything that Stella-Rondo or Papa-Daddy has ever said.

[A]t 6:30 A.M. the next morning, he threw a whole five-cent package of some unsold one-inch firecrackers from the store as hard as he could into my bedroom and they every one went off. Not one bad one in the string. Anybody else, there'd be one that wouldn't go off.

Well, I'm just terribly susceptible to noise of any kind, the doctor has always told me I was the most sensitive person he had ever seen in his whole life, and I was simply prostrated. I couldn't eat! People tell me they heard it as far as the cemetery, and old Aunt Jep Patterson, that had been holding her own so good, thought it was Judgment Day and she was going to meet her whole family. It's usually so quiet here. (53)

As this superbly comic passage develops, Sister's language becomes less controlled and ironic. Self-praise and self-martyrdom converge, and by the end she imagines that the entire town heard the indignities perpetrated against her, and the perfectly timed concluding phrase, "It's usually so quiet here," adds a new twist to the humor. The sentence is comic because its speaker does not realize that we have to take it as an absurdity; we have heard nothing but noise since the story began. This comment also has a sinister edge to it, for the longing for separation and silence that it reveals foreshadows the dark edge to the ending of the story, when "quiet" at great cost is finally achieved.

Once we begin to doubt the narrator's reliability, evidence to increase our doubt begins cropping up everywhere when the story is reread. The tale's wonderful opening paragraph is a case in point. "I was getting along fine with Mama, Papa-Daddy and Uncle Rondo until my sister Stella-Rondo just separated from her husband and came back home again. Mr. Whitaker! Of course I went with Mr. Whitaker first, when he first appeared here in China Grove, taking 'Pose Yourself' photos, and Stella-Rondo broke us up. Told him I was one-sided. Bigger on one side than the other, which is a deliberate, calculated falsehood: I'm the same. Stella-Rondo is exactly twelve months to the day younger than I am and for that reason she's spoiled" (46).

As this passage reveals, the causes for Sister's anger lie much deeper than any resentment she has for specific things that Stella-Rondo has done to her, such as taking Mr. Whitaker from her and marrying him. The paragraph begins and ends with references to Stella-Rondo's being the younger sister whose birth caused her parents to spoil her and slight her older sister. In returning home with her child, Stella-Rondo clearly disrupts the privileged status of the parent's favorite child that Sister has managed to regain during her sister's absence. Because the two sisters share the same birthday, moreover, their rivalry is all the more galling to the older one; Stella-Rondo seems to have come on the scene exactly a year after Sister's birth to usurp her identity along with her birthday. Welty enforces this point by having Stella-Rondo's name mentioned repeatedly throughout the story, whereas the narrator, when she is addressed at all, is called merely "Sister," as if she has no identity except in (subordinate) relation to her favored younger sibling.

The status that Sister briefly had in the family with Stella-Rondo gone was much more various than the role of only child. Because of her job as the postmistress at the post office of China Grove, she is also able to hold the honored (and traditionally male) status as the family's principal breadwinner. (The fact that Papa-Daddy is rich and Uncle Rondo a pharmacist is, to Sister's mind, irrelevant; of the immediate family, she is the only member with a salaried position of authority in the outside world.) Indeed, Sister may even be said *to have become the family's father:* no husband for Mama is mentioned in the story, a telling omission; there is only Uncle Rondo and Papa-Daddy, Mama's father. With Stella-Rondo gone, Sister thus seems (at least in her own imagination) to gain the two most prominent positions of authority possible within a family—that of the head male breadwinner and that of the favorite child. Upon Stella-Rondo's return, however, she is immediately relegated to the role of female servant. Welty emphasizes the trauma of this demotion early in the story by having Sister indignantly portray herself "over the hot stove, trying to stretch two chickens over five people and a completely unexpected child into the bargain, without one moment's notice" (46). As the story continues, the baby Shirley-T. takes over the role of the favored child, Stella-Rondo and Mama play the only available authoritative female roles, and both Papa-Daddy and Uncle Rondo reassert their place as male authority figures.

Originally, Welty's story used the name Adam rather than Rondo,

implying that issues of gender, priority, and power are indeed centra
to Welty's conception of the root cause of the family's feuding. By
fleeing to the P.O., Sister tries to gain a new family and new authority.
The citizens of China Grove who must use the P.O. every day will see
her, listen to her story of her family's cruelty, and commiserate. Raid-
ing her home of all the possessions that will make her feel at home in
the back room of the P.O.—including a cot, an oscillating fan, a
charm bracelet, a fern, a ukelele, a sewing machine motor, a ther-
mometer, a calendar, and many jars of preserves, fruits, and vegetables—Sister reconstructs an orderly and quiet Eden-like world in the
back of the P.O., a public rebuke to her family. Welty's revisions to
the list of possessions Sister carries away with her well shows her genius as a writer of comedy: by changing "sewing-machine" to "sewing-
machine motor," for example, she makes Sister's actions even more
comically futile, and by changing "bottle-opener" to "the Hawaiian
ukelele" she stresses Sister's need to feel in touch with a world of
broader horizons she feels has been unfairly denied her (54). Sister's
paradise regained at the P.O. becomes an Eden as it might be imagined in a Woolworth's advertisement.

In the last three paragraphs of the story Sister's picture of self-
reliance darkens considerably, though, as the language Sister uses becomes less pastoral and the social dimensions of her domain suddenly
shrink. For in cutting herself off from her family, she is more or less
cutting herself off from any larger "world." Despite vague references
to other "people" and "folks" in China Grove, the only other resident
of China Grove who is named in the story, significantly, is the dying
old Aunt Jep Patterson, her family's last surviving member.

> Of course, there's not much mail. My family are naturally the main
> people in China Grove, and if they prefer to vanish from the face of
> the earth, for all the mail they get or the mail they write, why, I'm not
> going to open my mouth. Some of the folks here in town are taking up
> for me and some turned against me. I know which is which. There are
> always people who will quit buying stamps just to get on the right side
> of Papa-Daddy.
> But here I am, and here I'll stay. I want the world to know I'm happy.
> And if Stella-Rondo should come to me this minute, on bended

knees, and *attempt* to explain the incidents of her life with Mr. Whitaker, I'd simply put my fingers in both my ears and refuse to listen. (56)

The "world" and the authority that Sister will have at her P.O. thus seem largely self-created, a poor substitute for the position she had in her family before Stella-Rondo's return.

The most sinister aspect of the story's last paragraphs is not the sudden shrinking of Sister's world but the gruesome combination of a need to speak and a determination to be silent. Sister's flight and silence, like so many other elements in the story, are reminiscent of a child's temper tantrum caused by jealousy towards a sibling who seems to be favored by her parents. In a fit of pique Sister resolves never to speak to her family again, but like a child sulking in her bedroom she comically cannot but help break her resolve sooner or later—her family surrounds her. Sister's story is wholly constructed of desperate refutations and retellings of Stella-Rondo's stories, but the only audience that we are shown Sister convincing is one that she herself has imagined.

Thus we may revise one of the summarizing sentences at the end of "Why I Live at the P.O." to say "I want *myself* to know I'm happy." Despite the many legitimate reasons Sister has for feeling that she has been unfairly treated by her family, her story proves she knows that her own vanity, jealousy, and insecurity are at least partly to blame for her having to live in a post office's back room. The secret target of Sister's refutations is not only Stella-Rondo but herself, and her narrative at its deepest level is tragicomically inspired by her own guilt as well as Stella-Rondo's. Like Stella-Rondo's hilarious description of her as being "bigger on one side than on the other" (46), Sister's narrative is both monomaniacal and lopsided. What she intends to assert as the story develops becomes increasingly unbalanced with the weight of other secrets that she does not know are there: as Welty said of her in *One Writer's Beginnings*, "how much more gets told besides!" (13). These other secrets include her desire to be the authority figure in her family and to play the traditional role of the fashionable, worldly wife, but her secrets also include her own self-revulsion—her lingering belief that her family's view of her as a monster may be right. She has internalized all of her family's words against her and seems condemned to try forever to talk them down. The slapstick comedy that makes much of the story so hilarious changes somewhat near the end, as unsuspected pain and self-torment sound through the pratfalls, darkening the cartoon-bright narrative surface of the story like a bruise.

❦

Much has been said by Welty's commentators about her comic sensibility as a whole. Ruth Vande Kieft has stressed Welty's complex use of fertility rituals involving testing and renewal, and she notes, quoting Welty's own phrase, "the terror adjoining the comedy" in much of her comic short fiction (53–69). Alfred Appel borrows from Vande Kieft's discussion and adds consideration of Welty's roots in the frontier humor of American men (35–72). Seymour Gross sketches Welty's comic corpus as a whole; Carol Manning traces its roots to the oral storytelling culture of the South (27–49); Elizabeth Evans catalogues examples of Welty's use of such comic devices as mixed diction, exaggeration, absurdity, and comic migrations (21–50); Patricia Yaeger applies Mikhail Bakhtin's theories of "dialogic" quotation and parody to Welty's writing, particularly "June Recital"; and Peggy W. Prenshaw's essay "Woman's World, Man's Place" stresses differences between men's and women's personalities in Welty's fiction and its relevance for comedy. All of these pieces are suggestive, but I find Ruth Vande Kieft's distinction between "outside" comedies and her "comedies of love" (53–86) especially helpful and will adapt it here, renaming it a distinction between comedies of rigidity and comedies of rebirth. Comedies of rigidity involve characters such as those in "Petrified Man" whose behavior, language, and thoughts have petrified, and they essentially validate Henri Bergson's famous dictum in *Laughter* that laughter increases in direct proportion to mechanical rigidity in behavior and distance in sympathy. Comedies of rebirth, on the other hand, celebrate transformation, release selected characters from imprisoning behavior, and have a point of view as sympathetic as possible to the comic protagonist(s). Using Northrop Frye's terms in *Anatomy of Criticism*, we might say that the first kind of comedy is closest to the "winter" mode of irony and satire; the second, to the "spring" mode of romance (131–239). Distinguishing between these twin forms of comedy helps focus analysis, but only if we remember that these comic strains are *interwoven* in most of Welty's best comic stories, not kept separate: consider "The Wide Net," for example, which includes many wonderfully stylized, two-dimensional characters like the Malone boys but also turns upon the transformation of the main character, William Wallace, and presents crucial scenes in the story from his point of view.[4]

Pairing "Why I Live at the P.O." and "*Women!! Make Turban in Own Home!*" suggests some new directions that can be taken in considering particular aspects of Welty's comedy, and will allow this discussion to build on the points made in Chapter One about Welty's earlier portraits of characters who to some extent break through the barriers that restrict them. A quick glance at *The Collected Stories* as a whole suggests a hypothesis about the development of Welty's comic stories: a majority of her early comic stories (including her two most famous stories, "Why I Live at the P.O." and "Petrified Man") satirize rigidities in behavior, especially in women, whereas later collections, especially *The Golden Apples,* shift the comic balance slightly to include a much greater role for the satirization of men (such as King MacLain) and a corresponding rise in interest in comedies of rebirth—stories featuring motifs of escape and transformation. Beginning with *The Golden Apples,* these comic transformations in Welty's stories occur most often in women's lives: consider Virgie, who over the course of *The Golden Apples* displaces King MacLain as the central figure, or the female protagonist of the title story in *The Bride of the Innisfallen.*

Such a fruitful tension between rigidity and rebirth, comedies of imprisonment and comedies of escape, certainly can be seen when "Why I Live at the P.O." and "*Women!! Make Turban in Own Home!*" are juxtaposed. "P.O." is about obsessive behavior of all kinds, and as we laugh we are very conscious of the sharp difference between the characters' limited understanding of their grotesquely funny behavior and ours. The narrator in "*Women!!*" is much more distanced and ironic in her participation in American popular culture and its clichés, suggesting a sensibility that is not imprisoned within the language she uses. (Such an intelligence governs "P.O." as well, of course, but in a hidden way, revealing itself only when we learn to distinguish between a character's voice and the silent authorial presence.) Welty's later comedies of rebirth tend to be grounded in characters not like Sister or Leota but like Powerhouse or Phoenix Jackson or the persona created to narrate "*Women!!*"

The purpose of this chapter will be to evaluate the above generalizations, with particular emphasis on whether the role of women in Welty's comic stories changes. I will argue that Welty's first long work of prose, *The Robber Bridegroom* (1942) and her second volume of stories, *The Wide Net* (1943), mark a particularly revealing shift in her comic art from comedies of rigidity to comedies of transformation or rebirth in which women are prominently featured. Welty does not drop the earlier comic form, of course, but increasingly from the mid-1940s to the mid-1950s in her short fiction her most innovative comedies are of the second type, focusing on rebirth.

Older women never appear as fruitful role models for younger women in *A Curtain of Green*. Instead, they tend to be either purely conformist and repressive like the "ladies" in "Lily Daw" and "Old Mr. Marblehall" or thwarted and enraged women like Old Addie in "A Visit of Charity" or Octavia in "Clytie." As a consequence, many of the most well-balanced women in *A Curtain of Green* are profoundly isolated from other women, such as Marjorie in "Flowers for Marjorie," Phoenix Jackson in "A Worn Path," or Ruby Fisher in "A Piece of News." Although "A Worn Path" celebrates the potential for absolute, self-generated heroism, "A Curtain of Green," the volume's title story, questions that ideal and warns of the frustrating strictures that circumscribe all private acts of rebellion by a heroine. In Welty's second volume of stories, *The Wide Net and Other Stories* (1943), five tales have powerful heroines: Hazel Jamieson in "The Wide Net," Cora, Phoebe, and Irene in "Asphodel," Josie and Cornella in "The Winds," Livvie in "Livvie," and (perhaps) Jenny in "At the Landing." Of these, only Jenny and Livvie are isolated in a way comparable to any of the women in Welty's first collection. Both Livvie's and Jenny's stories, interestingly enough, have more conventional "romantic" plots, at least in outline form: both deal with a young woman's sexual awakening when the father figure in her life is displaced by a male lover close to her own age. The role played by other women in the lives of these two heroines is not depicted, unless we count Miss Baby Marie, the cosmetics saleslady in "Livvie"; the heroines are dependent upon, and generally deferential to, the men who are to "rescue" them. The other heroines in *The Wide Net*, in contrast, have the support of a small community of women who exist largely independent of male authority—who are not surrogates for the town's patriarchal power structures as are the "ladies" in "Lily Daw," "A Curtain of Green," or "Clytie." Welty's portrait of such a community of women in *The Wide Net* varies from affectionate parody in "Asphodel" to the glimpses she gives us of the profoundly powerful human and supernatural women in the volume's title story, women who may be said to orchestrate the comic action of the story from the beginning to the end. Of the stories in this volume with strong heroines, "The Winds" is arguably the most intriguing, for not only is it highly experimental in form but it also is Welty's first story to focus on the relation between an older woman artist and a younger girl.

If Welty's portrait of such a community of women begins in *The Wide Net*, it reaches its fruition in the novel *Delta Wedding* (1946) and the short-story cycle *The Golden Apples* (1949). *Delta Wedding* contains almost as many plots and subplots as it has characters, but certainly one of the most important is the story of how the young heroine, Laura McRaven, gains a new family and, most importantly, many new female role models, especially her aunt, Ellen Fairchild. In *The Golden Apples*, similarly, its three major comic stories feature heroines who pick unconventional women to be their mentors, allowing them to challenge directly Morgana's stereotypes of proper masculine and feminine behavior. "A Shower of Gold" satirizes stereotypes of male heroism, and "Moon Lake," following "The Winds" in *The Wide Net*, explores the role models that an older female may provide for a girl on the edge of adolescence. The volume's concluding story, "The Wanderers," is Welty's most dramatic merging of her tragic and comic modes, as her heroine, Virgie Rainey, confronts and subdues the specter of the woman-as-Medusa that haunts all of Welty's heroines who seek some measure of independence from men. In doing so, she forms a spiritual bond uniting herself, her dead teacher, and all rebellious women. Of all Eudora Welty's short stories, "The Wanderers" portrays most fully the values that inspire her comedies of rebirth, and is appropriately given pride of place in this chapter.

Welty's last volume of stories, *The Bride of the Innisfallen* (1955), has several stories in Welty's two comic modes, all focusing on women. Both "Kin" and "Ladies in Spring" are comedies of rigidity satirizing overbearing women somewhat in the mode of Welty's earlier stories in this vein, though their edge seems slightly less sharp and their tone more fluid than their earlier counterparts. (Welty's nearly contemporaneous comic novel, *The Ponder Heart* [1954], is comparable, juxtaposing Uncle Daniel Ponder's irrepressible generosity with the narrator Edna Earle's comic repressions and rigidities—her clichés, malapropisms, denials, and self-justifications, all endlessly imposed upon her captive audience.) Other comic stories in *The Bride of the Innisfallen*, including the volume's title story, which opens the collection, and "Going to Naples," which closes it, are tales of travel and renewal in which women play a major role. For my purposes, however, the most interesting comic story in *Innisfallen* is "Circe," since it does not fit well into either of my categories of comedy. A reading of it will provide a fitting coda to the discussion of Welty's comic stories because the story represents a fascinating rethinking on Welty's part of the issues of women's power and responsibility raised by her earlier women's comedies.

At the heart of this selective discussion of Eudora Welty's comic stories featuring women, therefore, will be works in the two collections published in the middle of her career, *The Wide Net* and *The Golden Apples*. They do not focus on women who are isolated from society and already powerful (such as Phoenix Jackson or Circe) but on the process by which such power may be created within a highly articulated social and historical context, shared by other women, and passed on from one generation to the next. Their heroines are not women who live outside of time and history, as Phoenix Jackson and Circe do, but immersed in time, required to face the contradictions between their visions of women's potential power and the often constrictive realities of social history.

✿

Originally entitled "Livvie is Back," "Livvie" is often read as a celebration of Livvie's comic rebirth—a retelling of Persephone's return from the underworld that sets the tale among black sharecroppers in Mississippi. But the ending is more ambivalent than parallels with the Greek myth may at first suggest. Certainly Welty's final choice of a title is more ambiguous. For Livvie's liberation from her oppressive husband is accomplished more through the efforts of another man than through her own. The unsatisfying features and unanswered questions at the end of "Livvie" thus provide a useful introduction to the innovations that make Welty's women's comedies special.[5]

Several details of Solomon's and Livvie's house may be taken as emblems of the status that each hopes to achieve through their "respectable" marriage, even though it is a "May/December" wedding between a healthy teenage girl and an infirm, acquisitive old man who is a parody of his biblical namesake. Welty portrays Livvie's naïveté by repeating the word "nice" three times in the first two pages of the story to describe how Livvie judges her new surroundings. As for Solomon's expectations, they are well illustrated by the catalog of his possessions—a list that now includes Livvie.

> Behind the front room, the other room had the bright iron bed with the polished knobs like a throne, in which Solomon slept all day. There were snow-white curtains of wiry lace at the window, and a lace bedspread belonged on the bed. But what old Solomon slept so sound under was a big feather-stitched piece-quilt in the pattern "Trip Around the World," which had twenty-one different colors, four hundred and forty pieces, and a thousand yards of thread, and that was what Solomon's mother made in her life and old age. There was a table holding the Bible, and a trunk with a key. On the wall were two calendars, and a diploma from somewhere in Solomon's family, and under that, Livvie's one possession was nailed, a picture of the little white baby of the family she worked for, back in Natchez before she was married. (228–29)

A throne, a key, a quilt commemorating a mother's prodigious self-sacrifice, a diploma—all these signify authority and prestige, and they comfort Solomon when he becomes bedridden soon after his marriage. This list is then followed in the story by mention of a photograph, the only possession that Livvie brought to her husband's house after the marriage. The juxtaposition of the photograph with the diploma and the rest of Solomon's possessions in the bedroom suggests that both Livvie and Solomon thought that their marriage would "graduate" Livvie from being a servant to whites all her life. The picture portrays the white child that she nursed, not Livvie herself, as if her identity before her marriage were reducible solely to her role as servant. Ironically, however, Solomon has not freed Livvie from such a role but has confirmed her in it—she is now *his* nurse and servant, another one of his status-giving possessions. Her value to him is increased not just because of her youth and attractiveness but also because she allows him to have the illusion that he has heroically rescued her from servitude. In the catalog of Solomon's possessions, no image of Livvie appears, only objects that denote the past and present things that she must care for.

Solomon's patriarchal pride of ownership is also denoted, of course, by the "bottle trees" in front of the house that "kept evil spirits from coming into the house—by luring them inside the colored bottles, where they cannot get out again" (229). At first glance this passage may be read as an instance of Solomon's heroic protectiveness of his new bride, but as the events of the story are pondered, a series of ironic parallels between the bottle tree lures and Solomon's house begin to suggest themselves. Livvie, too, has been lured into an enclosed space, and even though her husband does not think of her as "evil" he does have an intimation that this May/December wedding of his is a rather unstable union, in need of all the protection and validation it can get. The objects he has collected, from his throne to his diploma to his bottles to his photograph of the white child, are meant to perform that function.

When Livvie begins to feel claustrophobic in her role as nurse, her impulses to explore the countryside and to buy make-up for herself from a traveling saleslady do seem "evil" to her, desires that she needs to learn to bottle up for the sake of her husband: "Her hand took the lipstick, and in an instant she was carried away in the air through the spring, and looking down with a half-drowsy smile from a purple cloud she saw from above a chinaberry tree . . . there was the home that she had left" (234). For the first time in the story we get a glimpse of Livvie's past, as if her homesickness suddenly wells up inside of her. When Cash, one of Solomon's field hands, meets her later while she is taking a walk with her make-up still on, she can be susceptible to his fancy clothes and flirtatious ways because the make-up has already inflamed her imagination. He is like a vision created by all the desires she has repressed, a comic god of Spring rather than a specter of Winter (235). Near the end of the story, when Cash and Livvie confront Solomon on his deathbed and in effect declare their love for each other, Solomon's apology for "carrying away too young girl for wife and keeping her away from her people and from all the young people would clamor for her back" (239) makes Livvie's liberation appear complete. The last words of the story imply that with Cash's help she has escaped out-of-doors, free from the imprisoning spell that Solomon cast over her: "the sun was in all the bottles on the prisoned trees, and the young peach was shining in the middle of them with the bursting light of spring" (239).

A more skeptical reading of Welty's portrait of Cash, however, at least partially clouds the "bursting light of spring" that is released by the story's ending. Cash's name may be meant to suggest that he possesses "natural" rather than artificial wealth—that he, unlike Solomon, knows the "origin and meaning" of what he labors for (238)—but it also points to the fact that he has apparently stolen money from Solomon (236) and is as proud of his possessions as the old man. The first view of Cash that Welty gives us is a catalog of what he owns, and the introductory sentence stresses his narcissism: "As soon as this man caught sight of her, he began to look himself over. Starting at the bottom with his pointed shoes, he began to look up, lifting his peg-leg top pants the higher to see fully his bright socks. His coat long and wide and leaf-green he opened *like doors* to see his high-up tawny pants" (235; my italics). It is as if he too is escorting Livvie indoors, into a house filled with the things he owns. It is true that the story ends with Livvie and Cash moving outdoors—"they moved around and around the room and into the brightness of the open door" (239)—but the fact remains that Livvie in the final paragraphs of the story is silent and passive. All the words and actions are Cash's: "she rested in silence in his trembling arms, unprotesting as a bird on a nest." And the colors of Cash's clothes are identical to those of Solomon's bottles.

Such a reading of the ending admittedly perverts the story's tone by emphasizing marginal rather than central details. We are surely meant to allow ourselves to be swept off our feet as Livvie is by her ecstatic sense of release and renewal, but that feeling can be kept only if we do not question too closely how "natural" and liberating Livvie's rescue by Cash is. Cash is actually no more "natural" in character than Solomon, and any bond Livvie makes with him must necessarily be

social, not natural or "mythical"—it will be subject to all of C
yet unstated conceptions about the proper role for his wife. Like "Lily
Daw," "Livvie" achieves its comic ending in part by excluding certain
questions that some of its own figures of speech—especially its architectural metaphors—have raised.

We need only examine the other story in *The Wide Net* about a
woman who loses the father figure in her life and becomes attached to
a younger man, "At the Landing," to see how dark the unexamined
aspects of "Livvie" may be. (Interestingly, it follows "Livvie" in *The
Wide Net,* concluding the volume.) Like Cash, Billy Floyd in "At the
Landing" seems like a god of Spring and carries away Jenny Lockhart,
the heroine, during a time of crisis, but unlike "Livvie" this rescue
occurs in the middle of the story, after which the rescuer has intercourse with Jenny and then abandons her. The heroine remains so
dependent upon him that after a brief period of regret and housecleaning she winds up waiting for him by a riverbank in a daze. She is soon
taken to a grounded houseboat near the river and forced to have sex
with an unstated number of men.

> "Is she asleep? Is she in a spell? Or is she dead?" asked a little old
> bright-eyed woman who went and looked in the door, and crept up to
> the now meditating men outside. She was so precise in her question
> that she even held up three rheumatic fingers when she asked.
> "She's waiting for Billy Floyd," they said.
> The old woman nodded, and nodded out to the flowing river, with
> the firelight following her face and showing its dignity. The younger
> boys separated and took their turns throwing knives with a dull pit at
> the tree. (258)

Cash is hardly a rapist, of course, and the ending of "Livvie" is not
the ending of "At the Landing." But the parallels remain sobering, as
if each story represented the inverse of the other: rescue and rape,
Livvie's "unprotesting" "silence" (239) and Jenny's "spell," the violation of the bottle tree and the tree at the end of "At the Landing."
What makes the ending of "At the Landing" most disturbing, however, is the contradictory way in which Jenny's rape is described by
the story's narrative voice. At some moments the narrator implies that
Jenny somehow transcends the experience by remaining pure at heart;

it stresses the "humility that moved now deep in her spirit" and even
suggests that the sounds of her rape "could easily have been heard as
rejoicing" (257–58). These details (and the nature imagery associated
with Billy Floyd) have influenced most of Welty's commentators, who
tend to argue that despite the violence done to her Jenny experiences
a mythic initiation, a necessary growth away from the regressive dependence upon father figures that she displays at the story's beginning.[6] I would argue, conversely, that at other moments the narrator
in the story's last pages creates distinct difficulties for such an interpretation. One crucial sentence stresses that Jenny's actions are those of
despair: "all things, river, sky, fire, and air, seemed the same color,
the color that is seen behind closed eyelids, the color of day where
vision and despair are the same thing" (257). Appropriately, certain
details in "At the Landing" align the story with "Clytie" in A Curtain
of Green. Like Clytie, Jenny imagines herself as many people in her
fantasies: "she dreamed that she lined up on both sides of the road to
see her love come by in procession. She herself was more people than
there were people in The Landing" (256). And in describing Jenny's
melancholy, Welty refers to mirror images in dark water: "if desperation were only a country, it would be at the bottom of the well. . . .
She thought she could see herself, fleet as a mirror-image, rising up
in a breath of astonished farewell" (246). (For the description of the
site of Clytie's suicide, a rainbarrel rather than a well, see Collected
Stories 90.)

Such a reading of "At the Landing" regards the story as a nightmarish (and possibly unconscious) undoing of the comic resolution of
"Livvie." Despite plentiful use of gorgeous metaphors describing how
mysterious and complex love is (such as the description of Jenny and
Billy Floyd watching butterflies on page 244), the narrative also stresses
that gender roles in this relationship are quite conventionally defined
as being full of "vaunting" for the male and "prostration" for the female (245). There are some indications that Jenny wants to protest
such sex-role stereotyping, but the troubling ending of the story, particularly its reference to her "spell" and its gruesome last sentence
about the knives striking the tree, implies that Jenny's romantic thralldom is complete and that male violence toward women is passed down
from one generation to the next.

The truly innovative women's comedies of The Wide Net, on the other hand, invent a different kind of comic ending from the one that is offered in "Livvie" then doubted in "At the Landing." They do so by displacing the male-centered plots of romance, enthrallment, and rescue that are essential to both "Livvie" and "At the Landing." "Asphodel," "The Wide Net," and "The Winds" were published in 1942—the same year as *The Robber Bridegroom*—and in very different ways construct comic endings that confront the issues of women's self-making that are evaded in "Livvie." "Asphodel" may perhaps be read as a parody of Faulkner. "The Wide Net" wittily reverses the conventional romance plot of "Livvie" and of fairy tales like "Sleeping Beauty" and "Cinderella" where the plot turns on the action of a rescuing prince. In Welty's version, the men are still cast in the role of rescuers, but it is the women who initiate the events that allow the men to perform their comically self-inflated acts of heroism, and the women's goals are not to be rescued but to transform the men using means that their limited imaginations will understand. "The Winds" (1942) focuses on a topic new to Welty's work: the liberating effect of an older woman artist on a young girl's imagination.

Of these motifs, all but the last are also explored in *The Robber Bridegroom*, and before moving on to a reading of *The Wide Net's* most innovative comedies it is appropriate to consider for a moment the role played by parody in this contemporaneous tale, Welty's first longer narrative. Welty's heroine, Rosamond Musgrove, is in some ways as dependent a figure as Livvie or Jenny—a conventional housewife in love with an unconventional husband: "So Rosamond stayed and kept house for the robbers. In the daytime, in the silence of noon, while they were all away, she cooked and washed and baked and scrubbed" (82–83). Like Snow White, Rosamond makes the transition from having to care for a host of unruly males to having a home of her own with one husband and the prospect of a nuclear family. But it would be a mistake, of course, to read *The Robber Bridegroom* for its plot alone, for the narrative is clearly a loving but also mocking amalgam of the plots and diction of European and American folktales and, not incidentally, earlier American women's sentimental fiction. A fuller accounting of the narrative's parody of women's popular fiction must wait until the next chapter, but for now we can mark how sharply the ending of *The Robber Bridegroom* undoes the endings of "Livvie" and "At the Landing," both of which feature a spell cast on the heroine making her dependent upon males. *The Robber Bridegroom* is filled with spells, transformations, and secret identities, but in this case they make the heroine more energetic, not less. Caught in a similar situation as Jenny Lockhart—thinking her lover has deserted her—Rosamond behaves quite differently:

> So Rosamond went on, and by dint of begging one mail rider after another, and trotting upon one white pony after another black horse, she made her way clear to New Orleans.
>
> The moment she reached the great city she made straight for the harbor.
>
> The smell of the flapping fish in the great loud marketplace almost sent her into a faint, but she pressed on bravely along the water front, looking twice at every man she met, even if he looked thrice back at her. . . . . And sure enough, there in the middle . . . was Jamie Lockhart, waving goodbye to the shore.
>
> "Jamie Lockhart!" she cried.
>
> So he turned to see who it was.
>
> "I came and found you!" she cried over all their heads. (180–81)

Welty's use of the name Lockhart in both tales may be just a coincidence, but its different designation (as "maiden" name in "At the Landing" versus married name in *The Robber Bridegroom*) suggests that these two tales may be understood as a kind of chiasmus, a crossing or reversal in which the one tale undoes the narrative premises of the other. By exuberantly parodying narratives of women's dependency in *The Robber Bridegroom*, Welty's comic fairy tale opens the way for "Asphodel," "The Wide Net," and "The Winds" in *The Wide Net*, which in different ways break other new ground for Welty's comic fiction.

🎜

> *Faulkner is not receding from us. Indeed, his work, though it can't increase in itself, increases us. His work throws light on the past and on today as it becomes the past—the day in its journey. . . .*
>
> *What is written in the South from now on is going to be taken into account by Faulkner's work; I mean the remark literally. . . . We inherit from him.*
>
> —Eudora Welty,
> *The Eye of the Story*

In the 1956 essay "Place in Fiction," Welty made the intriguing claim
that "in Faulkner's humor, even more measurably than in his tragedy,
[his knowledge of the world] is all there" (*Eye of the Story* 127). This
remark follows a cogent discussion of "Spotted Horses," Faulkner's
paradigmatic comic story, in which Welty praises his fidelity to "social
fact" as well as his comic genius for exaggeration and disguise. Given
the fact that Welty's best comedies, early or late, capture how women
either resist or are petrified by stereotypes of the feminine, it is instructive to compare Welty's sense of women in comedy with the roles
played in Faulkner's comic story "Spotted Horses" by its two female
characters, Mrs. Armstid and Mrs. Littlejohn. On the evidence of
"Asphodel," Welty appears to have needed to confront the power
of Faulkner as a predecessor before she could invent a new form of
comedy for herself. Her treatment of Faulkner's influence in "Asphodel" in 1942, when her career as an artist is just emerging, appears
somewhat different and more contentious than that depicted over a
decade later in her 1956 essay, when her identity as a Mississippi
writer in her own right was more securely established.

Faulkner's women in "Spotted Horses" live in a world rigidly separated from the male world of disguise, intrigue, competition, and fantasy. Throughout the story Mrs. Littlejohn's performance of household
tasks such as washing dishes and clothes functions as a rhythmic back-
drop to the actions of the men, which all revolve around Flem
Snopes's plot to make money selling wild horses at auction. The wom-
en's work is steady, unending, and entirely sober; Mrs. Armstid and
(especially) Mrs. Littlejohn keep track of every penny that their
households spend and have a fixed, thoroughly rational approach to
work: the way to get a job done is to plunge in and *do* it with the
resources that you have. In contrast, nothing seems to unite Flem
Snopes, Ratliff, Henry Armstid, and the hangers-on at Jody Varner's
store. Henry is impulsive and irrational, convinced that nothing will
bring him prosperity but having a new horse with his family's last five
dollars (money that his wife, not he, has earned). Flem is cold and
calculating, hardly seeming to be involved in the sale beforehand or
profiting from it afterwards. Ratliff and the others seem mere specta-
tors, unable to take their eyes off Flem as he makes chaos out of the
lives of others without seeming to bat an eyelash. But all of the men

are united by a combination of complete idleness and compulsive scheming: they want to get their money the new-fangled way, by steal-ing it. Of course they should not *seem* to steal it; their work must appear to be like women's work, honest and self-sacrificing. Thus Flem pretends to make money as a store clerk even while he is arranging a horse swindle; Henry Armstid thinks he needs the horse for plowing, not for his own vanity. Ratliff and the others clearly admire Flem's audacity even as they suffer from it: as Ratliff says, paying Flem what to him is the ultimate compliment, "he skun me in two trades, myself, and the fellow that can do that, I just hope he'll get rich before I do; that's all" (*Uncollected Stories* 166).

The women's sense of work is an old-fashioned one: all wealth and well-being come from brute physical labor. From Ratliff the traveling salesman of labor-saving devices to Flem Snopes the swindler, the men believe that wealth ought to be created by exchange, not by labor—labor is demeaning to their male pride. Moreover, the cleverer the trade is, the better it is. Their work methods should not be straightforward and public, like the women's, but complicated and disguised. As narrated by Ratliff, the humor of "Spotted Horses" de-rives not just from Flem's outwitting his male competitors but from the men's disdain for and disruption of women's work. At the story's end, Flem spits in front of Mrs. Armstid even as he courteously lies to her, and such a gesture epitomizes the sources of the story's humor.

In Welty's comedies from "Petrified Man" to "Kin," women are of-ten the butt of her humor, but they are mocked more because they are like Flem than because they are like Mrs. Littlejohn. (This is particu-larly the case with the vulgar Sister Anne in "Kin," who has taken over Uncle Felix's household and hired an itinerant photographer to take pictures of her and her friends in their best clothes.) From the beginning of Welty's development of a special form of women's comedy with "The Wide Net" and "The Winds" in 1942, however, she began to imagine women potentially as comic heroines as well as comic butts. Not coincidentally, a story that she wrote at the same time, "Asphodel," was placed between "The Wide Net" and "The Winds" in *The Wide Net*. It is not really successful as a story in its own right, for its comedy is handled with a very broad brush: the women are prim and Mr. Don McInnis very satyrlike. It becomes especially interesting, however, when read as a possible parody of Faulkner—as if in order to invent her form of women's comedy Welty simultaneously had to distance herself from him.[7]

"Asphodel" accomplishes this task obliquely, not so much by parodying Faulknerian comedy as by appearing to make fun of his most ambitious novel, Absalom, Absalom! (1936). The story's Sutpen figure is "Mr. Don McInnis," proprietor of Asphodel, a now-ruined plantation mansion whose decaying front lawn provides the story's setting. Rosa Coldfield's and Ellen Coldfield's parts are alluded to through "Miss Sabina," the domineering daughter of the only other aristocratic family in the area: she marries Mr. Don but later deserts him for infidelity and rages against him and others with all the passion of Rosa Coldfield. In this case, however, she kicks *him* out of the mansion, rather than the reverse. There is no murder or miscegenation in "Asphodel" (it is a parody, after all), but three old maids who are representatives from the next generation do return to the site of Mr. Don's mansion (like Miss Rosa and Quentin) to discover to their horror that a figure in their stories thought long vanished is secretly living in the house. It is like a slapstick version of *Absalom:* just as the ladies reach the climax of their story of Mr. Don's promiscuity, he appears stark naked from behind some vines at the edge of the lawn of Asphodel and chases them away with his goats. As parody, the story works quite delightfully: Mr. Don and Miss Sabina have all the obsessiveness of Faulkner's characters with none of their grandeur, and the narrative itself appears to make wily fun of *Absalom's* involuted plot and multiple narrators: "They pressed at the pomegranate stains on their mouths [the women are picnicking on the lawn in front of Asphodel]. And then they began to tell over Miss Sabina's story, their voices serene and alike: how she looked, the legend of her beauty when she was young, the house where she was born and what happened in it, and how she came out when she was old, in her triumphal way, and the pitiful end when she toppled to her death in a dusty place where she was a stranger" (201). *Absalom's* Gothic plot would seem comic too if it were summarized in a single sentence.

Alongside such techniques distancing the power of Faulkner's narrative, other events occur. One of the principal characters associated with the Faulknerian plot, Miss Sabina, is also characterized by the fact that she prohibits speech: "If there's one place in the solid world where Miss Sabina would never look for us it's Asphodel," they said.

"She forbade it," they said virtuously. "She would never tolerate us to come, to Mr. Don McInnis' Asphodel, or even to say his name" (200). Miss Sabina's prohibition of speech reaches its climax just before her fatal stroke: she descends upon them as they are picking up their mail in the post office, demands that they tear up their letters from their "lovers," and then grabs their mail away from them: "In her frenzy she tore all the letters to pieces, and even put bits in her mouth and appeared to eat them" (206). First Miss Sabina prohibits the women's speech, and then she attacks all forms of writing: could it be that through this figure Welty is embodying how Faulkner may intimidate his successors? After all, what this parody of a Faulknerian harridan does to the three old maids is similar to what Welty in the remarks quoted as an epigraph to this section said Faulkner does to all the writers who follow him—she holds them "accountable." (Welty's odd phrase states that *later* work by other southern writers will be "taken into account" by Faulkner's earlier work [*Eye of the Story* 158]—a revealing solecism, I think, especially when she says it is to be taken "literally," which is, of course, impossible.) Welty's comic ladies, however, escape Miss Sabina's attempts to hold them accountable and, the very day after her funeral, they retell her story aloud, in their own words, on forbidden ground.

The significance of this act of defiance can easily be overstated. Welty's position towards Faulkner is hardly equivalent to the ladies' relation to Miss Sabina and Mr. Don in "Asphodel." When she says that Faulkner's art inspired and empowered her own, her word is not to be doubted—we can see its truth throughout both her fiction and her literary criticism. But through the parody and the evasions of "Asphodel"—and the experimental comedies of *A Curtain of Green*, especially "Why I Live at the P.O."—Welty seems to gain space for her own work to grow. She interprets Faulkner's work, interposing her own voice within his, cracking and opening what was even by the early 1940s a magisterial and imposing canon.

The narrator's description of the ruin of Mr. Don McInnis's mansion may be read as a metaphor for what Welty's "Asphodel" does to Faulkner's massive narrative structures:

> A wind blew down from the columns, and the white dimity fluttered about [the women's] elbows.

"Look—"
"Asphodel."
It was a golden ruin: six Doric columns, with the entablature unbroken over the first two, full-facing the approach. (200)

The crack in the entablature comes after the first two columns and cannot be named, only described obliquely. Nevertheless this crack may be said to signify parody's ability to break the spell cast over Welty by the imposing edifice of Faulkner's work. The skittish comedy of "Asphodel" thus prepares the way for two daring experiments with comic form in Welty's comic masterpieces in *The Wide Net*, the volume's title story and "The Winds," in which she builds on the new directions charted by *A Curtain of Green* and boldly moves out of Faulkner's territory into a special Mississippi province of her own.[8]

The title story in *The Wide Net and Other Stories* is more obviously a comedy than "The Winds," for it lampoons its buffoonlike male characters and ends with a reunion. If we can judge by dates of first publication (Vande Kieft [1962] 195–96), it is the first comedy that Welty wrote in which the deflation of male rather than female pretensions is the heart of the comic business. Her earlier comedies containing caricatures of men, "Why I live at the P.O." and "Petrified Man," take the point of view of women who themselves are roundly mocked. But when "The Wide Net" is paired with "The Winds," we discover not only a continued ability to satirize men but a link between that ability and Welty's celebration of a spiritual bond between women in "The Winds" and "The Wide Net." In short, "The Wide Net" (along with "The Winds") points the way to the later women's comedies in *The Golden Apples*.

"The Wide Net" is set during the fall equinox and celebrates the beauty and mystery of all "changing times" in the cycle of a year and the phases of a person's life. "The Wide Net" does not seem to be about adolescence, for the principal characters, Hazel and William Wallace Jamieson, have just had their first wedding anniversary and are expecting a baby in the spring. But in many ways they are as childish as Josie and her brother Will in "The Winds"—especially William Wallace, who still has a boy's short attention span, bursts of uncontrollable jumpiness, and distrust of girls. He has barely begun to adjust to married life, much less understand it, and so, like "The Winds," which also occurs during the fall equinox, "The Wide Net" may be said to be an "equinoctial" comedy about the transformation of children into adults.[9]

If William Wallace found marriage difficult, his wife's pregnancy dramatically increases his problems. In the story's first paragraph, the narrator's voice comically captures William Wallace's mixture of jealousy and petulance as he tries to understand his wife's new behavior.

> William Wallace's wife Hazel was going to have a baby. But this was October, and it was six months away, and she acted exactly as though it would be tomorrow. When he came into the room she would not speak to him, but would look as straight at nothing as she could, with her eyes glowing. . . . So one night he went out with two of the boys down the road and stayed out all night. But that was the worst thing yet, because when he came home in the early morning Hazel had vanished. . . . He went through the house not believing his eyes, balancing with both hands out, his yellow cowlick rising on end, and then he turned the kitchen inside out looking for her, but it did no good. Then when he got back to the front room he saw she had left him a little letter. . . . After one look he was scared to read the exact words, and he crushed the whole thing in his hand instantly, but what it had said was that she would not put up with him after that and was going to the river to drown herself. (169)

It is impossible to read this without smiling—particularly at the detail of William Wallace turning the *kitchen* inside out looking for his wife, as if that were the only room in the house where she could surely be found. He is threatened by the changes that he sees occurring in Hazel, particularly her new sense of autonomy and power, even though he remains thoroughly in love with her. He envies her pregnancy because the baby seems all hers; he thinks she ought to act special only after it is born, when they can both share it. He is especially jealous of the glow in her eyes, because it is caused not when she is looking at him but when she is focusing on something he can't see, perhaps inwards on the wonder of her own body and the prospect of having a child. His retaliation (staying out all night drinking) is really a childish bit of bravado, revenge to show that he can be happy with friends from his bachelor days if she is going to be so happy with her womanhood.[10]

When William Wallace organizes an all-male band to drag the local river where he thinks his wife's body will be, the group appears to include the entire male population of the town. Like William Wallace, they are really boys in disguise, excitable, possessive, comically uncouth, and enraptured with any chance they can get to show off their physical prowess. One of the funniest portraits is that of the Malone boys, really just a pack of overgrown hound dogs: "eight giants with long black eye lashes . . . already stamping the ground and pawing each other, ready to go" (173). The most important man in the group is "Doc," the richest and best educated man in the town. His house overlooks the town, and he owns many things (like a fancy porch rocker and a wide net for the river-dragging) that no one else does. He may be a preacher, for he approvingly discusses a revival the previous Sunday and has a highly oratorical manner, but his interests are not merely religious. He believes that he has the right to expostulate on any subject from the state of the citizen's souls to the condition of their crops and the future of the weather, and he automatically assumes that he is to supervise and comment upon the expedition as well as lend it his wide net. Doc is best described as the town's preacher, politician, almanac, and radio all in one, the representative of male power in the town as embodied in its institutions, its economy, and its "educated" and public forms of speech. He wields his power with a humorously inflated sense of self-importance. Yet he too has no inkling of why Hazel acted the way she did. He can only puff himself up and intone, "Whatever this mysterious event will turn out to be, it has kept one woman from talking a while" (175). For him as well as for William Wallace women are rather threatening, a power that men do not understand but must reckon with.

As the river-dragging commences in Part II of the story, it becomes clear that most of the men present are there more for themselves than for William Wallace. The net brings up a whole host of things from the river bottom, from shoes and lost necklaces to heaps of succulent fish, and Welty adroitly draws a parallel between the river-draggers' belief that they have a right to ransack the natural world and Doc's aristocratic confidence that he has the right to do the same thing symbolically, through language. The issue of the men's possessiveness is first raised in the story at the end of Part I, before the river-dragging begins. As the men approach the river, Doc provides a running (or walking) commentary. He is a perambulatory Poor Richard's: "'We're walking along in the changing-time,' said Doc. 'Any day now the change will come. . . . Only today,' he said, 'today, in October sun, it's all gold—sky and tree and water. Everything just before it changes looks to be made of gold'" (176). Doc's voice has such a powerful effect on William Wallace that he not only has a vision of his wife's golden hair and eyes, but also distractedly forgets the name of the river they are searching. A crucial passage in the story follows: "They looked at him as if he were crazy not to know the name of the river he had fished in all his life. But a deep frown was on his forehead, as if he were compelled to wonder what people had come to call this river, or to think there was a mystery in the name of a river they all knew so well, the same as if it were some great far torrent of waves that dashed through the mountains somewhere, and almost as if it were a river in some dream, for they could not give him the name of that. 'Everybody knows Pearl River is named the Pearl River,' said Doc" (176).

In his involuntary wonder, William Wallace understands nature in a way that Doc cannot, despite the beauty of Doc's language. He sees the way a river (and Nature herself) is constantly changing, eternally evading all names and nets and their claims to possession. Doc's tautological response that the Pearl River is the Pearl River shows the comic poverty of what "everybody knows"—they do not really know the river as much as their own names for it and their own illusions of dominion. [11]

The men's comic delusions about ownership apply to women as well as to the Pearl River. In marriage as well as river-dragging, they think that a husband's right to rename the woman is linked to his right to possess her. During William Wallace's deepest dive in the Pearl River, however, he discovers what an illusion those "rights" are. Both the river and his wife once again seem shadowy, evasive, and threatening. "So far down and all alone, had he found Hazel? Had he suspected that . . . she had been filled to the brim with that elation that they all remembered, like their own secret, the elation that comes of great hopes and changes, sometimes simply of the harvest time, that comes with a little course of its own like a tune to run in the head, and there was nothing she could do about it—they knew—and so it had turned into this? It could be nothing but the old trouble that William Wallace was finding out, reaching and turning in the gloom of such depths" (180). William Wallace sounds the depths of his own fears and guilt about women as he dives beneath the river surface. He discovers that because he was so threatened by Hazel's elation over her pregnancy, Nature herself, not just Hazel's mother, may take her revenge on him and frustrate his possessive love for her—thus the mysterious mixture of elation and foreboding he feels.

Once William Wallace resurfaces and rejoins the men as they haul in the net, his old confidence returns even though they still have not found a sign of Hazel. They feast on fish, doze off, and then wake to see William Wallace cavorting with a huge catfish tucked under his belt buckle and dangling between his legs. His dance celebrates the phallic power of fathering and owning, as if the dance (and the all-male fertility ritual of the river-dragging) creates his beard, his manhood: "they all hollered, and the tears of laughter streaming down his cheeks made him put his hand up, and the two days' growth of beard began to jump out, bright red" (181). The men and boys then experience a collective hallucination, as they see what seems to be the god of male sexual prowess rising out of the river. It is the "King of the Snakes," moving with "an undulation loop after loop and hump after hump of a long dark body, until there were a dozen rings of ripples, one behind the other, stretching all across the river, like a necklace" (182). The "necklace" of water rings formed by the snake, although seemingly feminine, is actually very much like the net the men used for the dragging; it too stretches "all across the river" and proclaims male sovereignty over it. Such a deity, however, represents male visions of nature rather than Nature herself, and in the following paragraphs the natural world suddenly changes and turns on the males, reminding them of their weakness, not their power of possession. Collectively, they experience the same sense of guilt and awe that William Wallace felt when he was immersed in the river's deepest part (182–83). But after the storm passes, the men gain back their bravado with each step they take toward home. In Part III they parade their trophies up and down the town's main street: "The whole town of Dover began to throb in its wood and tin, like an old tired heart, when the men walked through once more, coming around again and going

down the street carrying the fish, so drenched, exhausted, and muddy
that no one could help but admire them" (184). Welty's portrait of
the men's sense of their own grandeur is affectionate, but she also
shows us how comically childish it is; the parade quickly degenerates
into a fight between William Wallace and his friend Virgil for bragging
rights: "'This wasn't your river-dragging! It wasn't your wife!' [William
Wallace] jumped on Virgil and they began to fight. . . . 'Say it was
my wife. Say it was my river-dragging'" (186).

In the story's very next paragraph, however, William Wallace's
troubled machismo is juxtaposed with a very different kind of power,
the power that belongs to women. After the fight, William Wallace
and Virgil

> walked along getting their breath, and smelling the honeysuckle in the
> evening. On a hill William Wallace looked down, and at the same time
> there went drifting by the sweet sounds of music outdoors. They were
> having the Sacred Harp Sing on the grounds of an old white church
> glimmering there at the crossroads, far below. He stared away as if he
> saw it minutely, as if he could see a lady in white take a flowered cover
> off the organ, which was set on a little slant in the shade, dust the keys,
> and start to pump and play. . . . He smiled faintly, as he would at his
> mother, and at Hazel, and at the singing women in his life, now all one
> young girl standing up to sing under the trees the oldest and longest
> ballads there were. (187)

For the first time in the story, a woman's voice is heard, and for the
first time as well we get a glimpse of the woman's world that the men
of the river-dragging have that day ignored. It is as much a vision of a
natural deity as their glimpse of the King of the Snakes—"he stared
away as if he saw it minutely"—but now William Wallace witnesses a
female deity, an imaginary girl not unlike his wife who presides over
the world of women even as he and Doc and the King of the Snakes
preside over the world of men. When William Wallace arrives home,
he has another glimpse of such a female power, in the form of a rain-
bow at night: "In the light of the moon, which had risen again, it
looked small and of gauzy material, like a lady's summer dress, a faint
veil through which the stars showed" (187). Curiously, this faint veil
of moonlight is of the same delicate texture as the "curtain" of leaves

that fell over all the men during the storm (183); it signifies a female power very different from male power, and is of a much finer weave than the river-draggers' net or even the King of the Snakes' "necklace" of ripples. At last such a maternal presence inspires wonder in William Wallace rather than jealousy or guilt or fear.

When Hazel magically reappears, wryly asking William Wallace where he has been and telling him to clean up for supper, it is as if she is an emissary from this maternal power returning not merely to restore William Wallace's peace of mind but to usher him into a new level of maturity.

> After supper they sat on the front porch a while.
> "Where were you this morning?" . . . .
> "I was hiding," she said. "I was still writing on the letter. And then you tore it up."
> "Did you watch me when I was reading it?"
> "Yes, and you could have put out your hand and touched me. I was so close."
> But he bit his lip, and gave her a little tap and slap, and then turned her up and spanked her.
> "Do you think you will do it again?" he asked.
> "I'll tell my mother on you for this!"
> "Will you do it again?"
> "No!" she cried.
> "Then pick yourself up off my knee."
> It was just as if he had chased her and captured her again. She lay smiling in the crook of his arm. It was the same as any other chase in the end.
> "I will do it again if I get ready," she said. "Next time will be different, too."
> Then she was ready to go in, and rose up and looked out from the top step, out across their yard where the China tree was and beyond, into the dark fields where the lightning-bugs flickered away. He climbed to his feet too and stood beside her, with the frown on his face, trying to look where she looked. After a few minutes she took him by the hand and led him into the house, smiling as if she were smiling down on him. (188)

Underneath this scene's playfulness and charm lie its sexual politics. William Wallace's assertions of power, however "playfully" made, are still linked to his earlier guilt and fears about women's sexuality and autonomy. He also seems to be claiming that he may continue to violate the rules of the marriage, while she may not. Then something entirely new happens: when William Wallace's comically muddled questioning of his wife ends, he abstains from contradicting her statement that she has the right to trick him into "capturing" her again. He also lets her initiate all the final action in the story and, in fact, recognizes that she has initiated the *entire* action of the story: it is she who wrote the note that inspired his display of male independence and prowess. Even more importantly, William Wallace now tries to accommodate himself to her point of view, not his. Whereas at the beginning of the story he was angered by her looking "as straight at nothing as she could, with her eyes glowing" (169), now he tries to "look where she looked"—to contemplate the same things that made her eyes glow at the story's start. He thus is no longer fighting for possession of the baby but willingly conceding her special power.

Such a gesture is not merely a willingness to let his wife be a mother. Rather, it accepts the fact that she has her own point of view, rights, and power—that she is indeed superior (or at least more adult) in all these things to him. This is not something that William Wallace can say out loud, but it is something that he silently concedes. The final sentence of the story thus marks a comic reversal of power in which William Wallace's illusion of male superiority is overturned. He now accepts his wife's dominance joyfully and without fear—though with some effort, as his frown of concentration shows.[12] The plot of "The Wide Net" also marks a witty rewriting of the romantic enthrallment and rescue plots that dominate fairy tales like "Snow White" and so much of women's fiction and are alluded to in stories such as "At the Landing." In this case, the woman does not need to be rescued but understands the man's need to believe he is the rescuer; and if there is one character in the story who is subject to enthrallment, it is William Wallace, who spends his time under a spell in as active a way as possible, rather than motionless as fairy-tale heroines (such as Sleeping Beauty) tend to be.

Intriguingly, when Welty read the galleys of *The Collected Stories* in 1980, she made only one substantial change to any of the stories: the scene in "The Wide Net" in which William Wallace returns from the

Pearl River and confronts Hazel's mother (185). She decided to have William Wallace give the fish away for free rather than charging three dollars, and she added a paragraph on Hazel's mother: "'What have you done with my child?' Hazel's mother shouted."[13] Made almost forty years after the story was written, this latter change reveals that the role of Hazel's mother in the story is obviously crucial to Welty and linked to the way in which the story is about male fears of women. From the beginning of the story, Hazel's mother is portrayed as a somewhat intimidating presence:

> "Her mama eats like a man. I had brought her a whole hatful of berries and she didn't even pass them to her husband. Hazel, she would leap up and take a pitcher of new milk and fill up the glasses. I have heard how they couldn't have a singing at the church without a fight over her."
>
> "Oh, she's a pretty girl all right," said Virgil. "It's a pity for the ones like her to grow old, and get like their mothers."
>
> "Another thing will be that her mother will get wind of this and come after me," said William Wallace. (170–71)

By the end of the story, though, William Wallace is no longer afraid of Hazel's mother; when she shouts at him as he's giving away his fish, he merely turns "his back on her . . . and on everybody, for that matter, and that was the breaking-up of the party" (185). This should not merely be read as an instance of William Wallace's machismo, now so inspired by his epic river-dragging exploits that he is no longer intimidated by a woman. William Wallace throughout the story has displayed great tenderness as well as machismo (the scene with the rabbit on page 172 is especially notable), and at the end of the story when he thinks of Hazel at a church sing, his imagination focuses not on men fighting over women but on women's artistic prowess (evidenced by the flowered cover on the church organ as well as by their singing and songwriting). Significantly, with this change in perspective comes a change in understanding of Hazel, her mother, and "all the singing women in his life," including his own mother. Such a change is necessary to bring to a climax the story's comic upending and revision of traditional gender roles.

At the conclusion of "The Wide Net," Hazel shows signs of curing William Wallace of his fear and jealousy of women (especially pregnant women and powerful mother figures) that torment so many of Welty's male characters, including Howard in "Flowers for Marjorie" and Ricky in "Acrobats in a Park." Unlike the comic closure of "Livvie," that of "The Wide Net" recognizes and heals rather than suppresses the story's tensions. The story plumbs the anxiety that lies beneath William Wallace's displays of power, locating its source in his envy of the child he thinks will replace him as the focus of the mother's affection. By staging her disappearance, "drowning," and return, however, Hazel cures her husband's anxiety: she allows him the healing illusion of performing heroic feats, but she also shows him how much he needs her and teaches him that he must acknowledge female as well as male power if he is ever to find his wife again. The rescue at the end of "Livvie" purports to be a beginning, but in fact it may be merely a repetition, the perpetuation of Livvie's dependence on men. "The Wide Net," on the other hand, ends with a promise of repetition—"'I will do it again if I get ready,' she said"—that actually represents a beginning, the crossing of a threshold in William Wallace's psyche. This time the *deus* presiding over the *machina* of the story's comic resolution is female rather than male, and the difficulties that set the narrative in motion in the first place are solved, not more deeply hidden.

In a Wonderland they lie,
Dreaming as the days go by,
Dreaming as the summers die:

Ever drifting down the stream—
Lingering in the golden gleam—
Life, what is it but a dream?

— Lewis Carroll,
Alice in Wonderland

"The Winds" is the most underrated story in *The Wide Net*, as "Clytie" was in *A Curtain of Green*, [14] but this later story is as assured a piece as "Clytie" was strained. Filled with shifting voices, synaesthetic figures of speech, a dreamlike fluidity of time, and a Chekhovian mixture of exuberance and melancholy, "The Winds" is really a long prose poem rather than a conventional short story—one of the most daring works in all of *The Collected Stories*.

"The Winds" takes place at night during a fall equinoctial storm in 1917 or 1918 (219), as a mother and father wake up their two children, Josie and Will, and take them downstairs to the living room to wait the storm out. (The house has no basement.) The texture of the story mixes the fantasia of Josie's dream-world with her waking perceptions of the comforting presence of her parents and the world she knows by daylight. Real objects and events merge with their imaginary counterparts, and remembered events from that summer and other times are envisioned as happening in the present tense. In the following passage, Josie's imagination is so charged from the flashes of lightning, the sound of the wind, and her own dreaming that familiar objects seem to have taken on a strange new life of their own, while frightening things seem oddly human, "beseeching" and beckoning her to come out into the storm to join other children. "They moved into the living room. The sheet of music open on the piano had caved in while they slept, and gleamed faintly like a shell in the shimmer and flow of the strange light. Josie's drawing of the plaster-cast of Joan of Arc, which it had taken her all summer to do for her mother, had rolled itself tightly up on the desk like a diploma. Were they all going away to leave that? Outside the beseeching cries rose and fell, and drew nearer" (210).

All the objects with which Josie has defined her childhood identity are as thoroughly transformed by the storm as is her sheet of music: they seem to have been cast up by the storm rather than belonging to a human world. A sense of time's passing pervades almost all of the details, from the falling rose petals to the hay wagon filled with teenage boys and girls (Josie is still too young to join such a ride, but will go soon), to the reference to Josie's drawing of Joan of Arc as a kind of "diploma" marking the end of one phase of life and the commencement of another. As it turns out, this "diploma" will mark a very different kind of change than did the diploma in "Livvie." As the storm continues, the story circles back and forth between Josie's waking and dreaming states, and the voices of her parents and her brother merge with other remembered and imagined voices from her entire childhood. Phrases from lullabies, stories, playing songs, the chant of a man selling dairy products and vegetables from a cart, scraps of conversations with her girlfriends, and her own private prayers to a fairy-tale queen and the moon and the tides all sing in the wind, an equinoc-tial chorus whose words seem to rise and fall with the storm: "'Lady Moon, Lady Moon, show your shoe . . . I measure my love to show you. . . . ' Under the fiery windows, how small the children were. 'Fox in the morning!—Geese in the evening!—How many have you got?—More than you can ever catch!'" (217–18; Welty's ellipses).

"The Winds" is haunted by figures of speech suggesting forward mo-tion and journeying. "The house moved softly like a boat that has been stepped into," the narrator notes early on (212), and near the end of the story Josie sees her childhood as if from a great distance ("under the fiery windows, how small the children were"). If Josie wonders what adolescence will bring, she also searches the memories of her childhood for what the stream of time has carried away. She no longer passively receives and trusts the presences of her childhood or thinks that they will be eternally present; she now uses her imagina-tion to try to project their sounds and images into the void left by their vanishing. This is the true meaning of the "metamorphosis" she hopes to accomplish: "For the first time in her life she thought, might the same wonders never come again? Was each wonder original and alone like the falling star, and when it fell did it bury itself beyond where you hunted it? . . . Had they after all asked something of her? There, outside, was all that was wild and beloved and estranged, and all that would beckon and leave her, and all that was beautiful. She wanted to follow, and by some metamorphosis she would take them in—all—every one. . . . " (219, 221; second ellipsis is Welty's).

Josie's "metamorphosis" is an act of the imagination that requires the art of language, of naming. As her childhood vanishes, she imag-ines that it pleads for her to catalog it, "taking it in" to the eternally present space created by language. As the night passes, Josie's sense of her own power increases dramatically. She passes from the panicky desire at the height of the storm to hold on to the physical objects of her childhood—"'I want my little muff to hold.' She ached for it. 'Mother, give it to me'" (219)—to her later, calmer confidence that she "would take them in—all—every one" to the world of words (221).[15]

Josie does not make this discovery of the power of language entirely by herself; two female figures whom she picks as role models teach her the art of metamorphosis. The first is Cornella, an orphan girl who lives along with many other temporarily adopted children and their foster parents in a huge house directly across the street from Josie's. Josie's parents have forbidden her to play with Cornella because they are afraid her rebelliousness will influence their daughter, but she has exerted an influence over Josie nonetheless—not only because the friendship she strikes up with her must be secret but also because she is older and more experienced. Cornella lives in a world far less sheltered than Josie's and seems to represent to her what her life may be like when she grows up and leaves home. Josie imagines her outside in the storm: "'I see Cornella. I see Cornella in the equinox, there in her high-heeled shoes. . . . ' 'Josie, don't you understand—I want to keep us close together,' said her father. She looked back at him. 'Once in an equinoctial storm,' he said cautiously over the sleeping Will, 'a man's little girl was blown away from him into a haystack out in a field'" (211). Cornella entrances Josie with her sexuality, her provocative "adult" clothing, public temper-tantrums, beautiful hair, general aloofness, and mystery. She seems to be both a social outcast, reeking of orphanages and her foster parents' cooked cabbage, and also a lady, wearing perfume, fancy skirts, and pumps with "the Baby Louis heels" (216). Above all, she has entered the mysterious world of puberty ahead of Josie: "I will never catch up with her," she thinks desperately (214). Cornella thus not only teaches Josie that her childhood is passing but seems to give Josie a way to replace the once-loved childhood objects with equivalents from adult life—high-heeled shoes instead of toys, dates with boys instead of children's games. Cornella's version of the "metamorphosis" of her childhood that Josie needs, however, involves replacing one kind of object with another; in a way, it is as dependent upon possessions (and being possessed) as was Josie's childhood sense of self. Josie's last thoughts of Cornella in the story are inspired by a scrap of paper belonging to her that Josie finds the morning after the storm. Apparently written in Cornella's hand, it is a fragment of a note to a real or fantasized boyfriend: "Oh my darling I have waited so long when are you coming for me?" (221). Associated with Rapunzel (214), Cornella, despite her rebelliousness, is ultimately linked with romantic enthrallment and marriage.

The second female role model in the story, conversely, teaches Josie both a very different use of language and a very different sense of self. She is a woman cornet player who appeared with a band that visited Josie's town several summers ago as part of the Chautauqua Assembly, a series of concerts and educational lectures given by a traveling Chautauqua group.[16] Josie dreams of her near the end of "The Winds," just before the storm breaks and the children are put back to bed. Her vision of the woman musician thus occupies the climactic place in the story. The woman musician is never named, but she is indelibly etched in Josie's memory:

> The woman with the cornet had stepped forward, raising her instrument.
>
> If morning glories had come out of the horn instead of those sounds, Josie would not have felt a more astonished delight. The sounds that so tremulously came from the striving of the lips were welcome and sweet to her. . . . The cornetist was beautiful. There in the flame-like glare that was somehow shadowy, she had come from far away, and the long times of the world seemed to be about her. She was draped heavily in white, shaded with blue, like a Queen, and she stood braced and looking upward like the figurehead on a Viking ship. . . . The breaths she took were fearful, and a little medallion of some kind lifted each time on her breast. Josie listened in mounting care and suspense, as if the performance led in some direction away—as if a destination were being shown her. . . . It came over her how the beauty of the world had come with its sign and stridden through their town that night; and it seemed to her that a proclamation had been made in the last high note of the lady trumpeter when her face had become set in its passion, and that after that there would be no more waiting and no more time left for the one who did not take heed and follow. . . . (220; final ellipses are Welty's)

The musician mixes domestic and heroic images of women, showing Josie that a woman's life can involve both cultivating morning glories and leading a Viking ship. It is not just her "passion" that entrances Josie but her ability to shape and express that passion through her art. Playing a cornet (which, unlike a piano, violin, or voice, is conventionally played by men), the musician becomes for Josie a "sign" that she now wants to learn to read: "the beauty of the world had come with its sign."

The woman's performance in "The Winds" should remind us of "Powerhouse," for it too involves a transgression of the stereotypes that the audience may use to typecast musicians. But unlike the white audience at the beginning of "Powerhouse," Josie closely identifies with the performer from the start; her deepest thrill comes because for her the concert is a "proclamation" to follow, a demonstration of skills to be passed on. Thus immediately after her dream of the cornet player, Josie realizes that her now vanishing world of childhood has "asked something of her," is waiting for her to respond. When she closes her meditation with the resolve that "she would take them in—all" (221), her confidence comes from the fact that the woman musician has taught her how she may do it.

The woman musician has taught her that any pursuit of the world's "beauty" requires rebelling against the world's codes of behavior for what women and men may properly do. When Josie associates the woman cornetist with a "striving of the lips," she is describing how the woman musician has taught her how to answer the questions about her vanishing childhood and its sacred objects, and she is also learning from her how to question the ready-made answers of the adult world she is entering. Josie notices that her parents "were far back in the crowd" at the concert; "they did not see her, they were not listening" (220). The cornetist thus becomes a surrogate parent, a potential replacement for the other mother figures in the story who are either repressive and monstrous (Cornella's foster mother) or kindly but overprotective (Josie's mother). Significantly, the cornetist has neither the conventionality of Cornella's high heels nor the monstrousness that is associated with eccentric women in stories like "Clytie" and "June Recital." For Josie, she may play a man's instrument yet still remain "beautiful" (220)—indeed, she seems beautiful partly because she is so unconventional. Medusa's specter is present in "The Winds," lurking beneath the surface of Josie's dreams, but, significantly, it appears in Josie's memories of Cornella: "Cornella herself would stand still, haughtily still, waiting as if in pride, until a voice old and cracked would call her too, from the upper window, 'Cornella, Cornella!' And she would have to turn around and go inside to the old woman, her hair ribbon and her sash in pale bows that sank down in the back" (216–17). This passage (so reminiscent of "Clytie") implies that an obsessive desire to be a "lady" in fashionable pumps may eventually turn a woman into a repressive old maid like Cornella's foster mother, with a "cracked" voice and unfashionable ribbons in her hair. The cornetist, on the other hand, signifies how such a fate may be escaped. As their names suggest, Cornella and the cornetist seem like doubles, paired images of what Josie's future may be. Welty portrays them both as if they were dream-selves, projections of Josie's unconscious. Cornella lives directly across the street from Josie in a "double-house" that is described as if it were a face (211), and Josie's view of the musician at the concert is so detailed that it is as if she is facing her close up: "as the song drew out, Josie could see the slow appearance of a little vein in her cheek" (220). More than any other character in the story, the musician embodies the revolutionary heroism of Joan of Arc, whose portrait Josie has been working on all summer. That picture is described as a "diploma" (210), and while Joan of Arc's rebelliousness presides over the commencement of Josie's adulthood, the woman musician and her "proclamation" (220) do so as well. Both of these images of heroic women stand in striking contrast to the specter of the Medusa.

Also the musician's "striving of the lips" has taught Josie that such a transformation must be wrought by *language*. In *One Writer's Beginnings*, there is an eloquent passage describing Eudora Welty's first discovery of the power and presence of words, which she defines in physical terms, as John Keats did:

> In my sensory education I include my physical awareness of the word. Of a certain word, that is; the connection it has with what it stands for. At around age six, perhaps, I was standing by myself in our front yard waiting for supper, just at that hour in a late summer day when the sun is already below the horizon and the risen full moon in the visible sky stops being chalky and begins to take on light. There comes the moment, and I saw it then, when the moon goes from flat to round. For the first time it met my eyes as a globe. The word "moon" came into my mouth as though fed to me out of a silver spoon. Held in my mouth the moon became a word. It had the roundness of a Concord grape Grandpa took off his vine and gave me to suck out of its skin and swallow whole, in Ohio. (10)

The origins of this paragraph in *One Writer's Beginnings*—and of others in that memoir, such as the description of an upstairs sleeping porch, musical refrains, and lightning bugs (15–16)—lie in "The Winds" and "Beautiful Ohio," an earlier and very different version of "The Winds" that Welty has dated "1936 (?)."[17] If anything, the link between music and the sensuous power of language is made even more strongly in "Beautiful Ohio" than in "The Winds."

In "The Winds" the woman musician teaches Josie that although "the beauty of the world" passes in time, it can be recreated through the metamorphic power of language (220). One of the most haunting images in the story of the passing of time is of children playing evening games under "fiery windows" reflecting the sunset; it is reminiscent of Blake's *Songs of Innocence* and *Songs of Experience:* "the children were rose-colored too. Fading, rolling shouts cast long flying shadows behind them, and to watch them she [Josie] stood still" (217–18). These sentences are then followed by lines about the moon's roundness, which *One Writer's Beginnings* has now taught us to read as essentially being about the muse of language: "Above everything in the misty blue dome of the sky was the full white moon. So it is, for a true thing, round, she thought, and where she waited a hand seemed to reach around and take her under the loose-hanging hair, and words in her thoughts came shaped like grapes in her throat" (218). Such a vision transforms the allusions to Rapunzel's hair in "The Winds." Elsewhere, they are associated with Cornella's waiting to be rescued by a man (214); here, they envision a relationship between an older woman (here personified by the moon) and a girl to whom the older woman teaches what it means to be an artist.

The earlier draft of the story entitled "Beautiful Ohio" portrays the woman musician as a writer's muse even more directly. Here too she is associated with "strong lips" and the "beauty of the world" (the story links her twice with Botticelli's Venus), but the most revealing scene includes a long passage explicitly about language. Taking a bath later in the evening after hearing the woman musician, the girl (here named Celia) becomes entranced with the raised lettering of the brand name of a water heater by the bathtub. She "trailed her fingers in farewell" across the letters spelling "Kankakee" on the water heater, and then begins "hugging the sides of [it] and pressing her lips on every part of Kankakee, raised to her mouth in thick tin letters from which the warmth had not yet died. . . . 'O Kankakee, O Kankakee,' she whispered against the tin word." As a portrait of the artist as a young girl discovering the sensuousness of words, this passage was unsurpassed in Welty's writing until she reconceived it in *One Writer's Beginnings*. While we may be struck by the physical, even erotic, presence language has in this scene, we should remember that Welty is also suggesting that words fill the void left by things as they vanish: "she trailed her fingers in farewell." Both "The Winds" and "Beautiful Ohio," like Wordsworth's "Intimations" ode and Whitman's "Out of the Cradle Endlessly Rocking," are elegies as well as narratives of initiation into an understanding of the power and limitations of art.

Comparing "Beautiful Ohio" and "The Winds" with an eye to the later stories Welty wrote leads to the discovery of important connections between Cornella, Josie, the woman musician, and some of Welty's later heroines. Once again, several of the most important links are harder to see unless "Beautiful Ohio" has been read. Of all Welty's earlier stories, only "The Winds" anticipates the formal experiments in "June Recital," particularly in its dream-like, spiraling movement both backwards and forwards in time. One scene especially recalls "June Recital": when Josie imagines that during the storm she hears Cornella playing the song "Beautiful Ohio" on the piano in the orphan's house next door, and the song releases a flood of memories (215ff). Josie and Cornella in "The Winds" cannot be simply cast as prototypes for Cassie and Virgie in *The Golden Apples*, however, for these early portraits intermingle many details and traits that are given even more richness in the later story. Cornella, like Miss Eckhart, is associated at one point with a face behind a waterfall: Cornella's hair "was bright yellow, wonderfully silky and long, and she would bend her neck and toss her hair over her head before her face like a waterfall" (214). This passage links Cornella with several of Welty's later rebellious heroines, including Easter in "Moon Lake" and Virgie Rainey and Miss Eckhart in "June Recital" (compare the passage in which Miss Eckhart plays Beethoven, page 300). But this passage in "The Winds" is immediately followed by the lines already quoted that give a much more conventional, Rapunzelean interpretation of Cornella's hair, thus implying contradictions (and different possible fates) in Cornella's identity that are only fully worked out in the stories of the various characters linked with her in *The Golden Apples*. Josie, similarly, is an *ur*-portrait not only of Cassie but of Virgie; she too is linked with an inspirational older woman musician, and with Cornella she makes a clover-chain and hangs it on a statue (215), foreshadowing the much more complex scene involving Virgie and Miss Eckhart in "June Recital" that also links clover-chains and a statue (298, 300).

The most interesting link between the woman musician in "The Winds" and Miss Eckhart in *The Golden Apples*, however, exists only in the story's early draft, "Beautiful Ohio." There, the cornet player is described using the word "vaunting" ("a vaunting of the scale and a long calling note . . . ended the marching song"), and at the end of the story this word inspires Celia to imagine herself "with her arm raised, alone in a field" throwing rocks. Both the word "vaunting" and the image of a raised arm, of course, are associated by Virgie with Miss Eckhart's heroism at the end of "The Wanderers" (460). In revising "Beautiful Ohio" to create "The Winds," however, Welty edited out all references to "vaunting" and raised arms, even though she kept her portrait of the woman musician resonantly heroic. ("Vaunting" is also an important word in *One Writer's Beginnings*, where it is again associated with art [39]. Note the contrast between how this word is used in "The Winds," *The Golden Apples*, and *One Writer's Beginnings* with how it is used in "At the Landing," where it is associated only with men and contrasted with women's "prostration" [245]). Welty also discarded the linear narrative and sometimes sentimental tone of "Beautiful Ohio" for a complex cyclical narrative built around dream images and musical motifs, and she added the presence of Cornella and a storm to give more drama and contrast. In the process, she thus discovered some of the central plot elements and the narrative form she would later use for "June Recital." The buried meanings that "vaunting" and a raised hand had for her—particularly in association with Perseus and Medusa—were explored only in *The Golden Apples*, which undertakes a much more multifarious investigation of the challenges facing a woman artist than "The Winds" or "Beautiful Ohio." When "Beautiful Ohio" is read, therefore, "The Winds" emerges as an absolutely central story in *The Wide Net* as Welty undertook to move from the issues of *A Curtain of Green* to those of *The Golden Apples*.

If the equinoctial storm in "The Winds" signifies the turbulent transition from summer to fall and innocence to experience, it also refers to Josie's (and Welty's own) difficult crossing from one image of women's power to another. With "The Winds" and "The Wide Net," Welty invents a new kind of comic ending for her stories, in which a woman with a powerful imagination no longer must be isolated from other women and dependent upon male rescuers to survive. In this new kind of comedy, she forms a spiritual bond with another powerful and independent female mentor; she is neither as self-created as Phoenix nor as dependent upon men as Livvie or Cornella. Such a comic structure may properly be called "feminist" because it substitutes a potentially revolutionary role model, the woman cornetist, for Cornella and the mothers in the story, who in their various ways represent constricting or overprotective definitions of what a woman's identity may be. By the end of "The Winds," admittedly, Josie does not choose the cornetist over Cornella; rather, she holds those potential future identities suspended before her. Yet the fact that she now has an alternative (as Clytie and other earlier heroines did not) is reason enough for us to think that she may indeed accomplish the metamorphosis (221) she desires.

Heroic women in Eudora Welty's stories are usually associated with the power of music—from Ruby Fisher's and Phoenix Jackson's humming, to the woman cornet player in "The Winds," to the women whom William Wallace imagines singing. As both "Powerhouse" and "The Winds" show, for Welty the power of music represents far more than "feminine" emotionalism or even a woman's ability to master singing or piano or violin playing, the performing arts traditionally thought appropriate for women. Their musical skills (at least potentially) are as sibylline as Powerhouse's; they have the power to revise the cultural "scores" that determine how women are defined, as Powerhouse changed his audience's perception of him, as Hazel changed her husband's, and as the cornet player changed Josie's.

The Golden Apples presents both Welty's fullest tragic portrait of a woman who suffers the difficulties of the sibyl's role (Miss Eckhart) and four of her richest, most powerful comic heroines: Miss Katie Rainey, the narrator of "Shower of Gold"; Easter and Nina Carmichael of "Moon Lake," two girls who extend Welty's portraits of Cornella and Josie in "The Winds"; and Virgie Rainey in "The Wanderers,"

Miss Eckhart's prize student. All of these heroines change the way in which their society views them, and are often compared by Welty to sibyls.

The Golden Apples is also distinguished by the fact that for the first time men rather than women become the primary targets of Welty's comedy and satire. As her heroines grow in power, her male protagonists become the subject of closer scrutiny, resulting in the affectionate comic portraits of Loch Morrison in "June Recital" and "Moon Lake"; Mr. Fatty, Old Man Moody, and Barney Holifield in "June Recital"; and Mr. King MacLain in "Shower of Gold" and "The Wanderers"—as well as in her tragic portraits of Ran and Eugene MacLain in "The Whole World Knows" and "Music from Spain." This is not to say that Welty's later stories contain no satire of women (consider "Kin," for example), or that there was no criticism of men in her early stories—any reader of "The Hitch-Hikers" or "A Still Moment" knows differently. What has changed is the balance between male and female comic portraits, and the tone of the female ones. No longer do female grotesques dominate Welty's work as they did in A Curtain of Green, and no longer do her portraits of such women seem to be shadowed by the fear that the fate of a Clytie or a Mrs. Larkin may be the fate of a woman writer as well.

The opening story of The Golden Apples, "Shower of Gold," well illustrates the gentle mockery of men and the celebration of bonds between women that was first explored in "The Wide Net" and "The Winds." Like Old Mr. Marblehall, King MacLain in "Shower of Gold" can gain a sense of his own importance only when he breaks other people's rules. For King MacLain, though, his other life must not remain hidden: first he marries Snowdie Hudson, a rich woman whom the women of Morgana had decreed was ineligible for marriage because she was born an albino, and then he flouts that marriage by periodically vanishing to live the life of a roving bachelor.[18]

The narrator of "Shower of Gold," Snowdie's neighbor and friend, Mrs. Katie Rainey, superbly voices the Morgana women's righteous (and also somewhat jealous) indignation at King's behavior: "marrying must have been some of his showing off—like man never married at all till he flung in, then had to show the others how he could go right on acting. And like, 'Look, everybody, this is what I think of Morgana and MacLain Courthouse and all the way between'—further, for all I know—'marrying a girl with pink eyes' " (263). Even worse, during his bachelor escapades King fathers illegitimate children, "known and unknown, scattered-like" (264)—including some, perhaps, in Morgana itself.

Snowdie turns out to be a stronger-willed woman than King bargained for when he married her. He soon feels cooped up in the house her family built for her, hemmed in by her campaigns to preserve domestic order and by his obligation to be the family's breadwinner, either as a lawyer (his original training) or, later, as a traveling tea-and-spices salesman. The latter job helped his claustrophobia temporarily because it allowed him to travel away from Snowdie's hometown, but it was an imperfect solution because Snowdie's father is a "storekeeper down at crossroads past the Courthouse" (265), just the kind of authority figure whom King can never escape as a tea-and-spices salesman. Gradually he begins disappearing on his "travels" for longer and longer intervals. After one such absence, he writes to his wife commanding her to meet him in the Morgana woods at night, impregnates her, and then vanishes for three more years. He always returns to Morgana sooner or later, though, as if he cannot really measure his independence except in terms of how it violates Morgana's sense of order.

To the husbands of Morgana, King's freedom makes him a hero, even though they are rather jealous of all the attention he gets. Katie Rainey's husband, Fate Rainey, for example, testily comments after one of King's disappearances, " 'Well now, let's have the women to settle down and pay attention to homefolks awhile' " (265). But he also boasts about seeing King once in Jackson, Mississippi, during the inauguration of the new governor. "He was right up with the big ones and astride a fine animal"; "King MacLain could steal anyone's glory" (268). As Welty's title for the story makes clear, the men without knowing Greek mythology tend to think of King as a Zeus-like god who appears to his wife and then disappears with his power and independence intact. As Mr. Rainey's first name, "Fate," implies, the men perhaps secretly aspire to have the same superhuman power that "King" does; their last names may tie them to families, work, and local history, but their first names (to them at least) may be emblems of their inborn heroic stature.

The women of Morgana tell King's story somewhat differently. Three years after meeting his wife in the woods, King decides to treat her to a brief visit on Hallowe'en. He apparently is not prepared for the possibility that he might have fathered a child—much less twins—during his last visit, for he arrives on her porch carrying only one present. But the sons he does not know about see him before his wife does and burst out of the front door on skates wearing their Hallowe'en costumes, Eugene dressed as a wicked-looking Chinaman and Ran as a lady with a floppy hat and "an almost scary-sweet smile on her lips" (269). (The boys of course do not know whom they are scaring; they are just trying out their masks on the visitor.) "The minute come, when King just couldn't get out quick enough. Only he had a hard time, and took him more than one try. He gathered himself together and King is a man of six foot height and weighs like a horse, but he was confused, I take it. But he got aloose and up and out like the Devil was after him—or in him—finally. Right up over the bannister and the ferns, and down the yard and over the ditch and gone. He plowed into the rough toward the Big Black, and the willows waved behind him, and where he run then, Plez don't know and I don't and don't nobody" (272).

There is more than a little comic irony in this Hallowe'en turning-of-the-tables; even Fate Rainey, who so admires King, has to admit that King's prank "come back to him" (274). (In Welty's typescript, the sense of the joke's rebounding was expressed even more strongly: "it come right back at him.")[19] Not only is the trickster treated to a trick that outdoes his own, but it is a trick that (unwittingly) mocks his own phobias about family life. Children and women scare him and confine him, and now he is suddenly surrounded by both. His crossing the Big Black this time is considerably less heroic than the last, and once the story of his flight gets out, Mrs. Rainey and the other women of Morgana realize that they have finally gotten a measure of revenge. Thus Katie Rainey's dry humor: "he was confused, I take it."

Like Welty's other first-person narrators, Mrs. Rainey is not entirely in control of the tale she tells or aware of the impulses that motivate her. Her listener is a "passer-by" who "will never see her [Miss Snowdie MacLain] again, or me either" (263). Such a situation allows a certain amount of fantasizing, particularly on the matter of King's freedom and sexual prowess, a subject that both attracts and repels her.

During much of her narration, Mrs. Rainey voices the disapproval of the women of Morgana at King's behavior, but often her expressions betray admiration as well. During her description of King's Hallowe'en return, for example, she protests, "Oh, don't ask me to go on!" yet admits that she could have seen him if she would have only looked up from her work: "I was a fool and didn't look" (271). Most revealing of all is the secret that leaps out of her at the end of the story, which implies that King may have paid her a visit once. She is at least enticed by such a prospect as she imagines it: "I bet my little Jersey calf King tarried long enough to get him a child somewhere. What makes me say a thing like that? I wouldn't say it to my husband, you mind you forget it" (274). Mrs. Rainey's monologue thus contains a secret, like Welty's other monologues, and is motivated both by indignation against and guilty involvement in the events she recounts.

Mrs. Rainey also sharply contrasts with Welty's other monologists because she is less isolated, less guilty, and more reliable. Much of her tale represents not her own private interpretation but what the "whole world" knows—the version of King's story believed by the women of Morgana. Furthermore, her story both expresses the view of this community and also dramatizes their power: in telling their version of King MacLain's story, the women appropriate and revise the version of King's heroism that the men of the town (and King himself) believe.

Mrs. Rainey's deflation of King begins when she describes his first "return" to Snowdie, a prelude for the Hallowe'en appearance three years later. The veneer of gentlemanly courtesy that surrounds King's "invitation" to his wife to meet him in the woods, Mrs. Rainey sees, hides his real disdain for her, his taking for granted that she will leap to follow his every command. She exposes King's arrogance with her comic asides, deflating just the sort of phrase that he might use—"both decided on what would be best"—with her own interpretation: "Best for him, of course." King wants to return on his terms, never on his wife's; it is Snowdie who must "cross the distance" and meet him more than halfway. As Mrs. Rainey comments sarcastically, "Beware a man with manners!" (264).

Snowdie MacLain's seemingly complacent behavior surprises Mrs. Rainey and the other women of Morgana, who seek to turn her into a martyr to her scoundrel of a husband, but Mrs. Rainey also celebrates the fact that once Snowdie becomes pregnant her power increases and King's diminishes. Her face and body glow—"it was like a shower of something bright" (266)—and King must now "cross the distance" to her, not the reverse, when he decides to return: "At her house it was like Sunday even in the mornings, every day, in that cleaned-up way. She was taking joy in her fresh untracked rooms and that dark, quiet, real quiet hall that runs through her house. . . . I'll tell you what it was, what made her different. It was the not waiting any more" (266–67). Ironically, King can act out his role as Zeus only when he returns to his wife's town and the sphere of her power, not when he is away from her. In fact, he has been placed in the position of courting his wife all over again. It is her family's house that he must approach, after all, and when he does so on Hallowe'en it recalls his original courtship, which also took place while Hallowe'en decorations were up (265). The result of King's Hallowe'en visit gives the women of the town another story about him, as was his intention all along, but the story they now tell is not quite the one he had in mind.

Mrs. Rainey's version of the events, however, may not be entirely equated with that of the other Morgana women. In Mrs. Rainey's hands, the tale of King's comeuppance is not solely vindictive. (Miss Lizzie Stark's version probably would be; as Katie says of her, she "hates all men" [267].) Mrs. Rainey's response to the men's stories also celebrates Snowdie MacLain's heroism. If Jenny waited for her man to return at the end of "At the Landing," Mrs. Rainey's Snowdie is not a victim of romantic enthrallment: "I'll tell you what it was, what made her different [after her pregnancy]," Mrs. Rainey says; "It was the not waiting anymore" (266–67). Mrs. Rainey unknowingly revises the Greek myth of Zeus and Danaë that lies behind this story of King's "descent" on Snowdie: "It was like a shower of something had struck her, like she'd been caught out in something bright. It was more than the day. There with her eyes all crinkled up with always fighting the light, yet she was looking out bold as a lion that day under her brim" (266). In Mrs. Rainey's (and Welty's) retelling of the myth, the shower of gold continues to rain down after "Zeus" has disappeared; it is not connected with impregnation so much as with nurturing, and the powers of transformation seem to belong just as much to Snowdie as to King: she has become a new woman, a "lion." Snowdie also stakes out her self-reliance linguistically; she names the twins fathered by King in the woods using names drawn from her own family, not his. As Mrs. Rainey comments wryly, "some women don't name after their husbands, until they get down to nothing else left" (267).

Such an interpretation of the events is Mrs. Rainey's own. Her idealization of Snowdie's independence goes far beyond (though it also has some elements of) the other women's rather condescending desire to treat Snowdie as a martyr. It also apparently clashes with Snowdie's own version of the events, for Snowdie resents gossip about her husband and remains in love with him, as Katie concedes in the midst of her discussion of how Snowdie named the twins (267). The real Snowdie is an essentially unlionlike character, "fighting the light" that hurts her eyes and standing for domestic order at its most restrictive. In "The Whole World Knows," for example, her nagging pleas to her son Ran to return to the safety of her family's home are one of the sources of his problems. (This picture of Snowdie is tempered somewhat by the sympathetic view of her given at the end of *The Golden Apples* in "The Wanderers," where she is one of the few people who behave honorably at Mrs. Rainey's funeral.) The "shower of gold" in Mrs. Rainey's monologue is something neither Snowdie nor other Morgana women such as Miss Lizzie Stark would put in their versions of the events.

Hence the central comic action of "Shower of Gold" is not King's Hallowe'en appearance but the interpretation that Mrs. Rainey puts upon it. She mocks King's heroic pretensions even as she is in awe of them, and she creates a picture of her neighbor that may not be true to the Snowdie MacLain we come to know but that perfectly captures Mrs. Rainey's own dreams of women's self-reliance. "Everybody to their own visioning" (268), she says of her theories about King MacLain's whereabouts. (Welty in her draft originally used the inferior word "opinions," then substituted "visioning.") But Mrs. Rainey's statement about "visioning" may be taken more broadly to describe her creation of a form of female heroism for herself. Although in important ways it is uniquely her own and incapable of being shared with anyone but an out-of-towner, its authority is also firmly rooted in the women's friendships and taletelling that form the heart of Morgana's social life.

At one point in the story, in fact, Welty implies that this story's comic point of view toward marriage problems represents the next logical step for her as a humorist after "The Wide Net." She alludes to her earlier story near the beginning of "Shower of Gold" as Katie Rainey recounts one of King's disappearances:

> It was sure enough nine months to the day the twins come after he went sallying out through those woods and fields and laid his hat down on the bank of the river with "King MacLain" on it.
> For Snowdie's sake—here they come bringing the hat, and a hullaballoo raised—they drug the Big Black for nine miles down, or was it only eight, and sent word to Bovina and on, clear to Vicksburg, to watch out for anything to wash up or to catch in the trees in the river. Sure, there never was anything—just the hat. They found everybody else that ever honestly drowned along the Big Black in this neighborhood . . . . I think with the hat he ought to have laid his watch down, if he wanted to give it a better look. (266)

In this retelling of a river-dragging, it is the husband rather than the wife who fakes suicide, but he does so not with the goal of reforming a spouse, as Hazel did, but because he is unable to bear the responsibilities of marriage. Like William Wallace, King finds his manhood threatened by his wife's pregnancy. In "Shower of Gold" women have moved from being the behind-the-scenes initiators of the action to controlling how those actions are interpreted, and the affectionate mockery of men's pretensions that dances lightly around the edges of the narrative in "The Wide Net" now, in "Shower of Gold," takes center stage, with women becoming the primary storytellers. Such a step beyond "The Wide Net" provides a key to interpreting the role women story-tellers will play in The Golden Apples.

The stories of Welty's that follow "Shower of Gold" in The Golden Apples render King MacLain much as Mrs. Rainey does, dismantling his epic swagger through mockery (as at the ending of "Sir Rabbit") and through direct criticism (as in Ran's and Eugene's stories). Mrs. Rainey's unconscious revision of the Greek story of Zeus's shower of gold also sets a precedent. Danaë was the mother of Perseus, and the myth of Perseus plays a prominent part in the later tales in the collection, but not as a precise transposition of the old story to modern times. The Perseus figures are Miss Eckhart of "June Recital," Easter and Loch Morrison of "Moon Lake," and Virgie Rainey of "June Recital" and (in particular) "The Wanderers." With the exception of Loch Morrison, these are all female—true inheritors of the ideal of woman's heroism that Mrs. Rainey sketches out in the first story in *The Golden Apples*. If "June Recital," the story that follows "Shower of Gold in the sequence," is a tragic retelling of the Perseus myth, the next story in the collection, "Sir Rabbit," continues the mock-epic interpretation of King MacLain begun by Mrs. Rainey. As if to emphasize its link with "Shower of Gold," Welty sets "Sir Rabbit" in the same Morgan's Woods that figured in Ran's and Eugene's engendering.[20] The next story, "Moon Lake," returns to focusing on the comic possibilities in the Perseus legend as they may be applied to women's heroism.

One way to read "Moon Lake" is as a revision and expansion of "The Winds." It takes place outdoors at the end of summer rather than indoors during the fall equinox, but it too is about an adolescent friendship between an orphan girl and a girl from a "respectable" family. It has sustained passages of dreaming, as "The Winds" does, yet it also explores the relationships among a wide range of characters over the course of several days, as "The Winds" cannot.[21] The fascinating character of Easter is this story's version of both Cornella and the woman trumpeter, and the role played by the heroine of "The Winds," Josie, is split between the thoroughly conventional Jinny Love Stark and the half-conventional, half-rebellious Nina Carmichael.

Jinny Love is the daughter of Miss Lizzie Stark, perhaps the richest woman in Morgana. Her mother makes a daily trip in her electric car to the summer camp three miles outside of town on Moon Lake and loves the great splash of attention she receives when she shows up with watermelons and other treats for a picnic. Her comically inflated sense of self-importance measures everything that happens—even Loch Morrison's rescue of Easter from the lake—in terms of how it affects her plans. Jinny Love takes after her mother. Her main use for the many orphans at the camp is to confirm her own sense of high social standing. The first time we hear her in the story, she is proposing to "let the orphans go in the water first and get the snakes stirred up" [i.e., get them away from the girls' swimming area] (344). When

her best friend, Nina Carmichael, begins befriending Easter, Jinny
Love uses every comment she makes to hint to Nina that such a
friendship ought to be beneath girls who can take hand-made hand-
kerchiefs with them to camp: "'Who would ever want to know?'" she
asks, when Easter proposes playing a tomboyish game of mumblety-
peg rather than the lady-like card game of cassino (346). In spite of
herself, however, Jinny Love is also fascinated by Easter: "Jinny Love's
gaze was fastened on Easter, and she dreamed and dreamed of telling
on her for smoking, while the sun, even through leaves, was burning
her pale skin pink, and she looked the most beautiful of all: she felt
temptation. But what she said was, 'Even after all this is over, Easter,
I'll always remember you'" (358).

Nina Carmichael is also from one of Morgana's best families, and
like Jinny Love carries emblems of her status such as a collapsible
metal drinking cup around with her at camp. She too feels the thrill
of thinking she is superior: when she and Jinny Love notice a ring of
dirt on the back of Easter's neck, they share "a feeling of elation"
(347). But Nina is more independent than Jinny Love and is fascinated with Easter's status as leader of the orphans. When we first meet
Nina, we see her (quietly) rebelling against one of the camp's rituals
designed for the youngest girls: "Nina Carmichael thought, There is
nobody and nothing named Mr. Dip, it is not a good morning until
you have had coffee, and the water is the temperature of a just-cooling
biscuit, thank Goodness. I hate this little parade of us girls" (343).
The following meditation of Nina's shows her ambivalence toward
Easter: it begins condescendingly, full of aristocratic disdain, but soon
expresses both respect and envy: "The reason orphans were the way
they were lay first in nobody's watching them, Nina thought, for she
felt obscurely like a trespasser. They, they were not answerable. Even
on being watched, Easter remained not answerable to a soul on earth.
Nobody cared! And so, in this beatific state, something came out of
her" (352). For Nina, the very orphanhood that made Easter ostracized also gives her special power: instead of inheriting her identity
from her family, Easter's seems entirely her own creation. (Note, incidentally, how close the last sentence of the above quotation is to a
similar phrase, "There was something in her that never stopped," used
to describe Ruby Fisher in "A Piece of News" [13].)

Part of Easter's power over Nina has to do with the fact that Easter has entered into adolescence earlier than any of the other girls; she seems in touch with a world of which they are just becoming aware. Easter's sexual mystique is well shown when Nina, Jinny Love, and she go on a hike around Moon Lake and far away from camp discover an unused boat moored to a stump just offshore. All the girls associate boats and the lake with sexuality, for they are very self-conscious of the fact that they are allowed to swim only within a roped-off area supervised by adults, whereas their counsellor, Miss Parnell Moody, goes boating in the middle of the lake on dates with men from town (360). When the girls reach the boat, Easter hops quickly in, as if she has been there before, but Nina and Jinny Love linger longer on shore, as if sensing some invisible barrier. Easter lies on her back with her head and arms over the prow of the boat, a "figurehead, turned on its back, sky-facing" (356), as if leading them on their journey into puberty. Disturbingly, however, she seems to be also falling backwards, as if away from her childhood self, with her eyes "rolled back" so that only the whites are visible (354). As in "The Winds," the world of adolescence frightens as much as it entices.

Easter's position in the boat foreshadows her position on her cot in her tent a few nights later, when Nina again envisions her as a kind of guide. In this scene it is the night rather than the lake that represents Nature's power to transform a girl into a woman, and now Nature is a decidedly masculine rather than feminine figure, a lover rather than a mother. This change eloquently testifies to how Nina's imagination has been changed by Easter. Nina's fantasies are now thoroughly sexual; it seems to her as if Easter is beckoning for the darkness to enter the tent.

> The pondering night stood rude at the tent door, the opening fold would let it stoop in—it, him—he had risen up inside. Long-armed, or long-winged, he stood in the center where the pole went up. . . . Easter's hand hung down, opened outward. Come here, night, Easter might say, tender to a giant, to such a dark thing. And the night, obedient and graceful, would kneel to her. . . .
>
> Nina let her own arm stretch forward opposite Easter's. Her hand too opened, of itself. She lay there a long time motionless, under the night's gaze, its black cheek, looking immovably at her hand, the only

part of her now which was not asleep. Its gesture was like Easter's, but Easter's hand slept and her own hand knew—shrank and knew, yet offered still.

"Instead . . . me instead. . . ." (361–62; final pair of ellipses is Welty's)

In the morning, Nina's arm has fallen asleep and stings her as it comes back to life. Welty's subtle references to Easter's rolled-back eyes and Nina's arm falling asleep hint that adolescence when it comes will involve a kind of sleep—a death—of their childhood selves. Nina may momentarily enter such a state, but she does not stay there for long: the time has not come for her to leave her childhood entirely behind.

Nina experiences the same feeling even more forcefully when Easter later nearly drowns. While the camp's lifeguard, Loch Morrison, clumsily performs his version of artificial respiration, it seems to Nina and the other horror-stricken girls that she has entered another world and is "calling" for them to follow her:

[Easter's arm] was turned at the elbow so that the hand opened upward. It held there the same as it had held when the night came and stood in the tent, when it had come to Easter and not to Nina. It was the one hand, and it seemed the one moment.

. . . They looked at Easter's mouth and at the eyes where they were contemplating without sense the back side of the light. . . . [W]as there danger that Easter, turned in on herself, might call out to them after all, from the other, worse, side of it? Her secret voice, if soundless then possibly visible, might work out of her terrible mouth like a vine, preening and sprung with flowers. Or a snake would come out.

The Boy Scout crushed her body and blood came out of her mouth. (369–70)

This scene may be a parody of the rescue of Andromeda by Perseus. The Greek myth involves a serpent whom Perseus kills, thus possibly explaining the presence of allusions to snakes in the above quotation, and although Andromeda is not in danger of drowning she is chained to a rock at the edge of the sea before her rescue, somewhat like Easter immobile in the chained boat (354–56; Hamilton 146–48). (A snake's presence also figures in the boat scene: 354.) Easter's story is different enough from Andromeda's to warn us to pursue such parallels very carefully; even more revealing, I think, are the social and sexual rather than mythical inflections in the episode. Never having seen artificial respiration performed before, much less seen it done so poorly, Nina involuntarily transforms what she sees into a vision of the sexual act. Like many children who first imagine (or overhear or see) sexual intercourse, she interprets it as violent and terrifying. To Nina, Easter has suddenly become a monstrous rather than heroic figurehead, her body both violated and self-violating—invaded from without and monstrously transforming itself from within. Thus the threatening phallic objects in the scene (the vines and snakes) come out of Easter's *mouth*, as if the very voice with which Easter calls out to the other girls has become demonic. Similarly, when her lungs hemorrhage slightly from the water and Loch's pounding, the blood seems to have been caused both by the near-drowning and by what Nina takes to be the self-wounding and shame of menstruation. "There it remained—mystery, if only for being hard and cruel and, by something Nina felt inside her body, murderous" (372).

Easter suddenly revives with a gasp, kicks the boy off her, sits up bewilderedly, and slowly pulls "her ruined dress downward" (371). When she is "herself" again, she becomes a heroic figure to Nina and the other girls once more. They remember not the horror of the near-drowning but the spell-bound, miraculous moment when Easter seemed to be flying through the air as she fell from the diving board: "Their minds could hardly capture it again, the way Easter was standing free in space, then handled and turned over by the blue air itself" (372). Here the forces of nature that are "handling" Easter and transforming her from a girl into a woman seem tender and maternal, not violent and masculine—air and light rather than water and darkness. But such a fate of near-drowning seems to await all of them as well: "'Oh, my child, Moon Lakes are all over the world,' Mrs. Gruenwald had interrupted. 'I know of one in Austria . . . . ' And into each fell a girl, they dared, now, to think" (372–73).

Easter does not merely represent the biological changes that define womanhood, however: to Nina she is heroic because she also introduces her to the social aspects of what it is to be a woman. These are just as mysterious and frightening as the biological changes that adolescence brings—perhaps even more so. Because of Easter, Nina for the first time becomes conscious of the social construction of gender differences. The first act of Easter's that Nina remembers hearing about is her biting Mr. Nesbitt from the Bible Class, when he stared at her breasts: "It was wonderful to have with them someone dangerous but not, so far, or provenly, bad" (347). Easter also ignores most of the boundaries separating proper male and female behavior and, in doing so, makes Nina newly conscious of how gender is linked to role-playing: "The one named Easter could fall flat as a boy, elbows cocked, and drink from the cup of her hand with her face in the spring. Jinny Love prodded Nina, and while they looked at Easter's drawers, Nina was opening the drinking cup she had brought with her, then collapsing it, feeling like a lady with a fan" (346). Nina's first reaction to Easter's androgyny here is defensive: she unconsciously reasserts her own class and sexual status as a "lady." But after some games of mumblety-peg with Easter's jackknife, Nina has a quite different response: "Nina's grandfather possessed a box of coins from Greece and Rome. . . . The color in Easter's eyes could have been found somewhere, away—away, under lost leaves—strange as the painted color of the ants. Instead of round black holes in the center of her eyes, there might have been women's heads, ancient" (347–48).

The passage make's Easter's independence seem associated at least in part with nature, as if Easter is a kind of female nature deity for Nina. Yet as Nina looks deeply into Easter's eyes, she imagines ancient, regal women, perhaps portraits of sibyls or queens on coins. Unconsciously, Nina knows that Easter's rebellious independence does not evoke visions of a "natural" woman outside of society so much as a different and thus "dangerous" (347) conception of the power a woman may have in society. Revealingly, in an earlier version of the story these sibylline coins were owned not by Nina's grandfather but by "a queer old music teacher"—Miss Eckhart. [22]

The scene in "Moon Lake" that most profoundly reveals the true source of Easter's dangerousness occurs just after the boat scene discussed above. It may be thought of as a second, symbolic journey the girls take that day with Easter leading them on. This time, however, it is explicitly an exploration of the meaning of a woman's social identity, for it involves an argument about naming and writing. The scene has not had adequate commentary [23] and is worth quoting at length.

Nina dug into the sand with a stick, printing "Nina" and then "Easter."

. . . Easter's hand came down and wiped her name clean; she also wiped out "Nina." She took the stick out of Nina's hand. . . . In clear, high-waisted letters the word "Esther" cut into the sand . . .

"Who's that?" Nina asked.

Easter laid her thumb between her breasts, and walked about.

"Why, I call that 'Esther.' "

"Call it 'Esther' if you want to, I call it 'Easter.' "

"Well, sit down. . . . "

"And I named myself."

"How could you? Who let you?"

"I let myself name myself."

"Easter, I believe you," said Nina. "But I just want you to spell it right. Look—E-A-S—"

"I should worry, I should cry."

Jinny Love leaned her chin on the roof of her castle to say, "I was named for my maternal grandmother, so my name's Jinny Love. It couldn't be anything else. Or anything better. You see? Easter's just not a real name. It doesn't matter how she spells it, Nina, nobody ever had it. Not around here." She rested on her chin.

"I have it."

"Just see how it looks spelled right." Nina lifted the stick from Easter's fingers and began to print, but had to throw herself bodily over the name to keep Easter from it. "Spell it right and it's real!" she cried.

. . . "'Easter' is real beautiful!" Nina said distractedly. She suddenly threw the stick into the lake, before Easter could grab it . . . . "I thought it was the day you were found on a doorstep," she said sullenly. . . . (357)

Ironies proliferate here. Easter thinks she has named herself, yet she spells and writes her name quite conventionally—her script is as "high-waisted" and "formal" as a lady's. Nina also insists on correct spelling but does so to make "real" Easter's name, whose uniqueness both threatens and delights her. Jinny Love meanwhile remains a largely passive onlooker, still retreating (as Nina first did) into the security of believing that identity is simply and unproblematically conferred by family and society.

Trying to affirm the uniqueness of her friend's identity, Nina finds herself compelled to use a medium that makes that identity conventional. No name can be "real" unless it is spelled right, yet such rightness contradicts the very reality that she seeks: "'"Easter" is real beautiful!' Nina said distractedly." What confuses Nina even more is the fact that Easter not only thinks she can "let myself name myself," but she thinks she can *read* in her own way too. First she "calls" herself Easter, and then she calls "Esther" "Easter." She thinks she can completely dismiss conventional ways of reading to substitute her own, even while she adopts unchanged the formal, lady-like cursive style of writing she has learned in school.

The implications of Easter's and Nina's acts are just as revolutionary as Ruby Fisher's "misreading" of her name in Welty's earlier story, "A Piece of News." Both scenes involve a secret, subversive identity disguising itself under the name that society recognizes. In Easter's case, however, that name does not remain hidden; it is spoken out loud, made public. Nina, moreover, is already beginning to change the spelling of Easter's name in order to make it conform to her special identity, not her conventional one. Her "distraction" comes from the fact that she cannot make such a revolutionary revision complete: her very act of spelling Easter "correctly" is both a proud assertion of Easter's uniqueness and a capitulation to linguistic convention, to proper spelling. No wonder Nina throws her writing-stick into the lake in frustration. It is much easier speaking Easter's special name than writing it: orally, the girls can create a private world that seems as removed from society as their secret beach is from their camp, but once they begin commemorating that private world in writing, they are constrained by a medium whose conventions are much more recalcitrant.

Easter's name of course abounds with religious connotations that further enrich the scene's meaning. If to a child the onset of puberty is as frightening as imagining one's own death, then Easter is the figure who gives Nina the faith that there is life after summer camp, after the end of childhood. But "Easter" also suggests another kind of transformation, the escape of a woman's identity from being encrypted within a name that is not her own. The difficulties that the girls discover in first names are difficulties that apply to all forms of naming: there is a permanent tension between our desire to be unique and the fact that (as Jinny Love says) we are conventionally named "for someone" else. Such linguistic doubleness obtains for male as well as female names, admittedly, but it is particularly relevant to women because they are conventionally named for someone else twice in their lives, once when they are born and once when they are married. Easter's claim to having named herself is thus at least potentially the revolutionary claim to be able to keep her unique identity (however she spells its name) if she marries.

Easter's unusual first name allies her with the other characters in *The Golden Apples* with special first names. Significantly, when those other characters are male their special first names denote their high status ("Fate" Rainey, "King" MacLain), whereas in the only case in which a woman has such a special name, "Snowdie" MacLain, her name denotes her oddness, the chance genetic occurrence that made her an albino. Easter is the only female character in *The Golden Apples* to have a first name denoting both her oddness and her special status of living "for herself," and unlike her male counterparts she never really has her mythic status deflated. She retains her queenly power over the orphan girls while extending it to at least one and perhaps more of the respectable Morgana girls.

Like Cornella and the lady cornetist in "The Winds," Easter is the "double" for the story's heroine who represents the several future selves she may become. As "Esther" with conventional handwriting, she embodies Nina's potential to be little more than a Jinny Love with the delusion that she is acting independently. (This indeed appears to be Nina's fate, as we learn to our sorrow in "The Wanderers.") As "Easter," however, she may signify not every woman's right to name herself (even Easter, after all, really has not done that) but her right to make her identity her own, not something that primarily exists "for" others, such as one's original family or one's present husband. Easter's name for Nina is a "proclamation" and a "sign" just as the trumpeter's performance was for Josie—an event whose revolutionary meaning Nina wants to learn to read.

To a large degree, the Easter/Esther conjunction represents the same tension within Morgana's naming conventions indicated by women's names (like Miss Lizzie Stark or Virgie Rainey *Danke schoen*) that was investigated in "June Recital," and like Miss Eckhart, Easter has the uncanny ability to make people "distractedly" aware of the unresolved contradictions within the compensatory self-naming conventions that Morgana girls and women inherit. More than any other female in Morgana, Easter's name is also androgynous, embodying the special power associated with mythical first names—rather than a social marker like "Miss"—that conventionally belong to males only.

"Moon Lake" concludes on a tentative but beautifully right note, as Nina and Jinny Love spy on Loch Morrison standing by the opening of his tent one evening, posing naked and obviously swelling with pride over rescuing Easter. Nina may instinctively recognize the importance of biological and social differences between the sexes, but she is not yet ready to face them—she is still on the verge of adulthood, not yet crossed over. Like Loch's, Nina's interest in the opposite sex expresses itself obliquely rather than directly, as mockery and proud indifference, but she also makes fun of Loch because she has also newly discovered her own kind of sexuality and self-confidence, matching his.

The story's last words, ironically, are Jinny Love's: "You and I will always be old maids" (374). (The convention-bound Jinny Love is of course the *least* likely candidate of all the girls to remain unmarried, and we learn in "The Whole World Knows" that she marries Ran MacLain.) The narrator then notes that the girls go to join the others singing around the campfire. The "singing" that they walk towards signifies not just the conformist children's songs like "Mr. Dip" that Nina now finds so silly but (as always in Welty's stories when music is mentioned) an art that has the potential to give an individual a distinctive voice. It is no accident that Easter casually comments that she plans to be a singer (358) when she grows up: this detail identifies her with the heroism of Powerhouse-the-sibyl in "Powerhouse," the woman cornet player in "The Winds," Hazel and the other "singing women" (187) in "The Wide Net," and Miss Eckhart and Virgie Rainey in "June Recital." Easter has their sibylline power to change society's tune and rewrite its cultural texts. This power is not yet realized, admittedly, either in herself or in Nina, and it may be lost in adulthood if their respect for correct "scripts" takes over. Yet Nina's instinctive sense that Easter's name must be spelled in a way that captures its uniqueness suggests that a compromise may be possible, that a woman's independence may be shaped within a culturally bound medium (such as language) without destroying itself or ostracizing that woman as a Medusa-figure. Such a vision also means that

Easter's "dangerous" and "unanswerable" independence may become public and communicable, not private and forever secret.

"I must not lose the end of the picture and so miss the meaning of the whole, so far painfully perceived. I must hold on here or the picture will blur over and the sequence be lost. In a sense, it seems I am drowning . . . I know that I must drown . . . completely in order to come out on the other side of things (like Alice with her looking-glass or Perseus with his mirror). I must drown completely and come out on the other side, or rise to the surface after the third time down, not dead to this life but with a new set of values, my treasure dredged from the depth. I must be born again or break utterly.
— H.D.,
Tribute to Freud

"The central myth of the artist is surely not Narcissus but Perseus—with the artist in all roles, Perseus and Medusa and the mirror-shield."
— Reynolds Price,
Things Themselves

"The Wanderers," like "The Winds" and "The Wide Net," is set in late September, near the fall equinox (427), and on one of her working typescripts Welty originally wrote "present time" [i.e., ca. 1949] under the title.[24] But unlike the heroines of those other equinoctial comedies, Virgie does not seem to be on the threshold of a new life for herself; rather, she has just buried her mother beside her father and her only brother, and now, in her middle forties, appears fated to become yet another one of Morgana's old maids. She has more or less stopped playing piano, allowing her less-talented friend Cassie Morrison to become the town's piano teacher, and contents herself with working as a typist for the fundamentalist Christian businessman Mr. Nesbitt, the same Mr. Nesbitt who bothered Easter in "Moon Lake" and now, approximately twenty-five years later, runs a lumber company that is fast depleting Morgan's Woods on the outskirts of Morgana. (Miss Lizzie Stark has apparently sold Mr. Nesbitt the logging rights, and his rape of the woods parallels King's rape of Mattie Will Sojourner at the same site [336–37].) Even Eudora Welty herself has recently commented on the poor appearance that Virgie seems to make in "The Wanderers," contrasting her with Miss Eckhart and suggesting that "The Wanderers" shows her sadly "wasting" her talents (*One Writer's Beginnings* 102).

Yet in this story Virgie in fact emerges as the most powerful and most complexly drawn of all of Welty's comic heroines in her short fiction, the one who confronts and conquers the specter of an unconventional woman as a Gorgon. It is through Welty's portrayal of Virgie that she most fully resolves the anxieties of authorship expressed in *A Curtain of Green* and discovers and celebrates the power that is properly hers. Virgie's outer life is a series of blunderings and misunderstandings, ending with her in the ignominious position of being a secretary, a transcriber of someone else's words, but as she responds to the crisis of her mother's death her inner life radiates authority. Through Virgie, Welty draws together the two most important images of women's power in the earlier stories—the woman as musician and the woman as sibyl—into a revolutionary synthesis. More than any other character in the stories, Virgie Rainey is the true heroine of Welty's women's comedy. It is for these reasons, as well as because of chronology, that "The Wanderers" makes such a magnificent conclusion to *The Golden Apples* sequence.

At the start of "The Wanderers," Virgie seems destined to be more a tragic than a comic heroine. Indeed, the parallels with "Clytie" are striking, as are those with "June Recital." Like Clytie caught in the rain, Virgie's unorthodox behavior is a perennial subject for the Morgana gossips. Near the beginning of the story, just before her death, Virgie's mother imagines she can hear all the town's voices gossiping about her daughter.

> Circle by circle it twittered, church talk, talk in the store and post office, vulgar man talk possibly in the barber-shop. Talk she could never get near now was coming to her. . . .
>
> "Daughter wouldn't run off and leave her [her mother], she's old and crippled."
>
> "Left once, will again."
>
> "That fellow Mabry's been taking out his gun and leaving Virgie a bag o' quail every other day. Anybody can see him go by the back door."

"I declare."

"He told her the day she got tired o' quail, let him know and he'd quit and go on off . . . . "

"Do tell." (429)

Virgie is wild and brazen, known (like King MacLain) for her lovers and for leaving town and then reappearing later. She is thought to be incompetent at doing traditional women's tasks such as gardening, sewing, quilt making, and cooking. At Virgie's mother's funeral reception, a neighbor just outside of Virgie's line of vision is overhead remarking that she "might get a little bit of dairyfood savings now" (from her mother's cows) but that "she'll spend it on something 'sides the house, hm? . . . What does Virgie care about housekeeping and china plates without no husband, hm?" (436). Jinny Love Stark's treatment of Virgie is representative: she looks "at the burns and scars on Virgie's hands, as Missie Spights had done, making them stigmata of something at odds with her womanhood" (444).

Throughout the story, Virgie's hands are associated with unladylike behavior, with her ignoring the behavioral conventions separating class and gender. She holds a typing job in town, unlike any of the other women with whom she grew up; milks her mother's cows after work at five (also too "country" an activity to be truly ladylike); and like a man owns and knows how to operate a pistol that she keeps in her car—a racy coupe. She also began supporting herself with her hands even before she'd finished high school: in "June Recital" her classmate Cassie recites to herself the mildly scandalous fact that Virgie "plays the piano at the picture show" and has become "unpopular" with proper girls (286). Throughout the funeral reception in "The Wanderers," the women are constantly touching her, as if trying to guide her and smooth her, and Virgie instinctively pulls back in revulsion: "she felt their hands smooth down her and leave her, draw away from her body and then give it a little shove forward" (435).

Virgie's version of the reasons for her "stigmata" are very different: "the strength in her hands she used up to type in the office but most consciously to pull the udders of the succeeding cows, as if she would hunt, hunt, hunt daily for the blindness that lay inside the beast, inside where she could have a real and living wall for beating on, a solid prison to get out of, the most real stupidity of flesh, anguish for anguish" (453). As in Welty's other stories focusing on how women perceive their bodies, this passage dramatizes not their "natural" imprisonment within a physical self as much as the fact that this corporal confinement is really social. The references to heaviness, narrowness, and "stupidity" may seem to signify the cow's body, but they may also be read as references to the mindless body politic of the town against which Virgie rebels—the social conventions that dictate that a secretary ought not to be also a farmgirl and that proper ladies have nothing to do with either. A similar moment of frustration occurred earlier in Virgie's life, when she tried to butt her brains out against the basement wall of her school during an indoor recess ("June Recital," 291).

Like Clytie and Miss Eckhart, Virgie holds great rage within her, rage at others and rage against herself for being enraged at others. One scene in "The Wanderers" alludes to Clytie's cursing in the garden in "Clytie" and Mrs. Larkin's anger in "A Curtain of Green." On the day of the funeral Virgie decides that the front lawn must be properly cut, and waking in a frenzy goes outside to do it. "Virgie took her sewing scissors from the little bundle of plaid material in her room, and went outdoors. She crouched in the pink early light, clipping and sawing the heads off the grass—it had all gone to seed—a handful at a time. The choked-out roses scratched, surprised her, drew blood drops on her legs. She had to come in when Miss Snowdie, whose presence she had forgotten, stepped out on the porch and called her. As though for a long time she had been extremely angry and had wept many tears, she allowed Miss Snowdie to drive her inside the house and cook her breakfast" (441). Like Clytie, Virgie rebels even as she performs the tasks expected of her—or rather, she expresses her rage through her "mad" performance of a task. Yet elsewhere in the story, Virgie's temporary flashes of anger give her great anxiety, not relief; she unconsciously fears that her fate will be like that of Miss Eckhart (who died in the madhouse in Jackson), Cassie Morrison's mother (who led a "normal" life as a housewife and then suddenly killed herself), and Maideen Sumrall in "The Whole World Knows" (who killed herself after Ran MacLain raped her). Virgie's frightened attempts to distance herself from these three women by saying to herself that she "hates" them (449–50) only exposes the deeper kinship that she feels. Like Miss Eckhart's hands, her own are marked with the stigmata of her anger and despair.

Of all the women of Virgie's generation, including Nina Carmichael and Jinny Love Stark, only Cassie Morrison treats Virgie decently at the funeral and seems somewhat unscathed by what has happened since she and Virgie were piano students together. She has apparently not married and still lives in her family's house, taking care of her senile father and renting out the extra rooms to lumbermen working for Virgie's employer, Mr. Nesbitt. She has not lost any of the vanity that was evident at the start of "June Recital"; when she is first introduced in "The Wanderers," the narrator notes that "Cassie had chosen the one thin, gold-rimmed coffee cup for herself, and balanced it serenely" (432). She is generally a rather sympathetic character in the story, for her love and concern for Virgie are much appreciated. Yet her incessant desire to worship her mother's memory is troubling. She bought an expensive stone for her grave, a carving of a seated angel (449), rather like some of the monuments in Jackson's Greenwood Cemetery that Welty photographed in the 1930s that feature angels or women in eternal postures of mourning (Marrs 104, 114). She has also planted narcissi on the Morrison's front lawn spelling out her mother's name in huge letters. Both of these acts (as well as her comment to Virgie that Virgie herself will "never get over" her mother's death [449–50]) suggest that Cassie is trapped in mourning. Any anger that Cassie feels against her father and Morgana society for causing her mother's suicide is not evident in her mourning, but the thoroughness with which she sanctifies her mother's memory perhaps implies much buried anger and guilt. Interestingly enough, Cassie feels that she must write out her mother's name in large letters, as if subconsciously trying to compensate for her mother's not being able to make her mark on the world when she was alive. (The story of Cassie Morrison's mother is never told in The Golden Apples, but hints of her dissatisfaction with her marriage and her despairing renunciation of music may be found throughout "June Recital" [295, 324–29, for example]. Her husband, conversely, is frequently linked with writing and power, both through his ownership of the Morgana-MacLain Weekly Bugle and through his support of various political candidates whose circulars and posters are mentioned in the story [277, 295, 298,

303, 316].) In the case of Mrs. Morrison's narcissi, writing commemorates the loss of power, not its acquisition. We shall see later in "The Wanderers" that writing for Virgie signifies something very different.[25]

In "The Wide Net," "The Winds," "Shower of Gold," and "Moon Lake," Welty suggests that a spiritual tie between women may give them something that isolated heroines such as Clytie in *A Curtain of Green* did not have—a sustaining sense of their own importance that is not necessarily connected to how well they perform the role of married lady or spinster. It is just such a bond between Virgie and certain other women—especially Virgie's mother and Miss Eckhart—that helps Virgie ignore the other women of Morgana who would treat her as a freak and a monster.

Of these friendships of Virgie's, the one with her mother is treated most fully in "The Wanderers." Before her death, Mrs. Rainey often seemed to treat her daughter as poorly as Octavia treated Clytie, ordering her about and vehemently resenting whatever time she had to herself: "'Look where the sun is,' she called as Virgie did drive up in the yard in the old coupe [after she arrives home from work]" (430). But Mrs. Rainey also loves her daughter's independent nature and is hurt by the town's gossip about her supposed promiscuity and indifference toward her mother. The last thought she has before her stroke exemplifies this: "There nothing Virgie Rainey loves better than struggling against a real hard plaid," she thinks admiringly as they sew together (430). (Note how this contradicts the townspeople's view of Virgie's domestic incompetence: Vande Kieft 113). Not coincidentally, this sewing scene parallels the central scene of the first story in *The Golden Apples*, "Shower of Gold," in which Mrs. Rainey and Snowdie are sewing together. Like Mrs. Rainey's friendship with Snowdie, her bond with her daughter, though troubled, is too strong ever to be broken, and it has a golden wealth of its own that surpasses any "shower of gold" that may be associated with a man. Welty's language alludes to "Shower of Gold" as Virgie says goodbye to her mother on her deathbed: "Behind the bed the window was full of cloudy, pressing flowers and leaves in heavy light, like a jar of figs in syrup held up. A humming bird darted, fed, darted. Every day he came. He had a ruby throat. The clock jangled faintly as cymbals struck under water, but did not strike; it couldn't. Yet a torrent of riches seemed to flow over the room, submerging it, loading it with what was over-sweet" (431–32).

One of the original titles for "The Wanderers" was "The Humming-birds" ("The Kin" and "The Golden Apples" were others); if "The Hummingbirds" is not as richly suggestive a title as the present one, it nevertheless does underline the importance of this passage in the story. Unlike the riches that King represents, these belong wholly to women, like the bed and its counterpane, the mantel clock, the flow-ering yard trees, and the jar of figs. They commemorate the impor-tance for women of what one feminist scholar, Carroll Smith-Rosen-berg, has called the "women's world of love and ritual." Associated with pretwentieth century habits of women performing domestic tasks together, it contrasts strikingly with the isolation (except for certain formal occasions) that characterizes the life of a more "proper" and "modern" lady such as Miss Lizzy Stark, who sends proxies like her servant Juba to perform tasks that originally linked women.

The importance—and rarity—of such a spiritual tie between women in Morgana in the 1940s is also shown during three scenes in which Virgie is entirely alone. These scenes conclude the three prin-cipal sections of "The Wanderers" and offer a counterpoint to the comic vanity-fair of the funeral reception and its aftermath. In all three cases, they involve action that is thoroughly unladylike: swim-ming naked, smoking in one's car late at night, and walking in the rain without an umbrella. Such scenes show that Virgie does not merely restrict her acts of rebellion within a conventionally domestic domain, as her mother did. She represents the independent thinking of a new generation. Virgie's flouting of Morgana's standards increases in audacity from the first scene to the second to the third, but inter-estingly enough her most subversive act of all is a mental, not a physi-cal, one: it occurs while she is simply sitting still. Taking the last several pages of "The Wanderers" to unfold, this epiphany transfigures the various meanings that earlier scenes in The Golden Apples give to a spiritual bond between women.

In the first scene, concluding Section I, Virgie goes to the Big Black River after being sleepless during her first night after her mother's death. She strips, swims in the water, and washes away the touches and memories of the women who crowded into the house that afternoon to "help": they have made her feel soiled. It may be the best description in American literature of swimming naked—Mark Twain would have admired it. Its delicacy and tenderness also provide a comic counterpoint to King's "heroic" crossing of that same river many years ago when he left Snowdie. For Virgie, too, the river signifies strength and independence, but a kind that King MacLain may hardly imagine: "All seemed one weight, one matter—until as she put down her head and closed her eyes and the light slipped under her lids, she felt this matter a translucent one, the river, herself, the sky all vessels which the sun filled. She began to swim in the river, forcing it gently, as she would wish for gentleness to her body. Her breasts around which she felt the water curving were as sensitive at that moment as the tips of wings must feel to birds, or antennae to insects" (440). Virgie's heroism shows its power by merging with nature, not conquering it. (Contrast the above passage with this sentence from "Shower of Gold," added in revision: [King] "plowed through the rough toward the Big Black" [272].) The light in this scene from "The Wanderers" is Virgie's own shower of gold, but it does not involve a man at all: it comes from Virgie, returns to her, is one with her.

Welty's second meditative scene, concluding Section II, also takes place late at night, after the funeral, as Virgie goes out to her car and smokes. This scene also contrasts with an earlier example of male heroism in *The Golden Apples*, Ran MacLain's violent demonstrations of his masculinity with his car in "The Whole World Knows." Ran's reckless driving temporarily satisfied his urge to overpower women, to get revenge for his wife's adultery (389–90). Virgie uses her car to display her independence too: it is hard to say which scandalizes her neighbors more, her various affairs or her having a car of her own in which to leave town whenever she wants to. She also carries a pistol in her car, as Ran does, but Virgie does not feel orphaned by her parents or by nature. She is linked with both as if by an indestructible umbilical cord: "She knew that now at the river, where she had been before on moonlit nights in autumn, drunken and sleepless, mist lay on the water and filled the trees, and from the eyes to the moon would be a cone, a long silent horn, of white light. It was a connection visible as the hair is in air, between the self and moon, to make the self feel the child, a daughter far, far back" (454).

The final scene of Virgie's meditating in "The Wanderers" takes place early in the morning the day after the funeral and involves a very different kind of transgression of proper behavior. Virgie has just decided to sell all her family's belongings and leave Morgana. She drives to MacLain, the county seat seven miles away, and sits on a stile under a tree in front of the courthouse listening to the rain. These last pages of "The Wanderers" (457–61) are Virgie's hail and farewell to Morgana and the world of The Golden Apples, and they are perhaps the most spacious and revelatory pages in all of Eudora Welty's short stories. Virgie's meditation is in two parts, the first concerned with the history of the MacLains (457–58), the second with her own history (459–61). Not coincidentally, the first is largely the public history of men; the second, the private and unacknowledged stories of women.

"The land across from the courthouse used to be Mr. Virgil Mac-Lain's park," Virgie remembers as she begins to retrace the stories of the town's past in her mind. Then she remembers the recent history of the lives of many of the characters that we met in other stories—like that of Eugene MacLain, who eventually left his wife in San Francisco and came home to Morgana to die of tuberculosis. Always, though, the very language that Virgie uses shows that the history she is remembering is primarily about men: "all of Mr. King's family lay over there, Cedar Hill was bigger than the courthouse; his father Virgil in the Confederate section, and his mother, his grandfather—who remembered his name and what he did? The name was on the stone. Didn't he kill a man, or have to, and what would be the long story behind it, the vaunting and the wandering from it?" (458). Virgie's questions here imply not that the men's stories are lost but that they are stored in the town's public memory, needing only to be recalled. This entire quoted passage was added in revision to the story, to heighten the contrast between the proud tombstones of the men (and the "vaunting" stories that go with these markers) with the next paragraph's discussion of Miss Eckhart's humble grave, a "dark, squat stone" (459).

Footsteps on the sidewalk interrupt her thoughts, which then turn to the various men who have dominated her life: Mr. Nesbitt as her boss; Mr. Mabry as her present "suitor"; and various lovers and would-be lovers from the past. The men seem comically self-important and preoccupied, like the passerby who is "hurrying, bent on something, furious at being in the rain speechless." Mr. Mabry also shows up, so intent on an early-morning errand that he glances at Virgie and looks "right through her" without seeing her. Virgie views her relations with men with considerable wryness, realizing that she has come a long way from the affairs that so scandalized the town: "Mr. Mabry imagined he was coming to her eventually, but was it to him that she had come, backward to protection? She'd have had to come backward, not simply to stand still, to get from the wild spirit of Bucky Moffitt (and where was he? Never under the ground! She smiled, biting the seed in the pepper grass), back past the drunk Simon Sojourner that didn't want her, and on to embarrassed Mr. Mabry, behind whom waited loud, harmless, terrifying Mr. Nesbitt who wanted to stand up for her. She had reached Mr. Mabry but she had passed him and it had not mattered about her direction, since here she was" (459).

Virgie's memory of Mr. Nesbitt is particularly telling: falling under his power is truly falling "backward to protection." At the funeral he was brilliantly characterized as a loud boor showing off his power to a new employee. (He became newly rich plundering the Morgana woods, causing the main road through Morgana to be filled with lumber trucks and many of the large houses in town, like the Morrison's, to take in lumbermen as boarders. For Welty his manners and business practices personify the changes that were "modernizing" the South in the 1930s and 1940s.)[26] Only Bucky Moffitt (also known as Kewpie Moffitt, the sailor she slept with in "June Recital") escapes Virgie's disdain. As the first part of Virgie's meditation closes, we see how both the public history of Morgana and the public history of Virgie herself are dominated and defined by men.

Virgie's thoughts then swerve in a new direction—returning to Miss Eckhart and running over the unknown story of her heroism rather than the public scandal of her failure. Now the "vaunting" heroic adjectives that were previously used to describe men's lives (458) are applied to a woman's life—without, however, turning her into a saint. "Miss Eckhart had had among the pictures from Europe on her walls a certain threatening one. It hung over the dictionary, dark as that book. It showed Perseus with the head of the Medusa.

'The same thing as Siegfried and the Dragon,' Miss Eckhart had occasionally said, as if explaining second-best. Around the picture—which sometimes blindly reflected the window by its darkness—was a frame enameled with flowers, which was always self-evident—Miss Eckhart's pride. In that moment Virgie had shorn it of its frame. The vaunting was what she remembered, that lifted arm." Virgie is at last, in middle age, able to see beyond Miss Eckhart's public arrogance to her inner nobility, the invaluable gift (her own "shower of gold") that she gave her favorite student.

> Because Virgie saw things in their time, like hearing them—and perhaps because she must believe in the Medusa equally with Perseus—she saw the stroke of the sword in three moments, not one. In the three was the damnation—no, only the secret, unhurting because not caring in itself—beyond the beauty and the sword's stroke and the terror lay their existence in time—far out and endless, a constellation which the heart could read over many a night.
>
> Miss Eckhart, whom Virgie had not, after all, hated—had come near to loving, for she had taken Miss Eckhart's hate, and then her love, extracted them, the thorn and then the overflow—had hung the picture on the wall for herself. She had absorbed the hero and the victim. . . . She offered, offered, offered—and when Virgie was young, in the strange wisdom of youth that is accepting of more than is given, she had accepted *the* Beethoven, as with the dragon's blood. That was the gift she had touched with her fingers that had drifted and left her.
>
> In Virgie's reach of memory a melody softly lifted, lifted of itself. Every time Perseus struck off Medusa's head, there was the beat of time, and the melody. Endless the Medusa, and Perseus endless. (460)

If Virgie as a girl could see only her teacher's strangeness and be frightened by her breakdown—her sudden transformation into an enraged, insane Medusa figure—the older Virgie is able to see the Perseus in Miss Eckhart, her heroic struggle to counter both the town's and her own belief that her independence and her passion for music were monstrous. The reference to Perseus here thus must not be misread as a reference to the way in which the town (and Miss Eckhart's own failings) destroy her. Rather, it symbolizes Miss Eckhart's struggle against seeing herself as a Gorgon. If like Clytie she eventually succumbed to that Medusan self-image, she also, Virgie recognizes, struggled until the very end against such a betrayal of herself. Her struggle is the struggle that any independent woman must accept: "Endless the Medusa, and Perseus endless." As shown by earlier passages in the story, particularly Virgie's troubled identification with the town's other martyred women, Maideen Sumrall and Cassie's mother, Virgie knows that she too has to fight seeing herself as a Medusa.

A piece of evidence from another story in The Golden Apples about the pictures on Miss Eckhart's walls is relevant here. In revising "Music from Spain," Welty caused Eugene MacLain to remember not the picture of Perseus but a picture of a sibyl: "The Spaniard with his finger on the page of a book, looking over his shoulder, as did the framed Sibyl on the wall in his father's study—no! then, it was old Miss Eckhart's 'studio'—where he was muscular, but in a storylike way womanly. And the Spaniard with horns on his head—waiting—or advancing! And always the one, dark face, though momently fire from his nostrils brimmed over, with that veritable waste of life!" (408).

Eugene's vision is thoroughly troubled; not only does the sibyl in his vision turn into a dragon, but the figure is frighteningly androgynous, expressing all of his sexual turmoil and guilt. In the process, Eugene apparently conflates the picture of the sibyl with that of Perseus and Medusa, then turns Medusa's head into the head of a dragon. But he precisely captures Virgie's later understanding of what that Medusa's/dragon's head means: it is the self's dark, despairing double, "that veritable waste of life." (Prompted by Miss Eckhart's comment about Wagner's Siegfried, another Perseus figure, Virgie also associates Gorgons and dragons.) Welty implies that Miss Eckhart may have had portraits of both the Perseus/Siegfried figure and the Sibyl on her walls because she wants to link their heroism: they all inspired Miss Eckhart to try to subdue the demons within.

As well as being further proof that we ought to read Miss Eckhart's Perseus as an essentially female rather than male figure, the Sibyl picture Eugene remembers is important for reading the ending of "The Wanderers" for another reason. A sibyl may defeat the Medusa with a pen, after all, as well as a sword. That is, her powers are the powers of reading, writing, and interpreting—in short, of shaping a society's texts. This is why she is portrayed in the above passage from "Music from Spain" and in "Powerhouse" (131) with her "finger on the page of a book." If we read the Medusa allusions in Welty primarily as allusions as to how society may turn independent and passionate women into monsters, then a sibyl's power to defeat the Medusa is essentially a power to rewrite the stereotypes—the cultural texts—by which a woman's proper and improper identities are defined.

Immediately after the passage about the Medusa in Virgie's meditation, she is joined by another woman on her seat under the trees, an old black "thief" with "a red hen under her arm." It is as if Virgie has suddenly become associated in Welty's imagination with the secret survival stratagems of Phoenix Jackson, the indomitable heroine of "A Worn Path." [27] Virgie also finally confronts a vision of herself rather than others as a Medusa, in a sentence that recalls the ending of "Clytie" when Clytie saw her face reflected in the water of the rainbarrel: "she smiled once, seeing before her, screenlike, the hideous and delectable face Mr. King MacLain had made at the funeral" (461). The face that Virgie sees may be male, but it is no less threatening to her; as the narrator comments earlier in the story when King MacLain first made the face during the funeral reception: "he made a hideous face at Virgie, like a silent yell . . . at everything—including death, not leaving it out" (446). If King and Phoenix combat the despair of old age, however, for Virgie such a death's-head grimace contains overwhelming associations with the Medusa's head—and with the early deaths of Miss Eckhart, Mrs. Morrison, and Maideen Sumrall. The terror that she faces is less the terror of old age than the terror of allowing the world to turn her into a monster, a living death's-head. (In such circumstances, it is tempting for a woman to end the struggle entirely; this is why the "featureless" water in which Clytie drowns herself is described as "kind" [90]). Yet Virgie faces the death's-head down—or, rather, like a Perseus or a sibyl she outwits it. What sustains her is simply the presence of the strong woman beside her and the sweet sounds of the rain: "the magical percussion, the world beating in their ears." Unlike Clytie, she is able to believe in that inner music.

A page earlier in the story, the narrator makes one comment about Virgie's strength of character that seems somewhat out of place: the "gift" of music and passion that Virgie had received from Miss Eckhart "had drifted and left her" like her skills at playing (460). We know that Eudora Welty herself more or less agrees with this judgment of the narrator's, for in *One Writer's Beginnings* she qualifies her praise of Virgie by saying that compared to Miss Eckhart she is wasting her gifts (102). I agree with such an assessment to some extent, but it also does not tell the whole story. Virgie may have mostly given up piano playing, but the last pages of "The Wanderers" are filled with references to music, particularly the final sentences. Virgie has made her imagination her instrument. Miss Eckhart's gift has not left her; it has simply become more deeply internalized.

The magisterial last sentence of the story (also added in revision) shows us that Virgie's imagination has attained an unprecedented power, transforming her at once into a Perseus, a musician, a bringer of wealth, and a sibyl: "They heard through the falling rain the running of the horse and bear, the stroke of the leopard, the dragon's crusty slither, and the glimmer and the trumpet of the swan." Every phrase of this final sentence reverberates with associations from the rest of *The Golden Apples*. The words "stroke" and "dragon" recall the combat of Perseus and Siegfried with the beasts, but now these male heroes have been displaced in Virgie's imagination by their female counterparts: true heroism, she has learned, is required even more for a woman's struggle against Medusa than it is for a man's. The allusion to Perseus and the phrase "the running of the horse and bear" recalls Cassie Morrison's meditation about Miss Eckhart in "June Recital," in which she says that such great events seemed "to be by their own nature rising . . . and crossing the sky and setting the way the planets did. Or they were more like whole constellations, turning at their very centers maybe, like Perseus and Orion and Cassiopeia in her Chair and the Big Bear and Little Bear, maybe often upside down, but terribly recognizable. It was not just the sun and moon that traveled" (302).

This passage in turn recalls Virgie's thoughts a few moments before the last sentence of "The Wanderers," when she compares memory's revelations with stargazing: "beyond the beauty and the sword's stroke and the terror lay their existence in time—far out and endless, a constellation which the heart could read over many a night" (460). The story of Miss Eckhart's heroism thus does not reveal its full meanings to Virgie or to the readers of *The Golden Apples* all at once; like a huge constellation rising and setting in the night sky, it must be "read over" as its "runs"—as it gradually reveals and then conceals itself in the context of Welty's volume as a whole. Memory does not just break up a single event into "three moments" (before, during, and after), but it also learns to blend original views and hindsight into a single vision, a cluster of experiences revealing themselves over time like constellations rising and setting with the seasons.

As for the concluding words "the glimmer and the trumpet of the swan," they recall all the images of light that radiate throughout *The Golden Apples* (particularly in "Shower of Gold" and "June Recital"); the allusions to Leda and the swan in "Sir Rabbit"[28]; and the references to music and music teachers throughout Welty's short stories—Miss Eckhart, the lady cornetist in "Beautiful Ohio" and "The Winds," and Powerhouse himself. Since all these figures are associated not merely with music but (in Miss Eckhart's words) with learning to be "heard from in the world" (303), it is not an exaggeration to say that "The Wanderers" ends with Virgie's having a moment of self-knowledge that reveals all her music teacher has taught her. Since the last word of the story is "swan," we can only conclude that Miss Eckhart has now become transformed by Virgie's imagination: no longer the town's ugly duckling, she is reborn radiant and powerful, a sibyl whose story can never be entombed beneath a dark, squat stone.

I say "story" because Virgie unconsciously sees Miss Eckhart as a heroine of language as well as of music. She may not remember that her teacher had a sibyl on her wall (as Eugene MacLain does), but she does link the portrait of Perseus with a huge book that Miss Eckhart owned: "Miss Eckhart had had among the pictures from Europe on her walls a certain threatening one. It hung over the *dictionary*, dark as that book. It showed Perseus" (459; my italics). For all we know, admittedly, Virgie does not include either writing or music in her plans for the future after she leaves Morgana. How we imagine her future is irrelevant: Virgie's epiphany at the end of "The Wanderers" exemplifies what a writer may do. Virgie does not merely recover her own voice, she recovers all the repressed voices and stories within her community. And if she takes on sibylline powers of rewriting the "texts" of her community, she also commits herself to a continual battle with a destructive shadow self, her own guilt and anxiety about desiring such powers.[29]

By choosing to call her story "The Wanderers" rather than "The Hummingbirds," Eudora Welty commemorates not only Virgie's private moment of communion with her mother but also the public implications of her independence. *The Golden Apples* as a whole has frequently focused on histories of male wandering—King MacLain's, his two sons', Loch Morrison's—and indeed it has been plausibly argued by most critics that the main narrative thread connecting all the stories in the volume is the effect King's absence (or sudden reappearance) has on the various protagonists of each story. As Virgie so aptly understands near the end of "The Wanderers," these are not just stories that are told with "vaunting and wandering" but stories that are *about* the vaunting and the wandering of men—their compulsion to believe (as King wants to in "Shower of Gold") that their exploits are eternally the center of attention. During the course of "The Wanderers," Virgie displaces King MacLain as the real wandering hero of *The Golden Apples,* even as in her imagination she transforms Perseus from a male into a female hero. Thus all three major comic stories in *The Golden Apples,* "Shower of Gold," "Moon Lake," and "The Wanderers," trace a pattern whereby male heroism is first mocked and then confronted with particularly feminist forms of wandering and subversion—both in the lives the heroines lead and the stories they imagine and tell. Appropriately, the most heroic moment of wandering in all of *The Golden Apples* occurs when Virgie is sitting still; under a tree in the rain at the end of the volume she trangresses all the stereotypes and histories that have imprisoned the lives of women. Against such revolutionary perspectives, King's aggressive exploits seem rather comically self-deluded, mere shadows of Virgie's adventures in defining her identity.

Virgie's epiphany of course changes nothing. Ran MacLain and Mr. Nesbitt will continue to be respected figures in Morgana, and the old conservatism of Miss Lizzie Stark and Miss Perdita Mayo will undoubtedly be replaced by the new conservatism of women such as Jinny Love. But in "The Wanderers" Virgie has not only made her individual voice heard in Morgana loudly and clearly, but her private moment of self-discovery gives her the energy she needs to cast off the despairing complacency that has quietly been encoiling her. In transforming and appropriating the Perseus myth for women, she has redefined what women's heroism may be.

🔖

> *A woman in the shape of a monster*
> *a monster in the shape of a woman*
> *the skies are full of them*
> . . . .
> *Galaxies of women, there*
> *doing penance for impetuousness*
>   —Adrienne Rich,
>   "Planetarium"

Welty's last volume of stories, *The Bride of the Innisfallen*, contains five stories that may conceivably be called comedies, "Kin," "Ladies in Spring," "Going to Naples," "Circe," and the title story. "Kin," perhaps the best story in the collection, marks a return to the mode of "Petrified Man," although it is less savage in its mockery of modern vulgarity. ("Kin" is also the most important source in Welty's earlier work for her longest novel, *Losing Battles*.) "Ladies in Spring" is a lightweight, gently satiric portrait of Miss Hattie Purcell, the matriarch of a small southern town, who is an authority on sorting mail and rainmaking but is also comically oblivious to a love affair that is going on under her nose. "The Bride of the Innisfallen" celebrates the newly awakened senses and emotions of a wife who has set out on a trip to Ireland without her husband. But none of these stories centers on the comic transformation of a protagonist in the way that "The Wide Net," "The Winds," "Moon Lake," and "The Wanderers" do. To me, "Circe" is the most intriguing story in the group. Certainly it is the story with the greatest "vaunting," the most risks taken.[30]

Welty's decision to recreate Circe directly rather than indirectly (as she represents mythological characters in *The Golden Apples*) is daring; Circe's monologue is made to sound slightly archaic and Homeric: "When you dig the grave for that one, and bury him in the lonely sand by the shadow of your fleeing ship, write on the stone: 'I died of love'" (536). Welty's interest in the heroism of Circe rather than the wanderer Odysseus is certainly consistent with her revision of the story of Perseus in *The Golden Apples*, for Circe has wiles and powers of transformation to rival those of Odysseus. Indeed, the legend of Circe seems a logical one for Welty to turn to, given that the subjects of her feminist comedies are the dangers and potential rewards of unbounded women's power. Of the seven stories in *Innisfallen*, "Circe" is the only one published in the 1940s—in fact, it appeared contemporaneously with "Moon Lake" and "The Wanderers" in 1949 (Vande Kieft [1962] 196). It thus may be taken to be a kind of afterthought, a late (and perhaps overly self-conscious) look at the issues *The Golden Apples* raises.

Miss Eckhart is the only character in *The Golden Apples* who is compared to Circe, when she is at the height of her public power during the June recital (314), but certainly the sibylline powers that Welty's comic heroines dream of recovering are related to Circe's powers of transformation, as are those stories' gentle mockery of men. It is as if after imagining women characters who could define their identities independently from men, Welty needed to ask the question of how a woman should use the new-found power that she had conceived. She approached the question by turning to Circe, the figure in Greek mythology who represents both the triumph and the dangers of women's power.

Welty's portrait of Circe is hardly idealized. She has a wicked, misanthropic sense of humor that enjoys pranks such as feeding her victims pork broth before turning them into swine. The story presents itself as a meditation on the difference between immortal and mortal vision: Circe wonders what it is like to be mortal, to know grief, uncertainty, mystery as well as Odysseus does (533). A draft of the story, called "The Wand," demonstrates that Welty labored at length to find the proper balance between earthy details and Circe's necessary grandeur; Circe's charming imperiousness is present in the draft, but many of the details giving the story its humor and drama were added later. The scene in which Circe finds that her broth has not worked on Odysseus (532), for example, is not dramatized nearly as well in the earlier version, in which Circe shows little surprise or anger. Her eroticism is also not as strong: a crucial phrase suggesting that she strips naked in front of Odysseus, "as I came forth" (532), is not in the draft, and the sentence "I took him by the locks of his beard and hair" (533) is rendered with a cliché: "I flung myself against his senseless breast."

Circe, like Virgie, makes love to her sailor, though in Welty's retelling of this episode from the *Odyssey* it is not clear whether Odysseus is conscious or whether he could even see Circe if he were (532).

Curiously, there are two possible allusions to the Perseus story in this tale, though the myths of Circe and Perseus are not usually linked. Near the end of the tale Circe claims that she would be a wanderer like Odysseus, "if I were not tied to my island" (537). Apparently pregnant from the union with Odysseus with a son who will eventually slay his father—a detail not in the *Odyssey*—Circe has compared herself to Andromeda, who also was tied (literally) to an island. (She also compares herself to Andromeda's mother, Cassiopeia [537].) But she needs no rescuer and feels no grief. Commentators on the story have rightly stressed that for Welty an experience of grief, mystery, and time is necessary for narrative, but in suggesting that Circe is somehow "beyond" narrative, Welty is also implying that by imagining a figure like her we also imagine the limitations of narrative itself—especially, narratives of a woman's romantic enthrallment to a male rescuer. Thus Welty's wry allusions to the difference between Circe and Andromeda: "I stood on my rock and wished for grief. It would not come" (537). Circe's wand gives her a power that is not unlike that of Welty's other women artists—the power to revise narratives, to imagine other endings for them. (Strikingly, Welty does the same with the *Odyssey*, adding the detail of Circe's pregnancy, inventing a new ending for Odysseus' story, and telling the whole Circe episode from a different point of view.) Being immortal, admittedly, Circe can experience little of what Welty's other heroines can, but her woman's power shares with Welty's mortal heroines the powers of revision and transformation.

The other possible allusion to Perseus' story in "Circe" is considerably more problematic. Welty mentions that Circe feeds Odysseus and his sailors her magic potion in "bowls" (531), but in the seduction scene she mysteriously uses the word "glass" in such a way that it seems to mean both a drinking glass and a mirror. It certainly has the same effect on Odysseus that Perseus' mirror had on Medusa: "When I held up the glass he opened his mouth. He fell among the pillows, his still-open eyes two clouds stopped over the sun, and I lifted and kissed his hand" (532). A mirror, a raised hand, a stunned body: the details are uncannily similar to the moment in which Perseus slays Medusa. Yet here gender roles are reversed; the female "slays" the male and violence is transformed into an act of great tenderness, one that belies Circe's reputation as a witch and a monster. It is as if Medusa were to reimagine another completely different version of her meeting with the warrior-hero. This strange subtext in Welty's story—if that is what it is—even more audaciously links Circe with the powers of revision than the other allusions to Greek myths in the story, and it casts her as the most extreme—indeed, immortal and inhuman—example of the freedom from the inherited bonds of male-centered narrative that all of Welty's comic heroines aspire to. Read in this light, "Circe" appears to be a parable in which Welty posed for herself moral dilemmas about the uses and abuses of women's power.

Perhaps the most fascinating detail in the entire story is one of its original titles, "Put Me in the Sky!" (Vande Kieft [1962] 196). This makes the story a kind of coda to Virgie's meditation at the end of "The Wanderers," comparing women's stories and constellations in the sky. Although the story of Miss Eckhart's heroism may be likened to a constellation, Virgie realizes, it is also an untold story, a constellation that has not yet been named. There is only one list of constellations in The Golden Apples, Cassie's list in "June Recital" (302), and it contains only one woman, Cassiopeia, whereas several male heroes' names are listed, including Perseus. Moreover, Cassiopeia is hardly as heroic a figure as Perseus, at least in Welty's mind; in "Circe," when this constellation is mentioned again, Cassiopeia is described as being totally passive: "I looked up at Cassiopeia, who sits there and needs nothing, pale in her chair in the stream of heaven" (536). Welty's original title, "Put Me in the Sky!" thus voices the quiet frustration that Virgie experiences at the end of "The Wanderers" and that the contemporary poet Adrienne Rich, among many, has expressed: women's stories have not yet been fully told. Perseus is there, but where is Medusa, his female victim? And where are constellations—and the narratives linked to them—celebrating women as victors rather than as victims?

"Circe" is admittedly a better title for the story, because "Put Me in the Sky!" would have been uncharacteristically polemical for Welty—no other story in The Collected Stories has a title with an exclamation point. Yet this suppressed title may also be taken to be the hidden credo—the secret "vaunting"—of Welty's comedies of women's rebirth.

🐚

When *The Collected Stories* is read as a whole, Eudora Welty's women's comedies provide a special and invaluable perspective on the shape of her career. The early stories, we notice, are dominated by threatening matriarchal figures—older sisters like Octavia and repressive mother figures such as the "ladies" in "Petrified Man" and "Lily Daw and the Three Ladies." Many of the stories that are told using the point of view of a young girl (especially "A Visit of Charity" and "A Memory") verge on being matriphobic. "A Memory," for example, is usually discussed as a portrait of the artist as a young girl, but I find it much more strikingly a story about a girl's anorexic-like horror at older women's bodies: "the fat woman . . . bent over and in a condescending way pulled down the front of her bathing suit, turning it outward, so that lumps of mashed and folded sand came out. I felt a peak of horror" (79). In other stories, especially "A Curtain of Green," "Old Mr. Marblehall," and "Clytie," the narrative voice seems divided between supporting and censuring the female characters' angry rebellion against social restrictions: "Old Mr. Marblehall" buries the stories of Mrs. Marblehall and Mrs. Bird beneath the story of their husband, and in different ways both "A Curtain of Green" and "Clytie" punish the heroines as the stories seek closure. In short, anger in the narrative voice at social restrictions to some degree becomes converted into anger at the figures who challenge those restrictions. The greater the anger (as in "Clytie"), the greater the repression that follows, as if in guilty compensation and fear. Even more deeply sublimated than the heroine's anger is the *narrator's* anger at the society that has produced the social restrictions that drive the stories and make victims of their leading women characters. Using Welty's own vocabulary in *One Writer's Beginnings* to describe the way stories may hold secrets within secrets (17), we may speak of the apparent misogyny of stories like "Clytie" or "A Visit of Charity" as the first "secret" of their narratives and those stories' feminist anger as their even more deeply hidden secret, the one that when it is named will be even more startling to its hearers than the first.

Such a perspective gives special insight into Welty's comment else-where in *One Writer's Beginnings* that she associates the desire to write with the mixture of guilt and pleasure she felt whenever she acted independently in childhood. The guilt she describes, crucially, is in-separable from the fact that she is a woman. Her dilemma first sur-faced, she tells us, when her mother gave her gifts.

> When my mother would tell me that she wanted me to have some-thing because she as a child had never had it, I wanted, or I partly wanted, to give it back. All my life I continued to feel that bliss for me would have to imply my mother's deprivation or sacrifice. . . .
>
> In the Century [movie theater]'s first-row balcony, where their seats always were, I'd be sitting beside my father at this hour beyond my bedtime carried totally away by the performance, and then suddenly the thought of my mother staying home with my sleeping younger brothers, missing the spectacle at this moment before my eyes, and doing without all the excitement and wonder that filled my being, would arrest me and I could hardly bear my pleasure for my guilt.
>
> There is no wonder that a passion for independence sprang up in me at the earliest age. It took me a long time to manage the independence, for I loved those who protected me—and I wanted inevitably to protect them back. I have never managed to handle the guilt. In the act and the course of writing stories, these are two of the springs, one bright, one dark, that feed the stream. (19–20)

All children may feel such a passion for independence and guilt for indulging that passion, but in this case the fact that Welty is female complicates her feelings in a way that would not be so if she were male. She feels guilty not merely for acting independently (as any child might) but also because her most intense pleasure at the movies somehow breaks an unspoken rule she has learned—women are sup-posed to be self-sacrificing, not self-involved. There was no question of her father's not going to the show; it was her mother's duty to deprive herself for her child. If we extend the meaning of Welty's references to "pleasure" and "passion" and "independence" to include other episodes in her life and other arts than the movies, then we must conclude that writing for Welty also involves a refusal to deprive oneself of pleasure, passion, and the powers that the imagination may bestow.

This credo may seem at odds with the plots of stories like "Clytie" or "A Curtain of Green" (not to mention "Petrified Man" or "June Recital"), but it really is not. The learned guilt that Welty says she experienced when she felt most deeply the pleasures of art is quite analogous to the guilt that characters like Clytie or Mrs. Larkin feel (or the narratives express), except that in the case of Welty's fictional narratives the women characters' guilt is much more strongly laced with anger and social criticism. Not surprisingly, the fields through which Welty's memory ambles in the pastoral *One Writer's Beginnings* seem marked by more bright springs than dark ones. The opposite is true of her first volume of stories, which is rarely pastoral, despite its title.

The buried anger against matriarchal figures in Welty's early stories, furthermore, must *not* be read simplistically and autobiographically, as a veiled attack on her own mother and the paradox of having literary ambitions while returning to live in her parents' house, as Welty did after leaving New York City in 1931. (After her father's death in 1931, she lived with and cared for her mother until 1966, the year of her mother's death.) Welty has eloquently expressed in *One Writer's Beginnings* how deeply she loved her parents and how they fostered her desire to be a writer, first by teaching her to love literature and later by supporting her education, buying her a Smith Corona portable, and countless other ways. She also has stressed that her mother and her mother's family were especially good storytellers, and that she feels that much of her knack for telling stories comes from her (53). She also says in no uncertain terms that her "chief inheritance" from her mother was her "fierce independence" (60). The repressive female figures in the early stories should be seen as part of Welty's unfolding meditation on the deprivations and sacrifices that are required of women and the price their psyches must pay for such repressions. Welty's petrified women are made monstrous, not born so; it is not nature but culture that enrages a Mrs. Larkin in "A Curtain of Green" or a Miss Eckhart in "June Recital." The guilt Welty says helps feed the stream of all her stories is thus not guilt for being angry with her parents but guilt for desiring the "unladylike," sibylline powers that her imagination holds. For this reason, Welty notes in *One Writer's Beginnings* that her mother well knew the problems her independent-minded daughter would face growing up: "that independent spirit . . . was what she so agonizingly tried to protect me from, in effect to warn me against. . . . To grow up is to fight for it, to grow old is to lose it after having possessed it" (60).

For this reason, surely, Welty made the point in *One Writer's Beginnings* that in making Miss Eckhart "out of my most inward and most deeply feeling self, I would say I have found my voice in my fiction" (101). This comment has a special resonance for readers who examine Welty's manuscripts. At the heart of "June Recital" Miss Eckhart is shown working with texts: "from her gestures of eating crumbs or pulling bits of fluff from her bosom, Loch recognized that mother-habit: she had pins there. She pinned long strips of the newspaper together, first tearing them carefully and evenly as a school teacher. She made ribbons of newspaper and was hanging them all over the parlor, starting with the piano, where she weighted down the ends with a statue" (282).

Welty also used pins with her manuscripts, precisely pricking them to the corners of cut pages to affix new typescript additions to older pages (Prenshaw, *Conversations* 89, 244–45). In Welty's case, of course, her use of pins represents mastery, not madness, but the parallels and contrasts between Miss Eckhart and her creator are haunting—mute testimony to the psychic risks Welty knew she was taking in her "most inward and most deeply feeling self" with her visionary art and her aspirations for sibylline powers. Paradoxically, her art became a Persean mirror that allowed her safely to diagnose the forces that destroyed Miss Eckhart and to envision alternatives.

In Welty's tragic stories from "Keela, the Outcast Indian Maiden" to "The Demonstrators," a stereotype has been imposed on a human being: the grotesque Indian costume on Lee Roy; the mask of "beauty" on Mrs. Fletcher; the mask of a madwoman on Clytie and Miss Eckhart; the masks of either a passive mother or a grotesque monster on the women in Ran and Eugene MacLain's stories; a businessman's clichés about a woman having an affair in "No Place for You, My Love"; and racist slurs on blacks in "The Demonstrators" and, in particular, "Where Is the Voice Coming From?" In stories told in the third person, such as "Petrified Man" or "The Demonstrators," the narrator obviously is not as implicated as an "unreliable" narrator may be in a guilty monologue such as Ran's. In those stories the narrator's voice is often dominated by a "text" or a series of stereotypes that are analogous in a way to how poor Steve the carnival barker in "Keela" cannot forgive himself for the lies he has unwittingly told. In "The Demonstrators" this is done in a fairly straightforward manner, by having a large chunk of the final pages of the narration be devoted to an obviously distorted newspaper account of the story's events. In "Petrified Man," or "June Recital," it is done more subtly. The women at the beauty parlor and Cassie putting on make-up in her room are shown to be so strongly influenced by stereotypes of feminine beauty that they largely misread the meaning of the tragic events that are occurring before their eyes. Such stereotypes so dominate the point of view of both stories that the stories' "omniscient" narrators are really that in name only. (Needless to say, Cassie's misreading of the story's events is neither so complete nor so blameworthy as Mrs. Fletcher's and Leota's.) The "texts" that influence these stories' narratives may not be an actual piece of writing, as the text in "Keela" was, but they are just as powerfully coercive.

As "Keela" demonstrates, however, such stereotypes cannot completely subdue their material, nor can the storyteller entirely neutralize his or her feelings of guilt for employing them. Like Steve's search for an audience or Mrs. Fletcher's trips to the beauty parlor, Welty's guilty narrators are doomed forever to retell their unconvincing stories—forever unconsciously seeking to absolve in the telling the guilt that they feel. In her tragic (or tragicomic) stories the texts that so oppress the teller and the tale are never overthrown, and the stories are forced to be endlessly retold: Steve, Sister, Ran, Eugene, and the unnamed murderer in "Where Is the Voice Coming From?" can never stop talking. Their stories' guilty subtexts can neither be successfully repressed nor successfully liberated, and the contradictions between the "layers" of the narrative fester like an uncleansed wound. All of Welty's tragedies ask the terrifying question, "Where is the voice coming from?" Yet they can never answer the question—and quiet the voice—because they can never uncover the sources of the guilt that drives their characters to talk. The essence of tragedy in Eudora Welty's short stories is a lonely, endless cry of terror and anger—a cry that calls and calls and is never answered.

Welty's comedies of rebirth from "A Piece of News" to "The Wanderers" and beyond, in contrast, are characterized by either indirect or direct acts of comic release: the dominating "text" is overthrown or temporarily incapacitated by the story's subtext, its revolutionary hidden meanings. Ruby Fisher retains her private identity, despite her husband's "correction" of her; Powerhouse changes the way his audience "reads" him; Hazel Jamieson writes a suicide note, hides, and then returns to prove to her husband that his nightmares are groundless; and the heroines in Welty's mature women's comedies overturn stereotypes and inspire themselves and sometimes others to find a "vaunting and a wandering" that they can call their own. Rather than ending in spiritual isolation, Welty's comic heroes and heroines (even if physically alone) conclude their stories united with their actual or imagined audience. Hence Hazel may lead William Wallace to bed, Mrs. Rainey regale her listener on her front porch, and Virgie and the anonymous black woman at the end of "The Wanderers" sit "alone and together" (461) listening to the sounds of the morning rain. (Circe is the exception that proves the rule.)

The year Welty published *The Robber Bridegroom*, "The Wide Net," and "The Winds," 1942, thus emerges as the pivotal point in her career for her portrayal of male and female characters. *The Wide Net*, published the next year, contains several male characters who may be called either gods of sexual initiation or rapists, depending upon a reader's interpretation—most notably the patrician satyr Mr. Don McInnis in "Asphodel" and Billy Floyd in "At the Landing." The most complex male characters of Welty's fiction later in the decade, George Fairchild and King MacLain, may perhaps be thought of as volatile mixtures of the bouyancy of Jamie Lockhart, Cash, and William Wallace Jamieson with the neuroses of characters like Howard, Mr. Marblehall, and Tom Harris in *A Curtain of Green* and Lorenzo Dow in *The Wide Net*. Indeed, to a degree unprecedented in Welty's work, King so absorbs and transforms all of the previous male character types in Welty's fiction that it is impossible to categorize him. In turn, we may use King's character as a benchmark to measure that of other male characters in *The Golden Apples* and later fiction. King's psychoses are bequeathed, unfortunately, to his twin sons, whereas his sexual energy and independent thinking are most marked in two female characters, Easter and Virgie Rainey, whom he may have fathered. Daniel Ponder of *The Ponder Heart* is closest to King of all Welty's male characters in the 1950s, though if Daniel has King's exuberant generosity he seems somewhat stripped of his sexual energy.[31] Similarly, we may say that Jack Renfro in *Losing Battles* represents a later example of a "cure" for King's problems that keeps all of his best elements. Uncle Nathan Beecham in *Losing Battles* and the unnamed narrator in "Where Is the Voice Coming From?" are the most intriguing portraits in Welty's later fiction of the psychopathology of male repression first diagnosed in *A Curtain of Green* and depicted more fully in *The Golden Apples*.

As far as the evolution of Welty's portraits of women are concerned, repressive women characters play a much more minor role in Welty's short fiction after 1942. In fact, Salome in *The Robber Bridegroom* so embodies and parodies this sort of figure (who as we shall see in the next chapter is also a staple of fairy tales and popular women's fiction) that she may represent a kind of exorcism of the power such figures held over Welty's imagination in *A Curtain of Green*. After that book these figures are always evaluated in a more controlled and ironic way, whether they be the aunts in *Delta Wedding* and *Losing Battles* or figures like Miss Eckhart's mother or Miss Lizzie Stark in *The Golden Apples*. These repressive and often older women are also more frequently balanced with other female characters who become empowering role models in the manner of the woman musician in "The Winds."

The next important step that Welty took in portraying such a positive female figure after 1942 was of course *Delta Wedding*, in which we find the story of a girl who loses her mother and is taken into the Fairchild family by her Aunt Ellen. The most positively portrayed maternal presence in Welty's fiction up until that time, Ellen Fairchild best represents Welty's shift of focus in the early and mid-1940s from repressive relations among women to nurturing and empowering ones. There are no women like Ellen Fairchild or the cornet player in *A Curtain of Green*, though we can perhaps see elements of them in Phoenix Jackson. To some degree, these new women are heroines of the maternal and are associated with the nurturing forces of nature, but these women are associated with culture as well, art and music along with the skills of mothering. As has been mentioned previously, Ellen Fairchild is once described as having taught her older children to play the piano (110), and several later scenes involving the powers of music (especially those on pages 156 and 176) anticipate "June Recital," the next work of fiction that Welty wrote. Somewhat muted in *Delta Wedding*, Welty's interest in the role of women artists in southern culture as role models for young girls became a central theme of *The Golden Apples*.

Comparing *Delta Wedding* and Welty's later long fiction allows further insights on Welty's changing portraiture of women characters. Welty's first long narrative, *The Robber Bridegroom*, is a comic roustabout of a tall tale that stands with "Asphodel," "The Wide Net," "At the Landing," and "The Winds" in importance for the ways in which it parodies stereotypes from fairy tales and women's sentimental fiction. *The Ponder Heart* (1954) is a superb adaptation to a longer narrative of the comic woman's monologue explored in stories like "Why I Live at the P.O." and "Petrified Man," and like those earlier narratives it is essentially a comedy of rigidity whose heroine never changes. *Delta Wedding* and *Losing Battles* are less easily categorized. Both novels center on a family reunion (the former for a wedding; the latter for a birthday and a return from prison). Both are told in highly episodic ways, focusing on the families' successive retellings of stories central to their identity as families, along with their absorption of new events occurring during the reunion into the families' sprawling chronicles of themselves. *Losing Battles* retains some of the densely metaphorical and elliptical description of the earlier work, but Welty's decision to tell the story almost entirely from the "outside," using dialogue, seems correct for such an epic conception of domestic history where storytelling and story revision are oral, collective, contentious, and continual.

Most important, perhaps, for a discussion of how Welty's comedy evolved is the fact that although both *Delta Wedding* and *Losing Battles* feature many outsiders both male and female who challenge the values of the dominant families, the handling of the most important female outsider figures, Robbie Reid and Gloria Renfro, respectively, is quite different. Each women is married to the central male figure in the family at the heart of the novel, the Fairchilds and the Renfros. Robbie Reid and her mother were aspiring (but failed) schoolteachers (*Delta Wedding* 160), while Gloria and her mentor Miss Julia Mortimer in *Losing Battles* have between them tried to educate just about every other character in the book. Instead of being mother and daughter like Robbie and her mother, Miss Julia Mortimer and Gloria are more properly understood to be cultural mentor and initiate, somewhat like Miss Eckhart and Virgie Rainey: their relationship is not maternal as much as it is sibylline.

The clearest difference between the role played by female outsiders in *Delta Wedding* and *Losing Battles* comes, however, when the characters of Robbie Reid and Gloria Renfro are compared. Gloria's (and Jack Renfro's) restlessness with the Renfro/Beecham clan in *Losing Battles* is cast largely as an irreconcilable conflict between two principles of human identity—the one, in Ruth Vande Kieft's words, a commitment to "progress" and "change" in history (represented by the schoolteachers and, in a different way, by Jack); the other, an expression of the Renfros' and Beecham's "mythical or archetypal mode of existence, which is cyclical and repetitive" (156). To some extent this eternal conflict is represented as well in *Delta Wedding* between the principal family and a married couple, George Fairchild and Robbie Reid, but Robbie's rebellion against her husband's family is portrayed as being considerably more petty and self-deluded than Gloria's, and her criticism of the Fairchilds is hardly sanctioned by her husband, as Gloria's is. Since *The Golden Apples* was published between *Delta Wedding* and *Losing Battles* and is the volume most concerned with the relations between women mentors and their students, it should be credited as the work that spurred Welty to reconceive the role such female schoolteacher figures and quester figures could play in her long fiction. Such an analysis of Welty's portraits of women also demonstrates how her evolution as an artist occurred at a much more drawn-out pace with her long fiction than with her short stories, where the crucial changes occurred with meteoric intensity between 1939 and 1949.

With *The Optimist's Daughter* (1972) Welty achieves her most truly tragicomic work, as Reynolds Price first pointed out when it was published ("The Onlooker Smiling" 76). Rigid and rootless characters like Fay are treated much more sympathetically than their predecessors were in "Petrified Man," though their faults—and those of the "modern" age that created them—are unsparingly exposed. Furthermore, this repressive figure is also for the first time in Welty's fiction a character younger than the heroine rather than older—an ironic twist of the well-used formula of repressive stepmother and rebellious daughter. Judge McKelva's mixture of wisdom and self-delusion is as tied to the needs of his male ego as that of earlier characters like King MacLain, but he never verges on becoming a satyr or a demon or a magician, as King did; such archetypal categories seem much too general to do justice to Welty's subtly shaded portrait of him. Laurel for her part may be the most mature and successful heroine in all of Welty's fiction, the crowning depiction of what the comic powers of transformation may create. Yet her story in the ironically titled *The Optimist's Daughter* is the story of facing limits, not creating unbounded opportunity. The heroine (whose name before marriage, Laurel McKelva, interestingly echoes Laura McRaven's in *Delta Wedding*) is the familiar female outsider figure, but ironically she feels that she has been orphaned from her *own* family with her mother's death and her father's remarriage to Fay. Laurel has a successful career and a confident, well-balanced, middle-aged adult identity that none of her predecessors possessed, although Gloria (and probably Virgie) show some promise of developing such a self. Laurel returns to her family because of an illness and then a death rather than for a marriage or a birthday, and except for Laurel's confident identity as a career woman in Chicago and a superb passage describing her short "morning" life with a husband who would be killed in World War II (186), this heroine's history is a Chekhovian tale of the recovery of dignity in the face of tragic loss—of Laurel's mourning rather than Laura's morning world. To leaven the book's somber truths, Welty periodically returns to the satiric mode initiated with *A Curtain of Green*, but the energy that anger provides in the later text is bittersweet rather than acidic.

Several comments of Welty's in *One Writer's Beginnings* about her *Collected Stories* are especially telling on the matter of transformative role models for women in her fiction: "As certain as I was of wanting to be a writer, I was certain of not wanting to be a teacher. I lacked the instructing turn of mind, the selflessness, the patience for teaching, and I had the unreasoning feeling that I'd be trapped. The odd

thing is that when I did come to write my stories, the longest list of
my characters turns out to be schoolteachers. They are to a great extent my heroines" (82). Curiously, this statement is a slight misre-
membering of her short stories, though not of her novels. There are
strictly speaking only two characters in the *Collected Stories* who are
schoolteachers, and both are minor figures: Miss Parnell Moody in
"Moon Lake" and Miss Pruitt in "Ladies in Spring." Welty's short
stories simply do not abound with Miss Jean Brodies, but music teachers and musicians *are* prominent in the short stories. Similarly, in the
novels the central female character in *Delta Wedding*, Ellen Fairchild,
taught music to her older children, and Gloria Renfro's and Julia Mortimer's duties as schoolteachers in *Losing Battles* included the teaching
of music, especially singing. As Welty says later in *One Writer's Beginnings*, Miss Eckhart "derived from what I already knew for myself,
even felt I had always known. What I put into her is my passion for
my own life work, my own art. Exposing yourself to risk is a truth Miss
Eckhart and I have in common. What animates and possesses me is
what drives Miss Eckhart, the love of her art and the love of giving it,
the desire to give it until there is no more left" (101). Moreover, in
One Writer's Beginnings Welty also notes in passing that her mother
played the cornet as a child—like the woman musician in "The
Winds"! Her mother's father "sent off for the instruments, got together a band, and proceeded to teach [the members of the family] to
play in concert, lined up on the courthouse lawn: he had a strong
need of music. His children had an instrument to play too: he assigned
my mother the cornet" (50). In fact, when Welty revised "Beautiful
Ohio" to turn it into "The Winds" she carefully changed the story to
have the woman play a cornet, not a trumpet. By equating music
teachers and school teachers Welty implies that both kinds of teachers
may teach their students what Miss Eckhart did: to read, revise, and
invent, not merely perform scores that others have written.

By stressing the musicians' roles as teachers in her stories, furthermore, Welty quite rightly recognizes the revolutionary and sibylline
powers she has bestowed on the heroines of her women's comedies.
Indeed, the single most notable feature of Welty's comic short fiction
as it evolves is the emergence of female characters who successfully
challenge the established order after learning to do so from older fe-

male mentors. Except for the absence of such mentor figures, the primary elements necessary to create such a new form of comedy were present in the two crucial comic pieces Welty wrote in 1941, "Why I Live at the P.O." and "*Women!! Make Turban in Own Home!*"

With the exception of Welty's praise of Willa Cather and Katherine Anne Porter, she has suggested that she had to look outside of the United States for female role models for her art. (Male mentors, however, were another matter; she found many in the United States, especially Twain and Faulkner.) Welty's disdain for earlier American women's fiction such as Augusta Evans Wilson's *St. Elmo* (1867) is clearly a disdain for what she takes to be badly written fiction that promotes mindless conformity (*One Writer's Beginnings* 7; Prenshaw, *Conversations* 8). Readers who have attended to the crucial role played by women teachers and artists in Welty's fiction, however, have a right to wonder whether the question of Welty's relation to her female American predecessors may be more complex than this. Are there precedents in earlier American women's fiction for the comedy and the sibylline scenes of instruction that so mark Welty's imagination? This is a provocative and difficult question, and it deserves a chapter to itself.

CHAPTER 4

Sibyls

Eudora Welty and American Women's Literature

"Not to get married is to confess one's self simply a — a Gorgon."
— Grace Elizabeth King
Monsieur Motte

she carries a book but it is not
the tome of the ancient wisdom,

the pages, I imagine, are the blank
pages
of the unwritten volume of the new;

. . . .

but she is not shut up in a cave
like a Sibyl; she is not

imprisoned in leaden bars
in a coloured window;

she is Psyche, the butterfly,
out of the cocoon.

—H.D.,
Trilogy

In *One Writer's Beginnings* Eudora Welty refers selectively to American writers or books. Several of the authors she mentions, Hawthorne, Twain, and Faulkner, come as no surprise, nor does her praise of them. When she mentions two sentimental romance novels by American women writers, however, her manner is markedly different, gently mocking rather than commendatory. The first mention involves a favorite quotation of her mother's: "*St. Elmo* was not in our house; I saw it often in other houses. This wildly popular Southern novel is where all the Edna Earles in our population started coming from. They're all named for the heroine, who succeeded in bringing a dissolute, sinning roué and atheist of a lover (St. Elmo) to his knees. My mother was able to forgo it. But she remembered the classic advice given to rose growers on how to water their bushes long enough: 'Take a chair and St. Elmo'" (7). The second comment was prompted by the young Eudora Welty's receiving her first library card. "'Eudora is nine years old and has my permission to read any book she wants from the shelves, children or adult,' Mother said. 'With the exception of *Elsie Dinsmore*,' she added. Later she explained to me that she'd made this rule because Elsie the heroine, being made by her father to practice too long and hard at the piano, fainted and fell off the piano stool. 'You're too impressionable, dear,' she told me. 'You'd read that and the very first thing you'd do, you'd fall off the piano stool'" (29).

Further evidence for Welty's disdain for the sentimental romance may be found in her story "Moon Lake" (351), in which several girls comically try without success to read the best-selling romance *The Re-Creation of Brian Kent* (1919) by Harold Bell Wright, in which Kent is the novel's Byronic figure who needs reforming; and in her novel *The Ponder Heart* (1954), in which Welty wryly named the delightfully vulgar narrator after the pure and formal heroine of *St. Elmo*, a novel she freely confesses she has never read.[1]

Elsie Dinsmore (1867) was the first in a series of books written by Martha Finley featuring the heroine named in the title. It is instructive to compare Welty's mother's description of the piano-stool episode with that of a contemporary critic, Nina Baym: "In the same year Evans [Wilson] published *St. Elmo*, Martha Finley published the first Elsie Dinsmore book, where little Elsie, resisting her father's command to sing for his guests on Sunday, falls off the piano stool and gashes her forehead, taking the strategy of self-abuse for the purposes of manipulating others further than it had been taken before, and more crudely" (296). Baym's comment on *St. Elmo* is also worth comparing with Welty's. Baym argues that *St. Elmo* is unusual for nineteenth-century American women's fiction in that it emphasizes the heroine's reform of a dangerous rake. Almost no marriages in the fiction, Baym claims,

> represent rescues of the man by the heroine. A woman will accept her obligation to save an errant father or brother, but she does not solicit

like opportunities among the male population at large. She looks to
marry a man who is strong, stable, and safe. She is canny in her judgment of men, and generally immune to the appeal of a dissolute
suitor. . . . The most famous confrontation of this sort occurs in *St.
Elmo*, where Edna Earl steadfastly withstands the appeal of an irresis-
tible blackguard and tells him to go away and save himself. In its employment of a rake hero, however, *St. Elmo* is itself a rarity. The conventional hero of woman's fiction is solid, ethical, generous, frank,
hard-working, energetic, an admirer and respecter of women who likes
the heroine as much or more than he lusts for her. . . . Although the
authors of woman's fiction all accepted certain fundamental differences between the sexes as reason for differences in social roles, they
were idealizing, in their marriage patterns, something like a union of
equals. (41)

Together, these paired comments well represent the differing interpretations that recent readers have given of popular nineteenth- and
twentieth-century American women's fiction. Welty's mother remembers Elsie's suffering because of patriarchal pressure, and Baym emphasizes the irony that acts of resistance against others in these texts may
turn into self-defeating acts of self-mutilation. But both imply that
issues involving victimization are at the heart of *Elsie Dinsmore*, and
indeed it can be said to be a feature uniting *all* American fiction written by women during the nineteenth century.

It is with these women's comments on *St. Elmo*, however, that
their different premises reveal themselves most strikingly. Welty and
her mother criticize *St. Elmo* in a way that is thoroughly congruent
with much recent feminist criticism, particularly work by Ann Douglas, Alfred Habegger, Rachel Blau DuPlessis, and Thelma Shinn.
These critics argue that whatever forms of resistance may be present
within these romance texts—and they emphasize that these works
display many, especially via subplots and figures of speech—they are
finally undercut by the form's reliance on the proper ending of either
marriage or death for the heroine. As DuPlessis stresses, there is a
fundamental contradiction in these bildungsroman novels between
the *bildung* chronicling the heroine's quest to find a productive place
in society and the *roman* or romance plot defining that quest primarily
in terms of a successful marriage. In the end, the heroine's quest must

be "set aside or repressed, whether by marriage or by death" (3–4); if the heroine behaves properly, she is rewarded with marriage; if she has been too rebellious, death is the only "proper" ending.

Such readings argue that although Edna Earl may seem all-powerful near the end of *St. Elmo* as she brings the hero-villain to his knees, that power is actually an illusion, since the heroine is merely "reforming" her husband into an acceptance of the new pieties of Victorian America, with their emphasis on separate men's and women's spheres, the home and the workplace, where the woman's sphere of power is completely circumscribed by the man's. What began as an attempt by women writers to create a heroine who could resist the male seducer figures in popular novels based on Richardson's *Pamela* and *Clarissa* ended, these critics argue, with heroines whose values ultimately sanction patriarchal power. Welty's dry skepticism regarding the illusions of women's power in a book like *St. Elmo* invigorates much recent feminist commentary as well. Critics who attack the influence of women's romances concede that these novels were sometimes agents of social change, but they argue that the change they promoted merely exchanged one outdated form of patriarchal power that was essentially pre-industrial and aristocratic for a new one that was Victorian and capitalist.

Nina Baym, Annette Kolodny, Jane Tompkins, Cathy Davidson, Janice Radway, and others, in contrast, argue that to place so much weight on the endings of these books is to confuse the point, which is that the majority of these novels offer many instances of critiquing stereotypes and revising cultural scripts regarding proper women's behavior, and that rather than merely being agents for the new doctrine of the "woman's sphere" in a newly industrializing society such fiction actively taught its readers to question the dictates of their culture and imagine alternatives.[2]

It is overly simplistic, of course, to divide recent criticism on nineteenth-century American women's fiction into the schools of Ann Douglas and Nina Baym, the former more or less attacking the work and the latter defending it. Both Baym and Douglas are eloquent in discussing alternative readings of the cultural phenomena they analyze and they are able to show how both individual novels and the trend of women's fiction writing as a whole are divided on the matter of social and literary innovation, so it is impossible to label these novels as being either "progressive" or "regressive." Similarly, critics like Tompkins or DuPlessis who have followed the ground-breaking books of Baym and Douglas do not merely align themselves with one or the other, and they carry forward the project of attending to the often contradictory messages these works of fiction give us. Nevertheless, differences and divisions are present, and the conclusions of Ann Douglas can hardly be easily reconciled with those of Cathy Davidson, for example.

Such disagreement over how to interpret nineteenth-century American women's fiction comes with a rising crest of renewed interest in that fiction, which was read avidly by hundreds of thousands of readers (mostly women) in the nineteenth century and then fell into neglect until the increase in women writing literary history after the 1960s spurred renewed interest in it. Despite Welty's implication in *One Writer's Beginnings* that none of her *own* beginnings can be found in nineteenth-century American women's fiction, her stories in fact give us an invaluable entry into both that literature and its recent commentary. For in trying to come to terms with her heritage as an American woman writer, Welty's stories struggle with the same difficulties contemporary criticism confronts in interpreting the meaning and value of that heritage. Welty's stories assay the social and artistic values that heritage bequeathed later women writers. In the process, her stories may in fact suggest one way to resolve the divisions in current study of nineteenth-century American women's fiction.

This struggle with how to assess the cultural work performed by earlier American women's fiction is made all the more acute by the fact that many of the most popular writers of nineteenth-century sentimental romances in the United States, like Welty, were southern, including the author of *St. Elmo*. Baym indeed argues convincingly that that there is a distinctly southern style in nineteenth-century American women's fiction, and that rather than being conservative it was the most experimental and iconoclastic:

> In style, plotting, and attitudes Evans [Wilson] brought together the two divergent schools of woman's fiction: the prudent, cautious, measured writing of the northerners Warner and Cummings, with its correlative sense of limiting circumstances, its emphasis on self-control,

calculation, and safety; and the open-ended, flamboyant, colorful work of southern writers like Southworth and Holmes, who emphasized experiment, risk, and adventure. . . . Evans endows her heroines with Byronic qualities usually reserved for the lady villains of melodrama and romance: alienation, tempestuousness, pride, vengefulness. Yet at the same time her heroines are moral, virtuous, and pious. These yokings create a kind of unquietness of tone which makes Evans' novels intense, turbulent, and exciting . . . . (279)

In fact, far from being restricted to a single-minded focus on the marriage ceremony as the only proper goal for the heroine, such fiction is remarkable for the extensive variety of plots and the many heroines it deploys. A novel like E. D. E. N. Southworth's *The Mother-in-Law* (1851) features seven major female characters and seems to aspire to be exhaustive in its catalog not of the whaling industry but of the imaginable possible identities a woman might have. Aside from the title character in *The Mother-in-Law*, there are, Baym tells us, "six varieties of heroine": "her daughter, Louise, a totally passive and compliant person, the end product of a ferociously repressive education; Zoe, a foundling and a 'dove,' that is, a gentle, domestic woman; Anne, a noble, intellectual mulatto slave; Susan, her mistress, a serene, self-dependent, benevolent person; Brittania O'Riley, Louise's governess, a self-centered, luxury-loving, high-spirited, energetic woman; and finally Gertrude Lion, a nordic beauty who is six feet tall, rides, hunts, eats roots and berries, cannot bear to be indoors, and generally upsets every notion on conventional femininity while remaining a woman with the 'majesty of Juno and the freedom of Diana' " (120).

Through the 1970s and 1980s, Welty criticism by and large has been much more skeptical about the value of nineteenth-century American women's fiction than Baym, Tompkins, Davidson, and others. Following Welty's lead, it has argued that if nineteenth-century American women had any "influence" on her it was mostly by giving her endless examples of what *not* to do in fiction. The two critics who have written most extensively on the matter, Albert Devlin and Jennifer Lynn Randisi, have stressed Welty's independence from the literary forms she inherited, particularly those two most favored by southern writers, the "plantation" novel and the sentimental romance. Devlin has shown how thoroughly Welty's novel *Delta Wedding* critiques the plantation novel tradition—a tradition formed predominately by male rather than female authors, incidentally. Randisi caustically sums up her sense of Welty's attitude toward the romance tradition in her book's title: *A Tissue of Lies: Eudora Welty and the Southern Romance.* Certainly both these readings of Welty's work (which primarily focus on her novels) are persuasive, for the independent and vigorous way in which Welty borrows from and then revises the plantation novel is clear. Welty's commentators have argued that her liberating models for women writers were different: Sarah Orne Jewett, Willa Cather, Jane Austen, Virginia Woolf, and Elizabeth Bowen, for example.

The importance of these writers to Welty is indisputable. Yet a reader who has read Welty's stories and then read representative works by nineteenth-century women writers such as Southworth, Stowe, Chesebro', Fern, and Evans Wilson has a right to feel that this consensus in Welty criticism regarding influences on her work has come too soon. There are in fact all kinds of parallels between popular motifs in the plots of nineteenth-century American women's fiction and Welty's stories; read with an eye toward her American women predecessors Welty's stories begin to seem almost encyclopedic in their absorption and reworking of their plot elements. This chapter will focus on several such elements in the plots of Welty's stories, with the dual goal of reopening the issue of what earlier writers meant to Welty and what they may mean for us today as we reassess the nineteenth-century American canon.

A quick (not exhaustive) list of shared plot elements between Welty's stories and nineteenth-century American women's fiction would contain the following:

- prominent use of motifs from folklore and mythology, as well as the writing of certain works that are "historical" rather than contemporary in setting
- cruel or indifferent fathers, dangerous male suitors
- an important role played by orphans or by children separated from their parents. Wanderers are also featured. These character types can figure both as minor characters and as heroines. Many of the heroines in the best-sellers by women were orphans.

- a "Miss Asphyxia" figure, tyrannical spinsters, cruel mothers or step-mothers versus "Grandmother Badger" types, generous spinsters who aid the heroine
- the "Medusa/Hagar" motif: heroines confronting anger, despair, ostracism, and madness, either themselves or through a character who is an alter ego
- the "Sibyl" motif: heroines who become musicians or writers or teachers and who often have a crucial scene of instruction from an older female role model
- prominent use of satire and vernacular speech, including often comic first-person monologues written in dialect, and "provincial gothic" motifs demonstrating the constrictions of provincial or regional culture
- short-story collections that often feature story-cycles, linked tales all set in a particular place, usually a small town, and sometimes sharing characters from one story to the next

Much has been made of Welty's superb use of mythology in her fiction, especially allusions to Greek and Celtic narratives, and her use of colonial and nineteenth-century American history, especially in "First Love," "A Still Moment," *The Robber Bridegroom*, and "The Burning." But there are precedents for both of these practices in nineteenth-century American women's fiction. Many nineteenth-century American woman writers tried their hand setting a novel in a distant time and place: two examples are Lydia Maria Child's *Hobomok* (1824), set among Puritans and Indians in Massachusetts, and Evans Wilson's *Inez: A Tale of the Alamo* (1855). As far as the use of folklore and mythology in women's fiction goes, consider the following discussion of the novelist Mary Jane Holmes: "Holmes delighted . . . to use folk and fairy tale motifs in her novels, a trait which may partly explain both her facility and her popularity. Her special approach to these age-old motifs gave them a more contemporary, active, rendering: Cinderella takes a conscious part in calling the attention of others to her neglected virtues; Griselda demands contrition and restitution before she consents to return to her wifely duties; Euridice lives a full, busy life in the underworld" (Baym 195).

The primary source for allusions in all nineteenth-century American women's fiction, however, is undoubtedly religious literature. Recently Jane Tompkins has argued that biblical narratives—particularly the story of Job and *Pilgrim's Progress*—are even more important prec-

edents for the basic plots of women's fiction than folklore and fairy
tales; Tompkins calls them American Protestant bildungsromans,
"spiritual 'training' narratives in which God is both savior and perse-
cutor and the emphasis falls not on last-minute redemption but on the
sorrows of the 'way.' " The husband whom the heroine eventually
marries "provides her with a way to live happily and obediently in this
world by obeying the dictates of heaven. He is the principle that joins
self-denial with self-fulfillment, extending and enforcing the discipli-
nary regimen of the heroine's life, giving her the love, affection, and
companionship she had lost when she was first orphaned" (183). Such
an emphasis on an education in submission for the heroine is well
captured by the subtitle of a novel by Almira Hart Phelps: *Ida Nor-
man; or, Trials and Their Uses* (1848). Because of the authority the
Bible had, its narratives were much harder for women writers to revise
than folklore motifs, especially if revisions were undertaken with an
irreverent spirit like that of Holmes. Biblical allusions are relatively
rare in Welty's work, implying that she felt that narratives focusing on
a woman's "trials and their uses"—at least defined in predominately
Christian terms—were no longer appropriate sources for women's fiction. The topic of how Welty's use of the Bible, mythology, and folklore compares with that of earlier American women writers is a subject
that is beginning to receive attention in Welty criticism, but much
more work needs to be done. I just note its importance here, passing
by it in favor of other motifs in the above list.

Of all the motifs listed, those involving male characters seem to be
least shared between Welty and her predecessors. There are really no
cruel fathers in Welty's short fiction, except Lily Daw's father. (There
are several rather distant ones, though, such as Mr. Morrison in *The
Golden Apples*.) "At the Landing," interestingly, clearly implies a link
between how a daughter sees her father figure (actually her grandfather) and how she sees the other men in her life. ("Livvie" does also,
first with Solomon then with Cash as the replacement for the father
she has left behind.) Both stories suggest that the roles fathers play are
absolutely crucial, even though they are barely depicted in the text,
and like earlier women's stories both feature innocent heroines who
lose the idyllic unity of home life and then try to restore it through
marrying. In much nineteenth-century American women's fiction,

the traditional concluding marriage is disturbing to a modern reader in part because it seems so patently a regressive fantasy of a lost childhood world. In Catherine Sedgwick's early novel *A New-England Tale* (1822), for example, the heroine, Jane Elton, marries the wealthy middle-aged Quaker widower who bought her parents' house after she was orphaned and sent to live with her aunt. In *St. Elmo*, its heroine, Edna Earl, reforms St. Elmo by making him into a minister who is more of a father figure than a husband, a deliberate re-creation of the kindly elderly pastor who acted as a father to her after she was orphaned. (Evans Wilson's *Beulah* [1859] and Finley's *Elsie Dinsmore* are two other novels that fit into this pattern of father figure and daughter romance.) Although the authors of such fiction promoted the Victorian ideology that women had supposedly supreme moral authority in the limited spheres of Christianity and the home, their plots reveal that they yearned to return to childhood, as if none of the spiritual "powers" that the proper Victorian marriage offered women could compensate for the loss of their power and status as Victorian girls.[3]

To put it mildly, the endings Welty gave to "Livvie" and "At the Landing" show how skeptical she was concerning such a solution. Livvie is able to repeat her childhood not once but twice, with two different father figures, and a knowledge of Welty's skepticism regarding earlier American women's romances supports those readers who sense that the apparent sunny optimism of the story's ending may be shadowed. As I argued in Chapter Three, in contrast, "At the Landing" seems devastating in its deconstruction of the way earlier women writers handled the romance plot, both those like Susanna Rowson who wrote cautionary novels about fallen heroines who failed to resist seducers (*Charlotte Temple,* 1794) and those like Evans Wilson whose heroines were as "pure" as possible.

Mr. Don McInnis in "Asphodel" and King MacLain in *The Golden Apples* present other interesting cases. One way to read them is as parodies of the male seducer figures popular in earlier women's fiction; certainly their Byronic and Richardsonian lineaments remain distinctly visible, along with other elements from Greek mythology. Like King MacLain, rakes such as St. Elmo Murray spend years wandering the world over because of their egomania and cynicism. Welty's handling of a figure like King seems in marked contrast to the earlier tradition, however, for King is clearly a successful rogue in a way that St. Elmo is not. Welty's innovation in *The Golden Apples* in one sense comes by turning the plot of *St. Elmo* upside down, having a heroine (Snowdie MacLain) who not only is not afraid of the seduction plot but meets King, literally, more than halfway (in the Morgana woods) to ensure the seduction's success. Grounding her version of the story in Greek mythology, especially the story of Zeus and Danaë, allows Welty to reject the biblical, even Augustinian morality of predecessors like Evans Wilson in *St. Elmo*. But *The Golden Apples* also demonstrates that Welty's narratives retain much from earlier women's fiction regarding this male figure, particularly their trenchant analysis of male needs for violence and domination. If one of the tasks of Evans Wilson's and others' novels as Baym defines them was to provide a critique of contemporary masculine behavior, then Welty's analysis of such masculine faults in her fiction is a bold continuation of that tradition. Indeed, it appears that she reworks the tradition in all its aspects, rejecting its general fear of sexuality but also continuing and enriching its investigation into the causes of sexual pathology.

Other motifs in the above list offer even richer cases for comparison and contrast. Orphans or children estranged from their parents appear in a number of crucial Welty stories, as they do in much earlier American women's fiction. Critics such as Baym, Josephine Donovan, and Nancy Miller have pointed out the parallels between the basic plot or "heroine's text" of the sentimental romance and the plots of the Cinderella and Griselda stories. The former features an orphan girl, a wicked stepmother, a series of trials, and a rescuing prince; the latter emphasizes the importance of the heroine's proving her worthiness by resisting would-be seducers. (Sentimental romances, however, tend not to portray married heroines, in contrast to the Griselda story; like fairy tales, they usually dramatize how girls are socialized to be women and assume that once this process is completed successfully all will continue happily ever after.) Pointing out the Cinderella story as a master text of the sentimental romance is valuable because the relative simplicity of the folktale allows us to see a crucial truth that may be obscured by the labyrinthine complications of the plot when it is extended to sustain a two- or three-volume novel. The truth is this:

whatever independence and spunk the orphan heroine displays, including her rebellions against her tyrannical stepmother, her identity as an adult is still thoroughly dependent upon a prince who may be lured into rescuing her with a proper marriage. Even when the heroine goes so far as to engineer her future husband's moral reform (as Edna Earl does), she merely arranges it so that the Cinderella plot may be properly concluded in a marriage. The whole point of her taking the initiative as a young unmarried woman is to be able to give it up to her husband as a wife. Overly strict agents of socialization, the stepmother and other such figures, are exchanged for a more proper but still thoroughly conventional one, her rescuing husband, and her status as an orphan ends as she is finally surrounded by an idealized family unit that replaces the one she lost at the narrative's beginning.

Several of Welty's best stories feature orphans or characters estranged from their families. Cornella and Easter in "The Winds" and "Moon Lake" are the most prominent examples and show the function of this character in Welty's stories most clearly: she is to be a foil for the main female protagonist, an example of greater daring and freedom from social ties, but the tale is also cautionary, an example of a road not to be taken. Lily Daw, Joel Mayes, and Jenny Lockhart (of "Lily Daw," "First Love," and "At the Landing," respectively) are other variations of this type, revealing instantly how innovative Welty is in handling this motif. When an orphan is present in a nineteenth-century sentimental romance, it is conventionally as the main character, since so many of those works are structurally based on the Cinderella story. (Susan Warner's The Wide, Wide World [1850] is a classic example.) But in Welty when the plots are closest to this model—arguably "First Love" and "At the Landing," both of which have orphans as protagonists—Welty mixes new elements into the formula: homoeroticism and deafness in the former story; in the latter, a suggestion that the heroine's dutiful submissiveness is a "spell" (258) leading to rape. As if instinctively aware of the heavy freight of conventions associated with orphans in earlier American literature, Welty chooses in her stories to make the orphan character secondary or, if central, depicted with a new twist. The way I read "At the Landing" in Chapter Three as a revision of the seduction plot ultimately aligns it closely with the fiction of Welty's American female predecessors, for as Baym and Davidson and others have argued such a critique of the seduction plot was central to earlier women's fiction.

One cannot understand the role played by repressive mother figures in Welty's stories—particularly those of the 1940s—without a consideration of their central role in earlier women's fiction. This stereotype may be called the "Miss Asphyxia" figure, after one of its most memorable embodiments, the repressive Calvinist aunt who disciplines and mistreats the orphaned heroine in Harriet Beecher Stowe's *Oldtown Folks* (1869). Her role is essentially that of the wicked stepmother or aunt in fairy tales such as Cinderella, and her chief function in these works seems to be to teach the heroines the art of self-control, restraint, repression, and obedience. Yet she also fosters deep inner anger and defiance, and depending on the author and the novel this rebelliousness is either criticized or sanctioned. In Stowe's novel, we are clearly meant to side with the orphan girl as she rebels; the narrator is quite categorical in her denunciation of the forces that have created such a creature as Miss Asphyxia (principally Calvinism) and her belief that parenting is a matter of discipline and punishment rather than love. Frequently in women's fiction, however, the Asphyxia type dominates the heroine in a way that the novel may tacitly approve, as with Aunt Fortune and the orphan Ellen in Warner's *The Wide, Wide World*. Though Warner's narrative sympathizes with the orphan, Aunt Fortune and a neighbor teach her Christian virtues of "untiring gentleness, obedience, and meekness" that prove invaluable for the heroine; through them, Ellen learns to control her anger and rebelliousness. In Warner's text, then, unlike Stowe's, the function of the Asphyxia type is a microcosm of the structure of the narrative as a whole, the goal being to teach its heroine to aspire only to the powers inherent in meekness and submission—in short, proper feminine behavior as defined by the ideology of Victorian womanhood.

Many characters in Welty's stories, from Miss Eckhart and her mother in *The Golden Apples* and the old crone in "At the Landing" to Octavia in "Clytie" and (possibly) the three "ladies" in "Lily Daw," share some of Miss Asphyxia's qualities, with Octavia closest to the model. In the spectrum of evaluations of this figure offered by earlier women's fiction, a story like "Clytie" clearly is closer to Stowe than to Warner; for Welty's estranged heroine, this repressive older woman represents everything in the world that seeks to kill her growth. *The Golden Apples,* however, adds the twist of giving the witch-like figure (Miss Eckhart) a mother of her own who seems even more irrational and repressive than her daughter appears to be, so we see that the tyrannizer ironically is even more tyrannized than those under her power. The narrative also performs the miracle of turning this figure into a heroine, not by reforming her but by showing us how two of the girls who chafed under her charge change their views of her later in life. Welty's ties to what Lawrence Buell has called the "provincial gothic" elements in nineteenth-century American women's writing is marked by the presence of such witch-like figures and their association with large, run-down houses—such as Lily Daw's, Clytie's, and Miss Eckhart's. As in earlier women's fiction, gothic and melodramatic elements—especially those involving imprisonment, hallucinations, insanity (or its threat), and even witchcraft—are used "to anatomize the pathology of regional culture" (Buell 351–70) that seems embodied in these Asphyxia figures and others.

Many of the heroines under the restrictions of a Miss Asphyxia of course do not repress their anger as successfully as Warner's model heroine Ellen. They turn it inward, only to have it rebound upon them redoubled in strength and often directed now toward the heroine herself as well as toward her oppressor. Evans Wilson's heroine Beulah in the novel of the same name is a case in point. An orphan who cares for a younger sister and her friend in an orphanage, she undergoes a crisis when her two young charges are adopted by an elegant lady and she is rejected because she is ugly. Sent instead to be a nurse and a babysitter—i.e., a worker rather than a family member—for another lady, Beulah responds, in Baym's words, "by developing masochistic delight in berating herself for her ugliness and stupidity, and in doing her job to the point of exhaustion" (283). Beulah is eventually rescued from this cycle of self-hatred by an older man and becomes one of the more independent and well-balanced heroines in all of nineteenth-century women's fiction, but her need for outside intervention or rescue strongly implies that the very energies in her that later prove so creative could just as easily have become self-destructive. The temptation to wound oneself is arguably one of the key scenes in nineteenth-century women's fiction; each heroine must pass it to continue her career, through successful repression (Warner's Ellen), through a well-timed rescue (Beulah), or through her own will and determination to ignore criticism, as does Fanny Fern's iconoclastic heroine in *Ruth Hall* (1855).

One clue as to how pivotal such a confrontation with masochism was for the woman's bildungsroman is provided by Margaret Fuller, the famous nineteenth-century feminist and journalist. She never published fiction, but in her papers is a draft for a short story entitled "Mariana," which deals with a precocious girl's traumatic introduction to the peer pressures of a girl's boarding school. (In this text school itself performs the Asphyxia role of socializing and disciplining.) After several months of defying her peers in matters of social behavior, she finally breaks down when she is publicly accused of lying: "she suddenly threw herself down, dashing her head with all her force against the iron hearth, on which a fire was burning, and was taken up senseless. . . . She returned to life, but it was as one who had passed through the valley of death. The heart of stone was quite broken in her,—the fiery will fallen from flame to coal. When her strength was a little restored, she had all her companions summoned, and said to them,—'I deserved to die, but a generous trust has called me back to life. I will be worthy of it, nor ever betray the trust, or resent injury more. Can you forgive the past?'" The narrator seems to approve, calling the changed heroine "wonderfully instructed," but the story's last paragraph is more ambiguous: "The terrible crisis . . . probably prevented the world from hearing much of her. A wild fire was tamed in that hour of penitence at the boarding-school, such as has oftentimes wrapped court and camp in a destructive glow" (Chevigny 99–101). Although hidden, Mariana's rebellious spirit is still smoldering, and in the last sentences Fuller focuses on what has been lost not just by the "crisis" but by its repressive cure. That a woman of Fuller's independence could write such a story—simultaneously fantasizing and censuring rebellion—shows the strong pull of the conventions of women's fiction and the social mores their motifs of self-punishment supported.

Welty's stories reflect this pull as well. Despite Welty's implication in *One Writer's Beginnings* that the melodrama of *Elsie Dinsmore* was

disdained by both her and her mother, her stories in fact contain numerous heroines who respond to oppression in a self-destructive way
that is analogous to Elsie Dinsmore's: consider Clytie or Miss Eckhart,
to mention just two. There are also several telling instances of Welty's
heroines' responding to stress as Evans Wilson's Beulah does, by performing a task to the point of exhaustion: think of Mrs. Larkin's gardening in "A Curtain of Green," Jenny Lockhart's housecleaning in
"At the Landing," or Virgie Rainey's trying to use sewing scissors to
cut the front lawn on the morning of her mother's funeral. By linking
Virgie's own despairing action to Miss Eckhart's, however, a story like
"The Wanderers" allows us to understand the *causes* of such masochism and to watch a heroine successfully combat it. Yet the way in
which Jenny Lockhart's behavior in "At the Landing" has been evaluated by the majority of Welty's commentators shows that even for
some contemporary readers a heroine's self-punishment may be "justified" using rhetoric that essentially derives from the sentimental romance tradition. That this tradition has been so little discussed by
Welty criticism, yet seems to have influenced some of its commentary,
suggests just how pervasive if invisible its influence has been. Welty is
influenced by it too, but in her fiction she makes a conscious effort to
evaluate its worth.

Nineteenth-century American women's bildungsromans show their
ambivalence toward independent heroines no more clearly than in
how they handle the prospect of a heroine with her own career. Three
such careers are most frequent: schoolteacher, music teacher or musician, and writer of either fiction or journalism. As with the motifs of
orphans and spinsters, the fiction exhibits a stunning variety of ways
of evaluating these possibilities for women, from punishment to
praise. Sometimes these disparities are evident not only in a comparison of different writers but within the same writer, or even within a
single work. Caroline Chesebro's *Isa, A Pilgrimage* (1852) is exemplary
of the last instance. Isa is an orphan who ends up living in Europe out
of wedlock with a radical freethinker; they both pursue successful careers in teaching and writing. Her counterpoint is Mary Irving, who
in Baym's words is "a brilliant and talented young singer who, lacking
the courage equal to her talent, made a mercenary marriage rather
than suffer the demands and difficulties of a career. . . . As she accepts

his gifts, his indulgences, and his caresses she is tormented by the sense that she has sold herself. She lives in an agony of self-deprecation and self-loathing." As Baym concludes her discussion about Chesebro's use of such a contradictory set of heroines: "[h]owever compassionate the author is toward Mary, and however she admires her for withstanding temptation as best she can, she clearly looks forward to a time when Isa's extraordinary heroism will be natural to the whole female sex" (212–14).

Augusta Evans Wilson represents the best case of a woman writer who seems thoroughly inconsistent from book to book in her evaluation of a woman with a career. She is the creator of the heroine in *Beulah* (1859), who rejects a male suitor in favor of a teaching job and, later, a successful writing career (though she marries at the novel's end), and she is the creator of Edna Earl in *St. Elmo*, who is determined to earn a living as a teacher and writer but uses her independence to argue against women's rights. Evans Wilson is also the author of *Vashti; or, "Until Death Us Do Part"* (1869), a novel so regressive that it causes Baym to claim (wrongly, I think) that it marks the end for the most innovative period in nineteenth-century American women's fiction. In *Vashti*, Baym argues, "defiance of convention is equated with assertion of the impulse to gratify the self and hence is forbidden" (295). This ideology is most clearly represented in the novel's subplot, which features an aspiring opera singer portentously named Salome who pays the price for prideful self-assertion by losing her singing voice on the night of her debut recital; she spends the rest of her days as a penitent lace maker. "The woman's fiction which had been so importantly limit-breaking," Baym concludes, "became with a slight shift of balance a limit-enforcing genre" (279).

Like Evans Wilson, nineteenth-century American women writers tended to pair their images of women artists or teachers, so that examples of success and confidence were shadowed by cautionary instances of failure and self-recrimination. This may occur on a macroscopic level, when the stories of several heroines are juxtaposed (as in Southworth's *The Mother-in-Law* or Chesebro's *Isa*), but the most haunting instances of the mixed messages these novels give occur on a microcosmic level, in their figures of speech and their naming of characters, not just their plotting. Hagar should be at least as well-known a name for readers of nineteenth-century American fiction as Ishmael, for example, for Hagar is Ishmael's mother and like him is a generic name for outcast (Gen. 21). At least three nineteenth-century America novels use heroines named Hagar: Alice Cary's *Hagar* (1852), which features a fallen woman who redeems herself and then casts herself out of her community; E. D. E. N. Southworth's *The Deserted Wife* (1855), which features a heroine named Hagar who pursues a career as a singer after being deserted by her husband, only to be reunited with him at the end of the novel and discontinue her career; and Harriet Marion Stephens's *Hagar, A Story of Today* (1858), which uses the seduction plot to portray a sexually emancipated woman. Due to the rise of Melville's reputation and the simultaneous eclipse of women writers such as Southworth who were his contemporaries (and his targets in *Pierre*), the male version of the outcast myth in nineteenth-century American fiction is famous, the female one largely forgotten. (Southworth also wrote a novel called *Ishmael*; see Baym 114.) Of the three novels just mentioned with heroines named Hagar, two out of the three (Stephens is the exception) display a profound ambivalence toward their protagonist, both drawn to her and thoroughly threatened by her, so that in each case closure in the novel is accomplished by an attempt to contain the energy the heroine represents. These writers' dilemmas are similar to that experienced by Hawthorne in *The Scarlet Letter* (1850), and it is reasonable to argue that a balanced understanding of Hawthorne's treatment of his outcast heroine is impossible without the perspective given by these three contemporary Hagar narratives.

Fanny Fern's *Ruth Hall* (1855) represents an even more intriguing case. Joyce W. Warren has claimed that its heroine is the most independent of all the major heroines in nineteenth-century American fiction by either male or female authors ("Introduction" ix-xxxix). As Baym succinctly puts it, the "unconventional aspect of *Ruth Hall* is that it generalizes from the heroine's unfortunate experiences, not to the formation of a superior family structure centered on the heroine [the usual pattern], but to a repudiation of the kin and marriage structure entirely. At the end of the novel the autobiographical heroine, who has taken the pen name 'Floy,' is satisfied with an independent career and has no wish to enter any domestic situation" (252). It also must be conceded that Fern's heroine would never have embarked on her career as a writer except for the death of her husband that left her in need of an income to support herself and her child. Her "independence" therefore is justified to herself (and to the reader) by Fern because it is used to fulfill her responsibilities as a mother in the original family unit. Ruth Hall's financial independence as a successful writer is symbolized by a stock certificate presented to her in the penultimate chapter and reproduced in facsimile in the text. It is however only a *substitute* for the lost family unity that was once represented by her marriage certificate: one form of writing, now lost, has been exchanged for another. Fern caustically shows the dangers of a woman's being financially dependent upon her husband or her relatives, but she also makes it difficult to imagine how her heroine would have been led to discovering such truths without the drastic intervention of her husband's death.

Such a paradoxical limitation on Ruth Hall admittedly differs widely from the kind of censure that is heaped on Salome in *Vashti,* for if Evans Wilson censures Salome's energy as scandalous Fern treats her heroine's energy as an honorable necessity. But fears of the stigma of being made an outcast—a Hagar or a Medusa—haunts even such an iconoclastic author as Fern. Revealingly, the one reference to Medusa in *Ruth Hall* occurs not in the main plot but in a Dickensian comic subplot that also features an independent woman, Mrs. Skiddy. Her husband is as much a scoundrel as Ruth's was a model, and when he seeks to return to her after deserting her for the California Gold Rush, she asserts her rights and refuses to pay for his return or accept him back into her household. The scene ends with a remarkable image: "through her set teeth hissed out, like ten thousand serpents, the word 'N-e-v-e-r!' " (109). Fern's narrative makes it clear that we are to side with Mrs. Skiddy and enjoy her husband's humiliation, but the sudden appearance of the image of Medusa's snakes during Mrs. Skiddy's moment of triumph reveals the dark image of a powerful woman as a monster shadowing Fern's attempts to cast such independent women as the new kind of heroine. Unlike the representation of the Miss Asphyxia types in these narratives, such shadow portraits of the heroines definitely threaten the limit-breaking energy of the novels in this genre, and when this shadow portrait becomes as central to the narrative as it is in *Vashti* rather than as suppressed as it is in *Ruth Hall*, the limit-breaking energy of the genre becomes successfully circumscribed.

≈

Two kinds of pairing of women characters in nineteenth-century fiction by American women have been discussed so far: the Miss Asphyxia/orphan-girl pairing and the heroine/Hagar-Medusa pairing. Each of these focuses on a scene of instruction that is ultimately cautionary and disempowering. A third kind of pairing is equally important, and features an *empowering* link between an independent older woman and a young heroine. Being influenced by Welty's stories, I call this motif the "sibyl" motif, but it can be shown that images of sibyls in fact play a very important role in the writing of Welty's female predecessors, from Willa Cather and Sarah Orne Jewett back to southerners like Southworth and Europeans like Madame de Staël. Like the younger heroines, these older women are often successful teachers, musicians, or writers—or women who run a business such as farming. Some of the most energetic heroines have no such steady role models, admittedly: Fern's Ruth Hall, or Wilson's Beulah. But representative examples of those that do exist are worth examining closely, for this motif potentially involves how a woman's limit-breaking power may be transferred from one generation to the next.

Two novels by Caroline Lee Hentz give early examples. Hentz was born in Massachusetts but after her marriage lived in North Carolina and other southern states and set her novels in the South. In *Rena; or the Snowbird* (1851) the older mentor for the heroine is named Aunt Debby. A widower who inherits a farm and then manages it so successfully that she is able to invest and then lend her profits to others at modest interest, she becomes the heroine's guardian and trains her "in industry and self-control"; in return, the widow learns to value companionship and to trust another. In *Eoline* (1852) the title character, a music teacher, comes to work for a supervisor, Miss Manley, who as her rather allegorical name suggests has chosen education as a career and seems perfectly happy living the life of a single woman. Sometimes pompous and overly strict, she nevertheless provides inspiration for the heroine, who once again tempers her mentor's faults even as she comes to recognize her virtues (Baym 131–33). These older women, a spinster and a widow, are sometimes seen as tyrannical by their students, but they can be differentiated from the Miss Asphyxia types because they are treated much more sympathetically by the narrator, and they teach the heroine to question the ways she has been taught to define her identity. Rather than being a blocking character for the heroine, these older women open doors for her.

In considering the issue of the limit-breaking potential of women's fiction Nina Baym locates the decline in inventiveness in women's fiction around 1870 but does not explain it. The evidence shows, however, that most of the limit-breaking American women writers in the nineteenth century felt some anxiety and guilt for their actions even as they justified them, and the "shift" that Baym sees is actually present all along. An author like Warner explores much more restrictive possibilities for women's fiction while authors like Fern or Chesebro' are investigating its revolutionary potential. Augusta Evans Wilson causes such difficulties for Baym's thesis because she is so remarkable for the intensity with which between 1855 and 1870 she seems to have explored the genre's limit-breaking and limit-enforcing capabilities with equal interest. Furthermore, Baym's book largely ignores the work of such writers as Alice Cary, Rose Terry Cooke, Mary Wilkins Freeman, Sarah Orne Jewett, and others whose careers began to flourish after the Civil War—particularly in what came to be known as the "local color" short-story genre—when the multivolume, serialized women's bildungsroman gradually ceased to be innovative. Unlike women's novels, the women's short-story tradition reached maturity in the 1870s and continued strong through the early years of the next century. Moreover, unlike earlier women's fiction, which was generally published by males because of the huge profits they could make but largely disdained by male reviewers and authors, women's local color fiction in the latter half of the nineteenth century received somewhat less prejudicial treatment. Two important figures in the male critical and publishing establishment, William Dean Howells and James Ticknor Fields, recognized them as excellent examples of the new "realist" movement and actively promoted their work (Donovan 38–49; Habegger).

Recent work on what has been known as nineteenth-century women's local color literature gives particular emphasis to the mentor or sibyl figure for the heroine, for such characters often play an important role in local color fiction by women; when they are absent, the heroine's career suffers for it. This figure may be easily simplified and sentimentalized, as she was in Stowe's *Oldtown Folks*, where she is named Grandmother Badger. In Josephine Donovan's book, *New England Local Color Literature: A Woman's Tradition*, she argues that realistic local color literature by American women ought to be seen as an alternative women's literary tradition to the sentimental romance. In her view, the local color tradition is predominately a *short-story* rather than novelistic tradition; it begins to break down the master plot that dominates the sentimental romance—the Cinderella narrative concluding in marriage—to explore other plots for its heroines, other roles for them to play both before and after marriage.

The progenitor of the local color tradition in America in Donovan's view is Tabitha Tenney's popular picaresque novel, *Female Quixotism: Exhibited in the Romantic Opinions and Extravagant Adventures of Dorcasina Sheldon* (1801). This work debunks many of the conventions of the sentimental romance in England and France which were to influence the later American romances, particularly the classical beauty of the heroine's features and her unwavering virtue in the face of unscrupulous suitors. Donovan concedes that such a novel influenced later American women novelists, particularly the more irreverent ones like Southworth, Holmes, Chesebro', and Evans Wilson, but she argues that it was also crucially influential on early American short-story collections, including Caroline Kirkland's local color stories of settlers in Michigan, *A New Home, Who'll Follow? Or, Glimpses of Western Life* (1839); Harriet Beecher Stowe's sketches, particularly *The Mayflower; Or, Sketches of Scenes Among the Descendents of the Pilgrims* (1843); Charlotte A. Fellebrown Jerauld's *Chronicles and Sketches of Hazelhurst* (1850); Alice Neal's *The Gossips of Rivertown* (1850); and Frances M. Whitcher's satirical *Widow Bedott Papers* (1856). In these local color works, stereotypes for proper feminine behavior are mocked, local communities and manners (including dialects) are portrayed in intimate detail, and strong older women appear who are not necessarily tyrannical stepmother figures.

Donovan's case for a separate local color tradition in American literature by women is undoubtedly overstated, for with the exception of the short-story form each of the characteristics she cites as identifying this tradition—especially its use of dialect speech, humor, and satire; its emphasis on a network of local social relations; and its interest in the highly varied lives of women, from young to old, married to unmarried, dependent and passive to independent and aggressive—is demonstrably present in the novels she claims such a tradition is criticizing. It is also undeniable that Donovan's book represents the new critical interest in nineteenth-century short stories by women, and a recognition that these tales often strikingly asserted their independence of the Cinderella masterplot that circumscribed many women's novels. Such a tradition of regional writing is hardly limited to women—Washington Irving's *The Sketch-Book* (1820), for example, was an important early success in the mode—but from the beginning of the nineteenth century women played a central, even dominant role in the tradition, particularly in the latter half of the nineteenth century and the beginning of the twentieth (Buell 301–3).

Rose Terry Cooke provides an example. She began publishing stories in popular magazines like *Putnam's* and *Harper's* in the 1850s—her first pieces in *Putnam's*, interestingly enough, appeared contemporaneously with stories by Herman Melville—but she became prominent upon book publication of her stories: *Somebody's Neighbors* (1881), *The Sphinx's Children* (1886), and *Huckleberries Gathered From New England Hills* (1891). Not only do her best stories often parody the heroines and villains of romance, but they feature strong-minded spinsters and unidealized depictions of the problems that can occur after marriage; unlike the writers of most sentimental romances, Cooke assumes that her heroines' real stories begin after their marriages, not before. Several of her heroines, perhaps most notably Polly Mariner in *Somebody's Neighbors,* remain unmarried but actually increase their importance and stature in their villages. Cooke unflinchingly portrays how husbands and wives adjust the balances of power in their marriages, yet she also shows the network of friendships among other women in New England villages that were often at least as important to the women, if not more so, as their husbands. To do this, she featured a device that became a staple of later women's local color stories, that of having the story told largely through the conversation of women as they perform a chore together—sorting apples, shelling peas, quilting (Donovan 70–71). Such elements show how Cooke builds on earlier American women's writing, both romances and local color stories, even as she creates her own variations on those traditions.

Donovan singles out two aspects of the work of the later local colorists, Sarah Orne Jewett and Mary Wilkins Freeman, to be particularly important: first, their emphasis on the role of matriarchal power in the small towns, particularly the bonds created among an extended family of grandmothers, aunts, village spinsters, and other women; and, second, their analysis of how this network of friendships was increasingly threatened at the end of the nineteenth century by mores decreeing that such ties should be subordinate to the duties that the married women owed their husbands (113). Rapid industrialization and urbanization of many formerly rural communities in the second half of the nineteenth century—particularly in New England—began to break apart the old social networks of those communities that had been dominated by women, as did (ironically) the increased opportunities for women to be educated and employed outside of their communities.[4] Without idealizing either the hardships or the provincialism of rural life, both Jewett and Wilkins Freeman sound a sharply elegiac note in their stories portraying the woman-centered, matriarchal world of the small town. Although such structures had always been subordinate to masculine authority, what power and autonomy they had possessed was becoming sharply restricted, and our most detailed picture of it in the work of Jewett and Wilkins Freeman comes at the moment of its disintegration.

Jewett's most famous story, "A White Heron," sounds the keynote of this change and also demonstrates how the local color tradition at its best emphatically does not promote an education in submission. The story turns on the heroine's rejection of a suitor who wants her to show him the secret nesting place in the woods of a white heron that he wishes to add to his collection of stuffed birds, but Jewett recognizes also that the heroine's power lies only in refusal. The heroine values the heron because it symbolizes her closeness to her grandmother, rural life, childhood, and Nature herself, but a tree that she climbs to be close to the heron also gives her a view of the sea and the world dominated by men beyond her grandmother's home. If the suitor's demands on her make her conscious for the first time of how important her grandmother's Edenic, matriarchal world is to her, they also cause her to experience a "fall"; she is drawn to the suitor and his wider, more "modern" horizons in spite of herself.[5] Jewett's short-story sequence, *The Country of the Pointed Firs* (1896), exhibits such paradoxes even more complexly, for while it portrays the strongest country matriarch in all of American local color literature, Mrs. Almira Todd, the narrator is a younger woman who is visiting the community only for the summer—she makes her living as a writer in an unnamed eastern city. In Donovan's words, "The ambivalence of the narrator-visitor may be seen to represent the historical anxieties of this generation of women, their distance from the matriarchal world of their foremothers, and their longing to reconnect with it. The world of rural Maine, the land of the pointed firs, however, emerges as a place on the edge of historical time; it is an almost timeless female realm that stands as a counterreality to the encroaching male world of modern technology" (113).

Many of Mary Wilkins Freeman's stories also focus on women's friendships and how they may be threatened by men. Sometimes the stories depict the heroine's actual or secretly desired rejection of a suitor in order to examine the reasons for the woman's feeling threatened; in the process the stories make single life seem singularly attractive ("A New England Nun," "Evelina's Garden"). Others tell of major and minor acts of rebellion by women against men in order to protect their interests and their self-respect ("A Village Singer," "A Mistaken Charity," "The Revolt of 'Mother'"). But Wilkins Freeman also chronicles with ruthless clarity how little real power such women have and how the Cinderella model of the sentimental romance heroine haunts their imaginations even as they seek to rebel against it. Especially notable in this regard are her stories of women who remain enthralled by lovers they might have had or husbands who died, such as "A Traveling Sister," "Sister Liddie," and "A Patient Waiter." Stories like these show that even as antiromantic a writer as Wilkins Freeman still felt the authority of the stereotypes she inherited and tried to dismantle.

The most prominent twentieth-century heirs of the American women's local color tradition who published their most important stories before 1950 are Willa Cather, Katherine Anne Porter, and Eudora Welty. Like the art of their predecessors, their stories cannot fully be appreciated unless they are seen as a response to *both* the local color tradition and the conventions and ideology of the sentimental romance, for if the former tradition had begun to identify itself as a separate tradition, the latter tradition retained its authority and popularity for women, as Welty's comments about the ubiquitous presence of *St. Elmo* in Jackson, Mississippi, attest (*One Writer's Beginnings* 7). All three women had to identify those conventions and values of the sentimental romance that they found liberating and those they found repressive, and this process was not a steady one; they occasionally reverted to its more restrictive conventions after publishing work that was radically revisionary.

Willa Cather's *A Lost Lady* (1923), for example, intends to portray a powerful and intelligent modern woman living in the Midwest, but by the end of the novel Cather has unconsciously lapsed into following the model of the fallen woman as defined by the sentimental romance; it is as if Susanna Rowson's *Charlotte Temple* were disguised and restaged more than one hundred years later in the Great Plains. Two of Katherine Anne Porter's most powerful stories, "The Jilting of Granny Weatherall" and "The Cracked Looking-Glass," also draw strongly on romance conventions for their portrayal of heroines who are dependent upon men for their self-esteem, although Porter's handling of these motifs (as always with her work) is ironic and inquisitorial. Granny Weatherall is a heroic matriarch in the manner of Sarah Orne Jewett's Mrs. Todd, doing such man's work as digging postholes as well as woman's work (she raises two generations of children). But on her deathbed all the self-doubt and guilt caused long ago by being jilted by her fiance on her wedding day returns to haunt her. In "The Cracked Looking-Glass," the rebellious young bride, Rosaleen O'Toole, gradually loses her energy and self-confidence, absorbing her neighbors' view that her character is cracked and misaligned: "She took down the looking-glass to see what kind of look she had on her, but the wavy place made her eyes broad and blurred as the palm of her hands, and she couldn't tell her nose from her mouth in the cracked seam" (Porter, *Collected Stories* 117). (Note how Porter's phrase about the "look" Rosaleen "had on her" implies that this self-image is imposed from without.) Such a scene is similar to Clytie's contemplation of her weeping face in the water in Eudora Welty's "Clytie," but her act ends in suicide, whereas Rosaleen's ends in quiet resignation.

Four specific features of the nineteenth-century local color tradition were especially influential for Cather, Porter, and Welty as they constructed a new form for American women's fiction in the first half of the twentieth century. Two of these features are formal—the story sequence and the comic monologue. The other two are crucial "scenes" in the heroine's life that the women's local color tradition gradually made central to women's narratives rather than peripheral and subordinate, as they tended to be in women's multi-volume novels that ended in the heroine's marriage. I shall call these central scenes from local color fiction the "scene of instruction" and the "scene of farewell." Both scenes dramatize the importance of pairing of sibyl-like older woman and a younger heroine and allow us to trace important lines of inheritance between Cather, Porter, Welty, and earlier American women writers in both the romance and local color traditions. These four features will be discussed in turn.

Story sequences characterize much American local color fiction because the plot conventions of the sentimental romance could more easily be evaded in a loosely linked series of sketches than in a long novel. The sketches of village life in Washington Irving's *The Sketch-Book* (1820) and in the English writer Mary Russell Mitford's *Our Village* (1824–32) provided models for later American writers both male and female. They could chose a general regional locale, as with Stowe's *The Mayflower*, or a specific community, as with Jerauld's *Chronicles and Sketches of Hazelhurst*, Cooke's sequence of stories set in Bassett, Connecticut, and Jewett's *The Country of the Pointed Firs*, the most famous story sequence of all (Donovan 25–37; Buell 304–18). Cather's late Great Plains stories ("Neighbor Rossicky," "Old Mrs. Harris," and "The Best Years") owe such sequences a debt, as do Porter's early stories set in Mexico and her later Miranda sto-

ries—"Old Mortality," "Pale Horse, Pale Rider," and her 1944 sequence, "The Old Order," set in Texas. Welty's 1949 sequence, *The
Golden Apples*, represents a kind of culmination and transformation of
the tradition. Despite their many virtues, Cather's and Porter's sequences are loose and rather monochromatic in comparison with Welty's; her sequence not only covers a greater period of time and a more
complex set of relations among its characters, but it is a *summa* of the
resources of her art, from tragedy to comedy, the monologue and the
story with multiple points of view. *The Golden Apples* was of course
influenced by Faulkner's Yoknapatawpha stories, particularly the
group published as *Go Down, Moses* in 1942, and Sherwood Anderson's *Winesburg, Ohio* (1919). But examples of story sequences by
women writers are at least as important to Welty; in her essay on
Porter in *The Eye of the Story*, she singles out several stories from "The
Old Order" for special praise, and her essay on Cather in the same
volume lauds the liberating influence on Cather of Sarah Orne Jewett
(48–49).

As Mary Louise Pratt and Josephine Donovan have pointed out,
there were several distinct advantages for a woman author working in
the short-story form, and especially in the story cycle. Story sequences
could comment upon and revise plot conventions associated with romance novels by changing the parts of the heroine's story they focused
on, thus changing the interpretation of the conventional atttributes a
heroine should have and, in some cases, the attributes themselves.
Because the stories were short, episodes or characters that would be of
marginal importance in a romance—such as a spinster mentor figure,
an act of rebellion by the heroine, or a story focusing on life after
marriage—could be given central importance. This encouraged more
freedom in choosing subject matter and in revising the conclusions
romances made about how to handle subject matter. The title of one
of Mary Wilkins Freeman's best-known stories, "The Revolt of
'Mother,'" is indicative of how local color narratives often brought
novelistic conventions under scrutiny. Linking stories into a sequence
with some shared characters also proved an advantage in critiquing
romance narratives. Because many stories were interlinked, no longer
did the narrative have to focus centrally on a young heroine's life and
to turn on her success at learning self-abnegation and in choosing a

husband. The emphasis instead was on a community of figures inter-dependent upon each other and on the life stories of characters who were old as well as young, peripheral to the standard romance narra-tive as well as central to it. Such linked narratives tended to be set in small towns, moreover, and they thus could also focus on the conflict between traditional rural values and those of modern urban and capi-talistic society. Often these stories featured at least one character from the "outside" world, such as the narrator visiting from a city in Jewett's *The Country of the Pointed Firs*. These narrative possibilities did not belong exclusively to local color sequences, of course; they were also found in some popular romances, especially those by authors like Kirk-land, Southworth, Chesebro', and Stowe. After 1870 these issues fig-ure strongly in the local color short story collections while they recede from view in longer women's fiction. Welty's *The Golden Apples* su-perbly demonstrates the changes wrought via modernization and mechanization (especially in the logging industry) in the South be-tween the late nineteenth century and the 1940s. Katie Rainey's nar-rative that opens the collection represents the turn-of-the-century South both in its leisurely pace and its handling of conflict between men and women. But the last story, "The Wanderers," set in the 1940s, mentions lumber trucks filled with timber from Morgan's Woods roaring through town, making old-fashioned porch sitting and taletelling impossible. Welty casts a Yeatsian cold eye on these changes and does not moralize or allow her narrative to become overly steeped in either nostalgia or the praise of change. The same forces that devastated the MacLain family and Miss Eckhart and then filled the old MacLain house with lumbermen as boarders, after all, also give Virgie Rainey a measure of freedom that would have been impossible in older Morgana. Welty's comments in her essay "Place in Fiction" about the importance of place and leisurely time in fiction could stand as a credo for the entire American local color tradition. In Welty's hands, however, the traditional modesty associated with local color authors is overturned; she argues that "regional" and "local color" are both condescending terms, and that a strong grounding in place and history is necessary for any ambitious writer. In her words, "art that speaks most clearly, explicitly, directly and passionately from its place of origin will remain the longest understood" (*Eye of the Story* 132).[6]

Comedy also links Welty and earlier local color writers. Of all of Welty's work her comic short stories are most famous, particularly "Why I Live at the P.O." and "Petrified Man." Commentary on Welty's place in the tradition of American comic writers by Vande Kieft, Appel, Evans, and others, however, has emphasized her male predecessors, especially Mark Twain and the frontier humorists specializing in hyperbole and exaggeration, as well as her sources in folklore and myth. Precedents among American women humorists have generally gone uninvestigated. Yet newly published work by Nancy Walker and Alfred Habegger on women's humor and American culture opens up a whole new direction for Welty scholarship, a new tradition within which Welty's work may be understood. The vigor and diversity of Welty's humor, in turn, allows us to test and in some cases revise conclusions that have been made about the forms and function of American women's humor.[7]

In her book *A Very Serious Thing: Women's Humor and American Culture*, Walker notes that women's humor has had a very problematic place in American culture because, until very recently, it has been assumed that a sense of humor was by definition masculine: women could be the butt of a joke but could never *tell* one. Three of the qualities thought essential to wit—intellect, social freedom, and aggressiveness—were also thought to be prototypically unfeminine, and a woman who displayed such qualities inevitably was thought to be threatening, a monstrous man-woman who deserved all the laughter men could direct against her.

In her reading of American women writers, Walker finds that a link between writing and humor extends all the way back to the colonies' first published writer, Anne Bradstreet. The anthology Walker and her colleague Zita Dresner published in 1988, *Redressing the Balance: American Women's Literary Humor from Colonial Times to the 1980s*, gives the lie to the claim that American women did not have a sense of humor. The volume begins with Bradstreet, includes Sarah Kemble Knight, Mercy Otis Warren, and Judith Sargent Murray from the eighteenth century, and then represents eleven nineteenth-century writers, many of whom (such as Tabitha Tenney, Fanny Fern, Frances Whitcher, Harriet Beecher Stowe, Louisa May Alcott, and Marietta Holley) satirized conventions defining womanhood in popular fiction.

Several of these writers, furthermore, are central to any canon of nineteenth-century women local colorists—Whitcher, Stowe, and Holley
in particular. *Redressing the Balance* inexplicably excludes other local
colorists, especially Rose Terry Cooke and Mary Wilkins Freeman,
whose sharp humor, realistic detail, and social criticism ought to have
earned them a place in such an anthology. Welty's work is also excluded, perhaps because Walker and Dresner felt that it was well
known and easily available elsewhere.

Walker argues that the special nature of women's literary humor
is defined by women's subordinate and marginal place in American
culture.

> America's male humorists have been quick to perceive that a nation
> founded on the promise of equality and freedom has largely failed to
> reach those goals, and have pointed out the distance between the ideal
> and the real. Women's humor also deals with incongruity—with the
> contrast between the official mythology and the daily reality—but it
> starts from different assumptions. Traditional male American humor
> rests on the premise that human events—including human fail-
> ures—are somehow within our control; there is in it a consciousness
> that the promises that get broken were made by the same sort of people
> who now seek, through humor, to do the mending. In contrast, wom-
> en's humor develops from a different premise: the world they inhabit is
> not of their making, and often not much to their liking, so their tactics
> must be those of survivors rather than those of saviors. (*Very Serious
> Thing* 36)

Walker then claims that at least three distinguishing features of wom-
en's humor result from such a cultural difference:

> The most obvious is subject matter. Until very recently, most Ameri-
> can women's humor could be called "domestic" in a broad sense, turn-
> ing as it does on the details of life *inside*—the home, the church or
> social group, the neighborhood—whereas men's humor typically takes
> place *outside* of this domestic world: on riverboats, in the legislature,
> in offices. The second major difference is the use of certain humorous
> forms, which is in turn related to subject matter and place. Both men
> and women have written comic plays, satiric sketches, humorous sto-
> ries, and light verse, but women have not written the traditional tall
> tale, and when they have written political satires, these have almost

uniformly dealt with the subject of women's role and rights, from "Fanny Fern" in the 1850s to Ellen Goodman in the 1980s. Finally, and most important, is the difference in the way the theme or message is presented—the manner in which the language of the text in women's humor reveals awareness of discrimination and oppression at the same time that it wears a gloss of amusement. (*Very Serious Thing* 44–45)

Walker's last point is especially important. Because of cultural prescriptions against aggressiveness in women, the open use of satire by women tended to be relatively rare until recently. Certain writers such as Fanny Fern scandalized their readers with the force of their satire, but Fern could be popular because she demonstrated the ability to write other pieces in the properly sentimental mode, thus making her less threatening, though still subversive. Other writers who were more consistently trenchant, such as Elizabeth Stoddard, found their works did not become best-sellers. Much more common for women writers than overtly "feminist" humor, Walker argues, was the ironic and often exaggerated appropriation of their culture's stereotypes of feminine and masculine behavior. They employ what Walker calls the "double text"—quoting clichés associated with those stereotypes only to undermine them and show the disastrous effects they have upon women and men (*Very Serious Thing* 13). In other words, women humorists often assumed the persona of the very qualities they were attacking. Historically, the stereotypes that women humorists have treated ironically have been predominately of two kinds. In Walker's words, "one group of images emphasizes women's tendency to submissiveness, and includes the 'clinging vine,' the sentimentalist, the 'dumb blonde,' and the weak, incompetent woman. The other is in many ways the obverse, including the nag, the gossip, the obsessive housekeeper, and the domineering bitch—images that derive from either feelings of uselessness or misguided efforts to perform well in women's 'proper sphere'" (*Very Serious Thing* 62–63).

Whitcher and Holley are representative examples of earlier women humorists who provide important precedents for Welty's work. Whitcher was most famous for creating the character "Widow Bedott," a gossipy and garrulous man-hunter who could think of nothing but how to arrange a second marriage. After Whitcher's death in

1852, the Widow Bedott character became a popular figure on the American stage. She was always played by male actors in female costumes, however, for actresses would not touch the misogynist portrait that the character had become for male audiences (Habegger 149–50). Whitcher's Bedott is quite a different character. In the following passage from the *Widow Bedott Papers* (an intentionally pretentious title), the widow rhapsodizes about her husband's wisdom, but she keeps getting distracted by digressions:

> He was a wonderful man to moralize, husband was, 'specially after he begun to enjoy poor health. He made an observation once when he was in one of his poor turns, that I never shall forget the longest day I live. He says to me one winter evenin' as we was a settin' by the fire, I was a knittin' (I was always a wonderful great knitter) and he was a smokin' (he was a master hand to smoke, though the doctor used to tell him he'd be better off to let tobacker alone; when he was well, used to take his pipe and smoke a spell after he'd got the chores done up, and when he wa'n't well, used to smoke the biggest part o' the time). Well, he took his pipe out of his mouth and turned toward me, and I knowed something was comin', for he had a pertikkeler way of lookin' round when he was gwine to say any thing oncommon. (*Redressing the Balance* 69–70)

Several hundreds of words later, comically, Bedott finally gets to the point: her husband's words of wisdom were merely, *"We're all poor critturs!"* The humor of such a piece—which can stand up to more than a few of Mark Twain's comic monologues—clearly lies in its satire of the husband's pretensions as much as the wife's. The parody of a wife's overly awed worship of male authority deliciously is increased by Whitcher's superb use of dialect, which implicitly contrasts the abstract pieties of the cult of true womanhood with Bedott's homely solecisms. As Walker concludes, "Whitcher's intentions in presenting women (and, not incidentally, men) as silly social climbers and talkative nags was not to endorse and perpetuate these stereotypes, but rather to write a cautionary tale for women and men she saw debasing and trivializing themselves" (*Very Serious Thing* 20).

Marietta Holley created Samantha Allen, who at the turn of the century was as recognized a synonym for American humor as Mark Twain. Holley published many books with Samantha commenting on the issues of the day, from the "race problem" to women's rights to the 1893 World's Columbian Exposition in Chicago. As Walker and Dresner note, "[a]s if to point up ironically women's subordination to men, Holley used the pseudonym 'Josiah Allen's Wife' for many of her books, and she used stereotypes to subvert the cultural assumptions that lay behind them: thus, Betsey Bobbet is the epitome of the sentimental, clinging female . . . and it is Samantha, rather than her husband Josiah, who is strong of both body and mind" (*Redressing the Balance* 98). Like Whitcher and other earlier women humorists, Holley is a talented user of dialect and a parodist of sentimental clichés.

Welty's famous comic portraits of overly aggressive or overly dependent women (including "P.O." and "Petrified Man" as examples of the former and "A Piece of News" of the latter) thus have many precedents in earlier women's writing. This link can be seen first in the formal methods they employ: dialect-filled monologues and dialogues in the first two stories and the parodic quotation of sentimental language in the third. The link is also evident because of the subversions and social criticism that Welty's stories hide below their surface. Nineteenth-century stories by Whitcher, Holley, and others teach us that it is crucial *not* to read these stories of Welty's as straightforward attacks on aggressive and "masculinized" women in the mode of the stage shows for men built around the crass Widow Bedott character. Like her predecessors, Welty presents such women not for us to laugh at self-righteously but to spur us to ask what has made them the way they are. Ultimately, she is intent on using humor to examine inequities caused by stereotypes, particularly the links between modern commercial culture and inherited nineteenth-century clichés about proper men's and women's behavior. Intriguingly, the comic stories in Welty's first volume (1941) tend to be comedies of rigidity, stories about characters who are as trapped within imprisoning stereotypes as Lee Roy was within his grotesque Keela the Indian Maiden costume. "*Women!!* Make Turban in Own Home!" and the comic stories in Welty's second volume of stories published two years later tend to emphasize ways in which those stereotypes may be undone. "Livvie," "Asphodel," "At the Landing," and "The Wide Net," in very different ways, parody and revise the conventions of popular women's fiction, especially those focusing on a dangerous seducer figure. "*Women!!*

Make Turban in Own Home!" is a brilliant analysis of the social construction of gender differences using the classic persona of a narrator
who appears to be a humble, innocent, and mechanically incompetent female. With "The Winds" and the comic stories in *The Golden
Apples,* we move into a different form of comedy, a comedy of rebirth
over which an older-woman artist figure usually presides. This latter
form of women's comedy, the "comedy of rebirth," is little discussed
in Walker's book or her anthology. To find a precedent for this other
form of comedy we must turn to Welty's sources in earlier local color
narratives and short-story sequences, many of which featured older
women characters who performed a crucial mentoring role for the
younger heroines.

In the "scene of instruction" an older woman with special skills and
self-reliance passes on her knowledge to the younger heroine. In the
"scene of farewell" the heroine says goodbye to her role model either
because the older woman is dying or because the younger woman must
go away. In either case, this scene raises questions about how to maintain the continuity of matriarchal power. Instead of involving the heroine's relations with a potential husband, it involves her efforts to
internalize the influence of a powerful female role model. It can properly be called comic because it represents a release and rebirth.

The matriarchal figures involved most frequently in such scenes of
instruction are mothers, foster mothers, or schoolteachers—Grandmother Badger types who may evolve into something more assertive
and sibyl-like. Sarah Josepha Hale's *Sketches of American Character*
(1829) uses plots derived from sentimental romance, but Josephine
Donovan contends that two of her stories contain "the first of a long
line of New England spinsters portrayed relatively positively [even
though they are] conceived primarily in terms of failed romance."
A. J. Graves's *Girlhood and Womanhood* (1844) juxtaposes the re-
warding relationship between a schoolteacher and her best pupil
(who becomes her successor) against the unhappy lives of the other
girls in the class after they grow up and marry. In Stowe's *Oldtown
Folks,* Grandmother Badger stands in opposition to the stepmother,
Asphyxia, and the gentleman rogue, Ellery Davenport; she and
several other strong female characters, including Esther Avery, an

independent-minded, scholarly schoolteacher, serve as loving surrogate parents for the orphaned hero and heroine and represent the bildung plot rather than the romance plot.

The potentially subversive roles of such parental figures are generally not explored by these earlier authors, however. The beneficent schoolteachers in Hale's and Graves's work have sharply limited spheres of power; they may represent the benefits of the single life for a few select women, but the majority of their female students are "graduated" to the world of marriage where men reign. Stowe's schoolteacher, Esther Avery, admittedly, is a "MAN-WOMAN . . . who unites perfectly the nature of the two sexes" and thus would seem to be a potentially revolutionary figure. But Stowe's novel is less an ironic critique of the sentimental romance than it is a counter-romance, a fantasy of a world almost entirely purged of patriarchal control: in the end, Esther becomes both a "MAN-WOMAN" and wife. To confect such a happy ending Stowe resolutely dodges any question of how improbable such a situation would be for a woman in America in 1869 (439; quoted in Donovan 66).

With Cooke and Jewett and Wilkins Freeman, the role played by such positive matriarchal figures begins to change; their stories focusing on such figures may dramatize not only their self-reliant power but the dilemma they pose for the heroine, who suddenly finds herself confronting for the first time the contradiction in her culture between matriarchal and patriarchal values. Definitive examples of the scenes of instruction and farewell in the local color tradition may be found in Jewett's *The Country of the Pointed Firs*. In the first chapter the narrator meets Mrs. Todd, with whom she will be staying the summer, and the last chapter features a farewell scene of richly understated power. Mrs. Todd was once married to a man from a "high family" but has long been separated from him. Her absent husband is both the unfaithful aristocratic suitor of the sentimental romance and the confidence man of the Gilded Age. Mrs. Todd pointedly criticizes his disdain for honest, old-fashioned labor: "he was above bein' a seafarin' man" and went west to earn a fortune quickly. The humiliation of her failed marriage has been converted into brave independence; she really began to forge her identity only after her husband left. Coming from a large eastern city, the narrator immediately is struck by the way in which Mrs. Todd has made a professional as well as a social identity for herself: she is the town's herbalist and its social arbiter. She also becomes for the narrator a figure of mythic power as well, a vision of a woman in the midst of a community of men and women who is entirely in control of her own identity: "She stood at the center of a braided rug, and its rings of black and gray seemed to circle about her feet in the dim light. Her height and massiveness in the low room gave her the look of a huge sibyl, while the strange fragrance of the mysterious herb blew in from the little garden." Her last glimpse of Mrs. Todd shows that she has internalized her solitary strength: "her distant figure looked mateless and appealing, with something about it that was strangely self-possessed and mysterious . . . . [A]t last I lost sight of her as she slowly crossed an open space on one of the higher points of land." The narrator may be leaving, but her tutelage in self-reliance has been completed (Solomon 51, 150).

Descendants of Mrs. Todd can be seen in the stories of Cather and Porter, particularly the title character in Cather's "Old Mrs. Harris" and Evangeline Knightly in "The Best Years," and Grandmother in Porter's Miranda stories, among others. Porter characteristically treats her version of this character ironically—her stubbornness and sentimentality are inextricably a part of her heroism, and the unwavering strength of Cather's matriarchs seems almost superhuman in comparison. The young heroines of "Old Mrs. Harris" and "Old Mortality"—Vickie Templeton and Miranda—learn from these older women, but there are no straightforward scenes of instruction or farewell as there are in Jewett or Cooke: the girls absorb what the women have to teach them largely without knowing that they are doing so, and their last scenes ironically, find them asserting their own independence against what they take to be the older women's antiquated and oppressive influence. But their very rebelliousness shows that they have absorbed their mentors' strength of character, and it is only later in their lives, usually after their mentors' deaths, that they look back and see how much they owe. In Cather's eloquent words, "when they are old, they will come closer and closer to Grandma Harris. They will think a great deal about her, and remember things they never noticed" (*Obscure Destinies* 158).

Such scenes are the precursors of Welty's rich portrayal in *The Golden Apples* of Virgie Rainey's changing relationships with her mother and with Miss Eckhart, young women who inherit both the noble and the overbearing qualities associated with matriarchs in American women's fiction. It is only when Virgie returns to Miss Eckhart's grave at the end of "The Wanderers," the concluding story in *The Golden Apples*, that she can fully appreciate what her teacher gave her. Her farewell to her mother at the beginning of the same story is as important. That scene pays homage to the deathbed scenes of both Cather's "Old Mrs. Harris" and Porter's "The Jilting of Granny Weatherall." Virgie realizes that her mother has showered her with gold, given her her character: "a torrent of riches seemed to flow over the room, submerging it, loading it" (432). Welty's most spacious and radiant comic story begins and ends with a scene of farewell, but the story as a whole is really one long scene of instruction, an act of remembering and restoration.

With the earlier writers in the American local color tradition, the heroic matriarch tends to be not an artist but a spinster, a divorced woman, or a widow who through her own efforts has gained special status working in her community—Cooke's Polly Mariner, who lives alone and makes her living as a seamstress, for instance, or Jewett's Mrs. Todd, whose role in the town includes that of herbalist. Welty's richest examples of the scene of instruction tend to involve the teaching of music. (The most significant exception may be the scene of instruction in "Moon Lake" in which Easter writes in the sand.) Women musicians of course are frequent figures in nineteenth-century women's fiction; perhaps the most provocative examples are Mary Irving in Caroline Chesebro's *Isa* (1852); Caroline Lee Hentz's Eoline and Miss Manley in *Eoline* (1852); E. D. E. N. Southworth's Hagar in *The Deserted Wife* (1855); Margaret Huell in Elizabeth Stoddard's "Lemorne *versus* Huell" (1863); Salome Owen, the foil for the heroine in Augusta Evans Wilson's *Vashti, or "Until Death Us Do Part"* (1869); Audrey in Rebecca Harding Davis's *Earthen Pitchers* (serialized 1873–74), who gives up a career as a violinist, singer, and composer after her husband is blinded in a train accident (Davis 140–45); Candace Whitcomb in Mary Wilkins Freeman's "A Village Singer"

(1891); and Mademoiselle Reisz in Kate Chopin's *The Awakening* (1899), who lives singly and devotes her life to her art. Most of these authors' handling of this character (especially in *Vashti*) demonstrates how conventional sentimental romances usually provide a *cautionary* scene of instruction for the heroine, showing her the price she will pay if she is too ambitious and iconoclastic. Davis's novel, in contrast, is elegiac, ironic, and obviously troubled by the convention of having the heroine renounce her art, as Tillie Olsen has shown (Davis 140–45). Stoddard's and Wilkins Freeman's stories are considerably more angry: Stoddard's story recounts an independent woman's betrayal by an evil fairy godmother figure, and Wilkins Freeman's caustically dissects the conflict between a church choir's premier soprano and church's male power structure. Chopin's *The Awakening*, interestingly enough, reverses the sentimental romance's generic pairing of heroines by having the primary heroine die and the secondary heroine survive: Edna Pontellier kills herself, but the older and single Mademoiselle Reisz lives. Edna's suicide highlights how impossible it is for Chopin to reconcile her novel's romance plot (in this case, one involving seduction and adultery) with the self-reliant bildung plot exemplified by Reisz.

Women musicians probably play such an important role in Welty's stories because of the influence of two works by Willa Cather, the novel *The Song of the Lark* (1915) and the story collection *Youth and the Bright Medusa* (1920). These works offer a complex combination of the cautionary scenes of instruction featured in romances such as *Vashti* and the empowering scenes of instruction that characterize women's local color writing. Of these stories, "Coming, Aphrodite" is the most interesting to the reader of Welty's short stories; not only does it retell tales from Greek mythology in a contemporary setting (as *The Golden Apples* does), but it can also be read as a story about Cather's own anxiety of authorship. On one level, the story may be read as a study of how even relatively unconventional male artists may be threatened by a woman artist: Eden Bower's would-be lover, Dan Hedge, is disturbed by how powerfully her sexuality is expressed in her art and in her unconventional lifestyle. Yet what most disturbs Cather's characters is the apparent necessity for an artist to lead a single life. Cather's story retells the myths of Hippolytus and Actaeon, both of whom were destroyed for admiring Diana, the virgin goddess of the hunt. She thereby dramatizes her own fears that an artist's rejection of marriage will be as destructive as the love of Actaeon and Hippolytus for the virgin Diana. The end of her story, moreover, makes it clear that she fears she could still be destroyed even if she should succeed in turning herself into a Diana. Her heroine sacrifices her private life for success as an opera singer, but one of our last glimpses of her shows her face under streetlights and stage lights to be hardened into a Medusa-like parody of beauty, a "plaster cast" (74). For Cather, as for Welty, the image of Diana turning into Medusa haunts the woman artist because she has been taught that pursuing a career in art rather than marrying will deform her face and soul. Underneath a consciously "modern" story of a liberated woman such as "Coming, Aphrodite," therefore, lies the disturbing subtext of a cautionary scene of instruction inherited from the sentimental romance. In Southworth's The Mother-in-Law (1851), for example, the most unconventional heroine, Gertrude Lion, is also compared with Diana, and having her story subordinated to that of other more conventional heroines, paradoxically, allows Southworth to handle her story in ways that are arguably more provocative and less wary than Cather's.

Cather's novel The Song of the Lark is a more extended treatment of the life of an opera singer and is more sanguine than her stories about women artists.[8] In Welty's essay on Cather in The Eye of the Story, she praises The Song of the Lark, among other novels, in the midst of a discussion of how Jewett taught Cather to "find your own quiet center of life and write from that"; she sees it as a novel of an artist's rebellion and self-discovery—how she trains herself to be reborn (48). The most important role models in this quest for its heroine, Thea Kronborg, are her music teachers. The first is Professor Wunsch, whose name in German means "desire." A homeless musician trained in Europe, he supports himself in Colorado with only a few students, of whom only Thea has any real talent. He boards with a family at the edge of town and has to fight bouts of depression, violence, and alcoholism. Like Miss Eckhart, he is a "wanderer" (Cather, Song of the Lark 23) whose career ends in madness, with his trying to chop down an orchard and dove-house while (as in "June Recital") children watch the events from their second-story bedroom windows. Thea's second teacher is Andor Harsanyi, a successful musician in Chicago. Welty singles out his credo in her essay: "every artist makes himself born. It is much harder than the other time, and longer" (*Song of the Lark* 175; *Eye of the Story* 59).

Later, when Thea rapidly achieves success as a singer, she speaks of her singer's voice not merely as her natural talent but as her re-created identity, a "second person in her" that was concealed until she learned to give it voice (*Song of the Lark* 217). Cather then audaciously parallels Thea's discovery with Walt Whitman's; hers is a mythic, Edenic conception of womanhood that usurps and stands aloof from any definitions of it that society decrees. She feels that when she sings for an audience, she brings out the Edenic selves in others. Cather even uses a Whitmanian word to describe it: "These faces confronted her, open, eager, unprotected. She felt as if all these warm-blooded people *debouched* into her" (232; my italics). Thea's discovery of a primal self has all the revolutionary subversiveness of Whitman's, yet Cather's counterpointing of Thea's joyful discovery of her own powers with the melancholia of Professor Wunsch subtly dramatizes how an artist is burdened with a double life: the new self must learn to coexist with its social identity; it can never displace it. Similarly, Thea's success as an opera singer does not allow her to remain free from dependence on the patriarchal powers that control the world of opera. (By Cather's design, we feel noticeably distant from Thea in the last part of the novel, seeing her only through the eyes of the men who surround her.) Still, in *The Song of the Lark* Cather generally dissents from the pessimism of stories like "Coming, Aphrodite." Thea Kronborg's story is not a cautionary tale to her female readers but a potentially revolutionary one: like Whitman's, her success teaches them to question how identity is defined, not merely to choose from among the patterns that society offers. The epigraph for Cather's novel could be the epigraph for "June Recital," especially the scene in which Miss Eckhart plays Beethoven during a thunderstorm: "It was a wond'rous storm that drove me" (from Lenau's *Don Juan*). And when Thea sings Frika's part from Wagner's *Das Reingold*, Cather describes her as having

> a distant kind of loveliness for this part, a shining beauty like the light
> of sunset on distant sails. She seemed to take on the look of immortal

loveliness, the youth of *the golden apples,* the shining body and the shining mind. (*Song of the Lark* 447; my italics)

Such a passage is a precursor to all the images of radiant and powerful heroines in *The Golden Apples,* from Snowdie MacLain at the beginning to Virgie Rainey at the end. When Welty alludes to this passage of Cather's, furthermore, she also joins it with Cather's other vision of the woman artist forced by her society to be a "bright Medusa": Miss Eckhart may be a heroic quester like Aengus and Perseus, but she is also characterized at the end of "June Recital" by her flaming hair—the "grave, unappeased, and radiant" (330) Medusa's-head of her madness that forever remains the frightening alter ego of the woman artist. No image of the "shining mind" is entirely separable from the threat of Medusa's shadow, in Cather or in Welty.

A full discussion of the influence on Welty of Cather's portraits of woman artists must go outside the American local color tradition, however. Cather's inspiration for Thea Kronborg came partly from her acquaintance with the singer Olive Fremstad; partly from Henry James's stories about art and artists; and partly from Evans Wilson's *Vashti.* But the primary influence was not an American work at all: it was Madame De Staël's *Corinna; or, Italy* (1807; U.S. translation 1808), the most famous nineteenth-century novel about a woman artist. De Staël's heroine was an "improvisatrice" in Rome, a national poet-sibyl who spontaneously composed and recited verses during great public exhibitions. She lost the man she loved to a conventionally pure woman, and like Willa Cather's opera singers she was as entrapped in her sibylline role as she was empowered by it.

In a chapter entitled "Performing Heroinism: The Myth of Corinne" in *Literary Women,* Ellen Moers traces the influence on nineteenth-century women writers of De Staël's novel. Quoting Margaret Fuller (who in her own lifetime was known as "the American Corinne"), Moers notes that discovering De Staël's portrait of Corinne was a turning point in the lives of practically every future woman writer who read it: "[f]emale authorship owed a great debt to Mme de Staël's intellect." Catherine Sedgwick, Fuller, Stowe, Kate Chopin, and Jewett—among many other American and European writers— began their own careers inspired by Corinne's example and more or less repressing the memory of her fate. Being a modern Italian sibyl, Corinne became associated with the Cumaean or Italian sibyl and her prophetic song, thus linking her as strongly with singing as with writ‑ing.[9] De Staël's Corinne, moreover, did not fit into any of the social roles played by other women in the novel; rather, her art inspired a revolutionary transgression of social roles.

Several passages about Corinne's public performances portray her as a sibyl in the mode of the Italian painter Domenichino (1581–1641), with black hair, beautiful blue drapery flowing from her shoulders, and a rich Indian fabric wrapped turban‑like around her head (Moers 274). As Sandra Gilbert and Susan Gubar have eloquently argued, the role played by the sibyl in women's fiction is essentially to initiate a femi‑nist scene of instruction. Discussing Mary Shelley's "Author's Intro‑duction" to *The Last Man* (1826), which contains an account of a woman's exploration of the caves associated with the Cumaean sibyl, Gilbert and Gubar note that the narrative may be read as a parable about a

> woman artist who enters the cavern of her own mind and finds there the scattered [Cumaean] leaves not only of her own power but of the tradition which might have generated that power. The body of her precursor's art, and thus the body of her own art, lies in pieces around her, dismembered, dis‑remembered, disintegrated. How can she re‑member it and become a member of it, join it and rejoin it, integrate it and in doing so achieve her own integrity, her own selfhood? Sur‑rounded by the ruins of her own tradition, the leavings and unleavings of her spiritual mother's art, she feels . . . like someone suffering from amnesia. Not only did she fail to recognize—that is, to remember—the cavern itself, she no longer knows its languages, its messages, its forms. . . . Bewildered by the incoherence of the fragments she con‑fronts, she cannot help deciding that "I have forgotten everything/ I used to know so long ago." (*Madwoman* 98)

These hidden sibylline powers are traditionally associated with oral rather than written authority—song rather than text, inspiration and improvisation rather than imitation. In Domenichino's most famous painting of a sibyl, for example, a new, handwritten scroll is juxta‑posed against an ancient printed text. Translated, the scroll in the picture reads, "One God, Who Alone Is Supremely Great [and] Un‑

Domenichino, *Sibyl*, ca. 1620. Musei Capitolini, Rome.
Photo credit: Istituto Centrale per il Catalogo e la Documentazione, Italy

born." [10] The sibyl appears to have just been inspired by these words, then to have written them down on a scroll. Although they have been received later than the bound script on which they rest, as a kind of orally dictated supplement, the sibyl's words in fact overthrow, or at least challenge, the authority of the earlier text. Representing the moment of *furor divinus* or divine inspiration, such a sibylline text overturns the traditional Western investing of greatest authority in written and codified texts. It celebrates the potentially subversive and revisionary prowess of oral discourse, seeing it as a return to the original, oral authority of God's Word. [11]

Three details are of particular interest in Domenichino's juxtaposition of pointing hand, handwritten scroll, and book. First, the sibyl's scroll may be written, but its form is more provisional than the bound text and thus is closer to their shared source of revelation. Paradoxically, the supplement supplants the earlier text, accruing priority and authority for itself. The content of the prophecy confirms this, for it stresses that the divine Word, like divinity itself, has not yet revealed itself in its entirety; it is not fixed; it may be added to. Second, the sibyl is not shown holding a pen, even though she has presumably just finished writing down the text she points to. The absence of a "proper" writing tool suggests not only the author's gender but the close link all her writing has to the original oral discourse that inspired it, and will inspire it again. The third detail may be the most important of all. The sibyl points not to the book or to her recently written text on the scroll but to the blank space following her writing. She indicates this space because her prophecies represent the power to open all texts, to make a "space" in them for revisions and supplementary revelations. In the poet H. D.'s eloquent words, the blank on the page represents "the blank pages/ of the unwritten volume of the new." Such a portrait of a sibyl's power is thus even more radically revisionary than that of Mary Shelley's parable as interpreted by Gilbert and Gubar; it argues that the true sibylline role is to write *new* texts, not only to recover and rearrange the fragments of the old. [12] When sibylline women appear in women's literature, they stage scenes of instruction that teach their initiates to identify, question, and alter the cultural "texts"—the stereotypes—that define what a woman's identity may be. Just as importantly, such authority is often associated

with recovering the lost power of *oral* discourse—the ability spontaneously to revise what society has tried to make permanently fixed.
Nineteenth- and twentieth-century women's fiction that appropriates
Western images of sibyls thus gives them an even more subversive
power than that bequeathed by Michelangelo and Domenichino. Now
the sibyl's authority is applied to social roles, not necessarily God's
Word, and it decrees that patriarchal society has not had the final
word on what a woman's identity may be.

At their deepest, most powerful level, the sibylline scenes of instruction in Eudora Welty's short stories teach the woman involved
how to recover the lost authority of oral discourse and transcribe it
into new and subversive written discourse. Characters such as Phoenix
Jackson, Powerhouse, and Ruby Fisher in *A Curtain of Green* celebrate
the power of oral rather than written language, and heroines like the
cornet player in "The Winds," Easter in "Moon Lake," and Miss
Eckhart in "June Recital" teach younger women how to identify the
stereotypes that have been governing them without their knowledge—the Cinderella and Medusa "texts" promoted by the sentimental romance—and how to create a new definition of women's heroism.
Seen from this perspective, the popular sentimental romances offered
a hypnotically powerful forgery of a Corinne-like heroine. Edna Earl
in *St. Elmo*, for example, appears to combine the intelligence of
Corinne with the morality of an upright American girl, but actually
she is much closer to Corinne's half-sister and rival, the thoroughly
proper precursor of the Victorian ideals of True Womanhood. Here is
Evans Wilson's revealing description of Edna Earl: "The young face,
lifted toward the cloudless east, might have served as a model for a
pictured Syriac priestess . . . . The large black eyes held a singular
fascination in their mild sparkling depths, now full of tender loving
light and childish gladness; and the flexible red lips curled in lines of
orthodox Greek perfection" (quoted in Donovan 20). Disguised behind this stylized profile is a heroine completely lacking Corinne's
revolutionary power even as she masquerades with her beauty and at
least some of her authority. Other women who more blatantly aspire
to Corinne's power, such as Salome Owen in *Vashti*, are punished for
their ambition. Such features of the sentimental romance give special
force to Gilbert's and Gubar's point that the feminist scene of instruc-

tion must involve a traumatic but liberating displacement of one kind of cultural text for another that has been dismembered and forgotten.

Acts of displacement, revision, and remembering characterize the comic heroines in Welty's stories, most notably Virgie Rainey. She appropriates the role of Perseus and slays Medusa, as Miss Eckhart, Jenny, Old Addie, Clytie, and others could not. With one stroke of the imagination, she assaults Morgana's deadly, stereotypical image of a strong and independent woman as a monster. To do this, like Perseus she reflects that dangerous image *back to itself*, identifying it *as* an image, a cultural fiction, thus taking the first step towards conquering its power to dominate her. And like the Cumaean sibyl in Domenichino, Virgie meditates on how a new tradition may replace the old, in which a woman may be Perseus, not merely Medusa. Her struggle, however, will be never-ending, always a part of the on-going struggle of women's history. In Welty's words in *The Golden Apples*,

> She might be able to see it now prophetically, but she was never a prophet. Because Virgie saw things in their time, like hearing them—and perhaps because she must believe in the Medusa equally with Perseus—she saw the stroke of the sword in three moments, not one. In the three was the damnation—no, only the secret, unhurting because not caring in itself—beyond the beauty and the sword's stroke and the terror lay their existence in time—far out and endless, a constellation which the heart could read over many a night . . . .
> In Virgie's reach of memory a melody softly lifted, lifted of itself. Every time Perseus struck off the Medusa's head, there was the beat of time, and the melody. Endless the Medusa, and Perseus endless. (460)

Such a passage is obviously inspired in part by Benvenuto Cellini's statue of Perseus, a reproduction of which Welty owns. Eugene MacLain in "Music from Spain" also remembers a picture on Miss Eckhart's wall, but unlike Virgie he recalls not Cellini's Perseus but a sibyl: "Eugene felt untoward visions churning, the Spaniard with his great knees bent and his black slippers turning as if on a wheel's rim, dancing in a red smoky place with a lead-heavy alligator. The Spaniard turning his back with his voluminous coat-tails sailing, and his feet off the ground, floating bird-like up into the pin-point distance. The Spaniard with his finger on the page of a book, looking over his shoulder, as did the framed Sibyl on the wall in his father's study—no! then, it was old Miss Eckhart's 'studio'" (408). *The Golden Apples* never resolves the question of just how many pictures Miss Eckhart had on the walls of her studio, much less what their meanings are. In effect, Welty has Miss Eckhart's walls contain a double image— pairing both Perseus and Medusa and Medusa and the Sibyl. This crucial sibyl reference, moreover, was added in revision to the "Music from Spain" typescript. [13]

It turns out that Domenichino's famous portraits of sibyls may have indeed inspired Welty's portraits of sibylline rather than Medusan powers. It is no absurdity that a music teacher in rural Mississippi might have a picture of a sibyl by Domenichino on the wall of her studio, perhaps next to her Perseus and the Medusa by Cellini. Domenichino's sibyls strike the exact pose that Eugene remembers, looking over a shoulder while laying a finger on the page of a book. By Domenichino's time, however, this pose was often transferred directly to portraits of St. Cecilia, the patron saint of music. Domenichino's Borghese sibyl has indeed been known both as a St. Cecilia portrait and as a Cumaean sibyl. Apparently, the Cumaean sibyl's indelible association with "prophetic song" in Virgil's Fourth Eclogue caused her to become associated with other kinds of music, and eventually with St. Cecilia. [14] Miss Eckhart's sibyl, fittingly, represents not merely the teaching and performance of music so much as a sibylline scene of instruction—the creation and transmission of a new text for women's heroism.

Throughout Welty's work, characters with sibylline powers are marked by several things: turban-like headdresses, a "secret face" revealed during their moment of vision, and a peculiar kind of light appearing under their eyelids that makes their eyes seem to roll back into their heads. In "Powerhouse," the moment when Powerhouse decides what tune to play is described this way: "Powerhouse reads each one, studying with a secret face: that is the face which looks like a mask—anybody's; there is a moment when he makes a decision. Then a light slides under his eyelids, and he says, '92!'" (132). Easter lying in the chained wooden boat in "Moon Lake," in a scene that prefigures both a later visionary moment for Nina in her tent and the episode of Easter's near-drowning, "looked falling over back-

Domenichino, *Sibyl*, ca. 1616. Galleria Borghese, Rome.
Photo credit: Istituto Centrale per il Catalogo e la Documentazione, Italy

wards. . . . [H]er eyes were rolled back, Nina felt. Her own hand was writing in the sand. Nina, Nina, Nina. Writing, she could dream that her self might get away from her—that here in this faraway place she could tell her self, by name, to go or to stay. . . . [I]f this was their ship, she [Easter] was their figurehead, turned on its back, sky-facing" (354–56). When Virgie swims in the Big Black in "The Wanderers" after her mother's death, she experiences a mystical connection to her: "all was one warmth, air, water, and her own body. All seemed one weight, one matter—until as she put down her head and closed her eyes and the light slipped under her lids, she felt this matter a translucent one, the river, herself, the sky all vessels which the sun filled. She began to swim" (440). Note how in these passages, Welty's grammar shapes complex sentences with quirky punctuation, as if under visionary pressure.

As I mentioned in Chapter Three, "The Wanderers" includes three such visionary moments, the second and third outdoing the previous one in scope and intensity. But perhaps the most sibylline epiphany in all of Welty's stories comes in "The Burning," a story in *The Bride of the Innisfallen* (1955) that features two half-crazed spinsters who have their ancestral home in Mississippi destroyed by General Sherman's Union soldiers near the end of the Civil War.[15] Eventually, in despair, they both commit suicide. The conclusion of the story belongs to their servant Delilah, who wears a turban-like headdress and returns to the rubble of the house after her mistresses' deaths. She finds a mirror that once hung above the hearth's mantle. Staring into it is a bit like looking into the shield Athena gave Perseus: in it she sees enacted in visionary flashes the entire tragedy of slavery and the Civil War. The passage is worth quoting at length:

> Though the mirror did not know Delilah, Delilah would have known that mirror anywhere, because it was set between black men. Their arms were raised to hold up the mirror's roof, which now the swollen mirror brimmed, among gold leaves and gold heads—black men dressed in gold, looking almost into the glass themselves, as if to look back through a door, men now half-split away, flattened with fire, bearded, noseless as the moss that hung from swamp trees.
>
> Where the mirror did not cloud like the horse-trampled spring, gold gathered itself from the winding water, and honey under water started

to flow, and then the gold fields were there, hardening gold. Through the water, gold and honey twisted up into houses, trembling. She saw people walking the bridges in early light with hives of houses on their heads, men in dresses, some with red birds; and monkeys in velvet; and ladies with masks laid over their faces looking from pointed windows. Delilah supposed that was Jackson before Sherman came. Then it was gone. In this noon quiet, here where all had passed by, unless indeed it had gone in, she waited on her knees.

The mirror's cloudy bottom sent up minnows of light to the brim where now a face pure as a water-lily shadow was floating. Almost too small and deep down to see, they were quivering, leaping to life, fighting, aping old things Delilah had seen done in this world already, sometimes what men had done to Miss Theo and Miss Myra and the peacocks and to slaves, and sometimes what a slave had done and what anybody now could do to anybody. Under the flicker of the sun's licks, then under its whole blow and blare, like an unheard scream, like an act of mercy gone, as the wall-less light and July blaze struck through from the opened sky, the mirror felled her flat.

She put her arms over her head and waited, for they would all be coming again, gathering under her and above her, bees saddled like horses out of the air, butterflies harnessed to one another, bats with masks on, birds together, all with their weapons bared. She listened for the blows, and dreaded that whole army of wings—of flies, birds, serpents, their glowing enemy faces and bright kings' dresses, that banner of colors forked out, all this world that was flying, striking, stricken, falling, gilded or blackened, mortally splitting and falling apart, proud turbans unwinding, turning like the spotted dying leaves of fall, spiralling down to bottomless ash; she dreaded the fury of all the butterflies and dragonflies in the world riding, blades unconcealed and at point— descending, and rising again from the waters below, down under, one whale made of his own grave, opening his mouth to swallow Jonah one more time.

Jonah!—a homely face to her, that could still look back from the red lane he'd gone down, even if it was too late to speak. He was her Jonah, her Phinny, her black monkey; she worshiped him still, though it was long ago he was taken from her the first time.

Stiffly, Delilah got to her feet. (*Collected Stories* 492–93)

Like antebellum southern culture itself, the mirror is an ornate edifice held up by slaves, now toppled, shattered, and burned. Delilah examines the mirror's frame, then stares into the mirror itself, which fills with visions, clouds over, then refills. She first sees the country-side and then the city of Jackson before the war, then a glimpse of the kinds of violence—including rape, murder, and miscegenation—on which the slave system was built: "what men had done to Miss Theo and Miss Myra and the peacocks and to slaves." Assaulted by her vision, she turns her eyes away, imagining she is being pummelled by a "whole army" of flying creatures and snakes, many hallucinatory and grotesque, with weapons and masks. (Readers who know Goya's work may think of his frightening *The Sleep of Reason*.) Delilah now listens rather than watches, but her "vision" of past and future is no less intense. In the magisterial run-on sentence that concludes the fourth paragraph in the above excerpt, Delilah sees the entire fabric of south-ern society coming apart, like "proud turbans unwinding." In this pas-sage we have yet another reference in Welty's stories to dragons, monsters, and conquering Perseus-like heroes wielding a sword, but these Perseus figures with their "blades unconcealed and at point" seem not heroes so much as riders of the Apocalypse, soldiers (both Union and Confederate) wreaking destruction. In prose that con-sciously seems to be rivaling Faulkner's, and Melville's in *Moby-Dick*, the paragraph ends with a reference to Jonah and the whale, linking pride and self-destruction. If these figures are Perseus-like, they seem demotic parodies as they destroy themselves with their own weapons ("one whale made of his own grave"). The images of southern society at the beginning of the passage are filled with references to gold, but by the end of the vision the sense of beauty, richness, and the infinite possibilities that the gold connotes has turned to darkness and destruc-tion—blood and ashes and a grave.

Typically, however, Welty ends this passage not on a climactic note but on a quiet and intimate one, and in a way this deepens unbearably the tragedy revealed by the mirror. It is not even clear that Delilah is looking at the mirror at this point, so strong is her vision. What she sees is apparently her own son Jonah as he is being taken away from her down a red dirt road. For Delilah (as for Stowe, Frederick Doug-lass, and Harriet Jacobs, incidentally) the violence of the slave system culminates in the most brutal act of all, the calculated breaking-up of black families to sell their members separately. In Delilah's case, her

child seems to have been taken away from her more than once, perhaps after a chance reunion. By ending one paragraph with a reference
to the biblical Jonah and beginning the next with a portrait of a lost
black boy with the same name, Welty ironically links the oppressors
and their victims via the shared name. If the former reference alludes
to Jonah the arrogant and self-destructive blasphemer and seems to
compare him to the white soldiers, the latter links his emergence from
the whale's belly with the emergence of blacks from slavery. Like
Jonah, Delilah is a survivor and, ultimately, a prophet whose vision
depicts the downfall of an entire corrupt society, an American Nine-
veh. In such a moment, truly Cumaean powers descend upon Delilah.
Given the story's date, 1955, and its references to Jonah, perhaps it is
not too far-fetched to wonder whether the story may prophesy the
reemergence of African American anger and pride in the Civil Rights
movement.

✍

To conclude, I would like to return to the larger issue of Welty's
inheritance from earlier American women's writing and ask a question that has been haunting this entire discussion. Studying plot sum-
maries alone, a reader could be forgiven for wondering whether nineteenth-century American women's fiction was more experimental in
its portrayal of women than most later women's fiction, including
Welty's. After all, how much pre-1970s prose by women has a character like Southworth's Gertrude Lion, who rides animals bareback
and at the altar breaks up weddings she does not approve of; or Southworth's Capitola in The Hidden Hand (1859), who has a series of adventures dressed as a boy; or Chesebro's Isa, a writer who lives with a
man out of wedlock and outdistances even Margaret Fuller in audacity? Perhaps the only equivalent for such characters occurs in the most
radical works by women modernists such as Djuna Barnes and H.D.,
or contemporary novelists influenced by the new feminist literary criticism and its recovery of "lost" earlier women's fiction—Joyce Carol
Oates, for example, who has written several novels such as The Bloods-
moor Romance in affectionate competition with the Brontës and earlier
American women novelists. As Westling and Shinn have noticed, in
comparison with Fern's Ruth Hall or Stowe's Esther Avery (Oldtown
Folks) the roles that Cather, Glasgow, Welty, McCullers, or Porter
gave their heroines seem somewhat less flamboyant and daring. In-

deed, until recently the only comparable experimentation with many varieties of highly independent roles for women occurs in American movies in the 1930s and 1940s, when, interestingly enough, the movie industry was at a moment analogous in its evolution to the tradition of American women's fiction in the 1850s. (I cannot think of Gertrude Lion or Capitola without being reminded of some of the roles played by Katherine Hepburn or Barbara Stanwyck, for instance.) Disturbingly, it seems as if many of the issues central to women's fiction, especially those of victimization, dependency, lost women's history, and the problems of empowerment, do not ever seem to be resolved. Miss Eckhart and Virgie Rainey confront the same prejudice in this century that blocked the characters in novels by Chesebro', Southworth, Hentz, and many others in the 1850s, and works like Glasgow's *Barren Ground* (1925) make points about women's necessary financial independence that are similar to Fern's *Ruth Hall*, published seventy years earlier. Are not the plots in the fiction of mid-twentieth-century women writers like Welty fundamentally less daring than those in American women's fiction a century earlier?

There is no easy answer to this question, of course, but if an answer is to be found it must be sought in the patterns of American history, not just within the fictional conventions and character types that women writers were drawn to. A glance at the history of various women's organizations promoting social change in the United States, for instance, displays similar cyclical patterns, with little apparent or easily measured long-term progress. In *Disorderly Conduct: Visions of Gender in Victorian America*, the historian Carroll Smith-Rosenberg makes some pertinent comments in this regard. The concluding chapter in her book focuses on the history of American women's rights groups between 1870 and the 1930s, particularly their efforts around the turn of the century to create a "New Woman" who repudiated the Victorian "Cult of True Womanhood" in order to become truly modern.

We identify the New Woman most directly with the new women's colleges. In her own mind and the minds of her contemporaries, education constituted the New Woman's most salient characteristic—and her first self-conscious demand. Complex economic, demographic, and institutional factors, factors that were largely external to the world of

women, led to the emergence of the women's college. These factors
included the growing need for a literate population; the delayed age of
marriage, especially among the affluent bourgeoisie; a quintessentially
bourgeois ideology that stressed upward mobility through education;
accumulated wealth, which permitted the bourgeoisie the luxury of en-
dowing education institutions—even ones for women. Young women
seized upon this novel institution for reasons of their own and so transformed the women's college into a potentially revolutionary social
force. (247)

Not coincidentally, I would argue, women's colleges proliferated in
the United States during the same decades—the 1870s and 1880s—
that the women's local color movement emerged at the vanguard of
women's fiction. Both of these literary and social movements felt a
profound ambivalence toward the rapid industrialization and urbanization that was occurring and the accompanying increase in power in
male-run institutions associated with the world of business and the
world of science and medicine. Like the promoters of women's colleges, the women local color writers sought to counterbalance these
changes in at least two ways: by critiquing new and old forms of patriarchal privilege and by imagining a protected "space" (either the cam-
pus or the small town) where women could be truly empowered in
their own lives and in the education of the next generation. Jewett's
Almira Todd thus gives herbal medicines along with her matronly
advice and examples of self-reliance to the narrator of *The Country of
the Pointed Firs*. Such a response to corporate capitalism and institutionalized science and medicine, admittedly, was profoundly contradictory. It repeated the separation of men's and women's spheres central to the earlier Cult of Domesticity that it sought to challenge. It
celebrated the passing of small-town America run by husbands and
ministers with near-absolute authority: a critique of the stifling conditions of these small towns as well as analyses of marital injustice lies
at the heart of Cooke's and Wilkins Freeman's fictions, for example.
But it also romantically sought to turn rural America into a source of
"color" and matriarchal values separate from the newly "grey," urban,
and industrial America that was growing up around it. The women
local colorists never resolved these contradictions in their work;

Jewett seems unable to imagine Mrs. Todd anywhere but in an isolated village.

Women activists who were Jewett's contemporaries created networks that linked the New Woman's campuses with new reform organizations in the cities. In Smith-Rosenberg's words, "the more politically radical of the New Women used the loving world of female bonding and traditional female familial concepts to forge a network of women reformers and social innovators into a singularly effective political machine. Settlement-house women spun out a delicate web of interlocking social-justice organizations led and staffed by militant (and, often, single) New Women. Residents of America's worst slums, familiar with the daily workings of industrial capitalism, they figured prominently within the left wing of the Progressive Movement" (255). "Rejecting the patriarchal family and their mother's domestic lives" (254), the New Women at the turn of the century tried, in effect, to establish as a norm the most radical identities for women that had been imagined but had been carefully kept circumscribed in earlier nineteenth-century women's fiction. Southworth's Gertrude Lion or Stowe's Esther Avery in many ways personify such a New Woman, but fifty years before the name was coined. This woman's identity would be defined primarily in terms of the career she held, the public work she accomplished. If she wanted also to marry, that was fine, but if she did not marry her life would not be regarded as a failed romance. Charlotte Perkins Gilman's major works, *Women and Economics* (1898) and *Herland* (1915), represent one culmination of the movement; the former uses Social Darwinism to argue that the racial health of humanity is best advanced by using women's natural abilities to the utmost, including allowing them to operate businesses as well as bear children; the latter is a feminist utopian novel imagining a society entirely of women who have perfected a type of parthenogenesis so that they may reproduce without males.

What happened to this New Woman? Smith-Rosenberg does not mince words: American men counterattacked. The newly organized medical establishment first argued that educating women's brains would necessarily weaken their nervous systems and their reproductive organs. Then in the 1890s, when these arguments were refuted by women physicians, they claimed that women who did not conform to bourgeois notions of proper womanhood were latent lesbians and therefore dangerous to the psychic health of the community. Smith-Rosenberg's sobering summary follows:

> Medical arguments and sensationalist literature began to exert an influence upon young women. The percentage of women college graduates who married increased significantly in the 1910s and 1920s. The percentage who attended graduate and professional schools and who pursued careers dropped proportionately. Between 1889 and 1908, 55 percent of Bryn Mawr women had not married; 62 percent entered graduate school. Of those women who married, 54 percent continued in a career and remained economically autonomous. (In fact, during these years only 10 percent of Bryn Mawr graduates did not work.) Between 1910 and 1918, as warnings against lesbianism proliferated, these figures reversed: 65 percent of Bryn Mawr women now married, only 49 percent went on for further training. Wellesley and other women's colleges mirrored the Bryn Mawr trend. (281)

Coupled with this attack by male scientists and doctors was an assault by male business leaders, who "orchestrated a campaign to return women to the home and transform the redomesticated woman into the bulwark of America's new consumer economy" (282). As Dolores Hayden chronicles in *The Grand Domestic Revolution: A History of Feminist Designs for American Homes, Neighborhoods, and Cities,* many of the business projects initiated by the New Women's groups, such as collective cooking and housekeeping services for apartment dwellers, failed in the first three decades of the new century due to the population shifts into new suburban housing, the rise of industries selling new consumer appliances to each household, and the fear of "Bolshevikism" after 1917 in anything that seemed socialist and collective. This trend was repeated in substantially the same form after World War II, when changes in the labor force caused by the depression and the war were reversed. Women in large numbers left the workforce and returned to the domestic sphere and the suburbanization of the middle class reached a new height. As discussed in Elaine Tyler May's *Homeward Bound,* in the late 1940s and the 1950s these changes were accompanied by a new Red scare, scientific and economic arguments

in favor of women's returning to the home, and depictions of androgynous women as monsters.

Such social changes in the early 1900s and in the late 1940s happened less dramatically in the South than in the North. As Anne
Firor Scott, Anne Goodwyn Jones, and Louise Westling have shown,
similar patterns can be found in the South, especially in fiction, non-
fiction, professional journals, and the media, where images of the
proper southern lady were portrayed as the antidote to disturbing modern changes in women's roles. Eudora Welty is hardly a Charlotte
Perkins Gilman, but in many ways her life represents the aspirations
of the New Woman that were so threatening in 1900 and 1920 and
1940. She was educated in part at a women's college, one of the southern equivalents of the more famous Seven Sisters in the North, and
after continuing her education at the University of Wisconsin she
moved to New York City to begin a career in that quintessentially
modern business, advertising. Even after returning to Jackson in 1931
to live with her mother after her father's death, she continued to have
a public career, first as a publicist for the W.P.A. in Mississippi and
then, of course, as a published writer. The addresses that she used at
the head of her typescripts tell an interesting story: at first they read
"Eudora Welty, 1119 Pinehurst, Jackson, Mississippi" (her home address), but then after she gets a New York agent she treats such head-
ings as a business address: "Eudora Welty, Russell & Volkening, Inc.,
522 Fifth Avenue, New York" (her agent's firm).

Smith-Rosenberg, Dijkstra, Gilbert and Gubar, and others have
shown why it was impossible for most American women writers in this
century to depict the New Woman in their fiction as directly and
boldly as she was imagined in the 1850s or the turn of the century.
Perhaps the situation has now changed (though I often doubt it), but
with the exception of Gertrude Stein and Djuna Barnes and a few
others who accepted ostracism, the majority of twentieth-century
American women writers from Cather, Glasgow, and Wharton on-
wards have been no more able than women activists to change the
stigma that was placed upon the New Woman. Indeed, both Cather
and Wharton made disdainful comments about the New Woman in
their fiction and elsewhere (Gilbert and Gubar, No Man's Land II,

174–75), making points similar to Welty's own criticism of overly
"feminist" fiction or social action (Prenshaw, *Conversations* 54). Welty's most daring heroines always exist in a profoundly *mediated* way,
still very constrained by social values they find asphyxiating, as Southworth's Gertrude Lion or Jewett's Almira Todd do not. Their most
subversive acts are largely private and meditative rather than public
and known to the world; they are not crusaders or social reformers:
Virgie "was never a prophet" (460). And like Wharton and Cather,
Welty has disparaged the popular nineteenth-century women ro-
mancers who preceded her and has been extremely cautious in depicting what may be taken to be "feminist" themes or New Woman
characters.

The image of Virgie Rainey sitting under the courthouse tree in the
rain at the end of *The Golden Apples* has been continually in my mind's
eye as I write these last paragraphs. Her meditations as she listens to
the sound of "the world beating in [her] ears" (461) seem to take the
pulse of the American woman's tradition in literature. Accompanied
by an old "wrapped-up" black woman (perhaps that turban-sibyl motif
again), Virgie thinks of people, especially men, who seem to rule the
world and control the stories. She then thinks of the women she
knows whose stories "they could not tell . . . right" (435): her
mother; the black woman next to her; Mrs. Morrison, who gave up
aspiring to be a singer (like so many characters in earlier women's
fiction) and then ended a suicide; and Miss Eckhart, Miss Eckhart
above all. There are no Gertrude Lions in Welty's work, except perhaps in "Circe," but Welty's development of Medusa and sibyl motifs
in her stories gives us a profound reading of her inheritance from earlier romance novelists and local color short-story writers. This allows
us to understand why American women's fiction seems to confront the
same problems eternally and gives us a way of negotiating the contradictory evaluations of that tradition offered by contemporary literary
criticism. Welty's stories show us that such an inheritance for women
writers is neither restrictive nor revolutionary in itself. It is simply
there, a discourse divided against itself, a word-hoard, a set of character types that, as Nina Baym has said, can be either "limit-breaking"
or "limit-enforcing" depending on how it is used. That images such as
the Medusa have often been used to stigmatize women who transgress

accepted conventions in society or in literature does not mean that the image necessarily must be used in that manner. Welty's references to sibyls and to the Medusa teach her readers to identify and change the cultural texts that confine them—to evolve from identifying with Medusa to identifying with a sibyl, from self-destructive rage and guilt to empowering acts of disguise and revision.

More work needs to be done tracing the iconography of the Medusa and the sibyl/writer figures in Western art and literature, following the leads Welty has given us. Recently Medusa images are more studied, as shown by Hélène Cixous's essay and by Bram Dijkstra's book *Idols of Perversity*, among other texts. I have found a fascinating pairing of the Medusa and a sibyl/Athena figure in one of Alice Rideout's designs for statues for the Woman's Building at the 1893 World's Columbian Exposition in Chicago (Weimann 172, 174), but so far have been unable to find commentary analyzing its iconography.[16] The design features a winged woman standing and spreading out her arms over two seated or crouching women. The one under the winged woman's right hand writes in a book held on her knee while glancing over her shoulder, in sibyl-like fashion, at the standing figure. Wearing a mortarboard, she may represent the proliferation of women's colleges in the United States in the two decades before the fair and the high hopes women placed in them. The other figure is under the winged woman's left hand and is harder to make out, for in the engraving illustrating the statue she is cast in deep shadow and appears to be crouching or falling, one arm upraised as if in distress, her head turning downward and away. Between these two women at the feet of the standing figure is an owl on a stack of books (a reference to Athena?) and, behind it, an oval image of Medusa. This Athena/Medusa pairing is of course duplicated in the pairing of the seated women: one writes and the other writhes, as if this allegorically represents the two fates women may have. The statue was given a prominent place atop the Woman's Building at the World's Fair, over the main entrance. At least two hypotheses may be drawn from studying the statue. First, its iconography of women (and perhaps even its comparative linking of Athena, sibylline poses, and Medusa) appears to have been conventional enough in the late nineteenth century to be thought appropriate for the major commemoration of the accomplishments of the

Alice Rideout's statue for the Woman's Building, World's Columbian
Exposition, Chicago, 1893.

women's movement, the 1893 Woman's Building. Second, women involved in reform movements and the arts may have had a fairly high degree of self-consciousness about the tension as well as the link between the Medusa and symbols of women's prowess juxtaposed so pointedly in Rideout's statue. Rideout's statue may thus be the crucial self-image that the nineteenth-century New Woman's movement in the United States assigned to itself, representing its fears and its aspirations. The statue represents a legacy for women in the visual arts as complex and contradictory as the legacy of nineteenth-century American women's fiction.

For women writers such as Welty and Porter who came of age during some of the most severe attacks against the New Woman, whatever criticism they felt of their culture's definition of gender differences apparently had to be disguised more thoroughly than it was in Southworth's, Fern's, or Evans Wilson's works. As Welty says with particular poignancy in *One Writer's Beginnings*, the legacy of independence that her mother taught her was also "what she so agonizingly tried to protect me from, in effect to warn me against" (60). Sibylline and Medusan images are buried deeply within Welty's stories, appearing only briefly within figures of speech before disappearing again, because of how powerful and dangerous she finds them.

Welty's struggle with the meaning of these images is profoundly relevant for artists and cultural commentators working today. Her indebtedness to male writers and to European women writers is indisputable, and this book should not be interpreted as implying that they were unimportant to her. A full accounting of Welty's relationship to earlier American women writers, moreover, would have to include a study of how her longer fiction incorporates and revises that tradition. But I would argue that from the beginning of her career at least through 1950 Welty's primary site of engagement with literary tradition was her stories, a supposedly marginal or "lesser" form that offered her more opportunity to deploy her sibylline sleight-of-hand tricks. It seems particularly apt that just when contemporary readers are recovering and rereading a lost tradition of American women artists Eudora Welty's short stories should be so instrumental in teaching us to understand their prophetic power.

Notes

PREFACE

1. For a fine overview of Eudora Welty's critical reception, including the 1950s and 1960s, I recommend Albert J. Devlin's *Eudora Welty's Chronicle: A Story of Mississippi Life*, especially pp. 3–15, 41–44, 82–85. Two invaluable recent checklists of publications by and about Eudora Welty are Noel Polk's "A Eudora Welty Checklist, 1936–72" and Pearl McHaney's "A Eudora Welty Checklist, 1973–86."

2. The lecture was reprinted in book form as *Short Stories* (1949); the quoted passages are from pp. 4 and 50–51, respectively. In revised and condensed form, it is reprinted as "Looking at Short Stories" in *The Eye of the Story* 85–106.

CHAPTER I

1. One version of what a male writer's "anxiety of influence" might be is of course notably developed by Harold Bloom. Gilbert and Gubar discuss their revision on Bloom's theory of influence in *Madwoman in the Attic* 45–92. Other discussions of the representation of women in American culture in the nineteenth century and their influence on twentieth-century images of women that were indispensable for this chapter and elsewhere include books by Scott, Douglas, Cott, Baym, Habegger, DuPlessis, Anne Jones, Donovan, Tompkins, Davidson, and Westling.

I should also mention that I am aware of at least some of the paradoxes involved in a male critic undertaking "feminist" or "gender" criticism. Particularly helpful and humbling for me have been the ideas in Laurie Langbauer's article "Women in White, Men in Feminism," which among other things contains an incisive reading of the ways male critics have often homogenized the voices of women feminist critics and used them to advance their own arguments with other male critics. In a way that made me especially reflective, Langbauer also analyzes references to mother figures in "feminist" criticism written by men. In my own case I cannot become fully conscious of that role other than to admit that (as my dedication indicates) such a figure, doubly absent, haunts this text.

2. A fine essay on "Lily Daw" is McDonald's "Artistry and Irony." As well as demonstrating how Welty's revisions of the story clarified Aimee Slocum's role, McDonald notes how ambivalent its comic ending is. For other discussions, see Appel, 42–46; Howard 27–32; Kreyling 6–8; and Weston. I cite Appel's book in these notes with some ambivalence, for after its publication in 1965 it became apparent that he had made use of Ruth Vande Kieft's book *Eudora Welty* (1962) without proper acknowledgment. In each case where I cite Appel, I have checked his discussion against Vande Kieft's. Unless otherwise noted, references to Vande Kieft refer to the 1987 revised edition of her study.

3. I.A4 Jackson, Marrs 31–32. Marrs's handy volume on Welty's manuscripts and documents now at the Mississippi Department of Archives and History in Jackson is an invaluable contribution to Welty scholarship. The book has an appendix compiled by Noel Polk listing Welty prose manuscripts (excluding letters) in other collections.

4. For a superb feminist reading of "Snow White," see Gilbert and Gubar, *Madwoman* 36–44. Two good introductory discussions of "A Visit of Charity" are by Vande Kieft 65–66 and Appel 39–42. See also Prenshaw, "Two Jackson Excursions" 3–4.

5. I.A4 Jackson, Marrs 31–32. Marrs notes that Welty "appears to have retyped from periodical versions, typically with some alterations, all stories published before 1941; 'Clytie,' 'The Key,' 'Why I Live at the P.O.,' 'A Visit of Charity,' and 'Powerhouse' had not yet been accepted for publication when EW prepared this typescript."

6. See Vande Kieft 37–38; Appel 24–30; Howard 10–14; Devlin *Eudora Welty's Chronicle* 18–19, 30–31, 81–82; and Detweiler. None of these critics does more than mention Mrs. Marblehall and Mrs. Bird in passing. Appel's is the fullest overall discussion, but I found Devlin's analysis is especially valuable for noting how Welty's story draws on Mississippi history: Marblehall is "the oldest family name in the city of Natchez, and his schizoid identity parallels the identity of Natchez, divided between aristocratic elegance and frontier violence." He also provides this insight into Mrs. Marblehall's "club work" and Welty's mention of the town's "Pilgrimage Houses" (93), which would have included the Marblehall mansion: "In 1932 the Natchez Garden Club sponsored the first Pilgrimage, an annual tour of antebellum homes designed to promote local history and restore the area's depressed economy" (19). Yet Devlin also argues that Mrs. Marblehall, unlike her hus-

band, is merely "patrician" and "complacent" (19). Incidentally, Mr. Marblehall was originally named Mr. Grenada; Grenada is a town near Jackson, Mississippi.

7. See, for example, Kreyling 16–17; Vande Kieft 29–31; Appel 30–34; and Burgess 136–38. Kreyling's is a representative reading that argues that Mrs. Larkin's anger is essentially metaphysical, a protest against chaos in nature, thus removing it from the social context in which Welty places it. The quoted claim that Mrs. Larkin finds "wholeness" is his.

8. Good introductory discussions of "Clytie" are by Vande Kieft 25–26, Appel 75–76, 80–83; Howard, 20–24; Manning 13–14; and Tarbox. Tarbox's psychoanalytical reading of the story (and of several other early ones, including "A Memory" and "Death of a Traveling Salesman") ought to be better known. Vande Kieft stresses the story's pathos; Appel places it within the tradition of Gothic fiction; Howard notes Welty's use of mythology in the story: Clytie is a lover of the sun, a potential bringer of light in a "house of death," but without the ability to recover her lost "vision," she is fated to remain a "shade in Hades." (For more on the mythological sources of the story, see William Jones; Jones argues, as I do, that Welty draws on Ovid's Clytie, who is eventually turned into a sunflower.) Robert Penn Warren's early essay on Welty is also relevant.

9. The story deserves more discussion than it has received by Welty's commentators. The best commentary is by McDonald, "Eudora Welty's Revisions of 'A Piece of News.'" See also Vande Kieft 30; Appel 13–16; and Hollenbaugh.

10. I.A4 Jackson, Marrs 31–32.

11. See Welty's comments on her readers' questions about the story in her essay "Is Phoenix Jackson's Grandson Really Dead?" in The Eye of the Story 159–62 and in Kuehl, "The Art of Fiction" 286, in which Welty quips that Phoenix Jackson's grandson is "not dead yet!" Welty's has also commented on the story's source of inspiration: Prenshaw, Conversations 167–68, 299–300. For other discussions of the story, see Appel 166–71; Keys; and Butterworth.

12. This sentence echoes Faulkner's description of Dilsey going down the stairs with Mrs. Compson's hot-water bottle in The Sound and the Fury: "she could hear Dilsey descending the stairs with a painful and terrific slowness" (334). Vande Kieft also notes some parallels between Dilsey and Phoenix Jackson (29). I read the presence of the diploma in the story differently from Welty, who equates it with Phoenix's "victory" (Eye of the Story 162).

13. See Vande Kieft: "she wrote [the] story rapidly just after going to a dance where the black jazz musician, Fats Waller, played with his band" (11).

Welty also refers to this incident in Prenshaw, *Conversations* 85. The best discussions of "Powerhouse" are by Vande Kieft 35–37; Appel 148–64; Stone; Pollack 60–69; and Burgess 138–41, who usefully contrasts Mrs. Larkin and Powerhouse as artist-figures in *A Curtain of Green*. Also recommended is the jazz critic Whitney Balliett's essay on Fats Waller. Vande Kieft and Pollack are especially prescient in discussing why Welty does not reveal whether or not Powerhouse's wife is really dead, while Appel and Pollack define the various shifts in the story's point of view and demonstrate the tension between Powerhouse and his various audiences.

14. I.A4 Jackson, Marrs 31–32. Further references to revisions in "Powerhouse" are based on this typescript, except as noted.

15. Welty's ending in I.A4, Marrs 31–32, reads as follows: "Well, we requested Hold Tight, and he's already done twelve or fourteen choruses, one in Fu Manchu talk. It will be a wonder if he ever gets through. His mouth gets to be nothing but a volcano. 'When I come home late at night I want my favorite dish—FISH. Hold tight—Fix me some that old Babylonian seafood, Mama—Yeahhh!' He does scare you. He really does. He has a mysterious face." This original ending was rejected by the editors of the *Atlantic Monthly*, probably because they thought the lyrics too sexually suggestive (Evans, *Eudora Welty* 56). But Welty kept her new ending in subsequent reprintings, I think, because although the lyrics of *Somebody Loves You* were not as quintessentially Walleresque as those of *Hold Tight*, they worked with the story in other important ways, as I have tried to show. Welty comments somewhat contradictorily about the story's ending in Prenshaw, *Conversations* 209, 266–67.

16. The sentence is absent in I.A4 Jackson, present in I.A5 Jackson, Marrs 31–33.

CHAPTER 2

1. I.A4 Jackson, Marrs 31–32. Three readings of "Flowers for Marjorie" are by Vande Kieft 17–19; Appel 20–23; and Manning 9–10. All three critics seem rather uneasy with the story, however, and Manning goes so far as to argue that its form and content should be separated: "Rather than being much disturbed by Howard's or other characters' predicaments . . . we applaud the author's clever imagination and enjoy the stories as stories." McDonald's article on Welty's revisions of "Flowers for Marjorie" focuses on the first half of the story and carefully contrasts the *Prairie Schooner* and *Curtain of Green* versions.

"Acrobats in a Park," which Welty dates as "probably" from 1935, is another early story about a man's fear of a woman's pregnancy; Welty originally included it next to "Flowers for Marjorie" in the *Curtain of Green* typescript before removing it in favor of "A Worn Path," the superior story that she chose to end the volume. In "Acrobats" a husband and wife are part of an acrobatic circus team that creates a human arch, but the husband does not want a child and thinking of her pregnancy in the midst of a performance causes him to shudder and make the arch collapse: "Last night, it was a difference in the weight, the moisture, and temperature of her body when she stepped into his hand that drove catastrophe into his very center." (Note that the pattern of a man stabbing or shooting a woman in the *Collected Stories* is here reversed: the wife's pregnancy is felt by the husband to be "stabbing" *him*.) The story has been published in the French journal *Delta* 5 (1977): 1–11. See also Graham's essay on "Acrobats" in the same issue of *Delta*. My thoughts throughout this chapter and the next on men's vs. women's behavior in Welty's works have been influenced by Prenshaw's essay "Woman's World, Man's Place"; Kerr's "The World of Eudora Welty's Women"; Bolsterli's "Woman's Vision"; and Evans's "Eudora Welty and the Dutiful Daughter," along with the particular sources cited below.

2. Appendix B, I.D.h Texas, Marrs 229.

3. Further circumstantial evidence in "June Recital" that Loch may be King's son includes the fact that the Morrison's black servant, Loella, calls him an orphan immediately after Loch and his mother have been discussing King's appearance, and (as Appel points out) that Loch's mother pointedly calls him "my" child in Cassie's presence, as if her relation to Cassie is not as close because Cassie's father is Wilbur Morrison. None of the evidence is conclusive, of course. For one discussion of the evidence for which of the characters may be King's unknown children, see Appel 205–37.

4. Welty has noted frequently how unpredictable and intense an experience writing *The Golden Apples* was: for representative comments, see Prenshaw, *Conversations* 43, 326 and *One Writer's Beginnings* 98–102. The best general discussion of *The Golden Apples* in a book on Welty remains Vande Kieft's, 87–125. Of the many journal articles that have been published on *The Golden Apples*, those by the following authors were indispensable, and because of their complexity they generally elude my strictures about "much" Welty criticism made in the text: McHaney, "Eudora Welty and the Multitudinous Golden Apples"; Messerli; Pei; Pitavy-Souques, "Technique as Myth"; and Yaeger's two articles. Selected authors of recent books and articles on Welty continue a basically archetypal approach to Ran's and Eugene's stories, with perhaps an even stronger emphasis on Welty's admixture of irony to myth: Howard 42–50, 62–66; Kreyling 77–105; Devlin, *Eudora Welty's Chronicle* 134–35; Westling 98–103; Manning 56–59, 97–117, 191–95; and McHaney, "Falling into Cycles."

5. For work of women psychiatrists who revised Freud and were Welty's

contemporaries, see in particular Horney, "The Dread of Women"; and Klein, *Contributions to Psycho-Analysis,* especially her articles focusing on the oedipus conflict, symbol-formation in infants, and the psychogenesis of psychotic states: 140–55, 202–14, 236–50, 282–320. Two fine introductions to Klein's and Winnicott's object-relations psychology have been published by Segal and by Davis and Wallbridge, respectively. For one account of how Horney and Klein have influenced recent feminist criticism, see Langbauer, especially 220–23; for one book-length treatment of how women have revised Freud, see Chodorow, *Feminism and Psychoanalytic Theory.* As far as I am aware, only one critic, Tarbox, has undertaken a sustained psychoanalytical reading of a Welty short story. All of these authors and others will be cited more specifically below, and in the bibliography. The works of Freud that have been most helpful in my own thinking on these matters in Welty have been the following: "Three Essays on the Theory of Sexuality"; "The Dream-Work"; "On Narcissism"; and "The Dissolution of the Oedipus Complex."

6. Compare Chodorow: "Because women are responsible for early child care and for most later socialization as well, because fathers are more absent from the home, and because men's activities generally have been removed from the home while women's have remained within it, boys have difficulty attaining a stable masculine gender role identification. Boys fantasize about and idealize the masculine role and their fathers, and society defines it as desirable" (*Reproduction of Mothering* 185). On this topic, see also Klein 202–14; and Lasch 172–76. Particularly relevant for a general understanding of misogyny are the following points of Chodorow's: "Women's early mothering . . . creates specific conscious and unconscious attitudes or expectations in children. Girls and boys expect and assume women's unique capacities for sacrifice, caring, and mothering, and associate women with their own fears of regression and powerlessness. They fantasize more about men, and associate them with idealized virtues and growth." In some cases, Chodorow believes, such feelings may result in men's "resentment and dread of women, and their search for nonthreatening, undemanding, dependent, even infantile women . . . . Through these same processes men come to reject, devalue, and even ridicule women and things feminine . . . . A boy represses those qualities he takes to be feminine inside himself, and rejects and devalues women and whatever he considers to be feminine in the social world" (*Reproduction of Mothering* 83, 185). Chodorow also cogently summarizes Horney's revision of Freud's views of misogyny: "Karen Horney, unlike Freud, does take masculine contempt for and devaluation of women as in need of interactive and developmental explanation. According to her, these phe-

nomena are manifestations of a deeper 'dread of women'—a masculine fear and terror of maternal omnipotence that arises as one major consequence of their early caretaking and socialization by women" (*Reproduction of Mothering* 183). See Tarbox for an account of characters in four of Welty's early stories ("A Memory," "Clytie," "The Purple Hat," and "Death of a Traveling Salesman") whose hallucinations merge visions of faces and breasts and reveal symptoms of both narcissism and misogyny. "The significance of these face-breast experiences for the study of Eudora Welty's fiction," Tarbox comments, "is that their occurrence is an unfailing sign that the Welty hero is in dire need of being saved, i.e., in dire need of being absolutely free of intense separation anxiety or persecutory fear" (71). Tarbox does not consider stories in *The Golden Apples*.

7. Compare Klein's chapters "The Psychogenesis of Manic-Depressive States" and "Mourning and its Relation to Manic-Depressive States," in which she discusses an infant's "splitting" of his images of his mother into feared and loved versions of her, one which he tries to destroy and one which he guiltily tries to restore. When what Klein calls symbolic acts of "reparation" for these imagined attacks are unsuccessfully made, the ego is unable to integrate its images of the mother or to be able to learn to treat her as a separate, autonomous human being with virtues and faults. When neurotic regression to such an infantile state occurs in adults (as it has, I would argue, in Ran's case), the fantasies are visualized and relived with little more control, "distance," or understanding than an infant possesses. See Klein 282–320; Jardine; and Tarbox: "The underlying reasons for the Welty hero's detachment are his intense oral rage over disappointment and a love which is impulsive and devouring; so devouring, that it provokes archaic fear reactions in the lover himself. The main focus of this hero's rage and love, appropriately, is the maternal breast or its equivalents" (73).

8. Note the parallels between this scene and the scene in which Tom Harris is alone in the motel room in "The Hitch-Hikers" (71–72). Now, however, the man is much more strongly threatened by women, and the imaginary space signifying his "independence" has been invaded.

9. In other words, Eugene is experiencing the classic symptoms of what Klein calls the inability to keep separate his "good" and "bad" objects—his loved and feared images of his mother (282–320). See also Tarbox: "The face-breast phenomenon or equation is often first experienced as good (enticing), but then may be suddenly experienced as bad (angry or forbidding)" (71). Representative critics who read Eugene's vision as a glimpse of redemption that his wife later destroys are Vande Kieft 110–111; Appel 228–30; Kreyling 98–99; and McHaney, "Falling into Cycles" 184.

10. This Traveler's Tree scene is absent in Welty's draft of the story in I.D3 Jackson, Marrs 34, as is much of the material from *Collected Stories* 406–9. Other references in Chapters Two through Four to Welty's revisions of "Music from Spain" apply to this draft.

11. I compute the chronology as follows. Ran, Eugene, and Maideen's mother are fifteen at the start of "Sir Rabbit" (*Collected Stories* 331, 333), and she appears to be only a few years older when she marries Junior Holifield and meets King in the woods (333). "The Whole World Knows" and "Music from Spain" are set when Ran and his brother are in their "forties" (393). Since we know that Maideen is eighteen in "The Whole World Knows" (376), the dates appear to work out. What happens in the interim to Junior Holifield, Mattie Will's first husband, is not clear. We must not assume that he is killed by King's buckshot in "Sir Rabbit"; the narrative implies that he is merely scared senseless by King so that King will be free to enjoy his wife (339). Perhaps if Mattie Will eventually married someone named Sumrall, she gave Maideen her new last name to disguise her parentage. The simplest hypothesis, however, is that Maideen's mother was another woman in the Sojourner clan and that Maideen's father is someone named Sumrall, not King MacLain. For another view, see Allen, where he claims that Maideen is Mattie Will Sojourner's granddaughter (32).

12. Readings blaming the women in the story are offered by Appel 93–99; Howard 73–74; and St. George Tucker Arnold, Jr., 21–27. Arnold speaks of a "savage matriarchal deity to whom human sacrifices, often male infants, were dedicated in the dawn phases of human society" and calls Welty's women "avatars of the Terrible Mother" (22). Appel even goes so far as to call the rapist, Mr. Petrie, the story's "only free man": "with the arrest of the petrified man the women seem to have succeeded in subjugating the only free man in the story—but not quite, for Billy Boy remains to be vanquished" (97). One partial exception is Vande Kieft 62–65. For two articles cataloguing the presence of Medusa allusions in the story, see Helterman and Robert C. Walker. For more on Medusas, mirrors, madness, and other relevant matters, see Auerbach; McGann; Irigaray; Cixous; and Dijkstra 137–38, 309–11, who focuses on Medusa images in late nineteenth- and early twentieth-century art. The art historian and anthropologist A. David Napier has recently published an especially interesting survey of the various incarnations of Perseus and the Gorgon Head in ancient mythology, in Greece and farther east, some of it pre-Homeric. He notes that the Gorgon was associated with rebirth and transformation as well as terror, and that it was often depicted androgynously. The Sanskrit root of the word Gorgon means "shriek" (83–134).

My understanding of advertising has been particularly influenced by Barthes;

Berger; Mulvey; and Ewen's *Captains of Consciousness,* a history of advertising in America focusing on the radical transformations that occurred between the 1920s and the 1950s. Boorstin's *The Americans* and Marchand's *Advertising the American Dream: Making Way for Modernity,* 1920–1940, provide general histories of the development of advertising in American in the nineteenth and twentieth centuries. Ewen notes the influence on advertisers of social psychologists and their theories of female narcissism (180), but does not connect his discussion of advertising's treatment of women as sexual objects to male narcissism or male rape fantasies.

Readers should know of other unpublished early work in which Welty satirizes advertising. "The Waiting Room" (IV.B.1 Jackson, Marrs 73), dating from 1935, is a farce set in a train station's waiting room. One of the characters in the opening pages is passing the time by trying to win a contest by coming up with a snappy description of what "White Spright Soap does to your skin," and another character later in the play, when provoked, blurts "Aw, if you're so smart, why ain't you rich." "What Year Is This" (IV.B2.a Jackson, Marrs 73; no date) is a series of musical sketches, some by Welty and others by Hildegarde Dolson. (For background, see Prenshaw, *Conversations* 207.) The following excerpt is from a delightful skit called "What Year is This," written by Welty in mock praise of *The New York Times:* "(She delivers like a school cheer): 'Sak's! Stern's! Sloan's for the house!/ With a hey nonny nonny and Abraham Straus!/ Wanamaker, Wanamaker,/ Peck and Peck!/ Here's a great big hug and a mail-order check!/ O the Times!' "

13. Compare Ewen on the role played by mirrors in advertising in creating anxiety: "In an informal survey of *Ladies Home Journal* and *Saturday Evening Post* ads through the 1920s, I have found that between eight and ten ads per issue depict a woman at or looking into a mirror. Many of these ads are *not* for cosmetic products" (177–83 and, in particular, 239, n121). See also Dijkstra's fascinating discussion "The Mirror of Venus" (127–46), which analyzes late nineteenth-century and early twentieth-century theories of women's narcissism and images of women looking into mirrors in the visual arts. Dijkstra's book provides many precedents for the conventions governing advertising's treatment of women and mirrors after World War I.

14. "June Recital" was the first story Welty wrote in the sequence that eventually became *The Golden Apples* (Pitavy-Souques, "Technique as Myth," 259n); an early version of it was published in *Harper's Bazaar* in 1947 (Polk, "A Checklist" 244). Portions of the heavily revised "June Recital" manuscript in Texas (I.D1c Marrs 228, Appendix B) that eventually became pages 311–13 in the *Collected Stories* are pasted onto newsprint from the *New York Times Book Review* of 20 February 1949, thus precisely dating one of

Welty's most intense periods of work on the manuscript; interestingly, the *Book Review* pages she used contained a review of Elizabeth Bowen's novel *The Heat of the Day*. Unlike "The Whole World Knows" and "Music from Spain," "June Recital" has received sustained and adventurous commentary. A reader should begin with Welty's own comments in *One Writer's Beginnings*, 100–102. With the exception of Vande Kieft 92–97 and Appel 210–18, the most thorough discussions are in journals or anthologies: McHaney's two articles; Messerli; Rubin, "Art and Artistry"; Pei; Pugh; Pitavy-Souques, "Watchers and Watching"; Yaeger, "'Because a Fire'"; and Wall. Kreyling discusses the relevance of Welty's allusion to the children's story "The Lucky Stone" (*Collected Stories* 292, Kreyling 81–83). Anne Goodwyn Jones, Scott, Westling (8–35), and Wall provide invaluable background for an understanding of Miss Eckhart's social predicament in Morgana; and Tick's and Neuls-Bates's works are especially recommended for those seeking histories of female musicians and music teachers in the United States in the late nineteenth and early twentieth centuries, to be read with a general discussion such as Evans's "Eudora Welty: The Metaphor of Music." For more on the subject of women and music as treated in American women's fiction, see Chapter Four.

15. Vande Kieft argues that Miss Eckhart is not consciously aware of Virgie upstairs (1987 edition, page 93; in the 1962 edition of her book she read the scene differently, page 119). McHaney agrees that Miss Eckhart is unaware of Virgie's presence in the house ("Eudora Welty and the Multitudinous Golden Apples" 601–2).

16. For information on the cotton crash of 1914, see Odum 13, 19–20; and Tindall 33–69. Another way in which Welty alludes to the cotton crisis as causing hard times for Mississippi is via Mr. Holifield, the nightwatchman at the town's gin mill. He has taken a second job in which he is supposed to "guard" the vacant MacLain house during the day for its new owner (307). (I place *guard* in quotation marks because, comically, this watchman sleeps through the entire events of "June Recital"!) The early draft of "June Recital" cited is I. D1 Jackson, Marrs 34; all other citations of an earlier draft of "June Recital" refer to this typescript carbon, except as noted. No Welty short-story typescripts in the Jackson and Texas collections show more revisions than those of "June Recital" and "The Burning."

17. "[Morgana is] a made-up Delta town. I was drawn to the name because I always loved the conception of Fata Morgana—the illusory shape, the mirage that comes over the sea. All Delta places have names after people, so it was suitable to call it Morgana after some Morgans. My population might not

have known there was such a thing as *Fata Morgana,* but illusions weren't unknown to them, all the same—coming in over the cottonfields" (Kuehl, "The Art of Fiction" 88).

18. For more on Loch's point of view, see Pitavy-Souques, "Watchers and Watching" 485–93; her reading, while sympathetic to him, is a needed corrective to critics such as Messerli (89–90), who have somewhat romanticized Loch's misreading of the events. She too stresses how Loch's point of view (in exaggerated form) parallels the town's.

19. Pitavy-Souques ("Watchers and Watching" 493–503) and Wall also stress how Welty uses Cassie's point of view to catalogue the town's prejudices. For a contrary view of Cassie, see Rubin's essay "Art and Artistry." Rubin's eloquent reading of Cassie's role in the story is ultimately overstated, in my view: it is one thing to argue that Cassie unconsciously appreciates Miss Eckhart's heroism, but quite another to claim that she is her true successor in Morgana.

20. For more on the rich blending of voices and "discourses" in the story's narrative, see Yaeger, "'Because a Fire'"; and Pitavy-Souques, "Watchers and Watching."

21. Interestingly, Rubin suggests that, because of the predominance of references to moonlight and the night sky in *The Golden Apples,* the unnamed Beethoven piano sonata played in this scene is the Moonlight Sonata ("Art and Artistry" 115–16). My vote, however, would be for the Appassionata: it would go better with a thunderstorm, and in *One Writer's Beginnings* Welty says that she associates Miss Eckhart with "passion" (101).

CHAPTER 3

1. "*Women!!* Make Turban in Own Home!" is listed as II.C1 Jackson, Marrs 195; the Jackson archives contain a copy of the entire November, 1941, *Junior League Magazine.* "*Women!!*" was republished in a slightly revised form by Palaemon Press in 1979 in two editions totaling 225 copies (McDonald, *Eudora Welty* 22) and was discussed briefly in Manning 208 n.5. For obvious reasons, I quote from the original 1941 article. Apropos of the upcoming discussion of Hedy Lamarr's relevance to "*Women!!*" is the following Lamarr quotation, which Welty no doubt would enjoy: "Any girl can be glamorous: all you have to do is stand still and look stupid" (Halliwell 612).

2. "*Women!!*" also anticipates the role paper cut-outs play in Loch's imagination in "June Recital" (282), and its reference to a witch and its use of the word "transformation" compare with the key role that word plays in Welty's later story about a woman with magical powers, "Circe" (531). Other stories

in which a woman's headgear plays a significant part include "The Purple Hat," "No Place for You, My Love," and "The Burning." For more on turbans and their connection with Welty's interest in sibyls, see Chapter Four.

3. For Welty's drafts of "Why I Live at the P.O.," see I.A2 and I.A4 Jackson, Marrs 30–32. All subsequent mentions of revisions to "P.O." refer to these drafts. My discussion of the story is in part inspired by two comments Welty has made about the story. The first describes its origin: "I once did see a little post office with an ironing board in the back through the window. This was in some little town—less than a town—some little hamlet in Mississippi. And I suppose that's what made me think of it. Suppose somebody just decided to move down there." The second reflects on the ending: "[the Rondos] live by dramatizing themselves. [Sister will] come back, they'll take her in, and it will start all over again." For the first remark, see Ferris, "A Visit with Eudora Welty" 161; for the second, Ascher 34. Enlightening readings of the story include those by Vande Kieft 53–55; Appel 46–51; May, "Why Sister Lives at the P.O."; Herrscher; Semel; and Romines. Appel's discussion is witty and adroit; it is also valuable for placing the story in the tradition of Ring Lardner and Mark Twain.

4. This chapter is also guided by general discussions and anthologies on comedy and American culture, including Rourke; Habegger 115–95; Rubin, *The Comic Imagination in American Literature*; Wallace; and—more than any other general source—Walker's book *A Very Serious Thing* and her anthology *Redressing the Balance*, edited with Zita Dresner. For further discussion of Welty's relation to earlier American women humorists (rather than the American male humorists who have generally been stressed by Welty criticism so far), see Chapter Four.

5. One example of such an optimistic reading of Livvie's liberation is Kreyling 24–25. Three prominent commentaries note the ambiguousness of Welty's treatment of Cash, Livvie's "rescuer," but more on the matter may be said: see Vande Kieft 48–51; Appel 193–99; and Howard 86–87. For a discussion of Welty's use of mythology in the story, see Prenshaw, "Persephone in Eudora Welty's 'Livvie.'" The presence of the Persephone myth in the story, of course, implies that Livvie's "liberation" may very well be temporary, as the original title, "Livvie is Back," does not.

6. The paradigmatic reading of "At the Landing" is by Vande Kieft 27–29. Her interpretation of Jenny's fate is essentially optimistic: she traces Jenny's painful initiation into the world of experience by Billy Floyd and the river in flood, which represent the "forces of life" causing Jenny to grow. Similar readings are made by Appel 188–93, and Kreyling 28–31; but see also Brookhart's and Marrs's article for historical and geographical back-

ground relevant for the story. Manning has perceptively compared "Livvie," "At the Landing," and "Asphodel," 90–97. My reading of "At the Landing" in particular has been influenced by definitions of "romantic thralldom" offered by Rachel Blau DuPlessis; for more on the subject of this story and women's nineteenth-century sentimental romance novels, see Chapter Four. Welty appears now not to like the story very much: see Prenshaw, *Conversations* 190. Given my discussion of "At the Landing," I should concede that it was apparently written *after* "Asphodel," "A Wide Net," and "The Winds," for they were published in 1942 and "At the Landing" was not published until 1943. I am more interested in intellectual development than in literal chronology, however; we hardly need assume that Welty's experimentation with comic form advanced progressively and consistently. (For bibliographic information on the first publication of Welty's stories, see Vande Kieft [1962] 195–98; or Polk, "A Eudora Welty Checklist.")

7. Insightful discussions of "Asphodel" include those by Vande Kieft 46–48; Appel 84–93; and Manning 91–97. For Welty on the subject of Faulkner, see *Eye of the Story* 126–27, 146–58, 169–73, 207–20; and Prenshaw, *Conversations* 220–21, 302, 321. Needless to say, much more work on the subject of Welty's relationship to Faulkner remains to be done.

8. One other strain of influence from Faulkner in Welty's comic stories deserves brief mention: their use of the popular folkloric image of the wily country peddler. As Rourke (15–36); Hoffman (33–82, especially 49–55); Buell (335–43); and others have shown, the peddler figure in American folklore is an amalgamation of several stock Yankee character types common in the eighteenth century. The peddler's character tends to undergo a significant change when he leaves the rural village to become a traveling salesman, so that native Yankee thriftiness and discipline become obsessive greed, predatory trickery, and egotism—he often trades for the sake of testing whether he can outwit his adversary. Twain portrayed his versions of such a national type with a special emphasis on how they sell not only clocks, notions, lightning rods, and spices but also visions of upward mobility through vast schemes for the investment of capital. Colonel Sellers in *The Gilded Age* is the most creative example, but more conventional variants are scattered through his stories—the wily lightning-rod salesman in "Political Economy" (possibly indebted to Melville's "The Lightning-Rod Man") and Twain's spoof of the whole tradition with the echo salesman in "The Canvasser's Tale." Faulkner has drawn the most memorable modern incarnations of the character, including Flem Snopes and Ratliff in "Spotted Horses" and *The Hamlet*, Jason Compson in *The Sound and the Fury*, and the metal-detector salesman in "The Fire and the Hearth" in *Go Down, Moses*. The contrast

between Ratliff and Flem is particularly telling, for although Ratliff conforms more closely to the traditional type, he is bested by Flem, who cheats people into believing that he is not even peddling and that they have not been had. Three of the most important characters in Welty's stories are traveling salesmen: R. J. Bowman in "Death of a Traveling Salesman," Tom Harris in "The Hitch-Hikers," and King MacLain in *The Golden Apples.* King has the braggadocio and ruthlessness that is long associated with the figure, a fast talker and a flatterer who (like Flem) knows when a well-timed gift is as important as a tight bargain. (Before Welty realized that "June Recital" and "Shower of Gold" were linked, incidentally, the outsider who walked into the MacLain house in the middle of the action in "June Recital" was a salesman named "Mr. Demarest, peddling 8-in-1 Song Conditioner for canary birds" [I.D1 Jackson, Marrs 34]). King's epic pretensions are dismantled during the course of *The Golden Apples* in the name of other, less traditionally masculine forms of heroism, while both Welty's earlier stories about salesmen focus on their difficult and sometimes infantile relations with women. Together, these portraits of Welty's demystify the peddler archetype that has so held the imagination of male writers. In contrast to them, she spends no time dramatizing the cleverness of the deals they strike; she focuses instead on the disastrous effect of their "heroic" mode of life on others and on themselves.

9. "The Wide Net" has received a good deal more attention than "The Winds." Especially recommended are readings by Vande Kieft 57–58; Appel 62–69; Howard 36–42, 68–69, 89–94; and an article by Cluck on the story as a comic epic.

10. For a scholarly discussion of the psychological and social causes of some husbands' jealousy of their pregnant wives, see Chodorow, *Reproduction of Mothering,* especially 201–5. For Welty, the success of William Wallace's quest to find his lost wife is measured by his ability to overcome his jealousy of her. See also my citations in notes 6–8 for Chapter Two. My reading of William Wallace's reaction to his wife's pregnancy may be contrasted with Appel's: "Hazel's pregnancy has filled her with a sense of mystery, making her hypersensitive and unpredictable" (63).

11. Vande Kieft, Howard, and Cluck treat Doc's presence in the story much less ambivalently; they see him as the incarnation of a "mythological" and "universal" point of view.

12. See also Prenshaw's suggestive but too brief discussion of the story's ending in "Woman's World, Man's Place," 62–63, in which she argues that Hazel, like many other heroines in Welty's fiction, acts as a Psyche figure

who rescues her man "first from naive innocence and then from threatening loneliness."

13. I.K6 Jackson, Marrs 50.

14. The best discussion of "The Winds" is Kreyling's 25–28; he stresses the importance of Cornella as a symbol of natural powers of transformation. But see also Appel 186–88; and Pearl Amelia Schmidt, "Textual Variants in 'The Winds.'" Apropos of my upcoming argument linking "The Winds" and the later story "June Recital" is the fact that in the 1980 galleys for the *Collected Stories* one of the few changes Welty made to the entire manuscript was to change Fate Rainey's street cry in "June Recital" to the present one (278) so that it would no longer be identical to the "Milk, milk,/ Buttermilk" song in "The Winds" (214).

15. This scene foreshadows a similar scene in the last pages of *The Optimist's Daughter* (1973), which is also about the contrast between physical versus imaginative possessions: in the case of Laurel Hand, she learns to do without a breadboard.

16. In *One Writer's Beginnings* Welty mentions attending Chautauqua events in Jackson during her childhood (32, 86). For background on the Chautauqua movement in the early twentieth century, two discussions by Case and Case and by Morrison are recommended, especially Morrison 161–92. While Chautauqua's educational lectures were sometimes reformist, women's rights appear to have been too radical a subject to be thoroughly debated; popular topics were more likely to be the need for banking reform or physical fitness. Josie's response to the woman musician is not prompted by any lecture that she may have heard. For information on women musicians in the late nineteenth and early twentieth centuries, see Tick: "By and large, women did not learn orchestral instruments in any significant degree until the 1870s, and here change was focused on string instruments rather than on winds or brass." Piano, harp, and guitar were most commonly studied in the 1870s, though a female cornet player was famous in the United States in that decade, partly because of her novelty; in the 1890s, violin was added to the group of instruments thought "acceptable" for women to play. Women's orchestras did become popular around the turn of the century (Tick 327–30), which is confirmed by the all-woman Chautauqua ensemble depicted in "Beautiful Ohio" and "The Winds."

17. IV.A4 Jackson, Marrs 72. The story is unpublished.

18. A good introductory discussion of "Shower of Gold" is Appel's, 60–62; he places King in "company with a long line of characters from American humor—the trickster tricked, a traditional figure who recurs in

the work of the Southwest humorists, in Twain, Lardner, and Faulkner." Most commentators celebrate King MacLain as a heroically rebellious Zeus figure, a god of fertility, though some also qualify this by mentioning Welty's use of irony: see Vande Kieft 55–56, 89–91; Devlin 133–34; Messerli 83–85; Howard 63–64; and Manning 97–100. The majority of critics over-simplify Katie Rainey's role in the story, arguing that even though she acts as a spokeswoman for Morgana's conservative values she reveals that she se-cretly idolizes King. This is true enough, but misses the way the story cele-brates Katie Rainey's storytelling, especially her ability to revise legends about King. Daniele Pitavy does stress Mrs. Rainey's creativity as a story-teller, as I do; see her "'Shower of Gold' ou les ambiguites de la narration."

19. I.Db Texas, Marrs 228, Appendix B. Other references to Welty's re-visions of "Shower of Gold" are based on this source, except as noted.

20. Excellent readings of "Sir Rabbit" that emphasize its mixture of mock-ery and mythology include those by Vande Kieft 91–92; Manning 100–3; and Kendig. I find when teaching the story, however, that students are dis-turbed by how the rape is portrayed and are not as willing as critics are to be-lieve that literary critical concepts such as "comic reversal" justify the story's methods. Welty's revisions of the story reveal that she was uncertain about the right tone for the story. An early version of the scene with Ran and Eugene (332) is both more graphic and more euphemistic: "One of the twins took hold of her and the other one ran under and she was down. One of them pinned her arms and the other one jumped her bare feet. One little paw blindfolded her eyes and two little paws took away her drawers" (I.D2 Jack-son, Marrs 34). Revising, Welty edited out the references to "paws" remov-ing Mattie Will's underwear and changed the mention of her eyes being blindfolded to a reference to the "blindness" of worms in the soil beneath her. These changes, in my opinion, do not resolve the problems of mixing cuteness and violence in how the scene is rendered. But Welty's revisions elsewhere in the story also clearly stress that the issue for her is Mattie Will's submission to power, whether voluntarily or involuntarily: when she has sexual intercourse with King, I.D2 Jackson, Marrs 34, describes it as "like knowing another way to talk," whereas the version in The Golden Apples has "like *submitting* to another way to talk" (338; my italics).

21. The most useful introductions to "Moon Lake" are by Vande Kieft 97–103; and Manning 107–16, but see also Pei 423–25, 429–30; Appel 217–22; Messerli 93–96; Thomas L. McHaney, "Eudora Welty"; and Yae-ger, "The Case of the Dangling Signifier." The best of these discussions may be Pei's and Yaeger's; Yaeger's is especially interesting for its use of Lacanian terminology to discuss the issues of sexual politics that the story raises. Arline

Garbarini discusses the relevance of Welty's sardonic allusion in "Moon Lake" to *The Re-Creation of Brian Kent* (1919), a sentimental romance by Harold Bell Wright; see also my own discussion of Welty's critique of the sentimental romance tradition in American fiction in the next chapter.

22. I.D5 Jackson, Marrs 35; this change is also made in ink in the manuscript of "Moon Lake," I.D1e Texas, Marrs 229, Appendix B.

23. Pei (423–24) and Yaeger ("Dangling Signifier" 436–37) have briefly argued for the scene's importance.

24. I.Dh Texas, Marrs 229, Appendix B. As with "June Recital," "The Wanderers" has been quickly recognized as one of Welty's best stories, and has inspired excellent commentary. In the books on Welty, see Vande Kieft 112–17; Appel 231–37; Howard 64–67, 95–96, 106–20; Kreyling 100–5; Devlin, *Eudora Welty's Chronicle* 163–66, 204; Westling 100–104; and Manning 57–58, 68–69, 104–6. In the journals and anthologies, see Messerli 98–100; Prenshaw, "Woman's World, Man's Place" 72–77; Thomas L. McHaney, "Eudora Welty" 17–24; Pei 426–33; MacKethan; Pugh; Pitavy-Souques, "Technique as Myth"; and Evans, "Eudora Welty and the Dutiful Daughter." Of these many interpreters, Pei captures best the story's ironic yet also affectionate portrait of the aged King MacLain; Evans superbly places Welty's portraits of Virgie and Cassie within the larger context of her varying portraits of mother-daughter relationships; and Vande Kieft and McHaney give the richest readings of the story's famous concluding epiphany.

25. Welty's typescripts for "The Wanderers" reveal that several of the most important details involving Mrs. Morrison were added in revision, such as the descriptions of how Mrs. Morrison told bad news with "a perfectly blank face . . . as if she repeated a lesson" and of how she reacted to learning of King's appearance (295, 326). It also should be noted that it was originally Mrs. Morrison rather than Miss Snowdie MacLain who gripped Cassie's hand so tightly when Miss Eckhart created a public spectacle of her anguish at the funeral for Mr. Sissum (299). I.D1 Jackson, Marrs 34; and I.D1c Texas (Marrs 228, Appendix B); all other references to Welty's revisions of "The Wanderers" are based these typescripts unless noted.

26. On Mr. Nesbitt's recent interest in lumbering, it is instructive to consult Odum's *Southern Regions of the United States*, 1936), a publication sponsored by the Southern Regional Committee of the Social Science Research Council. Odum took note of the disastrous effects on the South's economy of the boom-and-bust cotton-market cycles and advocated the exploitation of a far wider range of natural and agricultural resources. Odum's recommendations were quickly influential: see Michael O'Brien 13–93.

27. This scene also foreshadows Welty's portrait of the relationship between Laurel Hand and Missouri in *The Optimist's Daughter*.

28. Welty's "she had to put on what he [King] knew with what he did" (338) echoes Yeats's "Did she put on his knowledge with his power/ Before the indifferent beak could let her drop?" Welty, however, revises the line she alludes to, for in the very next sentence, the narrator says that Mattie Will's (her Leda's) experience is "like submitting to another way to talk." Several critics have pointed out the parallel but not the difference: see, for example, Thomas L. McHaney, "Eudora Welty" 605–6. Yaeger, however, does focus on the difference: "'Because A Fire'" 960–61. See also my comments on "Sir Rabbit" in Chapter Three, note 20.

29. Perhaps also relevant for Welty's linking of Miss Eckhart and texts is the following passage in the Texas "June Recital" manuscript (I.D1c, Marrs 228, Appendix B) describing Miss Eckhart's stopping children on the street after she is forced out of the MacLain house: she would load their arms with books and command, "Take these back to the public library and bring me eight more; I don't care to go inside." In the published version of the story her commands do not involve reading (*Collected Stories* 307). Perhaps Miss Eckhart was devouring some of the same romance novels that are discussed in the next chapter! Incidentally, in a 1980 interview Welty commented upon Virgie's future as follows: "Virgie had that power [learnt from Miss Eckhart] to feel and project her feelings, and she wanted to realize all of this. . . . I think at the end of the story she is saying good-bye to the life there in Morgana. I think she's got it in her to do something else" (Brans, "Struggling Against the Plaid" 305).

30. The best discussions of *The Bride of the Innisfallen* as a whole are by Vande Kieft 126–38 and Kreyling 118–39. Readers interested particularly in "Circe" may want to consult Devlin and Prenshaw, "A Conversation with Eudora Welty," in *Welty: A Life in Literature*, where she mentions that she wrote "Circe" after her Guggenheim Fellowship trip to Europe and the Mediterranean in 1949; it was inspired by wondering, "What would it be like to be condemned to live forever?" (19). Critical discussions of "Circe" include Vande Kieft 33–34; Goudie; and Romines, who stresses Circe's frustration and despair and places her within the tradition of earlier female monologists such as Sister. All references to revisions of "Circe" are based on the early typescript in Texas, where the story is entitled "The Wand" (I.F.1b Texas, Marrs 230, Appendix B).

31. But see Marilyn Arnold, who argues persuasively that the unnamed listener to Edna Earle's monologue is a woman not a man, as most critics

have assumed; she suggests that Edna Earle is sizing her up for Daniel Ponder's next wife.

CHAPTER 4

1. For a plot summary of *The Re-Creation of Brian Kent* and a brief discussion of its relevance to "Moon Lake," see Garbarini. For Welty's refusal to read *St. Elmo*, see Prenshaw, *Conversations* 8.

2. Besides the authors mentioned in the text, other influences on my understanding of nineteenth-century American women's fiction, both sentimental romance and "local-color" fiction, include works by Donovan, Buell 293–370, Huf, Petry, Anne Goodwyn Jones, Falk, McNall, Papashvily, Fletcher, and Miller. This field was largely dormant until the mid-1970s; the extraordinary amount of scholarship done since then is testimony to how newly unresolved our sense of the nineteenth-century American canon is, and to how much more work remains to be done. This scholarship is also inspired by the strength and popularity of American women's writing since World War II, particularly recent fiction. For bibliographic information on particular nineteenth-century works of fiction by women cited extensively in the text, see Works Cited.

3. On the general topic of women in America in the nineteenth century, histories by Cott, Welter, Conrad, and Smith-Rosenberg were also important to me, in addition to the works of literary criticism mentioned above.

4. On this issue, see in particular Smith-Rosenberg 53–76; Donovan 99–138; Sahli; and Faderman. Smith-Rosenberg's essay is a now-classic general survey, while Sahli's chronicles the changing attitudes toward close women's friendships during the turn of the century, the most important period for women's local-color literature.

5. Louis A. Renza has published an entire book devoted to an analysis of "The White Heron" and the shifting status of so-called "minor" literature in the canon. See also Deleuze and Guattari.

6. As exemplified by her essay "Place in Fiction" in *The Eye of the Story*, Welty is perhaps this country's most eloquent defender of "regional" or "local-color" literature, while attacking those names for it as being prejudicial. In essence, she claims that only a literature that has deep roots in a particular time and place can become universal. She finds a term like "regional" almost always used in a disparaging way, however, as shown by other passages on page 132 of the essay in *Eye of the Story*. Her various confrontations with New York writers criticizing "regional" or "southern" writing are expertly discussed by Devlin, *Eudora Welty's Chronicle* 3–15, 41–44, 82–85, includ-

ing an analysis of Welty's sharp letter to *The New York Times Book Review* in 1975 defending Reynolds Price after Richard Gilman had attacked his work and had claimed that southern literature was no longer "an ongoing cultural reality." See also Welty's eloquent brief 1954 statement "Place and Time: The Southern Writer's Inheritance" in the *Times Literary Supplement*; III.D2 Jackson, Marrs 71. Building on Anthony C. Hilfer's work, Devlin also usefully contrasts the "ideal communities" of earlier local-color writers, such as Jewett's Dunnet Landing and Zona Gale's Friendship Village, with later regional writers such as Sherwood Anderson, Sinclair Lewis, and Thomas Wolfe, who dramatize a "revolt from the village." He places Welty in the latter group: "Eudora Welty also examines critically the communal myth of small-town living, reserving various degrees of pathos and satire for Victory, Mississippi, China Grove, Farr's Gin, The Landing, and smug, complacent Natchez. In *A Curtain of Green* and *The Wide Net*, these and other fictional towns provide the atmosphere of 'binding perfection' that precipitates awakening and renewal or simply a vision of personal defeat. Eudora Welty's own 'revolt from the village' may not possess the same high level of environmental determinism, polemical warning, or bitterness that respectively impells Anderson, Lewis, and Wolfe, but it does permit a comprehensive description of her major themes and motifs" (80-81). Devlin does not consider Welty's relation to women local-color writers, beyond mentioning Jewett in this passage and briefly alluding to Katherine Anne Porter's Miranda during a discussion of Welty's "The Wanderers" (171). Also relevant is Donovan's book and Buell's chapter "The Village as Icon," 304-18. Critics who have briefly discussed Welty's debt to Porter's work are Russell; Bradbury 108-110; and Westling 63. The starting place for any consideration of Welty's relation to Porter and Cather, however, must be her essays "Katherine Anne Porter: The Eye of the Story" and "The House of Willa Cather" in *The Eye of the Story* and her essay "My Introduction to Katherine Anne Porter" (1990). McCullers and O'Connor of course were not predecessors or influences on Welty because they were younger contemporaries. For a balanced assessment of McCullers, O'Connor, and Welty, see Westling.

7. For other discussions of Welty and comedy, see Chapter Three, note 4. Lawrence Buell also has interesting though brief observations to make about the role women's humor plays in the "comic grotesque" tradition in local-color writing, especially via the motif of a tardy or awkward man's courtship of a woman (343-50). He finds a special importance for Wilkins Freeman in this tradition, while largely ignoring Frances Whitcher.

8. For further analysis of Cather's ambivalence towards the independent woman artist and towards the issue of women's sexuality, see Sharon O'Brien's excellent article; and Gilbert and Gubar, *No Man's Land*, 169-

212. Willa Cather's lesbianism further complicates such a reading of *Youth and the Bright Medusa* and other Cather texts: if social mores decree that a woman artist's necessary independence from men may "deform" her, lesbianism would do so even more. In general, Cather's successful female characters repress their sexuality to a great extent in order to gain independence; compare Alexandra's fate with that of Marie's in *O Pioneers!*, for example. Recommended readings of *The Song of the Lark* are those of Sharon O'Brien; Huf; and Fryer 291–301. For Welty on Cather, see especially *The Eye of the Story* 41–60 and Prenshaw, *Conversations* 195, 324.

9. Moers 263–319; she discusses Cather's novel in light of the Corinne myth on 287–92. See also Huf 81–104; curiously, Huf mentions Corinne only in reference to Carson McCullers's portrait of the aspiring musician, Mick Kelly, in *The Heart Is a Lonely Hunter* (1940). For the traditional association of the Cumaean sibyl with song as well as writing, see Virgil's Fourth Eclogue. For two histories of women musicians in the nineteenth and twentieth centuries, see Tick and Neules-Bates.

10. I thank William Turpin and Gilbert Rose of Swarthmore College's Department of Classics for translating and analyzing this Greek text of Domenichino for me, and Richard Spear of Oberlin College's Department of Art for answering my questions regarding Domenichino's sibyls and this Greek text. Spear translates the phrase as follows: "There is only one God, infinite [and] unborn." He notes that the Cumaean sibyl is traditionally associated with this prophecy (I, 232).

11. For two cogent discussions of the difference between the authority of oral speech versus the authority of written texts in the Western tradition, see Thoreau's distinction between the mother and the father tongue in his chapter on "Reading" in *Walden*, and Michel Foucault's *The Order of Things*: "[In the Renaissance, the spoken word] is stripped of all its powers; it is merely the female part of language, Vigenere and Duret tell us, just as its intellect is passive; Writing, on the other hand, is the active intellect, the 'male principle' of language. It alone harbours the truth" (38–39). Foucault, however, ignores the authority given in the Renaissance to God's spoken word. Derrida in *Of Grammatology* has written on the problems of subordination created by adding a "supplement" to a prior text, as well as on the vexed relations between oral and written discourse (6–26, 141–64).

12. Domenichino's portraits of such sibylline powers were of course indebted to Michelangelo, whose five sibyls on the Sistine Chapel ceiling dramatize the contrast between the oral and the textual, the authority of inspiration versus the authority of tradition. The Cumaean sibyl is given special authority in Michelangelo's sequence because the contents of her pro-

phetic song as recorded in Virgil's Fourth (or "Messianic") Eclogue were thought to foretell the coming of Christ and the founding of His church in Rome. The Cumaean sibyl thus anticipated the essentially oral moment of Christian revelation: her "song" was her strength, allowing her to contravene false prophets and centuries of written pagan law. At least four works are especially relevant for a survey of the role sibyls have played in Western art: De Tolnay, 57–62, 155–58; Wind; Schiller (volume I, especially plates 33 and 51 and commentary on pages 19 and 102–03); and Dotson. There is considerable disagreement among these critics—particularly De Tolnay and Dotson—about the meaning of Michelangelo's placement and posing of the Sistine sibyls, but all the commentators from Augustine to Aquinas to the Neoplatonic philosophers of the Renaissance stress that sibyls were thought to be among the most privileged of the pagan prophets. Especially relevant for the reader of Welty's stories is this sentence by De Tolnay: "The motif of the turned-away head, covered by a head-cloth, is an old one in Italian art, used to express the mysterious Cassandra-like female character" (157). Michelangelo's interpretation of the sibyls is revolutionary for the clarity with which it depicts the fact that the sibyls' authority comes from oral rather than written language: the first sibyl in the Sistine sequence, the Delphic oracle, hears the Word of God directly; the last, from Libya, puts down a book and prepares to rise, as if in preparation for the Day of Judgment. Domenichino's more secularized sibyls are strongly influenced by Michelangelo's Sistine sibyls. The standard work on Domenichino is Spear's; see 191–92, 232–33 of volume I, which discuss two of Domenichino's most important sibyl paintings, and plates 171–72 and 255 in volume II; see also color plate 6 in volume I. Relevant early literary texts mentioning sibyls include Plato, *Phaedrus* 224B; Virgil, *Eclogues* IV, *Aeneid* III.443ff. and VI.9ff.; Ovid, *Metamorphoses* XIV.143ff.; Dante, *Paradiso* XXXIII.66; and Milton, "Il Penseroso."

For a spirited discussion of the role of the "blank page" or empty space in women's writing, see Gubar. Langbauer's more recent essay "Women in White, Men in Feminism," however, makes the notion of a "free" blank or white space for writing considerably more problematic. For a meditation on the somewhat analogous role played in art and literature by the female figure of Melancholia (portrayed in Dürer's famous engraving), see Peter Schmidt, "'These.'" There are very intriguing parallels and contrasts between the standard poses of sibyls and those associated with Melancholy, not to mention the various meanings these allegorical female figures have accrued; more study needs to be done.

13. Welty's ownership of a reproduction of Cellini's *Perseus* is mentioned in a letter to the author, 1 August 1989. The entire passage in "Music from Spain" from "Eugene had been easily satisfied" to "a Filipino dropped a dish" (*Collected Stories* 406–9), including the sibyl reference, is absent in I.D3 Jackson, present in I.D5 Jackson, Marrs 34.

14. For an introduction to the iconography and legends of St. Cecilia, see Ferguson 197–98; and Kaftal 250–58; for a discussion of the contradictory interpretations that have been given Domenichino's Borghese sibyl, see Spear I, 191–92.

15. Valuable readings of "The Burning" may be found in Vande Kieft 128–31; Appel 138–43; Devlin, *Eudora Welty's Chronicle* 125–33; and Bloom, "Introduction" 6–10. Welty now disparages the story: Prenshaw, *Conversations* 220–21. Welty's typescripts of "The Burning" in Jackson demonstrate that she repeatedly revised the story, especially the excerpt quoted above; eight different versions are extant at Jackson. (For the typescripts, see I.F4–8 Jackson, Marrs 36–37.) A full collation of her additions, deletions, and transpositions has yet to be made, but a quick reading of the manuscripts reveals that neither the reference to "proud turbans" nor the most incisive details about the slave system—especially the references to rape and miscegenation—are present in the earliest draft, I.F4.a. The syntax of this quoted passage in the I.F4.a draft is also considerably simpler than in the *Innisfallen* version, with fewer long sentences filled with clauses treated as appositives. Even in a late draft very close to the *Innisfallen* text (I.F8.a), Welty is still making small changes to heighten her focus on the self-destructive violence, changing "one whale to be the grave of fire" to "one whale made of his own grave." As Appel noticed, an intermediate draft (I.F6.a, published in *Harper's Bazaar* in 1951) demonstrates that Welty was conscious of how her Delilah is inevitably indebted to Faulkner's Dilsey in *The Sound and the Fury*. One passage in particular, later deleted, is revealing both for its somewhat stilted and abstract language and its direct echoing of Dilsey's "I seed de beginnin, en now I sees de endin" (371): "[Delilah] let everything be itself according to its nature—the animate, the inanimate, the symbol. She would not move to alter any of it, not unless she was told to and shown how. And so she saw what happened, the creation and the destruction. She waited on either one and served it."

16. For more information on Alice Rideout and the Woman's Building at the 1893 fair in Chicago, see Weimann; an illustration on page 260 shows the placement of Rideout's statue on top of the Woman's Building. Jeanne Madeline Moore (formerly Weimann) notes that very little is known about

Rideout, except that she was a nineteen-year-old woman recently graduated from the San Francisco School of Art who of necessity had to employ men as assistants in making the sculpture. Apparently she did not continue her career as a sculptor after the fair, and her statue was destroyed. The illustration of Rideout's statue that I use is also reproduced in Weimann and is originally from William E. Cameron's 1893 book on the fair, p. 453; no other detailed reproduction of the statue is known to exist (Moore, letter to author, 22 November 1989). I am indebted to Moore for her research on Alice Rideout and the Woman's Building.

Works Cited

Allen, John Alexander. "The Other Way to Live: Demigods in Eudora Welty's Fiction." In *Eudora Welty: Critical Essays*. Edited by Peggy W. Prenshaw. Jackson: University Press of Mississippi. Pp. 26–55.

Appel, Alfred, Jr. *A Season of Dreams: The Fiction of Eudora Welty*. Baton Rouge: Louisiana State University Press, 1965.

Arnold, Marilyn. "The Strategy of Edna Earle Ponder." In *Eudora Welty: Eye of the Story*. Edited by Dawn Trouard. Kent: Kent State University Press, 1989. Pp. 69–77.

Arnold, St. George Tucker, Jr. "Mythic Patterns and Satiric Effect in Welty's 'Petrified Man.'" *Studies in Contemporary Satire* 4 (1977): 21–27.

Ascher, Barbara Lazear. "The Color of the Air: A Conversation with Eudora Welty." *Saturday Review* (November/December 1984): 34.

Auerbach, Nina. *Woman and the Demon: The Life of a Victorian Myth*. Cambridge: Harvard University Press, 1982.

Bakhtin, M. M. *The Dialogic Imagination: Four Essays*. Translated by Caryl Emerson and Michael Holquist. Edited by Michael Holquist. Austin: University of Texas Press, 1981.

Balliett, Whitney. "Fats." *Jelly Roll, Jabbo, and Fats: Nineteen Portraits in Jazz* (New York: Oxford University Press, 1983. Pp. 85–96.

Barthes, Roland. *Mythologies*. Translated by Richard Howard. New York: Hill and Wang, 1957.

Baym, Nina. *Woman's Fiction: A Guide to Novels By and About Women in America, 1820–1870*. Ithaca: Cornell University Press, 1978.

Berger, John. *Ways of Seeing*. New York: Viking, 1973.

Bergson, Henri. *Laughter*. Edited by Wylie Sypher. *Comedy*. Garden City: Doubleday, 1956.

Bloom, Harold. *The Anxiety of Influence*. New York: Oxford University Press, 1973.

———, ed. *Eudora Welty: Critical Views*. New York: Chelsea, 1986.

————. "Introduction." In *Eudora Welty: Critical Views*. Edited by Harold Bloom. New York: Chelsea, 1986. Pp. 1–10.

Bolsterli, Margaret Jones. "Woman's Vision: The Worlds of Women in *Delta Wedding, Losing Battles*, and *The Optimist's Daughter*." In Eudora Welty: A *Life in Literature*. Edited by Albert J. Devlin. Jackson: University Press of Mississippi, 1987. Pp. 149–56.

Boorstin, Daniel. *The Americans: The Democratic Experience*. New York: Random House, 1973.

Booth, Wayne C. *The Rhetoric of Fiction*. Chicago: University of Chicago Press, 1961.

Boyle, Kay. "Full Length Portrait." *The New Republic* 105 (24 November 1941): 707.

Bradbury, John M. *Renaissance in the South: A Critical History of the Literature, 1920–1960*. Chapel Hill: University of North Carolina Press, 1963.

Brans, Jo. "Struggling Against the Plaid: An Interview with Eudora Welty." In *Conversations with Eudora Welty*. Edited by Peggy W. Prenshaw. Jackson: University Press of Mississippi, 1984. Pp. 296–307.

Brookhart, Mary Hughes, and Suzanne Marrs. "More Notes on River Country." In *Eudora Welty: A Life in Literature*. Edited by Albert J. Devlin. Jackson: University Press of Mississippi, 1987. Pp. 82–95.

Brooks, Cleanth. "Eudora Welty and the Southern Idiom." In *Eudora Welty: Critical Views*. Edited by Harold Bloom. New York: Chelsea, 1986. Pp. 93–108.

Browning, Elizabeth Barrett. *Complete Poetical Works*. Boston: Houghton Mifflin, 1900.

Brownmiller, Susan. *Against Our Will: Men, Women, and Rape*. New York: Simon and Schuster, 1975.

Buell, Lawrence. *New England Literary Culture from Revolution through Renaissance*. New York: Cambridge University Press, 1987.

Burgess, Cheryll. "From Metaphor to Manifestation: The Artist in Eudora Welty's A *Curtain of Green*." In *Eudora Welty: Eye of the Storyteller*. Edited by Dawn Trouard. Kent: Kent State University Press, 1989. Pp. 133–141.

Butterworth, Nancy K. "From Civil War to Civil Rights: Race Relations in Welty's 'A Worn Path.' " In *Eudora Welty: Eye of the Storyteller*. Edited by Dawn Trouard. Kent: Kent State University Press, 1989. Pp. 139–45.

Cameron, William E. *The World's Fair, Being a Pictorial History of the Columbian Exposition*. N.p., 1893.

Cary, Alice. *Clovernook Sketches and Other Stories*. Edited by Judith Fetterly. New Brunswick: Rutgers University Press, 1987.

Case, Victoria and Robert Ormond Case. *We Called It Culture: The Story of Chautauqua*. New York: Doubleday, 1948.

Cather, Willa. *Obscure Destinies and Literary Encounters*. New York: Knopf, 1932.

———. *The Song of the Lark*. 1915. Rpt. Lincoln: University of Nebraska Press, 1978.

———. *Youth and the Bright Medusa*. New York: Knopf, 1920.

———. *A Lost Lady*. New York: Knopf, 1923.

Chesebro', Caroline. *Isa: A Pilgrimage*. New York: Redfield, 1852.

Chevigny, Bell Gale, ed. *The Woman and the Myth: Margaret Fuller's Life and Writings*. Old Westbury, N.Y.: Feminist Press, 1976.

Chodorow, Nancy. *The Reproduction of Mothering: Psychoanalysis and the Sociology of Gender*. Berkeley: University of California Press, 1978.

———. *Feminism and Psychoanalytic Theory*. New Haven: Yale University Press, 1989.

Chopin, Kate. *The Awakening*. 1899. Rpt. New York, Avon, 1972.

Cixous, Hélène. "The Laugh of the Medusa." Translated by Keith and Paula Cohen. *Signs: A Journal of Women in Culture and Society* 1 (Summer 1976): 875–93.

Cluck, Nancy Anne. "The Aeneid of the Natchez Trace: Epic Structure in Eudora Welty's 'The Wide Net.'" *The Southern Review* 19 (1983): 510–18.

Coleridge, Mary Elizabeth. *Fancy's Following*. Oxford, England: Daniel Press, 1896.

Conrad, Susan Phinney. *Perish the Thought: Intellectual Women in Romantic America: 1830–1860*. New York: Oxford University Press, 1976.

Cooke, Rose Terry. *"How Celia Changed Her Mind" and Selected Stories*. Edited by Elizabeth Ammons. New Brunswick: Rutgers University Press, 1986.

Cott, Nancy F. *The Bonds of Womanhood: "Woman's Sphere" in New England, 1780–1835*. New Haven: Yale University Press, 1977.

Dante Alighieri. *The Divine Comedy: Paradiso*. Translated by John D. Sinclair. New York: Oxford University Press, 1961.

Davidson, Cathy N. *Revolution and the Word: The Rise of the Novel in America*. New York: Oxford University Press, 1986.

Davis, Madeleine, and David Wallbridge. *Boundary and Space: An Introduction to the Work of D. W. Winnicott*. New York: Brunner/Mazel, 1981.

Davis, Rebecca Harding. *Life in the Iron Mills*. Edited by Tillie Olsen. Old Westbury, NY: Feminist Press, 1972.

De Staël [Staël-Holstein], Anne Louise Germaine (Necker). *Corinna; or, Italy*. London: Corri, 1807. Philadelphia: Fry and Krammerer, 1808.

De Tolnay, Charles. *Michelangelo*. Volume II: *The Sistine Ceiling*. Princeton: Princeton University Press, 1945.

Deleuze, Gilles, and Felix Guattari. *Kafka: Toward a Minor Literature*. Trans. Dana Polan. Minneapolis: University of Minnesota Press, 1986.

Derrida, Jacques. *Of Grammatology.* Translated by Gayatri Chakravorty Spivak. Baltimore: Johns Hopkins University Press, 1976.

Desmond, John F., ed. *The Still Moment: Essays on the Art of Eudora Welty.* Metuchen, N.J.: Scarecrow Press, 1978.

Detweiler, Robert. "Eudora Welty's Blazing Butterfly: The Dynamics of Response." *Language and Style: An International Journal* 6 (1973): 58–71.

Devlin, Albert J. *Eudora Welty's Chronicle: A Story of Mississippi Life.* Jackson: University Press of Mississippi, 1983.

———, ed. *Eudora Welty: A Life in Literature.* Jackson: University Press of Mississippi, 1987.

Dijkstra, Bram. *Idols of Perversity: Fantasies of Feminine Evil in Fin-de-Siècle Culture.* New York: Oxford University Press, 1986.

Dollarhide, Louis, and Ann J. Abadie, eds. *Eudora Welty: A Form of Thanks.* Jackson: University Press of Mississippi, 1979.

Donovan, Josephine. *New England Local-Color Literature: A Woman's Tradition.* New York: Ungar, 1983.

Doolittle, Hilda [H. D.]. *Trilogy.* New York: New Directions, 1973.

———. *Tribute to Freud.* New York: New Directions, 1956.

Dotson, Esther Gordon. "An Augustinian Interpretation of Michelangelo's Sistine Ceiling." *The Art Bulletin* 61 (1979). 2: 223–56, 3: 405–29.

Douglas, Ann. *The Feminization of American Culture.* New York: Knopf, 1977.

DuPlessis, Rachel Blau. *Writing Beyond the Ending.* Bloomington: Indiana University Press, 1985.

Evans, Elizabeth. "Eudora Welty: The Metaphor of Music." *Southern Quarterly* 20 (Summer, 1982): 92–100.

———. *Eudora Welty.* New York: Ungar, 1981.

———. "Eudora Welty and the Dutiful Daughter." In *Eudora Welty: Eye of the Storyteller.* Edited by Dawn Trouard. Kent: Kent State University Press, 1989. Pp. 57–68.

Ewen, Stuart. *Captains of Consciousness: Advertising and the Social Roots of the Consumer Culture.* New York: McGraw-Hill, 1975.

Faderman, Lillian. *Surpassing the Love of Men: Romantic Friendship and Love Between Women from the Renaissance to the Present.* New York: William Morrow, 1981. .

Falk, Robert Press. "The Rise of Realism, 1871–91." In *Transitions in American Literary History.* Edited by Harry Hayden Clark. 1954. Rpt. Durham: Duke University Press, 1967. Pp. 381–442.

Faulkner, William. *The Sound and the Fury.* 1929. Rpt. New York: Random House, 1946.

————. *Go Down, Moses*. New York: Random House, 1936.

————. *Absalom! Absalom!* 1936. Rpt. New York: Random House, 1964.

————. *Uncollected Stories of William Faulkner*. Edited by Joseph Blotner. New York: Random House, 1979.

Ferguson, George. *Signs and Symbols in Christian Art*. New York: Oxford University Press, 1954.

Fern, Fanny. *Ruth Hall and Other Writings*. Edited by Joyce W. Warren. New Brunswick: Rutgers University Press, 1986.

Ferris, Bill. "A Visit with Eudora Welty." In *Conversations with Eudora Welty*. Edited by Peggy W. Prenshaw. Jackson: University Press of Mississippi, 1984. Pp. 154–71.

Fiedler, Leslie. *Love and Death in the American Novel*. 1960. Rpt. New York: Dell, 1969.

Finley, Martha. *Elsie Dinsmore*. 1867. Rpt. New York: Garland, 1977.

Fletcher, Marie. "The Southern Heroine in the Fiction of Representative Southern Women Writers, 1850–1960." Ph.D. dissertation. Louisiana State University, 1963.

Foucault, Michel. *The Order of Things: An Archaeology of the Human Sciences*. New York: Random House, 1970.

Freeman, Mary Wilkins. *Selected Stories of Mary Wilkins Freeman*. Edited by Marjorie Pryse. New York: Norton, 1983.

Freud, Sigmund. "Three Essays on the Theory of Sexuality." *The Standard Edition of the Complete Psychological Works of Sigmund Freud*. Edited by James Strachey. 24 vols. London: Hogarth Press, 1953–1961. Vol. 7, pp. 135–243.

————. "On Narcissism: An Introduction." *The Standard Edition of the Complete Psychological Works of Sigmund Freud*. Edited by James Strachey. 24 vols. London: Hogarth Press, 1953–1961. Vol. 14, pp. 73–102.

————. "The Dissolution of the Oedipus Complex." *The Standard Edition of the Complete Psychological Works of Sigmund Freud*. Edited by James Strachey. 24 vols. London: Hogarth Press, 1953–1961. Vol. 19, pp. 172–79.

————. "The Dream-Work." *The Standard Edition of the Complete Psychological Works of Sigmund Freud*. Edited by James Strachey. 24 vols. London: Hogarth Press, 1953–1961. Vol. 15, pp. 170–83.

Frye, Northrop. *Anatomy of Criticism*. Princeton: Princeton University Press, 1957.

Fryer, Judith. *Felicitous Space: The Imaginative Structures of Edith Wharton and Willa Cather*. Chapel Hill: University of North Carolina Press, 1986.

Garbarini, Arline. "'Moon Lake' and *The Re-Creation of Brian Kent*." *Eudora Welty Newsletter* 2.1 (1978): 1–3.

Gilbert, Sandra M., and Susan Gubar. *The Madwoman in the Attic: The Woman Writer and the Nineteenth-Century Literary Imagination*. New Haven: Yale University Press, 1979.

————. *No Man's Land: The Place of the Woman Writer in the Twentieth Century*. Volume II: Sexchanges. New Haven: Yale University Press, 1989.

Gosset, Louise Y. *Violence in Recent Southern Fiction*. Durham: Duke University Press, 1965.

Goudie, Andrea. "Eudora Welty's Circe: A Goddess Who Strove With Men." *Studies in Short Fiction* 13 (1976): 481–89.

Graham, Kenneth. "'Acrobats in a Park': Performance and Catastrophe." *Delta* 5 (1977): 13–18.

Gross, Seymour. "Eudora Welty's Comic Imagination." In *The Comic Imagination in American Literature*. Edited by Louis D. Rubin, Jr. New Brunswick: Rutgers University Press, 1973. Pp. 319–28.

Groth, Nicholas. *Men Who Rape: The Psychology of the Offender*. New York: Plenum, 1979.

Gubar, Susan. "'The Blank Page' and the Issues of Female Creativity." In *Writing and Sexual Difference*. Edited by Elizabeth Abel. Chicago: University Chicago Press, 1988. Pp. 73–93.

Habegger, Alfred. *Gender, Fantasy, and Realism in American Literature*. New York: Columbia University Press, 1982.

Halliwell, Leslie. *Halliwell's Filmgoer's Companion*. 8th ed. New York: Scribner's, 1985.

Hamilton, Edith. *Mythology*. Boston: Little, Brown, 1940.

Helterman, Jeffrey. "Gorgons in Mississippi: Eudora Welty's 'Petrified Man.'" *Notes on Mississippi Writers* 7 (1974): 12–20.

Hentz, Caroline Lee. *Rena; or the Snowbird*. Philadelphia: A. Hart, 1851.

————. *Eoline; or Magnolia Vale*. Philadelphia: A. Hart, 1852.

Herrscher, Walter. "Is Sister Really Insane? Another Look at 'Why I Live at the Press. O.'" *Notes on Contemporary Literature* 5.1 (1975): 5–7.

Hilfer, Anthony C. *The Revolt from the Village, 1915–1930*. Chapel Hill: University of North Carolina Press, 1969.

Hoffman, Daniel. *Form and Fable in American Fiction*. New York: Oxford University Press, 1961.

Hollenbaugh, Carol. "Ruby Fisher and Her Demon Lover." *Notes on Mississippi Writers* 7 (1974): 63–68.

Homans, Margaret. *Bearing the Word: Language and Female Experience in Nineteenth-Century Women's Writing*. Chicago: University of Chicago Press, 1986.

Horney, Karen. "The Dread of Women." 1932. Rpt. in *Feminine Psychology*. New York: Norton, 1973. Pp. 133–46.

Howard, Zelma Turner. *The Rhetoric of Eudora Welty's Short Stories.* Jackson: University Press of Mississippi, 1973.

Huf, Linda. *A Portrait of the Artist as a Young Woman: The Writer as Heroine in American Literature.* New York, Ungar, 1983.

Hughes, Langston. *The Weary Blues.* New York: Knopf, 1927.

Irigaray, Luce. *Speculum of the Other Woman.* Translated by Gillian C. Gill. Ithaca, New York: Cornell University Press, 1985.

―――. *This Sex Which Is Not One.* Translated by Catherine Porter and Carolyn Burke. Ithaca: Cornell University Press, 1985.

Jardine, Alice. *Gynesis: Configurations of Woman and Modernity.* Ithaca: Cornell University Press, 1985.

Jones, Anne Goodwyn. *Tomorrow Is Another Day: The Woman Writer in the South, 1859–1936.* Baton Rouge: Louisiana State University Press, 1981.

Jones, John Griffin. "Eudora Welty." In *Conversations with Eudora Welty.* Edited by Peggy W. Prenshaw. Jackson: University Press of Mississippi, 1984. Pp. 316–41.

Jones, William. "Growth of a Symbol: The Sun in Lawrence and Eudora Welty." *University of Kansas City Review* 26 (1959): 68–73.

Kaftal, George. *Iconography of the Saints in Tuscan Painting.* Florence: Sansoni, 1952.

Kendig, Daun. "Realities in 'Sir Rabbit': A Frame Analysis." In *Eudora Welty: Eye of the Storyteller.* Edited by Dawn Trouard. Kent: Kent State University Press, 1989. Pp. 119–32.

Kerr, Elizabeth. "The World of Eudora Welty's Women." In *Eudora Welty: A Life in Literature.* Edited by Albert J. Devlin. Jackson: University Press of Mississippi, 1987. Pp. 132–48.

Keys, Marilynn. "'A Worn Path': The Way of Dispossession." *Studies in Short Fiction* 16 (1979): 354–56.

King, Grace Elizabeth. *Monsieur Motte.* New York: A. C. Armstrong, 1888.

Kirkland, Caroline. *A New Home, Who'll Follow? Or, Glimpses of Western Life.* 1839. Rpt. Edited by Sandra A. Zagarell. New Brunswick: Rutgers University Press, 1990.

Klein, Melanie. *Contributions of Psycho-Analysis, 1921–1945: Developments in Child and Adolescent Psychology.* 1948. Rpt. New York: McGraw-Hill, 1964.

Kolodny, Annette. *The Land Before Her: Fantasy and Experience of the American Frontiers, 1630–1860.* Chapel Hill: University of North Carolina Press, 1984.

Kreyling, Michael. *Eudora Welty's Achievement of Order.* Baton Rouge: Louisiana State University Press, 1980.

Kristeva, Julia. *Desire in Language: A Semiotic Approach to Literature and Art.* Edited by Leon S. Roudiez. Translated by Thomas Gora, Alice Jardine, and Leon S. Roudiez. New York: Columbia University Press, 1980.

Kuehl, Linda. "The Art of Fiction XLVII: Eudora Welty." In *Conversations with Eudora Welty.* Edited by Peggy W. Prenshaw. Jackson: University Press of Mississippi, 1984. Pp. 74–91.

Lamarr, Hedy. *Ecstasy and Me: My Life as a Woman.* New York: Bartholomew House, 1966.

Langbauer, Laurie. "Women in White, Men in Feminism." *Yale Journal of Criticism* 2.2 (1989): 219–43.

Lasch, Christopher. *The Culture of Narcissism.* New York: Warner Books, 1977.

McDonald, W. U., Jr. "Eudora Welty's Revisions of 'A Piece of News.'" *Studies in Short Fiction* 7 (1970): 232–47.

———. "Eudora Welty, Reviser: Some Notes on 'Flowers for Marjorie.'" *Delta* 5 (1977): 35–48.

———. "Artistry and Irony: Welty's Revisions of 'Lily Daw and the Three Ladies.'" *Studies in American Fiction* 9 (1981): 113–21.

———. *The Short Stories of Eudora Welty: The Evolution of Printed Texts.* Catalogue of an Exhibit [of W. U. McDonald's Welty Collection] at the Ward M. Canaday Center, the University of Toledo Libraries. University of Toledo, 1983.

———. *Eudora Welty: The Longer Fiction and Miscellaneous Prose.* Catalogue of an Exhibit [of W. U. McDonald's Welty Collection] at the Ward M. Canaday Center, University of Toledo Libraries. University of Toledo, 1988.

McGann, Jerome J. "The Beauty of the Medusa: A Study in Romantic Literary Iconology." *Studies in Romanticism* 11 (1972): 3–25.

McHaney, Pearl. "A Eudora Welty Checklist, 1973–1986." In *Eudora Welty: A Life in Literature.* Edited by Albert J. Devlin. Jackson: University Press of Mississippi, 1987. Pp. 266–302.

McHaney, Thomas L. "Eudora Welty and the Multitudinous Golden Apples." *Mississippi Quarterly* 26 (1972): 589–624.

———. "Falling into Cycles: *The Golden Apples.*" In *Eudora Welty: Eye of the Storyteller.* Edited by Dawn Trouard. Kent: Kent State University Press, 1989. Pp. 173–89.

MacKethan, Lucinda H. "To See Things in Their Time: The Act of Focus in Eudora Welty's Fiction." *American Literature* 50 (1978): 258–75.

Maclay, Joanna. "A Conversation with Eudora Welty." In *Conversations with*

Eudora Welty. Edited by Peggy W. Prenshaw. Jackson: University Press of Mississippi, 1984. Pp. 268–86.

McNall, Sally Allen. *Who Is in the House? A Psychological Study of Two Centuries of Women's Fiction in America, 1795 to the Present.* New York: Elsevier, 1981.

Manning, Carol S. *With Ears Opening Like Morning Glories: Eudora Welty and the Love of Storytelling.* Westport, Conn.: Greenwood, 1985.

Marchand, Roland. *Advertising the American Dream: Making Way for Modernity, 1920–1940.* Berkeley: University of California Press, 1985.

Marrs, Suzanne. *The Welty Collection: A Guide to the Eudora Welty Manuscripts and Documents at the Mississippi Department of Archives and History.* Jackson: University of Mississippi Press, 1989.

May, Charles E. "Why Sister Lives at the P.O." *Southern Humanities Review* 12 (1978): 243–49.

May, Elaine Tyler. *Homeward Bound: American Families in the Cold War Era.* New York: Basic Books, 1988.

Messerli, Douglas. "Metronome and Music: The Encounter Between History and Myth in *The Golden Apples.*" In *The Still Moment: Essays on the Art of Eudora Welty.* Edited by John F. Desmond. Metuchen, N.j.: Scarecrow Press, 1978. Pp. 82–102.

Miller, Nancy K. *The Heroine's Text.* New York: Columbia University Press, 1980.

Milton, John. "Il Penseroso." *Complete Poems and Major Prose.* Edited by Merritt Y. Hughes. New York: Odyssey, 1957. Pp. 72–76.

Moers, Ellen. *Literary Women.* New York: Doubleday, 1975.

Morrison, Theodore. *Chautauqua: A Center for Education, Religion, and the Arts in America.* Chicago: University of Chicago Press, 1974.

Mulvey, Laura. "Visual Pleasure and Narrative Cinema." *Art After Modernism: Rethinking Representation.* Edited by Brian Wallis. New York, Godine, 1984. Pp. 361–73.

Napier, A. David. *Masks, Transformations, and Paradox.* Berkeley: University of California Press, 1986.

Neuls-Bates, Carol, ed. "Women as Amateur Performers, Music Teachers, and Music Patrons." *Women in Music: An Anthology of Source Readings from the Middle Ages to the Present.* New York: Harper and Row, 1982. Pp. 179–91.

Oates, Joyce Carol. "The Art of Eudora Welty." In *Eudora Welty: Critical Views.* Edited by Harold Bloom. New York: Chelsea, 1986. Pp. 71–74.

O'Brien, Michael. *The Idea of the American South, 1920–1941.* Baltimore: Johns Hopkins University Press, 1979.

O'Brien, Sharon. "Mothers, Daughters, and the 'Art Necessity': Willa Cather and the Creative Process." *American Novelists Revisited: Essays in Feminist Criticism.* Edited by Fritz Fleishmann. Boston: G. K. Hall, 1982. Pp. 265–98.

Odum, Howard W. *Southern Regions of the United States.* Chapel Hill: University of North Carolina Press, 1936.

Ovid. *Metamorphoses.* Translated by Rolfe Humphries. Bloomington: Indiana University Press, 1955.

Papashvily, Helen Waite. *All the Happy Endings: A Study of the Domestic Novel in America, the Women Who Wrote It, the Women Who Read It, in the Nineteenth Century.* New York: Harper and Row, 1956.

Pei, Lowry. "Dreaming the Other in *The Golden Apples.*" *Modern Fiction Studies* 28 (1982): 415–33.

Petry, Alice Hall. "Universal and Particular: The Local-Color Phenomenon Reconsidered." *American Literary Realism, 1870–1910* 12 (1979): 111–26.

Petty, Jane Reid. "The Town and the Writer: An Interview with Eudora Welty." In *Conversations with Eudora Welty.* Edited by Peggy W. Prenshaw. Jackson: University Press of Mississippi, 1984. Pp. 200–210.

Pitavy, Danièle. "'Shower of Gold' ou les ambiguites de la narration." *Delta* 5 (1977): 63–81.

Pitavy-Souques, Danièle. "Technique as Myth: The Structure of *The Golden Apples.*" In *Eudora Welty: A Life in Literature.* Edited by Albert J. Devlin. Jackson: University Press of Mississippi, 1987. Pp. 258–68. Rpt. in *Eudora Welty: Critical Views.* Edited by Harold Bloom. New York: Chelsea, 1986. Pp. 109–118.

———. "Watchers and Watching: Point of View in Eudora Welty's 'June Recital.'" *The Southern Review* 19 (1983): 483–509.

Plato. *Dialogues of Plato. Selections from the Translation of Benjamin Jowett.* Edited by William Chase Green. New York: Liveright, 1932.

Polk, Noel. "Water, Wanderers, and Weddings: Love in Eudora Welty." In *Eudora Welty: A Form of Thanks.* Edited by Louis Dollarhide and Ann J. Abadie. Jackson: University Press of Mississippi, 1979. Pp. 104–10.

———. "A Eudora Welty Checklist, 1936–72." In Devlin, ed. *Welty: A Life in Literature.* 238–65.

Pollack, Harriet. "Words Between Strangers: On Welty, Her Style, and Her Audience." In *Eudora Welty: A Life in Literature.* Edited by Albert J. Devlin. Jackson: University Press of Mississippi, 1987. Pp. 54–81.

Porter, Katherine Anne. *The Collected Stories of Katherine Anne Porter.* New York: Harcourt Brace, 1965.

————. "A Curtain of Green." 1941. Rpt. in Eudora Welty: Critical Views. Edited by Harold Bloom. New York: Chelsea, 1986. Pp. 11–18.

Pratt, Mary Louise. "The Short Story: The Long and Short of It." Poetics 10 (1981): 175–94.

Prenshaw, Peggy W. "Persephone in Eudora Welty's 'Livvie.'" Studies in Short Fiction 17 1980): 149–55.

————. "Two Jackson Excursions." Eudora Welty Newsletter 2.1 (1978): 3–4.

————. "Woman's World, Man's Place: The Fiction of Eudora Welty." In Eudora Welty: A Form of Thanks. Edited by Louis Dollarhide and Ann J. Abadie. Jackson: University Press of Mississippi, 1979. Pp. 46–77.

————, ed. Eudora Welty: Critical Essays. Jackson: University Press of Mississippi, 1979.

————, ed. Conversations with Eudora Welty. Jackson: University Press of Mississippi, 1984.

Price, Reynolds. Things Themselves. New York: Atheneum, 1972.

————. "The Onlooker Smiling: An Early Reading of The Optimist's Daughter." In Things Themselves. Pp. 114–38. Rpt. in Eudora Welty: Critical Views. Edited by Harold Bloom. New York: Chelsea, 1986. Pp. 75–88.

Pugh, Elaine Upton. "The Duality of Morgana: The Making of Virgie's Vision, The Vision of The Golden Apples." Modern Fiction Studies 28 (1982): 435–51.

Radway, Janice. Reading the Romance: Women, Patriarchy, and Popular Literature. Chapel Hill: University of North Carolina Press, 1984.

Randisi, Jennifer Lynn. A Tissue of Lies: Eudora Welty and the Southern Romance. Washington, D.C.: University Press of America, 1982.

Renza, Louis A. "The White Heron" and the Question of Minor Literature. Madison: University of Wisconsin Press, 1984.

Rich, Adrienne. The Will to Change. New York: Norton, 1971.

Romines, Ann. "How Not to Tell a Story: Eudora Welty's First-Person Tales." In Eudora Welty: Eye of the Storyteller. Edited by Dawn Trouard. Kent: Kent State University Press, 1989. Pp. 94–104.

Rourke, Constance. American Humor. 1931. Rpt. Garden City, N.Y.: Doubleday, 1953.

Royals, Tom, and John Little. "A Conversation with Eudora Welty." In Conversations with Eudora Welty. Edited by Peggy W. Prenshaw. Jackson: University Press of Mississippi, 1984. Pp. 252–67.

Rubin, Louis D., Jr., ed. The Comic Imagination in American Literature. New Brunswick: Rutgers University Press, 1973.

————. "Art and Artistry in Morgana, Mississippi." *Missouri Review* 4 (1981): 101–16.

Ruskin, John. "Of Queen's Gardens." *Sesame and Lilies. The Works of John Ruskin, Library Edition.* Edited by E.T. Cook and Alexander Wedderburn. Vol. 18. London: George Allen, 1905.

Russell, Diarmuid. "First Work." *Shenandoah* 20 (1969): 16–19.

Sahli, Nancy. "Smashing: Women's Relationships Before the Fall." *Crysalis* 8 (1979): 17–27.

Schiller, Gertrud. *Iconography of Christian Art.* 2 vols. Translated by Janet Seligman. Greenwich, Conn.: New York Graphic Society, 1971.

Schmidt, Pearl Amelia. "Textual Variants in 'The Winds.'" *Eudora Welty Newsletter* 10.1 (Winter 1986): 3–7.

Schmidt, Peter. "Sibyls in Eudora Welty's Stories." In *Eudora Welty: Eye of the Storyteller.* Edited by Dawn Trouard. Kent: Kent State University Press, 1989. Pp. 78–93.

————. "'These': William Carlos Williams' Deepest Descent." *William Carlos Williams Review* 9.1–2 (1983): 74–90.

Scott, Anne Firor. *The Southern Lady: From Pedestal to Politics, 1830–1930.* Chicago: University of Chicago Press, 1970.

Sedgwick, Catherine. *A New-England Tale; or, Sketches of New-England Character and Manners.* New York: E. Bliss, 1824.

Segal, Hanna. "Notes on Symbol Formation." *International Journal of Psycho-Analysis* 38 (1957): 391–97.

————. *Introduction to the Work of Melanie Klein.* New York: Basic Books, 1964.

Semel, Jay M. "Eudora Welty's Freak Show." *Notes on Contemporary Literature* 3.3 (1973): 2–3.

Shinn, Thelma J. *Radiant Daughters: Fictional American Women.* New York: Greenwood Press, 1986.

Showalter, Elaine. *The Female Malady: Women, Madness, and English Culture, 1830–1980.* New York: Pantheon, 1985.

Smith-Rosenberg, Carroll. *Disorderly Conduct: Visions of Gender in Victorian America.* New York: Knopf, 1985.

Solomon, Barbara H., ed. *The Short Fiction of Sarah Orne Jewett and Mary Wilkins Freeman.* New York: Signet, 1979.

Sophocles. *Oedipus Rex.* Translated by David Green. Chicago: University of Chicago Press, 1954.

Southworth, E. D. E. N. *The Mother-in-Law; or, The Isle of Rays.* New York: D. Appleton, 1851.

Spacks, Patricia Meyer. *The Female Imagination.* New York: Knopf, 1975.

————. "Gossip and Community in Eudora Welty." In *Eudora Welty: Critical Views.* Edited by Harold Bloom. New York: Chelsea, 1986. Pp. 155–62.

Spear, Richard E. *Domenichino.* 2 vols. New Haven: Yale University Press, 1982.

Stoddard, Elizabeth. *The Morgesons and Other Writings, Published and Unpublished.* Edited by Lawrence Buell and Sandra A. Zagarell. Philadelphia: University of Pennsylvania Press, 1984.

Stone, William B. "Eudora Welty's Hydrodynamic 'Powerhouse.'" *Studies in Short Fiction* 11 (1974): 93–96.

Stowe, Harriet Beecher. *Three Novels: Uncle Tom's Cabin, The Minister's Wooing, Oldtown Folks.* New York: Library of America, 1982.

Sypher, Wylie. "The Meanings of Comedy." *Comedy.* 1956. Rpt. Baltimore: Johns Hopkins University Press, 1980. 191–255.

Tarbox, Raymond. "Eudora Welty's Fiction: The Salvation Theme." *American Imago* 29 (1971): 70–90.

Thoreau, Henry. *Walden and Civil Disobedience.* Edited by Owen Thomas. New York: Norton, 1966.

Tick, Judith. "Passed Away Is the Piano Girl: Changes in American Musical Life, 1870–1900." In *Women Making Music: The Western Art Tradition, 1150–1950.* Edited by Jane Bowers and Judith Tick. Urbana: University of Illinois Press, 1986.

Tindall, George Brown. *The Emergence of the New South, 1913–1945.* Baton Rouge: Louisiana State University Press, 1967.

Tompkins, Jane F. *Sensational Designs: The Cultural Work of American Fiction, 1790–1860.* New York: Oxford University Press, 1985.

Trouard, Dawn, ed. *Eudora Welty: Eye of the Story.* Kent: Kent State University Press, 1989.

Vande Kieft, Ruth. *Eudora Welty.* New York: Twayne, 1962.

————. *Eudora Welty.* Rev. ed. New York: Twayne, 1987.

Van Gelder, Robert. "An Interview with Eudora Welty." In *Conversations with Eudora Welty.* Edited by Peggy W. Prenshaw. Jackson: University Press of Mississippi, 1984. Pp. 3–5.

Virgil. *Eclogues, Georgics, Aeneid.* Translated by H. R. Fairclough. Rev. ed. 2 vols. Loeb Classical Library. Cambridge: Harvard University Press, 1974.

Walker, Nancy. *A Very Serious Thing: Women's Humor and American Culture.* Minneapolis: University of Minnesota Press, 1988.

Walker, Nancy, and Zita Dresner, eds. *Redressing the Balance: American Women's Literary Humor from Colonial Times to the 1980s.* Jackson: University Press of Mississippi, 1988.

Walker, Robert C. "Another Medusa Allusion in Welty's 'Petrified Man.'" *Notes on Mississippi Writers* 9 (1979): 10.

Wall, Carey. "'June Recital': Virgie Rainey Saved." In *Eudora Welty: Eye of the Storyteller*. Edited by Dawn Trouard. Kent: Kent State University Press, 1989. Pp. 14–31.

Wallace, Ronald. *God Be With the Clown: Humor in American Poetry*. Columbia: University of Missouri Press, 1984.

Warren, Robert Penn. "The Love and Separateness in Miss Welty." In *Eudora Welty: Critical Views*. Edited by Harold Bloom. New York: Chelsea, 1986. Pp. 19–28.

Weimann, Jeanne Madeline. *The Fair Women: The Story of the Woman's Building, World's Columbian Exposition, Chicago 1893*. Chicago: Academy Press, 1981.

Welter, Barbara. *Dimity Convictions: The American Woman in the Nineteenth Century*. Athens: Ohio University Press, 1976.

Welty, Eudora. "*Women!!* Make Turban in Own Home!" *Junior League Magazine* 28 (November 1941): 20–21, 62. Rpt. Winston-Salem, N. C.: Palaemon Press, 1979.

———. *The Robber Bridegroom*. New York: Harcourt Brace Jovanovich, 1942.

———. *Delta Wedding*. New York: Harcourt Brace Jovanovich, 1945.

———. *Short Stories*. New York: Harcourt Brace Jovanovich, 1949. Condensed and rpt. as "Looking at Short Stories." In *The Eye of the Story*. Pp. 85–106.

———. *The Ponder Heart*. New York: Harcourt Brace Jovanovich, 1953.

———. "Place and Time: The Southern Writer's Inheritance." *Times Literary Supplement* (17 September 1954): xlviii.

———. *Losing Battles*. New York: Harcourt Brace Jovanovich, 1970.

———. *The Optimist's Daughter*. New York: Harcourt Brace Jovanovich, 1973.

———. "Acrobats in a Park." *Delta* 5 (1977): 1–11.

———. *The Eye of the Story: Selected Essays and Reviews*. New York: Random House, 1979.

———. *The Collected Stories of Eudora Welty*. New York: Harcourt Brace Jovanovich, 1980.

———. *One Writer's Beginnings*. Cambridge: Harvard University Press, 1984.

———. "My Introduction to Katherine Anne Porter." *Georgia Review* 44.1-2 (Spring/Summer 1990): 13–27.

Westling, Louise. *Sacred Groves and Ravaged Gardens: The Fiction of Eudora Welty, Carson McCullers, and Flannery O'Connor*. Athens: University of Georgia Press, 1985.

Weston, Ruth D. "American Folk Art, Fine Art, and Eudora Welty: Aesthetic Precedents for 'Lily Daw and the Three Ladies.'" In *Eudora Welty: Eye of the Storyteller.* Edited by Dawn Trouard. Kent: Kent State University Press, 1989. Pp. 3–13.

Wharton, Edith. *The House of Mirth.* New York: Scribner's, 1905.

———. *Age of Innocence.* New York: Grosset and Dunlap, 1920.

Whitcher, Frances M. *The Widow Bedott Papers.* New York: J. C. Derby, 1856.

Wilson, Augusta Evans. *Beulah.* New York: Derby and Jackson, 1859.

———. *St. Elmo.* New York: Grosset and Dunlap, 1866.

———. *Vashti; or, "Until Death Us Do Part."* New York: Carleton, 1869.

Wind, Edgar. *Michelangelo's Prophets and Sibyls, Vol. LI from the Proceedings of the British Academy.* London: Oxford University Press, 1960.

Winnicott, D. W. *The Child and the Outside World: Studies in Developmental Relationships.* London: Tavistock, 1957.

———. *Playing and Reality.* London: Tavistock, 1971.

Yaeger, Patricia. "'Because a Fire Was in My Head': Eudora Welty and the Dialogic Imagination." PMLA 99 (1984): 955–73. Rev. and rpt. in *Eudora Welty: A Life in Literature.* Edited by Albert J. Devlin. Jackson: University Press of Mississippi, 1987. Pp. 139–67.

———. "The Case of the Dangling Signifier: Phallic Imagery in Eudora Welty's 'Moon Lake.'" *Twentieth Century Literature* 28 (1982): 431–52.

Yeats, William Butler. *The Collected Poems of William Butler Yeats.* New York: Macmillan, 1956.

Index